FELA
PHENOMENON AND LEGACY

MABINUORI KAYODE IDOWU (aka ID)

Copyright 2012 Black Art Productions
ISBN: 978-2-9543674-0-8
Front cover picture by Bernard Matussière
Back cover picture Africa 70 Photo Agency collection

DEDICATION

This book is dedicated to my late mother FOWOTADE IDOWU (nee ADEMOLA of the Abeokuta royal lineage), for her solid support in the wake of my association with Fela seen in family and friends circles as unambitious and going out of control. Today with the global explosion of the phenomenon that was Fela, critics of my dear mother's solid support can see where she was coming from. Dedicated also to my daughter ADERAYO, for my long absence from her side since the age of five deprived of my direct transmission of a life's experience and father's vision - two important selfish reasons on my part to desire her as a daughter.

ACKNOWLEDGMENTS

I acknowledge with gratitude the contribution to the making of this book of my long-time friend Jacqueline Grandchamp-Thiam, for her eagle eyes in spotting all the missing comas and full stops while reading over my manuscript. I first met Jacqueline in 1979 in Lagos, she was working as the secretary of the French Ambassador and writing her Doctoral theses on Pan Africanism and Music of resistance, she was presented to Fela and he in-turn presented me to her as the person competent in giving all the details about him and his struggles. Since that day, Jacqueline and I have remained friends and our friendship continues to blossom since my taking residence in Paris. Unfortunately due to health reasons, Jacqueline couldn't finish the necessary corrections. Special thanks to my brother Yomi Idowu, who generously finished the editing of this work. I will also like to acknowledge the strong support of my friend Olivier Lemaître of Absynthe Productions for his collaboration in making my website:www.radioshrine.com what it is and his contribution to the aesthetics and graphics of this book. Also to my wife Sylvie Aubanel-Idowu for all her love and support, and to those numerous to name here who one way or the other have given me the necessary boost to realise this work, to all of you from the deep bottom of my heart I say thank you!

CONTENTS

1.	PREFACE	06 - 18
2.	NO AGREEMENT	21 - 38
3.	COLO-MENTALITY	40 - 53
4.	EKO ILE (LAGOS SWEET HOME)	54 - 77
5.	VIVA NIGERIA! VIVA AFRICA!	78 - 90
6.	CHIEF PRIEST SAY	91 - 99
7.	ALAGBONCLOSE	100 - 112
8.	EXPENSIVE SHIT	113 - 119
9.	KALAKUTA SHOW	120 - 129
10.	YOUNG AFRICAN PIONEERS	130 - 148
11.	SECOND WORLD BLACK FESTIVAL OF ARTS AND CULTURE (FESTAC)	149 - 182
12.	UNKNOWN SOLDIER	183 - 226
13.	COFFIN FOR HEAD OF STATE	227 - 248
14.	THE IKEJA AFRICA SHRINE	249 - 271
15.	TEACHER DON'T TEACH ME NONSENSE	272 - 301
16.	LOOK AND LAUGH	302 - 329
17.	BEASTS OF NO NATION	330 - 370
18.	UNDERGROUND SYSTEM	371 - 381
19.	THE FELA PHENOMENON	382 - 413
20.	FEMI ANIKULAPO-KUTI	414 - 426
21.	SEUN ANIKULAPO-KUTI EGPYPT 80	427 - 430
22.	ANTIBALAS AFROBEAT ORCHESTRA	431 - 434
23.	COUP DE GUEULE (FIT OF RAGE)	435 - 444
24.	FELABRATION: ONE OF THE SOLUTIONS	445 - 451
25.	DISCOGRAPHY	452 - 524

PREFACE

Fela Anikulapo-Kuti in his life-time, was not only controversial he was an enigma and cultural icon. The circumstance of his transition from earth, was no less contentious and he has remained the subject of rave reviews, debates, and study even in death. To those who knew him and his countless followers he was in his own right the Black President, a Chief Priest, King, exponent of Black music and culture. However, to a class of elites with Christian and Moslem values (especially those in authority in Nigeria), he was an iconoclast, a hooligan, Indian hemp smoker, trouble-shooter and a "political non-starter".

Some of them articulate and privileged enough to write in journals and newspapers, have described him as an Afro-centric who personified a new counter-culture by the glorification of social rascality. In their criticisms and appraisal of Fela's several brushes with the authorities in Nigeria, Fela was considered as politically naïve and that he sought transmogrify from his indisputable and phenomenal stage success to a serious minded political actor especially at a most trying period for the nation which had been under military rule with zero tolerance for dissent. Fela may well not be the best friend or idol of many in the Nigerian establishment especially because he posed a formidable threat to their corrupt and exploitative dispositions.

However, this should not diminish his right to hold opinions and make comments on the affairs of his country as I affirmed in my first work: Fela, Why Blackman Carry Shit. His approach may not conform to their norms and possibly was seen as dippy, this does not erase the fact that many of his songs or comments - though biting satires or outright attacks on establishment, they remain profound and or altruistic. They remained pointers to genuine African self respecting ways, to keep our common patrimony as Africans and Nigeria in particular.

As expected of a ruthless government that had grown accustomed to being fawned at, deferred to and obeyed unquestioningly by the political and so-called educated elite, they regarded Fela's comments as a threat to their establishment. Taunted and afraid, of losing their grip on a society that for many years have been deprived of their basic liberties, such government normally does not take Fela's criticism lying low. They frequently returned his attacks which at best were verbal with brutal physical suppression applying instruments of state terror the police and the army.

The frequent nature of such attacks on the 'only' dissenting voice, has left us with a cajoled polity, and paranoid populace too scared to assert their collective rights let alone claim individual fundamental rights.

The average Nigerian has lost faith in his or her ability to be assertive. It was therefore against this backdrop, that some people in the society saw Fela as a depraved iconoclast daring to stand before the fable moving train which the authorities and their instruments of terror represented. It is ironical, that this same society harbours great pains in their hearts each time Fela is brutalized. They appreciate his stance and fight for the oppressed, but are rather too timid to challenge the authorities.

While I don't intend to sound like a show-off "frimeur" (like the French people say), I write as a living witness to all these events. A Fela ideologue and an associate who in 1974 after the famous "Kalakuta Show" attack, heard Fela's older brother Koye then professor of Paediatrics at the Lagos University Teaching Hospital say: "Fela do you know that those who did this to you wanted to kill you?" In response to his brother's observation he said: "Yes I know!" This was shortly after his doctor brother had put 18 stitches on his head, from the beatings he got from the Nigerian police attack – aptly dubbed "Kalakuta Show" in a song with the same title by Fela.

To my young mind, it was incredible to note the levity with which he treated the threat to his life. I remember discussing this with my other friends the artist Ghariokwu Lemi and Duro Ikujenyo (the three of us later became Care-Taker Committee members of the Young African Pioneers movement–YAP). Fela's courage and determination, convinced us to commit our lives to the struggle for the emancipation of our people from the slavery of mind defined as neo-colonialism. It also afforded us the opportunity to work and learn direct from the man himself.

In order to understand the reasons behind Fela's doggedness despite all the harrowing, anguish and tyranny he had been subjected to, I decided shortly after the police attack on Kalakuta Republic in 1974, to get acquainted with this controversial African personality. As a first step to achieving this end, I made attendance at the Friday Yabbis Night and Saturday Comprehensive Show at the Shrine more than a routine but more like a compulsory study time.

These sessions opened my mind to the vastness and richness of the African cultural endowment and accorded Fela's music in my heart a place beyond mere music to a profoundly authentic educational theme. It was almost like an apotheosis, a supreme or ideal example of the kind of wisdom that must propel a society. His unique and uncompromising use of music in disseminating wisdom and the enlightenment of the ordinary man in Nigeria and the Africans in the Diasporas in general unsettled the authorities. Rather than evaluate the message, the Nigerian authorities saw these as an affront to the established and so took recourse to pernicious measures which were the result of innumerable clashes with the state and its apparatus.

Another point I noticed from these visits, is that Fela was out there alone as political musician while Nigerian artistes like Sunny Ade, Ebenezer Obey and others, failed to grasp the potency of their music as instruments of social change and revolution. Rather, their genre of music celebrated the very corrupt aristocratic class who through their advantaged positions, have mortgaged the common patrimony of the people. Armed with this knowledge of Fela, I became increasingly curious to know more about him - especially off stage. I wanted to find-out about his domestic life. The answer came not long after on a Sunday afternoon, I chose to attend for the first time his Sunday Jump at the Shrine.

The first thing that made a big impression on me was the unprecedented crowd. They surpassed those I had seen during the night time shows I previously attended. Soon as I obtained my ticket, I edged my way through the teaming crowd into the venue. I managed to secure a stage-side seat, with the help of an old school mate who spotted me pushing my way through the crowd and offered me a seat next to him. "Duro Ikujenyo! So you too dey come here?" Was my remark to this friend as I settled next to him. "Man dey come learn here too," was Duro's response to my question. He then turned and introduced me to another friend sitting next to him. "Meet Lemi! Ghariokwu Lemi na my friend and him be artist. Na him dey design Fela album sleeves".

Without waiting any longer, I narrated to both of them how I had made the Friday and Saturday night shows regularly. I went further to explain that I was attending the Sunday afternoon Jump for the first time in order to get to know Fela closely. To my surprise, Lemi said: "ID! If you want to know Fela well-well, you can come with us to his house after show." Me to meet Fela at home?

I could not believe what I was hearing and I almost spoke the words out loud to my friends in the short space of time we got talking.For the first time since I started to attend Fela's Shrine sessions, I couldn't sit back smoke a joint and relax and listen to the music like I always did. The thought of meeting Fela at home after the concert kept distracting me.

At about 10.30 p.m., the show ended and Fela started to walk towards his house - Kalakuta Republic. He was surrounded, by a sea of people mostly tough looking men - a common description of members of his household by the Nigerian public. Soon as all of us that accompanied him from the Shrine were seated, Fela in view of all of us stripped off his clothes - leaving him in his tight fitting underpants.

Looking around, he brought his gaze on me and to my surprise he asked "Young man! Have I met you before?" I was too shocked with his sudden notice of me that it took me some time to stutter "No Sir!" in answer to his question.

Lemi seeing my discomfiture intervened in the exchange, by introducing me as a friend of Duro and himself. "ID! Make you no 'Sir' me - everybody around calls me Fela you hear?" Was his next statement to me. Meaning: "ID! Don't 'Sir' me as everybody around address me as Fela – do your hear?" He then went on to explain why he likes to be addressed by his first name.

According to him many, parents and elders in our society alienate themselves from the younger generation by creating a communication gap through fear – in the name of respect to the elder. In an attempt to demand respect from the younger generation, parents create an atmosphere of fear. This practice, Fela went on does not give room for the younger generation to get close and open-up their minds to their elders.

This talk went on for more than three hours. Fela was expanding his views using various issues to buttress his point.

He quoted from books he had read, and used logical lines of thoughts to drive his point home. It was as if we were in an 'Institute of African studies' as Fela revealed to us his intellectual side. From this day on, his house became a regular school for my friends and me. We were stunned, by this new education about Africans being a people who taught this world civilization.

This revelation, provoked a feeling of introspection in all of us to the extent that we started to question, the relevance of our educational system to the African environment particularly, an education system that debases the African as barbarian and savages. We wondered, why such realities about the African man were excluded from our school curriculum.

Unfortunately this intellectual aspect of Fela, was not exposed to the Nigerian public and the external audience as Fela's name and fame spread all over the globe. With these in mind and the controversial nature of Fela, the thought came to me to try and understand the man more in order to put his ideas into writing.

In order to erase all the misconceptions of him, I realised I needed to possess a deep knowledge and understanding of the Fela phenomenon. Today, I feel privileged to understand what the Fela phenomenon is all about. It took me almost a decade of close contact and association to know the real Fela.

What I learnt and went through with him within ten years I could never have acquired in a Nigerian university system given the same timeline. I feel privileged, to share so many intimate things with him. The only thing I never shared with Fela was his bed and women. This I believe is because we were both not inclined or oriented in that way, moreover he respected with a cordial distance, the women who shared my life throughout my involvement with the Africa 70 Organisation.

I cannot count how many times, Fela would be in bed with one of his many women and he would call-out to the security man at the entrance to his house, from his bedroom window a few meters away: "Gate Man! Call ID for me" or "Gate Man! Call me the YAP Boys." The gate man would come running to our part of the building shouting my name: "ID! Fela dey call you".

Summoned, I will go to his bedroom window and start to discus whatever issue that came to his mind, or information he listened to on the radio at his bed side that he wanted to discuss with us. Some other times the situation would be reversed. It was me or any of the YAP Boys, who heard some news item that we wanted to share with him. I will approach his bedroom window and call out "Fela! Did you hear the news?" Or just to discus something we felt needed to be treated urgently.

The conversation sometimes went on for so long, that he would say "come inside" – inviting me or whoever it was to come into his bedroom.

Fela always left his door ajar, he never locked his bedroom door with keys while sleeping. I guess locking his bedroom door reminded him of his various prison experiences. Fela would be there with one of the women whose turn it was to share his bed covered with a bed-sheet and without inhibitions, we will continue our conversations. We YAP Boys, got in the bad books of most of his women as a result of such interruptions of their 'love sessions'.

The only woman who didn't mind such interruptions was Remi. I guess if she was alive, I would be very much reluctant to discuss this aspect of her private life, but since I feel only very few of us had this privilege I guess we owe it to posterity to say it loud. I can remember that she was the only woman among Fela's women, who would get involved adding some intelligent and intellectual impute to the discussion at hand.

Sometimes, she misjudged him and other times she was right. I believe this was one of the reasons Fela encouraged we YAP Boys to visit her at her Ikate apartment where she lived with her mother and her three children. For instance, there was this issue where he wanted to take the 'kids' (Yeni, Femi, and Sola, as we called them) to Ghana to re-dub the sound track of his film Black President burnt in the house during the army attack in 1977.

Remi and her mother did not want the children to miss school, while Fela tried to convince them that the 'kids' would learn new things outside their school curriculum by travelling. We discussed this with Fela, and we came to the same conclusion that travelling would expose them to other kinds of education. Our judgment was based on the neo-colonial form of education curriculum in Nigeria.

Fela asked us to go and see Remi. However Remi and "mom" (her mother) had a contrary opinion, insisting that absence from school would inflict some damage on their educational pursuit and set them behind of their peers – even if consideration was given to a loftier concept their journey would expose them to. For the two women, the 'kids' deserved a formal education as a necessary insurance for progress in a society which places premium on certification.

Since we couldn't convince the two ladies to release the 'kids', Fela insisted on taking Femi alone saying he needed him to play the role of a young Fela knowing full well that at that age, Femi would never go away from home without his two other sisters. In the end he had his way bringing the three of them with us to Ghana. In a way sending us YAP Boys regularly to visit Remi and her mother in Ikate, was Fela's way of keeping his immediate family abreast of his political evolution – we were like his mouthpiece in the real sense of the word.

Contrary to what people have said about Fela's perceived autocratic dominance of women, Remi was highly respected by Fela. But for Remi's seemingly shy attitude she probably would have proclaimed in public the immense respect she enjoyed from her husband. She earned her respect and if other women possessed the strength of character of Remi they too would have earned the same level of attention and respect.

Since I was not there at the beginning in the sixties, thanks to our close contact with Remi and her mother Sadie Eileen Taylor (we called her mom like Fela or Nanny like the kids), I got to know about Fela's early life and his evolution from a tea-drinking mentally colonized African, to the visionary Pan-Africanist and anti establishment crusader.

Before her death, Remi was writing her memoirs but I guess she was too modest to share her personal experiences with Fela publicly like people close to pop stars and celebrities often do. I hope one day, her children will share these views with the public by publishing it for posterity.

In life and even after his death, people who did not know Fela well enough have called him a social pervert, who used his popularity to corrupt young girls. He was accused of living a lifestyle that espoused the subversion of family values. If one has his life as example, I guess I owe my well informed situation in life to the education I acquired around Fela.

For people like us who knew him, outright condemnations such as expressed above are pointers to what Fela went through in order to become the voice of the voiceless. I remember discussing with him my ambition to attend the university to study either history or philosophy.

In return, he asked me if I intended to study the works of so-called "Greek Philosophers" like Aristotle, Socrates, Plato, to which I answered in the affirmative. Fela then asked me if I was aware that these so-called philosophers were regarded as undesirables in their Greek homeland for propagating what the Greek government termed foreign ideas. I was not aware of this and he went on to borrow me and my friends books talking about the sudden about-turn of the Greek government and Africa being the base of our today's civilisation. Books like: "Blackman of the Nile" by Yosef Ben-Jochannan, "Destruction of Black Civilisation" by Chancellor Williams, "Stolen Legacy" by George G.M James, Cheikh Anta Diop's "Nation Negro And Culture," and "Civilisation or Barbarism", "How Europe Underdeveloped Africa", by Walter Rodney, etc.

All these books, talking about Africa being the mother of Western civilisation and "the Greeks not being the authors of philosophy but the people of North Africa commonly called Black Egyptians". This was the turning point in my life. I gave up the idea of going to the university to study philosophy. Instead, I started out as an auto didactic reading every book on philosophy, history and biographies of great men I could lay my hands on.

My mother was not happy with this turn of events. For her, I was being brainwashed by Fela and despite the fear people have of the latter, she was determined to confront him. She was convinced that no fear in this world could prevent her from visiting her son even if it's in a "lion's den".

Permit me to give a little background on my late mother. She was what we call in Fela's language, somebody with "Sense Wiseness". In his song with the same title, Fela explains that acquiring all the degrees in any university doesn't make you automatically wise. Being educated in western ways and mannerisms doesn't make you wiser than the average street-wise guy in Mushin, Ajegunle or Jankara (all these areas core of the Lagos ghetto). My mother understands the mentality of the ghetto and she could deal with it. She can be described as unlettered in the Western sense of the word, but I hate to use the word illiterate – particularly if one bears in mind the oral nature of education in Africa.

The word illiterate gives the impression of an un-educated person, which is not how I consider people who have been subjected to African traditional education system - my mother included. It is true that she couldn't read or write, but she was well informed about the Yoruba tradition and custom.

Fela left her an impression of a cultured man after her confrontation with him. I could recollect him walking towards her, and a few meters away from her he stopped and asked one of the boys around to fetch him a towel, which he later wrapped around himself before he finally acknowledge my mother in his presence as a sign of respect for her. He impressed my old lady with this gesture - bearing in mind that Fela received everybody in his house dressed in his underpants. Permit me another digression here, Fela was accused of being flamboyant in his attempt to attract attention. He was said to have often performed and conducted interviews wearing his underpants.

Those who knew him, are aware that he never went out of his house without his trousers on. It is true that he conducted interviews wearing his underpants, but definitely at home or somewhere he calls home at the moment of the interview. Whenever he had interviews outside his house, he was always dressed for the occasion.

Returning to my mother's confrontation with Fela, she asked him direct: "What have you done to brainwash my son? I know him to be ambitious and interested in furthering his studies but since he met you, I hear him condemn the university education system in Nigeria." Responding to her query, Fela explained how great the African culture is and how in the name of "modern" education, Africans are sacrificing traditional ways of life for Western values.

Telling her to count herself lucky to have a son, who has strong beliefs in African values and traditions. I believe, if every mother with a child in Fela's commune had chosen to dialogue direct with him as my mother did, a lot of the misconceptions about what he was doing would have been better understood.

Instead of taking the pains to talk with him and their children in Kalakuta, in order to understand why the child chose to run away from home those parents and guardians with government connections (magistrates, lawyers and judges) use their police and army connections to try and force the child to return home by attacking Kalakuta.

Since his passing, I have had people talk about Fela in terms of a mystic. He was even called to his face "ABAMI", which means in Yoruba language "A mystic". Fela as human being has nothing mystical about him except his convictions.

Femi Kuti asked what is his perception of Fela's mysticism today, and after his death if he feels drawn to it? He replied: "Fela's what did you call it - mysticism? He was not a mystic for me after-all he was my father. I hardly talk about it though except if I feel pressured. I know he is there watching over me and I feel his presence many times".

To those who knew him, there should not be any mystery if Fela is making history even after his passing. His family background played a big role in his life formation. For instance, it is important to understand the legend behind the Kuti family and its influence on each member of the family. Fela's early career like any other African child, was subjected to various irrelevancies in the name of an education.

He was born into Christianity, he attended the church, and learnt to sing and play the piano while in the church choir. The turning point in his life was when he went to America in 1969. He left Nigeria with the hope of making it big as an artiste. But the realities of the music industry ended up humiliating him.

Despite all the career setbacks in America he met Sandra Iszidore (nee–Smith), who at that time was aware of the Black Panther movement and their resistance drive in America. She took care of his financial needs and also set him on the African personality line of thought.

For the first time, he read books on the pioneers of the African struggle - names like Marcus Garvey, Malcolm X and Kwame Nkrumah, having hitherto emigrated from his culture these books ignited a new discovery of the richness of his culture which he held with ardour. On his return to Nigeria in March 1970, he decided to dedicate his music to the spread of the ideals of African Personality.

To realise them, he was aware that his musical career would play a big role hence his slogan: "music is the weapon of the future." Today, afrobeat music can be considered on the same level as other musical classics like jazz, and reggae, rich with political messages and cultural interests – the two important reasons behind the success of jazz and reggae music as world classics.

Like reggae music did with Bob Marley, and Peter Tosh, the message of Afrobeat music turned Fela into a role model to lots of today's revolutionary musicians.

From all indications, Fela can be considered a product of African history and a personified search for an answer to colonialism. For more than three decades, he remained one of Africa's most outspoken cultural figures. He attacked government corruption in his songs and took on wider social issues with songs like "LADY," which criticised the use of White Western values and standards for feminine beauty in Africa.

However to his detractors, songs such as these were interpreted as anti-feminist or simply "macho". In this volume I try to use his song titles and situate them in the proper cultural milieu of their rendition, to explain the Fela phenomenon and if possible make the reader understand his message as a legacy. Particularly, since most of the songs are very much relevant to the actual situation today world wide.

I have tried to capture the reasons behind his motivation, despite the price he had to pay for his outspoken criticisms. Also included in this volume, is an update on the relationship between the author and Fela. I have explained here, the sequence of events that led to my parting of ways with him and his organisation.

Death which is the ultimate end for all mankind on earth came knocking on Fela's doorsteps on August 2nd, 1997. He died in a hospital in Lagos Nigeria at approximately 5.30 p.m. According to a statement read by his elder brother Olikoye Ransome-Kuti, at a press conference held at the Africa Shrine situated at Pepple Street in Ikeja Lagos. The immediate cause of his death was heart failure, caused by many complications arising from the Acquired Immune Deficiency Syndrome (AIDS). According to Koye, if Fela knew he had AIDS he would have made it public knowledge.

The decision to take him to the hospital, was made by members of his immediate family after he fell into a coma. He refused to be treated or diagnosed by any western trained medical practitioner, and he was not in a position to comprehend in the end that he had the HIV virus. This should not come as a surprise, in view of his belief that western trained medical practitioners are biased towards traditional medical practices and beliefs. The last two decades of his life were spent as a semi-recluse. For an actively and politically involved person like Fela, to live a routine life of going to perform at the Shrine and back to Kalakuta can be described as semi-recluse.

Looking back after his death, it is obvious to the writer that he was tired of it all. He had done almost everything possible to stir the conscience of the Nigerian – paying a price that almost cost him his life and everything he had achieved or acquired. At the same time, the Nigerian public ostensibly complacent, failed to stand up for Fela who naturally might have felt or indeed felt abandoned, sloughed off, rejected, despised, by the same public he was championing their cause.

The only thing that kept him going, towards the end of his life was largely his music and women. Hence, one could understand why he sang songs like Look And Laugh and Condom Scaliwagy. Look And Laugh, was Fela's way of saying I have said it all it's up to you to rise up and fight this oppressive system. The latter song which he never recorded was his statement against the use of condoms in sexual acts.

According to Fela: "Africans cannot get AIDS. Africans eat fresh meat and vegetables. Most of our food are all fresh, as a result we have natural immunity against those white man diseases."

For a well informed man like Fela statements such as the one above, sounds like the man was out of his mind in view of the ravaging spread of the HIV virus world-wide. However, for those who knew him closely it is an evidence of turning his back to the realities around him in the last two decades. As far as he was concerned, the only realities he accepted were his music and women.

That should not come as a surprise considering that at the beginning of the AIDS epidemic, there was an attempt to place the origin of the virus in the African continent. However, the wide spread or prevalence of the epidemic in Europe and America makes it impossible to justify such claim.

Every evil in the world has been dumped on the door-steps of the Africans in order to justify the peerless dehumanization called slavery and colonization of the continent.

For a man like Fela who fought all his adult life trying to uplift a people from accepting the responsibility of these evil, it should not come as a surprise that he should call the devastation of the HIV virus in the world: "an imagination of the white man."

The distortion of the origin of man, by western writers for an example makes it hard for an informed person to accept it as fact all the information he or she gets - without questioning it. The inhumanity of colonization, is succinctly captured in the book:

"Toward the African Revolution" by legendary African revolutionary Frantz Fanon from which I would quote extensively. In his appraisal of the psyche of the colonized, Fanon said: "Having witnessed the liquidation of its systems of reference, the collapse of its cultural patterns, the native can only recognize with the occupant that God is not on his side."

The colonialists he emphasized, "through the inclusive and frightening character of his authority, manages to impose on the native new ways of seeing and in particular a pejorative judgment with respect to his original forms of existence." The situation has persisted even to the present age, in spite of the cosmetic independence wrestled and in some cases negotiated by the new crop of neo-colonial authorities.

Apart from Femi and his group Positive Force, Seun Kuti and Egypt 80, Antibalas Afrobeat Orchestra, who through their musical exploits can be considered as inheritors of the Fela phenomenon, it is most encouraging today to hear musicians like Tiken Jah Fakoly identifying with the Fela struggle and legacy. His first major-label album titled "FRANCEAFRIQUE" (Universal music France), can be considered like Fela's music the work of an engaged artist. An album critical of to quote the artist: "a capitalist society where morality is no more capital".

As other artists and activists keep the struggle alive in death, the truth of Fela's enormous following manifested itself in the huge turnout of Lagosians at a public viewing of his body lying in state. An estimated crowd of about one million people were reported to have filed-past the body and to make a seven kilometre march across Lagos to pay their respect to the Chief Priest. With all humility from one who knew and participated in his evolution for almost a decade, I invite you to discover the Fela phenomenon and Legacy – happy reading.

Mabinuori Kayode Idowu (Paris, France 2012).

Album cover design No Agreement

NO AGREEMENT

After Kalakuta Republic (Fela's abode) was maliciously scalded in 1977, 'friends' and childhood acquaintances of Fela tried to talk him out of confronting the Nigerian military authorities - stressing that "government can do no wrong" or "government is too powerful to be confronted" etc. In response to their defeatist attitude, Fela in the song titled 'No Agreement' stated clearly that he was in the struggle because he couldn't sit and watch fellow Africans going hungry or living homeless without talking against it. Particularly convinced that according to the estimation of Africa riches, every Black man should be a millionaire - why is the black man poor? It is time to investigate.

Fela, using the legendary Kuti family contributions to the evolution of modern-day Nigeria as further justification of his resolve not to compromise sang: "...my grand-papa talk! My grand-mama talk! My papa talk! My mama talk! Those wey no talk them see! I no go gree make my brother hungry! Make I no talk! No agreement today! No agreement tomorrow!" (Meaning "my father talked! My mother talked! Those that didn't talk could see! I won't sit down while my brother is hungry! No Compromise today! No compromise tomorrow!")

It shouldn't be a mystery if Fela made history, the Kuti family legend is history itself. It has its roots way down in the days of the late Reverend Canon Josiah J. Ransome-Kuti (1855–1930). According to Fela, he was a pioneer of Yoruba Christian (Anglican) church and a music composer whose music was first reduced to staff notation and recorded on gramophone record in Nigeria.

The patriarch of the Kuti family (an authentic African traditionalist), was against J.J. becoming a reverend. When the missionaries came, his mother took him to them. His father however was against the idea saying: "The White man was only here to steal our shear butter." The reader should bear in mind at this point, that this was the period shortly after the abolition of slavery and the beginning of the installation of colonial administrations in all the colonized territories.

The Christian and Islamic administrations, through-out Africa at this period was so strong. Africans were being brainwashed into thinking that with the coming of Christianity came salvation – that the installation of a colonial administration, saved Africa from her "savagery and "primitive ways of life".

With certitude we have to bear in mind that from the beginning to the end, the slave trade and the installation of colonial administrations was a denial of any standard except those of profit and loss. A black person was worth exactly, what his or her flesh could bring to their white owner in the market. If their flesh could bring nothing, they were tossed overboard like a horse with a broken leg.

Therefore, to preach against Christianity at that time was impossible. In those days if you didn't have an English (Christian) name, you could hardly make it in the society.

If you were not named: Williams, Doherty, Taylor, Braithwaite, Coker, Pearce, Bucknor, or Johnson, you could not make a head-way in life. It is the same practice where the Moslems were in charge with names like: Alhaji Abubakar, Alhaji Mohammed, Alhaji Ahmadu Alhaji, etc. This was why most of the educated elite in Nigeria and indeed Africa, have White (Christian) or Arab names added to their traditional names. Fela's grandfather had to add "Ransome" to the Kuti family name. J.J.'s father's wish for his son at that time could not supersede that of his wife.

The forces of colonialism were too strong for him to stand-up against. Fela's great grandfather realised that to stand-up against the forces of colonialism at that time, it could destroy whatever he stood for and in the process he may never get his point across. He had no choice but to let J.J. go to the missionaries. J.J. however, made an impact in the Yoruba Christian society during his life time - championing the course of the Christian church.

He almost got lynched trying to convert Western Nigerian Yoruba traditionalists into Christianity. He was left for dead from an attack on him by the traditionalists and only rescued by members of his church parish.

The irony of it all is that three generations after J.J.'s pioneering works, another Kuti (Fela) comes up trying to dismantle his colonial legacy. His son the late Rev Canon Israel Oludotun Ransome-Kuti 1891–1955 (Fela's father), was no less a victim of the same circumstances that colonialism has put the African man into today. According to Fela, his father wanted at an early age in life to be a lawyer and he told his father J.J. of his intentions.

Reverend Canon Josiah J. Ransome-Kuti 1855–1930 (Fela's grandfather), a pioneer of Yoruba Christian (Anglican) church and a music composer whose music was first reduced to staff notation and recorded on gramophone record in Nigeria. The irony of history is that three generations after J.J.'s pioneering works, another Kuti (Fela) comes up trying to dismantle his colonial legacy.
Picture copy from Anikulapo-Kuti photo collection.

Later, when it was time to choose a career he explained to his father his wish to study law, his father however told him he could not study law because he had only saved enough money for him to be a reverend father like him. It is obvious from his legacy in the political arena in Nigeria that Rev. I.O. Ransome-Kuti, was not someone out to spread the words of (the missionary gospel). He was never a pastor of any church like most reverends were.

He was more an educator - Principal of Ijebu Ode and Abeokuta Grammar schools. As a unionist, he was the first president of the Nigerian Union of Teachers. He rarely preached church sermons during church services, most times he was known to invite other reverends to preach sermons in his school's chapel.

A close look at Rev. I.O. Ransome-Kuti's life, would reveal that he realised that there was something wrong with the system being imposed on the people by the colonial powers and it was crystal clear, that he could do next to nothing to reverse the development. One reason for this is that it is not easy to say or do things one wants to, for the fear that it may destroy what one loves and stands for. If Fela's father could see the troubles his son Fela went through, I guess he would have contented himself with the words that he made the right decision not to confront the establishment. Rev. I.O. Ransome-Kuti was not a financially buoyant man but he was an honest, upright, and hard working man. It is these principles, and quality, that has endeared him to countless Nigerians of the time.

He like most other Africans, had to contend themselves with professions they did not like in order to get their points across. He turned Abeokuta Grammar School, into a model school for many generations after him. Abeokuta Grammar School was owned by the Abeokuta District Council, unlike most other institutions of the same educational orientation owned and run by the missionaries. As a result, he saw a challenge in front of him to make the school into a model with a standard worthy of emulation by any other institution.

In his drive to set a high standard for the school, being an ex student himself he saw himself as accountable to his community which entrusted him with the task of transforming the school into a citadel of knowledge. To this end he never allowed any missionary appointed school's inspectors to visit his school.

The one who tried to visit his school for inspection according to Fela, Rev. Kuti flogged out of the school's premises after the inspector had insisted despite Fela's father's decline of an inspection from any missionary. Reverend Kuti was a disciplinarian with very short fuse and could explode at the slightest irritation, he was a man who expected his students to learn quickly.

While teaching his students the tonic sol-fa, he made sure they sang every note correctly (Daudu as he was addressed by his peers) would call on all the students to sing after him. Usually, you found some of the students singing the notes wrongly. To such students there was no smile or parting on the back from Daudu.

In order to locate the culprit, all he did was to round-up all the students from where the wrong note was sounding from - and before you knew it all the people rounded-up would point out the culprit. As an example to the others, he would cry out his traditional funny slang to the culprit who by now would be standing in front of him "suu 'ke" (meaning hunch your back). Without any hesitations, Daudu would swing his atori (cane) across the hunched back of the offending student.

If there were more than one of them singing the notes wrongly, he took turns to flog each offending student. His creed like most educationist of that time was: "spare the rod and spoil the child". Meanwhile, there would be a graveyard like silence pervading the atmosphere except for the echo of the swipes of the atori (cane or horsewhip) lacerating the back of its victim.

Fela distinguished himself during these musical lessons, as a testimonial to his genius then which manifested in his iconic celebration as a musical talent later of world proportions.

On several occasions, he had the opportunity of being called upon by his father to conduct the whole school through musical lessons. I asked Fela to comment on how seriously his father took his music classes and his response was: "To show you how seriously he took his music lessons, my father had three different ways of beating offending students. One be! Touch your toe! This one if him don vex for you patapata, na him he go tell you say touch your toe.

Anybody wey him tell so, make that person know say my father go beat the shit out of him yansh" (butt). "Mark you!"Fela explained further, "As him dey whip your yansh (butt), he go dey shout out to the offender say: straighten your knees. If the offender no straighten him knees, my father go nearly beat the person yansh burst.

The second way to punish offending students be say if him dey for jovial mood, he will ask the offending student make him push him yansh out backward - he calls this style of flogging yoo booli! If you no yoo booli! He go flog your back bend by force". The third style his father used to punish offending students during his music classes is what Fela had explained earlier his father called: "suu'ke".

Describing his father's attitude towards his students generally, Fela said: "My father was so strict, but he was a very interesting man to deal with. He was always jovial in his moods except when you contravene any of his laid down rules. If you offend him while beating you, you will be wandering why such a jovial man can again turn to flog you so much without any twinge of emotion. However, to my father he was only trying to instil in you some sense of discipline Fela would rationalize as if defending the iconic Priest. He will admit in his school, any kind of school drop-out or expelled student from other schools without demanding for testimonial of good conduct.

In fact, Abeokuta Grammar School was well known because of my father's ability to control all kinds of rascally student regarded as beyond control or redemption by other institutions. When my father died, I did not really feel his departure because he was god-damned too strict with his students - his children inclusive. His strictness would have appeared to have created an alienation of affection in our relationships. To me at that time, despite the fact that I cried I was almost thanking God that the man died. If not for anything, I was sure to have my peace from any more floggings.

Contrary to the general opinion, we were all not too close to our parents especially my father. My parents treated us more like boarding house students, than their biological children which was an incontrovertible fact that we were actually fathered by them. The beatings I Fela alone received, from my father and mother individually is about 3,000 strokes of the cane. Every time, I always get beaten for doing one thing or another.

For an example, it was against my parents rule to lean against the wall or bend while you walk. It got to a point where everyone of us was afraid at the slightest sight of either of them, because you would not know what next you were going to be scolded for. In my father's case, whenever students heard the word "oga'nbo" (meaning the boss is coming in Yoruba language), there was always stampede at its best. The whole place will be in pandemonium as everybody is trying to runaway whether you are his child or not.

Those who were brave enough to wait for my father to pass bye, would stand motionless - with their chest thrown out like in the military, except that in his case the students bowed their heads in reverence. The only sound you hear during this moment is the student's usual salute to him "Good morning principal" depending on what time of the day it was.

The reason why most of those students bowed their heads while my father walked pass, was to pre-empt any of his usual questions ranging from why you were not smartly dressed or why were you standing and not pushing your chest forward? Many students ran afoul of my father's rules because a great percentage of the students in my school were from Lagos, where people tended to walk with strut. It was my father's belief, that those who had such tendencies were either rogues or that they harboured dubious character.

If you walked with a swagger close to him, my father would beat the daylight out of you. He was such an implacable disciplinarian, who believed nobody was too difficult to mend. Whenever the board of governors of our school met, you would always find him sitting behind the board members on the high table influencing deliberations.

He was so much an authority in his own right, he maintained in his school compound one of the most neatly kept flower landscape ever kept without exaggeration. Whenever a goat strayed into the school compound, he always made sure that students chased the goat out or seized it.

Students sent after such goats were obliged, to bring the goat back to the school compound and tied down even if they had to chase it to its owner's house. There was a day, I was sitting with other students - we numbered about twenty that day idling around chatting some funny tales among ourselves.

Suddenly, we heard that deep familiar voice of my father across the lawn from our house (the Principal's residence) saying: "Eyin ti e wa ni ibe yen!" (Meaning in Yoruba "all of you over there"), "Yes Principal!" we chorused back across the lawn. "Eran kan wa ni ehin yin!" (Meaning that there is a goat behind you all), we again responded "Yes Principal!" "E mo oruko e na?" (Meaning do you know its name?). We answered "No Principal". "Ko gbodo lo!" (Meaning it must not escape).

"What is it?" He cried out to us, we all replied in unison "Ko gbodo lo!" Spontaneously, there was a staccato of feet leading to something akin to bedlam as we all tried to catch the wandering goat. We were all aware that failure to catch the goat would bring our names in the punishment book. After chasing this particularly mulish nimble footed goat around the school compound for the best part of an hour we managed to apprehend it.

From the way we all stumbled altogether on the boy who seized the goat first, and firmly gripping its leg (goat and him together), it was like catching the most prized prey. Today, looking back, I can imagine my father laughing his head off as he watched us chase after those frequent and obdurate straying goats.

I begin to think it was fun for him too. Such goats when caught were tied behind the Principal's house until its owner came to bail it out with one shilling (ten kobo in the present day Nigerian decimal currency)" Fela concluded. From those who knew him, Rev. I.O. Ransome-Kuti was a rare character indeed. He was said to have kept his students alert almost all the twenty four hours of the day. Like his son Fela, he also had his brushes with the Nigerian military.

There was an incidence, where Fela's father was said to be walking through the military barracks in Itesi area of Abeokuta with his hat on. A soldier standing close to where Daudu was passing ordered him to take-off his hat while he walked past the British flag flying near bye.

He refused to comply with the soldier's orders, and the soldier tried to force the hat off Daudu's head with a bayonet. He almost lost an eye from the injury he received from the attack on him by the soldier. After this particular incidence, Daudu complained to the authorities so vehemently that in the end, the military barracks had to be reallocated from Itesi in the heart of Abeokuta city to its present location in Lafenwa area on the outskirts of the city.

Rev. I.O. Ransome-Kuti was a voice in the Nigerian political arena. These were the kinds of issues he took up with the authorities in Nigeria, he was said to have participated in the political scene in the country - though not on partisan basis.

However he left a legacy where whatever he stood for materialized one way or the other before the authorities concerned – Fela was every inch like him, very uncompromising and no middle way in his resolve to pursue a principle over which he zeroed his mind and this way of life, would be eloquently encapsulated in his song "No Agreement." Daudu was a member of the Elliot Commission responsible for the institution of university education in Nigeria.

Unfortunately for the country, those who ended up leading Nigeria to her independence did not possess the kind of vision he had for the country. His political vision was that of mass education, teaching the people how to know and fight for their rights and practicing in every day to day aspect of life, uprightness.

He lost any political impact he would have made as a result of the Nigerian "money politics". A not too rich Reverend and school Principal unlike his opponents, who were business men, lawyers, who had big business like the United African Company (UAC) behind them underwriting their campaign expenses.

Moreover, the demands of his professional calling, did not give him the opportunity to participate full time in partisan political scene. Whatever he contributed politically were done through his wife Funmilayo Anikulapo-Kuti (1900–1978), who herself was no less as dynamic as her husband.

The daughter of Daniel Olumoyewa Thomas (1869–1954) a farmer-trader and freed-slave that was liberated after the abolition of slavery. According to Fela, He was captured shortly before the abolition of slavery, set free by the abolitionists he walked back from Sierra-Leon to Igbogun village where he was originally captured and taken away as slave.

He later got married on his return to Omoyeni Adesolu (1874–1956) a trader and dress maker. Funmilayo like her husband had the enviable distinction of many 'firsts' in the Nigerian Society.

She was the first enrolled female pupil of Abeokuta Grammar School, and the first known female to own and drive a car in Nigeria. After her basic education at Abeokuta Grammar school, she left for England in 1919 where she spent the first two years in Wincham Hall College Manchester - a finishing school for young ladies and the third year, she spent studying Domestic science, Music and Dress making.

She returned to Abeokuta in 1922, where she joined Abeokuta Grammar School staff as a Domestic and General Teacher. She got married to I.O. Ransome-Kuti in 1925. The couple had their first child a girl named Dolupo in 1926, their second a boy named Olikoye in 1928. It took the couple another ten years before the birth of their third child named Olufela born in 1938 and their last son Bekololari in 1939.

"Bere" as she was fondly called by her peers (meaning first lady in Yoruba), could be considered as one of the mothers of Nigeria's nationalist struggle and a champion of the universal adult suffrage. She and her associates in the Market Women's Movement, won the rights for women to cast votes in general elections in Nigeria.

In their resistance against individual taxes imposed on women in Abeokuta by the late King of Abeokuta (Oba Alake) Sir Oladapo Ademola (who reigned from 1921–1962), the king was forced to abdicate his throne and went on exile in 1949 in Oshogbo in the northern part of Yoruba land. The king was only reinstated in January 1951, thanks to the British colonial administration for whom he played a stooge.

Throughout the period following this episode, Funmilayo's local leadership of the market women and in national politics steadily declined because her Abeokuta constituency like the rest part of Southern Nigeria was split as a result of the political conflict between the National Council of Nigeria and Cameroon (NCNC) and the Action Group (AG).

These crises led to the imposition of tribal politics in Nigeria – a kind of divide and rule that best suited the English colonial government. The fall-out from the power tussles between two political giants, led to another in-fighting within Chief Obafemi Awolowo's Action Group.

Rev Canon Israel Oludotun Ransome-Kuti 1891–1955 (Fela's father), member of the Elliot Commission responsible for the institution of university education in Nigeria. Unfortunately for the country, those who ended up leading Nigeria to her independence did not possess the kind of vision he had for the country. His political vision was that of mass education, teaching the people how to know and fight for their rights and practicing in every day to day aspect of life, uprightness. Copy picture from Anikulapo-Kuti photo collection.

The conflict, coming a few years after Nigeria's independence on October 1, 1960, would degenerate and engulf most of Nigeria's South West cities. It resulted in a conflagration of monumental proportions and social disruptions, with enduring scars on the Nigerian polity following disputations over the elections of the Western House of Assembly.

Although she served for a brief period, as an officer of the Western Region working committee of the NCNC and also as a member of the Egba Council (later the Abeokuta Urban District Council) for a number of terms. Funmilayo unsuccessfully contested twice as a candidate for the Western Region House of Assembly, in 1951 as the NCNC candidate and in 1959 as an independent candidate.

Expelled from the NCNC of which she had been a founding member since 1944, she founded her own party the Commoners' Political Party (CPP) which barely survived for a year. By 1960, she had petered out as a political force, and could not command any significant following among women in Abeokuta who were split between the two major national parties from the south. One should salute Funmilayo's courage as a politician and a woman at that, supporting and defending the banners of an NCNC Party considered as (Igbo party) in a Yoruba dominated region.

Problem started between the NCNC and the Action Group as a result of tribal politics introduced by the Action Group led by Chief Obafemi Awolowo. Prior to this, the NCNC was well accepted in the Western region despite its leader Dr Nnamdi Azikiwe being of Igbo origin from Eastern Nigeria. His party the NCNC, won the majority seats in the 1951 Western Region House of Assembly elections.

Chief Awolowo appealing to Yoruba tribal sentiments of the elected members, managed to convince most of them to cross-over to his party the Action Group. Thus overnight, most of the Yoruba elected members of the NCNC changed camps joining AG and thus began tribal and sectarian politics that would later lead Nigeria to the Biafra war. We shall discuss this war in the chapter ahead. Meanwhile to have a broader view of how these two political leaders arrived at manipulating their people to satisfy their personal ambitions, it is necessary to digress a little by asking the question who are the people of modern-day Nigeria?

On October 1, 1960, Nigeria gained what many today have described derisively as flag independence or political independence from its colonial masters but she has remained a member of the British Commonwealth a political contrivance designed to keep previous colonies in perpetual servitude.

As an entity Nigeria came into being on January 1, 1914, when the two British protectorates of Northern and Southern Nigeria were amalgamated by Sir Frederick (later Lord) Lugard. Sixteen years earlier Flora Shaw, a journalist for the London "Times" who became Lugard's wife had suggested that the several British Protectorates along the banks of river Niger be given the name "Niger-Area" (Nigeria). Later in 1961, Nigeria received a part of what was the British Cameroon. The area the country covers today (570.000 square km.) contains remnants of great Kingdoms and Empires that rose through the centuries.

In 1884-85 at the Berlin Conference after the scramble for Africa, the continent was divided between the western Powers. Under colonial rule, rich cultural areas were separated from their traditional sources. As a result, the present-day State-Nations in Africa contain a mixture of cultural heritages. Cosmogony mythologies play important roles in defining and it is not that this invaluable fact is not known to the colonial masters, but their choices were made for their own administrative convenience and essentially for mischievous reasons in African societies.

Though creation myths in African societies are as varied as the many cultures existing on the continent, some scientists and writers without the bias of Africa being the cradle of today's civilisation are of the opinion that various groups of Africans originated from the Nile valley region particularly Ancient Egypt.

Among the chain of evidence leading to this conclusion are similarities of language, traditional beliefs, ideas and practices, religion, plus the survival of customs and names. Concerning the Yoruba, one of the three major groups of people that inhabit present-day Nigeria, archaeological discoveries come in support of this theory.

The Yoruba progenitor Oduduwa, is said to have come from Ancient Egypt. This belief is based on the similarity of works of art (mainly sculptures) discovered in Ile-Ife, the mythological centre of Yoruba land with those found in Egypt.

Present-day Yoruba land is situated below the river Niger, starting at the fringes of the northern savannah grassland in the western part of Nigeria and covering the western high plains right to the tropical rain forest in the south. Yoruba cosmogony tells us about a God Olodumare, who lowered a chain from the sky at Ile–Ife, down through which Oduduwa the progenitor of all Yoruba people came down. Another story tells us that Oduduwa came from Egypt. He (Oduduwa), like several other African people, was forced to migrate from the great lakes region and the Nile valley as a result of wars.

This assumption is based on the resemblance between sculptures and other works of art, found in Ile–Ife and those found in temples and pyramids in Egypt. Today, Yoruba still refer to themselves as 'Omo Oduduwa' (the children of Oduduwa). After his death, his vast kingdom was divided up among his seven sons. Later divided into numerous independent kingdoms that share a cosmogony origin, the Yoruba kingdom broke up into numerous empires after several internecine wars – for which the slave trade was largely responsible.

A major factor in Nigeria's political dynamics is the similar cosmogony myth shared by the other two major peoples, notably the Hausa and the Igbo. Hausa cosmogony tells of the 'Hausa Bokwai' or the 'seven Hausa states' and the 'Banza Bokwai' or the 'seven bastards' referring to the 'seven legitimate' and 'seven illegitimate' children of the Hausa progenitor.

After his death like the progenitor of the Yoruba, his vast kingdom was shared among his children and later broken up into several geographically diverse and culturally varied states and empires – for which the Arab slave trade or the 'Jihad' were largely responsible.

Despite the propagation of Islam the similarity in the pottery works of the Nok people with those of the Yoruba, points to a common origin that has not been explored as a result of the divide and rule policy on which colonialism thrived. Present-day Hausa land is situated immediately above the Niger River, from the fringes of the northern savannah grassland in the western part, to the eastern end of Nigeria with a frontier with the republic of Cameroon - above the river Benue up to the fringes of the Sahara desert in the north.

The Igbo people of present-day Nigeria occupy the eastern half of the southern part of the country.

Historically, they reside in villages and towns smaller than those of the Hausa or Yoruba. Most of these towns and villages are headed by 'chiefs' called 'Obi' or 'Eze' who don't have the same stature, influence or authority as the kings in Hausa land and Obas in Yoruba land. The shared cosmogony between these three principal people who form the entity called Nigeria, gives credence to the notion of a common root for all the people. It is my conviction that when archaeological researches are done, more will be discovered that unite the people than the division on tribal lines that exist today.

Returning to the NCNC and Action Group crises, a brief history of the two political leaders will help put the reader in proper perspective. Dr Nnamdi Azikiwe started his political career in the then Gold Coast (re-named Ghana at Independence). After graduating from an American university, Azikiwe settled in Ghana as a journalist writing in "The African Morning Post" and championing alongside others the cause of the new African nationalism.

He was forced to leave Ghana in 1936, after he published an article considered seditious under the Gold Coast law and judged on appeal seditious by the West African Court of Appeal and later the Privy Council. Azikiwe returned to Lagos and started a new journal called "The West African Pilot". He was able to sell his brand of nationalism to a public that cut across tribal lines. According to Fela, a key reason why he attracted the followership of the likes of Funmilayo Ransome-Kuti as founding members of his party. At Independence, Azikiwe became the first

President of Nigeria thanks to an alliance with the party from the North. Chief Obafemi Awolowo "intelligentsia" lawyer and merchant, who became rich from defending big family and corporate interests like those of the colonial British conglomerate the United African Company (UAC). Awolowo had an ambition to rule Nigeria and was prepared to go to any length to archive his dream.

His support, for the Alake in Abeokuta despite the mass movement of women behind the market women protests might have been hinged on a desire to earn their support in view of his ambition. Shortly after independence a political fall-out between Awolowo and his deputy in the Action Group Samuel Ladoke Akintola, degenerated into a big political in-fighting the end result – a political crises that engulfed the West of Nigeria.

In 1962, Awolowo was charged and sentenced to prison for "treasonable felony". His son Segun Awolowo who returned to Nigeria presumably to defend his father, died in a mysterious car accident. Meanwhile Fela's mothers' alliance with NCNC, kept her out of the Western Nigeria political in-fighting and with all the political and social uprising, Funmilayo Ransome-Kuti's effective leadership of women had declined significantly.

This was due to developments in tribal and regional party politics as explained above resulting in the Action Group (AG), which supported the Alake becoming the majority party in the Western Region.

As a foundation member of the opposition party the NCNC, her chances for success in regional or national electoral politics shrank considerably, eventually ending in 1959 when the NCNC refused to nominate her as a candidate for the House of Representatives in the federal election. She also failed in her bid to create a strong representative national women's organisation.

Her Federation of Nigerian Women's Society, refused to co-operate with Action Group and instead supported women's leaders in Ibadan who established the National Council of Women's Societies. By the time Fela returned from his studies in the United Kingdom, his mother no longer commanded her former political influence at home.

She had become isolated, but found consolation in the recognition she received from the Women's International Democratic Federation - a Marxist organisation that sponsored her attendance at its international women's conferences as well as travel to Eastern Europe, China and other countries.

She was politically in contact with Dr. Kwame Nkrumah (first President of Ghana), and she also suffered from the Nigerian establishment for her international political impact, her passport was seized by the civilian government of Tafawa Balewa (1960–1966).

When Fela changed his name to Anikulapo-Kuti in 1975 she did too. It is a pity that by the Nigerian contemporary colonial African values and standards, all good people and things are always discredited while the bad things and people are celebrated and given places of honour.

Funmilayo Anikulapo-Kuti 1900–1978 (Fela's mother), fought for freedom and justice through-out her life, but in return she was paid back with uncommon vicious injustice and physical abuse and dehumanization. Her house where her son Fela lived was burnt down by Nigerian soldiers. She herself at a ripe age of 77 years, was thrown down from the balcony of the top floor of the one story building re-named Kalakuta Republic by her son.
Photo by Femi Bankole Osunla Africa 70 Photo Agency.

Funmilayo Anikulapo-Kuti fought for freedom and justice through-out her life, but in return she was paid back with uncommon vicious injustice and physical abuse and dehumanization. Her house where her son Fela lived was burnt down by Nigerian soldiers. She herself at a ripe age of 77 years, was thrown down from the balcony of the top floor of the one story building re-named Kalakuta Republic by her son.

More about this barbaric action of the Nigerian army is coming later in this volume. Critics have accused her of encouraging her son (Fela) to stand up against the colonial subservient regimes in Nigeria. If one may ask, how else does one expect her to act as a dynamic example to her children?

It is on record that during her life time, she fought against the ancestors of those her son is fighting against. Like her son later sang "No Agreement," Kutis don't compromise. This is the legend behind the Kuti family. They are born fighters for social justice and emancipation for the people.

This legacy is self-evident in all generations of the family Fela as we begin to read in this volume, with his frequent confrontations with the Nigerian establishment Fela was only stepping into the shoes of his ancestors. It was as if the family realized early in life like Frantz Fanon said in his book - Toward the African Revolution, on the need to be in the positive book of posterity and speak the truth to the oppressor.

According to Fanon: "The future will have no pity for those men who, possessing the exceptional privilege of being able to speak words of truth to their oppressors, have taken refuge in an attitude of passivity, of mute indifference, and sometimes of cold complicity". Similarly, a cousin of Fela and Nobel Prize Laureate Professor Wole Soyinka in his Prison memoirs, "The Man Died" was quoted as saying 'The man dies in him who keeps silent in the face of tyranny'.

Front cover Fela's London Scene album

Back cover Fela's London Scene album

COLO- MENTALITY

Colo-mentality is the title of a song Fela wrote in 1975, shortly after he dropped the "Ransome" tag from his family name and replaced it with "Anikulapo". The song is particularly critical of the African elite who prefer Western values, names and mannerisms to the African traditional names and way of life.

As inheritors of the colonial administration left behind after independence, they propagated a culture that made a great part of the African population develop negative images and resentment of their traditional values, indoctrinating Africans in a way designed to psychologically create an inferior people in them. Fela like many African youths growing-up on the continent was raised in this unfortunate cultural milieu.

For an outline of his early life, he was raised in the middle of the neo-colonial intelligentsia – educated middle-class lawyers, merchants, with Christian values. Born among the generation where colonial administration had flourished and had established "white" standards and values as symbols of a civilised man. Among these educated Nigerian elite of which his parents were leading actors, sending their children abroad was the symbol of a successful parent and status symbol. His other siblings Dolu, Koye and Beko were already in England studying nursing and medicine respectively while he was still struggling through high school.

According to Fela he was "the president of plan-less society", no ambition he was content to earn a little salary and go about Lagos night clubs having fun listening to highlife music. Fela had as collaborators in the "plan-less society" friends like Siji Shoetan, Dapo Tejuosho who later became the Oba of Oke Ona area in Abeokuta, St Mathew Daniel (nick-named Ajapa). Fela's nick-names at this time were "El Paso Kid" and "Simon Templer".

Many times they 'stole-out' of school at night went to Fela's house, silently pushed his mother's car out of the garage and let it role about two hundred meters from home before starting the engine. Once out of sight, they all got in the car and drove to Lagos about sixty Kilometres away night clubbing. They got back to school in the early hours of the morning. These escapades ostensibly explain, why he had low grades and had to struggle through high school.

Highlife music because of the introduction of electric instruments into the music, have been described by many Western writers to have been influenced by western music. However to those who know, it is an indigenous music with a lot of traditional rhythm from the accompanying drums and traditional call-and-answers vocal songs.

Highlife commanded national patronage and its popularity transcended the frontiers of most West African countries like Ghana, where E. T. Mensah's band was a pioneer and other groups like the Uhuru Dance band and the famous Ramblers International.

It was the music of choice in official circles, particularly during Independence celebrations. Very popular in Anglo-phone West Africa, with its variety in Franco-phone areas like Cameroon where it is called Makossa thanks to the contribution of Manu Dibango or in the Congo called Rhumba or Zoukous.

During this period Nigeria had an array of successful highlife band leaders like Victor Olaiya, Roy Chicago, Bobby Benson, Adeolu Akinsanya, and Cardinal Jim Rex Lawson. These were some of the major names, that were making waves in the swinging Lagos night life. Jimoh Kanbi Braimah, an older student from Ijebu Ode Grammar School was very much instrumental to Fela's taste of highlife music. J.K. (as he was known to everyone), met Fela during one of those inter-Anglican School's Sport meetings. They both hit it off as friends and regularly J.K. skipped school in Ijebu Ode, to join Fela and other members of "plan-less society" on their clubbing escapades.

Early 1957 after graduation from Abeokuta Grammar School, Fela moved to Lagos, took a clerical job with the then Ministry of Finance situated on Broad Street. He didn't have any specific ambition other than going out night clubbing listening to groups like Victor Olaiya with J.K. who also had moved to Lagos after his high school education in Ijebu Ode. Many times Beko, his younger brother wrote him letters inviting Fela to come-over to England like the rest of his siblings.

He even suggested that Fela could come and study music if he didn't find any other subject that interested him. All these to no avail, Fela was content with his little clerical salary and visits to Lagos night clubs. According to him, all that changed one day, when a girlfriend ditched him and left with another man.

He liked to go out regularly with her and she knew it. They had pre-arranged an outing and Fela arrived at the girl's home in his mother's car to pick her up for their date. He was told by the girl's younger sister that her sister couldn't make the rendezvous because she had to go on an errand for their parents. Disappointed, Fela got back into the car and as he was backing-out of the girl's house, his car headlight beamed into the garden next to the girl's home.

There she was in close embrace with another man kissing. Fela said he was so hurt with what he saw that he drove home forgetting his outing. Feeling his pride was badly hurt, he sent a telegram to Beko that night asking him to help enrol him in a music school in England. He wanted to go as far away as possible from this double-dating girl.

A little digression is necessary at this point because, contrary to certain claims that Fela went to England initially to study law because the educated middle class views of the Ransome-Kutis regarded music as a demeaning career for a family member of the ilk of a Kuti. I affirm here, that Fela left the Nigerian shores with the blessing of his mother to study music. I guess if his father were alive, he too wouldn't have objected to his son's choice of career, bearing in mind that his grandfather and father were renowned for their musical prowess.

The "Egba (Abeokuta) Anthem" was written by his grandfather. Without any hesitations as soon as he received the telegram, Beko enrolled Fela at the Trinity College of music and early 1958 he left the Nigerian shores for England. At the age of 19 he was considered too old for the beginner's class and the Principal of the college Mr. Greenhouse, who interviewed him almost cancelled his admission. However, Fela insisted on learning music saying: "it is the only thing I can do in life".

Considering that the young man came thousands of kilometres away from England, the school Principal accepted him in the school based on this declaration "that music was the only thing he wanted to do professionally". For his preliminary year in school, Fela was put in a beginner's class among children aged between eight and ten years old. According to him for the first time in his life, he had the urge to do something more serious than running after "skirts" and going night-clubbing. He wanted to major in trumpet, but at that time the trumpet was not considered a major instrument.

Hence, he chose the piano as a major instrument and the trumpet he played as a secondary instrument. He also built up some road experience by playing with different student groups mostly of West Indian origin. This was when he formed his first, group named Highlife Rakers playing jazz and calypso. They delighted their audiences with the works of musical greats like Lord Kitchener and Mighty Sparrow as well as Fela's songs which were rendered in Yoruba language. His old friend J.K. had joined him in England this time, Fela had a modest one bedroom basement flat in Cornwall Crescent, Ladbrokes Grove paid for by the £30 allowance his mother sent him monthly. He always had friends hanging out with him in the apartment even when he moved to Aberdare Gardens in Swiss Cottage.

The house was always filled with friends listening to music, in company of lots of women. There were also other students from the "plan-less society" school days people like Dapo Tejuosho, Bushura Tiamiyu, who later became a Lagos business man and Victor Akan, who later became a Senator during the Shehu Shagari administration in Nigeria (1979–1984).

Fela from all accounts at this time was shy with women, J.K. a year or two older was more forthcoming and street-wise than Fela and he was more successful in dating the girls. Beko (Fela's younger brother) detested J.K, from a long time and would continue years after their return to Nigeria decades after. Beko considered him as a bad influence and a parasite who lived off his brother Fela.

One of the reasons why Beko couldn't stand J.K. was that the latter usually skipped lectures at the Inns of Court where he was enrolled to study law, because he went night clubbing with Fela and found it difficult to wake-up next morning to attend lectures at school – and that was why JK never got to complete his Law school programme. Fela however at this time had become more focused and dedicated to his studies unlike J.K.

The turn around was essentially a manifestation of his love for music, he was interested in music and he did everything in this regard to advance. Things got bad for JK when his parents found out he was skipping school, they threatened to stop sending his monthly allowance hence he was forced to move out of London. They were thus separated in the early 60's, until Fela's return to England in 1971 to record at the famous EMI Abbey Road recording studio.

A transformational orientation, had occurred in Fela - gone were the days of "plan-less society", he knew he wanted to play music and he was ready to sacrifice everything for music. He went everywhere with his trumpet – anticipating any opportunity to play with other musicians, a habit that stuck with him even on the day of his first marriage.

Talking about his stay in London Fela said: "As a student in Trinity College, I worked very hard and passed my practical examinations majoring on piano and trumpet. To get a certificate as a professional, you are obliged to pass both practical and theory exams. The practical I was cool with, however the theory of music for me was not interesting. It covered the history of European music, which was irrelevant to me. Every time I had to sit for a theory examination, I would just read it hurriedly because I was not interested in this aspect of my studies.

As a result, I failed in my theory exams, but for the practical I made very good grades. To graduate however, if you passed the practical aspects of your examinations you had to also pass the theory within a space of three years. If at the end of the mandatory three year grace period the student failed the theory, he would be required to sit for both examinations again.

On my third and final attempt, I realised that it was my last chance and failure was not an option if I failed this time around I knew it meant starting all over again. Bearing in mind, that I was getting too far-out of that classic thing and I was deeply involved in Jazz. I was already experimenting with different mouthpieces to obtain some tone effects on my trumpet. To fail this time around the theory, I was sure to have problems with my practical too.

On this note I worked very hard on my theory and finally passed it". Recollecting these period in his musical history, he was asked by the author to explain what he thought was the most challenging experience he went through. In response Fela said: "There was this occasion when I thought I had learnt to play my trumpet well enough, I have been playing the instrument for almost a year and half so I assumed I was good enough because I could do some Duke Ellington solos with my trumpet. I decided to go to a club called MARQUEE, where I had seen some young White boys playing trumpet. I asked to play with them but they turned me down.

Fela pictured left with his ever present trumpet and Wole Bucknor third from left with friends in a London club. Copy picture from Anikulapo-Kuti photo collection.

Instead, they gave me an address of another place where they said professional musicians jam. So I carried my trumpet and went searching for the address given me. Luckily I was with Wole Bucknor (he was married to a cousin and latter became the director of music in the Nigerian Navy), he told me he had been to the place to see a concert before.

On our arrival, I saw musicians taking turns to play solos into different songs - mostly copy rights. I did not get an opportunity to join in the playing until after about four tunes had been played by the musicians present. Finally, one of the musicians beckoned on to me to join in.

The people watching the musicians play, were dancing and from all indications enjoying it too. Soon as I moved to take a solo, I noticed that the dancing audience was moving towards the stage. I thought being a new face, they wanted to hear me play my trumpet. But as I played on, instead of the merry mood I had witnessed in the audience this time they all just stood there starring at me.

At a point I realised that I was being mocked. It was really bad for me, because I kept playing my none-sense and I did not know how to stop. The more I tried to impress them, the more I realised that I was not getting anywhere with the audience. Suddenly, I heard the sound from an alto sax player just behind me this made me stop playing. It came out that the sax player was the late Joe Harriot - one of England's leading sax men at that time.

He masterfully drew the audience away from me, with some nice solo works and I could see that the audience had forgotten instantly about my poor performance. To make my situation worse, Wole Bucknor with whom I went to the venue had disappeared leaving with my trumpet case that I kept in his custody before I went on stage. Instead of walking out of the venue discreetly, I was forced to carry my trumpet in full view of the audience.

I was so ashamed of myself. Outside the club, I found Wole Bucknor waiting for me. It was clear he did not want himself to be identified with me. Without saying a word to him, I collected my trumpet case and headed home for almost a year, I could not step out of the house to play my trumpet anywhere for fear of being mocked again."

But Fela would psyche himself again and pick the broken pieces of a debased ego. He now resolved to put more energy to his trumpet playing and practice sessions, that lasted for several hours every day in order to improve and possibly achieve perfection. It was an experience he could never forget. Meanwhile Fela's sojourn in London, was not limited to just studying music and performing with his new band called Koola Lobitos at all the Nigerian student parties - there was also room in his heart for love.

During this period in his life, he met a young half Nigerian and half British girl Remi Taylor (1941-2002). The daughter of Alaba Taylor, a Nigerian and a Chartered Accountant resident in England and the younger brother, of Justice John Idowu Conrad Taylor who later became the Lagos State Chief Judge, her mother Sadie Eileen half British and Native American Indian and African American origin. As a child Remi had the opportunity to visit Nigeria with her parents, and Sadie Eileen too recounted very beautiful memories of these period in her marriage to Alaba Taylor.

How she visited the interior of the country - Warri and Abeokuta with young Remi and her sister Sonia. The country-sides of Nigeria she visited then, according to her are no longer the same peaceful countryside that it used to be she would recall later in life. Even Lagos, had undergone a remarkable change from the beautiful sea-side city it used to be she lamented.

In later years, Fela used to joke about how Sadie Eileen's father was so obsessed with cleanliness according to him, Remi's maternal grandfather used to brush the teeth of his dog. He too was a professional musician - a trombone player, and Remi's children had the opportunity to meet him while on tour with Fela in England, while he was resident in one of those homes reserved for retired artists where he lived till the late 1980.

Unfortunately for Sadie Eileen, her husband died young living her to cater for their two young daughters - Remi and Sonia. She worked so hard that she fell ill at the hospital, she was diagnosed with severe kidney problems that needed to be operated. After the operation she was left with one kidney, her doctors gave her a few years to live but Sadie Eileen is still very much alive almost four decades after her operation.

With her health problems and while recuperating from her operation, her two daughters were obliged to be transferred to a 'home'. Remi had to start working at an early age, but she kept contacts with her roots by attending Nigerian parties and it was at one of those parties she met the first and only love of her life - Fela.

At this party organised by Segun Awolowo, and Yomi Akintola, both children of Chief Obafemi Awolowo, leader of the Yoruba political party Action Group and first Premier of Western Nigeria and his Deputy Chief Ladoke Akintola respectively.

For Fela and Remi, it was 'love at first sight'. They dated and it seemed to both of them they were destined for each other. Fela met Remi's mother who was convalescing in a home for the sick. 'Mom' or 'Nanny' (as we all called her years later), is full of beautiful memories of the young Fela. For her he was a perfect 'gentleman'.

After they both had been 'going out' for about a year Fela still a student at the age of 22 and Remi a 20 year old working lady, got married on January 7, 1961 in Maidenhead, England, with Bushura Tiamiyu acting as best-man and Sonia (Remi's younger sister) the chief brides maid. Later in life, Fela claimed he cried on the day of his marriage because he never wanted to get married but his actions proved the contrary.

It was obvious he was in love and from all indications it was for both of them 'love at first sight'. Fela from his account admitted that he was the first and only man in her life. If he cried at his marriage, it must be his sudden realization of the enormous burden associated with marriage at a relatively young age of twenty-two the marriage institution apparently scared him.

One has to bear in mind, that his only regular source of income was still his £30 monthly student allowance from his mother back in Nigeria which barely took care of his rent and kept body-and-soul together. Fela proved to be a responsible father, husband and son-in-law to his immediate family as Remi and her mother explained many years after. Contrary to opinions in some quarters, there was no prenuptial agreement between Remi and Fela to stray out of the their legally contracted marriage to take on additional wife, let alone marry the history making 27 women at a single ceremony.

Fela still a student at the age of 22 and Remi a 20 year old working lady, got married on January 7, 1961 in Maidenhead, England. Even at his marriage, the musician Fela could not be separated with his trumpet. Copy picture from Anikulapo-Kuti photo collection.

People who knew the couple at this period (Remi and Mom did confirm this), claim that it was not the same Fela who many years later engaged in an unprecedented mass marriage to 27 women that Remi married way back then.

A woman of the strength of character of Remi, would never and could never have allowed the only man she ever knew such liberty through a prenuptial agreement. She knew what she wanted from the marriage, and her focus on the mission saw her give birth to three lovely children in quick succession. Moreover, his marriage kind of provided the stability he needed at that time to concentrate on his studies. Gone were the hanger-on's, the young couple moved into the Aberdare Gardens, Swiss Cottage apartment of Fela.

In the same year, they had the first of their three children - a girl named Omoyeni (named after Fela's maternal grandmother). The second child of the marriage, a boy named Olufemi Olufela was born in 1962. Their third child another girl named Olusoladegbin (Sola), was born on November 23, 1963 in Nigeria after Fela's graduation.

I believe Fela's return to Nigeria, was due to his new found family as most students that studied abroad usually stayed back after graduation, under the pretext of working to gain some more experience in the colony before returning to their home country.

However with Fela it was the contrary in 1963, shortly after graduating with a diploma from the Trinity College, he returned to Nigeria with his pregnant wife and two young children. On arrival in Lagos, he got a job as a program producer with the Nigerian Broadcasting Corporation (NBC).

He settled down with his wife and two kids into the Lagos home of his parents situated at 14A, Agege Motor Road and shortly after they sent for Remi's mother who later joined them in Nigeria. Sadie Eileen joined them in Lagos in 1964 and remained in Nigeria until the death of Remi in January 2002, after which she moved back to the United Kingdom with her younger daughter Sonia Nelson-Cole resident in London.

Fela's home coming party in Abeokuta 1963 from left: Fela's sister Dolu with her son Yomi, Fela's mother Funmilayo, Fela's Brother Koye with his son Dotun, Fela with first daughter Yeni and Remi with son Femi. Picture copy from Anikulapo-Kuti collection

Fela the strugglling days playing the piano at Kakadu Night Club

EKO ILE (LAGOS-SWEET HOME)

Eko is the traditional name for Lagos city, before the Portuguese renamed it Lagos – after the sea-side city with the same name in Portugal. In the song EKO ILE, Fela is talking about the popular adage 'no place like home'. Remembering the city with nostalgia, he sang in Yoruba - East, West, North and South, "there is no place I could head to that could be like Eko Ile (Lagos). If I go on a journey to London or New York, I will always return to Eko". Songs like this formed the repertoire of his group Koola Lobitos in London and later in Nigeria. As we shall discover soon, the early sixties theme of Fela's songs were complete contrast from those of the 70's and beyond.

One could conveniently say, he spent the final years of the sixties searching for direction and musical identity. Moreover, one of the conditions that attracted him to accept the producer's job with the Nigerian Broadcasting Corporation (NBC) was the offer for him to lead an NBC orchestra. This was shortly after independence, Nigerians who held degrees and diplomas from abroad were returning home to take-up jobs that hitherto were held by European members of the colonial administration.

All the political actors (military and civilians) of the 60's and the 70's were beginning to re-group at this time. People like Yakubu Gowon, Odumegwu Ojukwu, Murtala Mohammed, Theophilus Yakubu Danjumah, to mention a few. Fela's evolution in the society is like going through Nigerian history. The political climate in Lagos was tense but with his mother no-longer actively engaged in politics, Fela went about his business with lots of his energy dedicated to catering for his nuclear family.

Meanwhile, the orchestra he was supposed to lead at the NBC seemed a mirage and a forgotten story but the musician in him spurred him on. After exhausting his patience with no positive result, Fela decided to form his own band - independent of the NBC management. He called the band KOOLA LOBITOS, after his first group during his student days in London. The new group comprised of a contra-bass player from Cameroon named Ngomalloh, Tony Allen on drums, Uwaifor on tenor sax, Lekan Animashahun handled Baritone sax and Fela on Trumpet.

Like most of the musician of this generation and those that came after them, only very few of them could read or write music. The reason they could not read music, was because the opportunity to attend music schools was not available. Added to this handicap, was the plain fact that there was no school of music here in Nigeria at the time. This same problem persisted almost three decades after. Hence, most musicians of African origin merely learned to play from hearing. They also learned on the job, because they could not afford to buy their own personal instruments. Some learnt from the police and army bands.

Fela at this time, was said to have tried within the limits of time and opportunity to pass on knowledge to most of his musicians to enable them read and write music. The gusto to teach, was however not complemented by an equal passion by the musicians either due to mental laziness or some other remote reasons. Remi used to explain how Fela would set-up a black-board in the living room of their 14A Agege Motor road residence, and he would invite his musicians Tony Allen, Ngomalloh, Lekan Animashaun, and others, to learn to read and write music.

Years after, some of these musicians called Fela names ranging from "slave driver" to "exploiter" as his reward, for trying to impart knowledge but he was undeterred. Unknown to these crops of musicians, it was an opportunity on a platter of gold presented to them to learn and become independent professionally. The musicians didn't grab the opportunity. Like this generation and those after, they were too lazy to learn – preferring to learn by hearing only. We shall discus this when talking about the break-up of Africa 70. Fela meanwhile, continued to compose and write songs talking about social issues like I mentioned earlier. They were songs with theme clearly in contrast to the songs of the 70's.

Songs such as Obe! (Soup), Ako! (Braggart), Lover and Witchcraft all rendered in Yoruba language. The last song, "Witchcraft" is a nostalgic piece expressing his longing to return to his family after a long absence from them. In a homesick manner, he wishes the witchcraft would bring him home. Omuti Tide is about the alcoholic, who never takes his job seriously. In the end he lost his job to alcoholism, this song was also rendered in Yoruba language like most of the songs from the Koola Lobitos era.

One could hear the strong Latin jazz undercurrents in these songs, a legacy from Fela's London days experience out with West Indian brothers. There were also hints, of the mix of Latin jazz and the Afrcan American Diasporas influences in his Funky Horn. It is sad, Fela stopped playing the trumpet in the latter part of his life, as Funky Horn is a testimony to him being a great horn player. He did admit that he abandoned the trumpet, because he was lazy to keep the rigors demanded by the instrument.

Highlife Time another Koola Lobitos piece, delivered in English is about highlife music. Highlife music is one of the many contemporary urban music of West Africa, believed by some to have been influenced by Caribbean Calypso and Latin American Salsa.

Ololufe Mi is Fela's love song, declaring his affection for his lover and insisting that she is his one and only love. Fela's proficiency as a trumpet player can be heard in this track like in all the other pieces from his Koola Lobitos days. Wadele wa rohin, in Yoruba language, means 'you will go home and give news'. This is a song about Eko - the traditional name for Lagos city as earlier mentioned, Fela says: "you will go home and proclaim in what high esteem people hold Eko, the home of great sense! Smart city, Eko is a funky, swinging, crazy, ghetto".

Laise lairo another song in Yoruba, literally means "without any offence or provocation a man's wife is forcefully acquired and rewarded with imprisonment by the oppressor". Like most of Fela's songs of this era, they were addressing social malaise prevalent then. Wayo too, talks about dishonesty. Wayo in Hausa language translates to deviousness. Even though this song was rendered in Yoruba language, there has been a cross cultural relationship that made the word have the same meaning in both Hausa and Yoruba nations.

It has the same connotation and conveys the same feeling of consternation at the discovery that a person you trust is dishonest, a cheat, and fraudulent character. It is Fela's way of propagating virtues of up-rightness, in the society. To say the least, the going was tough for the young band-leader who had the problems of keeping the band together, coupled with the challenges of fending for his nuclear family, his devoted wife, and kids from pangs of hunger.

He was frequently running back to his mother, to borrow some money to put some food on the table for his family - a dependence that his younger brother Beko disliked. This time, all the four Kuti children were back in Nigeria from their respective studies in England. Dolu was working as a nurse at the General Hospital in Lagos, Koye a paediatrician at the Lagos University Teaching Hospital, and Beko a general medical practitioner at the Lagos State hospital.

According to Fela, many times he needed to fix something in his Opel car (with licence plate number LK 402), he went to his mother to ask for little loans. There was a time, the windscreen of his car was shattered and because he lacked the financial muscle to replace it, Fela improvised with a plastic sheet and drove it around Lagos.

When Beko discovered that their mother gave Fela money to fix the windscreen, he was so upset with her saying she was over-indulging him. One major problem for Fela and the band, was that the music scene in Nigeria had not become commercially rewarding to sustain an artiste. Not many people could afford to pay their way in at night clubs. And since most of them could not afford record players, and other accessories record sales could not have thrived under such atmosphere.

The political crises, in the Western region as the Southwest was known then aggravated the economic situation. With massive social uprising, people could not go out to night clubs due to insecurity and thus compounded the woes of industries related to showbiz. Curfews were imposed, thus restricting movements at night while the contrary was the case in Ghana. In Ghana, the music scene was much more vibrant compared with crises-torn Nigeria. The Nkrumah government, invested and had subventions for culture. As a result, Fela decided to explore the music scene there. On his arrival in Ghana, it did not take long for him to realise that highlife music was the brand of music making waves.

Most of the leading artistes were playing highlife all over the country, and the government of Kwame Nkrumah was encouraging artiste through their culture Ministry. Describing the state of affairs during this era in Ghana, Fela said: "I never see a country like that before anywhere in Africa. Only in Europe can you find such encouragement for cultural emancipation.

Fela many times needed to fix something in his "Opel" car (with licence plate number LK 402), he went to his mother to ask for little loans. There was a time the windscreen of his car was shattered and because he lacked the financial muscle to replace it, Fela improvised with a plastic sheet and drove it around Lagos.
Picture copy from Anikulapo-Kuti photo collection.

This visit was my second to Ghana on my first visit, I did not have the opportunity to see the country in a profound way and know its potentials fully because I was in transit. This time around, I had plans to stay long to see the country well. Everywhere I went, it was mostly highlife music, the whole country was swinging with this brand of music so much that I said to myself that this is the place to come and play music as a professional. Two weeks after my return to Lagos to make plans on how to bring my band to Ghana, it was reported in the news that Kwame Nkrumah had been deposed in a military coup."

The military coup that toppled Kwame Nkrumah February 1966, was invariably sponsored and financed by imperialists who preferred to keep Africa always as a dependent society. From all indications, despite western propaganda to mask imperialists imprints in the coup plot, the massive importation of American music to sway Ghanaians away from their favourite highlife music and in its place infuse American or Western type of music all bore marks of their agenda.

From the moment in 1958 when Nkrumah declared that, "the independence of Ghana is meaningless unless linked with the independence of the rest of the continent," and with his avowed ambition to unite the continent, he became a target for elimination by the imperialists if their design to continue to have a strangle-hold and explore unfettered, resources freely deposited in the bowels of Africa.

His publications from 1961, to the time he was toppled would testify further to Nkrumah's well articulated vision of Africa in: "Challenge of the Congo", "Africa Must Unite", "and Neo-Colonialism" all condemning in no mean term the role of the United Nations (UN), the United States and most Western powers that work to destroy the African unity drive.

Fela despite the change of political power in Ghana, went ahead with his plans to explore the music scene. He explained at a news conference in Nigeria his plans to tour Ghana with his band. Unfortunately Fela's employers the Nigerian Broadcasting Corporation (NBC), did not share his vision and perceived, his planned tour of Ghana as divided loyalty. But as far as Fela was concerned, a trip to Ghana was still in pursuit of the actualization of one of the terms of his engagement as a staff of NBC.

It would be recalled that I mentioned earlier, that NBC management had as part of the article of faith while Fela was to be engaged, to set a musical band which he would lead only to leave this promise unfulfilled once he started work - a clear breach of contract. Since there was no way for Fela to get redress for this breach, he decided to concentrate on building his career with the Koola Lobitos. As it turned out, it was the right decision because the NBC director of programs had resolved to sack him on his return from the tour and in anticipation of the possible sack, Fela resigned on his return to Lagos.

Meanwhile, he found a venue to perform with his band along Herbert Macaulay Street which then was considered down town of Lagos. The venue was called "KAKADU NIGHT CLUB". As part of the attraction for this club, he organised different concerts on a regular basis. Some of the shows he named "tea time dance" (a legacy of his colonial mentality), "miliki night "and the Sunday afternoon jump. With help from Remi his wife, some aesthetic transformation of the venue using local materials emerged, colourful and gorgeous.

The "Sunday Jump" was not limited to Kakadu subsequent venues he played after, had their own versions of the Sunday afternoon jump. It afforded, Fela the possibility of playing for the younger generation that could not stay out late at night. Special free Sunday afternoon jumps, were organised at the "Race Course" re-named "Tafawa Balewa Square".

He also organised the "jump" at the Ritz Hotel (on the Lagos Island), and the Crystal Gardens - situated in Ebute Meta, another suburb of Lagos as it was known then. These venues it must be pointed out, did not attract full capacity crowd most of the times for obvious reasons hitherto explained and for emphasis insecurity, occasioned by political crises, with homes and cars of political opponents being destroyed with impunity.

To make matters worse, there was also mass killings and exodus of Easterners (Igbos), resident in the North precipitated by the coup of January 15, 1966. We shall discuss this coup later but meanwhile for Fela, the gamut of political crises had insalubrious impact on his musical enterprise especially tasking his management genius to wield the group together.

After his last tour in Ghana and the fact that the situation was better than it was in Nigeria, he again decided to return to Ghana with his band in 1967. There was an initial encouraging turn-out of fans, but after sometime patronage started dwindling. It was so bad for the group, that they could not even pay their hotel bills.

The subsequent low turnout at his concerts, was not due to his brand of music which was called highlife jazz, but rather the impact of the change of government and the attempt by the new military rulers in Ghana, to obliterate all known legacies of the Nkrumah regime and highlife being one of such, was never given the kind of patronage or governmental support to the industry as was the case under Nkrumah. Highlife music which had widespread acceptance under Nkrumah, had now ceded ground through manipulative imperialist squeeze of the government of the day to their preferred and imported "soul" music.

The new rulers of Ghana in their attempt to please the western world, dissociated themselves from the Pan African policies of Nkrumah– substituting Western music for traditional highlife at official functions. To this end, subventions and encouragement of cultural activities were bunged or declared illegal by the new regime. In its place, massive importation of Western music became prevalent unmindful, of the effect on capital flight and the emasculation of the nascent and fledgling music industry.

Most night clubs that used to feature highlife music groups, now preferred disco and the soul music from Europe and America. It was "soul" music, that ruined the initial impact Fela and his group made on this second Ghana trip. Nigerian-Sierra Leonean born musician Geraldo Pino, who toured Ghana after Fela, was much more successful with his brand of "soul" music. He (Pino) also owned some modern musical equipment - a luxury Fela did not have.

Fela attested to the sophistication of Gerldo Pino's musical equipment thus: "Even when I was in England, the equipment used by most of the groups I came across, were no match for the sophistication of Pino's musical equipment." On the other hand, what Fela used as musical instruments were some improvised amplifiers - made from cutting-open boxes and fixing loud speakers and microphones inside. For a band trying to build a following, playing with this type of musical instrument was in itself a challenge, given that the sound quality could not but be substandard.

While Pino was touring Ghana, there was not much competition back home in Nigeria for Fela and his band. Rex Lawson, one of Nigeria's leading highlife musicians from Port Harcourt, had moved to the East because of the civil war.

He later died in a car crash before the end of the war. Before the war there was supposed to be a musical duel, to resolve an alleged "feud" between Fela and Rex Lawson. However, the musical "duel" between the two leading trumpet maestros in Nigeria at that time, never materialized by acts of providence. But, by 1968 Geraldo Pino left Ghana to return to Nigeria, making Lagos his base like Fela.

A potent scheme that would have foisted Fela masterly on the music scene, was hatched by Beko whose motivation was to assist Fela achieve financial liberation from his now incessant borrowing of money from their mother. Beko, proposed to have Geraldo Pino to accept a musical competition via a concert on an even kiln using the musical equipment of Pino. The latter, probably saw through the plot as a possible opportunity to have Fela leap-frog to limelight at his expense and so Pino declined the challenge.

Fela also at this time, dabbled into show promotions in collaboration with Faisal Helwani, a young Lebanese naturalised Ghanaian business man based in Accra. They called it Good Music Promotions (GMP), bringing different groups from Ghana to play at concerts with Fela's band. Among the well known groups that took part in these concerts were the Uhuru dance band and The Ramblers International. They toured with these groups in Nigeria and Ghana extensively.

Financially, the Good Music Promotions was successful. Fela said from most of the shows he made about 500 Naira (which then was about £500 due to exchange rate parity) per concert at that time. Meanwhile, Pino continued to perform throughout the country and for Fela it was really uneasy moments. Nigeria was in deep war of secession curfews were imposed in the big cities, and night clubs were forced to close down their operations. The only avenue open for performance for musicians and in that way make some money, was to be invited to various liberated zones in the Biafra war to entertain soldiers.

A brief history of how Nigeria arrived at this civil war is necessary at this point because as mentioned earlier, all the "actors" of the political scene of the 60's and 70"s profited from this war as they took over the reins of power, and were the new political players on the scene after the war in 1970.

Shortly before independence as earlier stated, Nigerians who attended foreign Universities and higher institutions abroad, returned home and since nature abhorred vacuum easily replaced the departing colonial administrators. Emeka Odumegu Ojukwu, was one perfect example of these new breed of Nigerian elite. The son of one of Nigeria's foremost millionaires, Chief Odumegu Ojukwu who made his fortune from transport business from the port city of Lagos to other parts of the country. Young Emeka was educated at England's elite college – Eton.

He graduated from Oxford University, with a master's degree in the early 50's. Emeka's father like other elites, nursed the dream that he would have a son in the heart of government business someday even though he was financially comfortable, yet he knew the additional benefits such foothold in government could harvest. Back in Nigeria, young Emeka had a different idea of a career in mind.

He drove his MG sports car to the Nigerian Army Barracks in Zaria in the Northern part of Nigeria, and enlisted in the Nigerian Army. From reports, the young man wanted to enlist where his father's financial influence could not pose an obstacle to his ambition.

While teaching the new recruits the names of the parts of a gun as part of their training, the regimental Sergeant (a Hausa man) un-aware of young Emeka's educational background called a "Safety catch" – "saplica". Emeka interjected saying the word is "safety catch" and not "saplica". Unknown to young Emeka, in the army such act of correction was tantamount to insubordination with severe consequences.

Everyone is expected to obey orders like Zombie in the army (apologies to Fela). Emeka was forced-match by the instructor Sergeant, to the presence of the Commanding Officer who happened to be an English man. Hearing the report of the instructor and the response of the young recruit, he realised immediately that in the young Emeka was exactly what they were looking for in the officer's cadre of the Army.

However, in keeping with army regulations discipline had to be maintained, insubordination could not go unpunished. An impression had to be created that the young recruit had been expelled, while in truth young Emeka was posted to Kaduna for officers training. He rose in rank to become Lieutenant Colonel Emeka Odumegwu Ojukwu, and was the commander of the 4th Infantry Division of the Nigerian Army based in Kano on January 15 1966, when a group of young Majors attempted to seize power.

The coup d'état was a welcome relief to most Nigerians, as there were jubilation on the streets throughout the country. The spontaneous jubilation from the public in support of the coup, was a proof that the citizens were tired of the political in-fighting and the subsequent atmosphere of insecurity that reigned since independence. Major Chukwuma Kaduna Nzegwu (spokesman for the coup plotters), in his radio broadcasts to the nation condemned the class politics for corruption and ineptitude.

He cited as part of reasons for the coup, a desire to 'clean the political scene of corruption and self-aggrandizing attitudes and ambitions of the political class'. This statement came as a relief for majority of Nigerians, who in over six harrowing years since independence had reeled under the burden of pervasive social uprisings and political in-fighting resulting in infernos and massive loss of lives. For about a week there was no government at the centre, some of the high profile casualties were the Prime Minister Tafawa Balewa, the Premier of Western Region Chief Ladoke Akintola, the Premier of Northern Region and the leader of the Northern political power Sir Ahmadu Bello (the Sardauna of Sokoto), a few federal ministers, and some top Army Generals accused of collaboration with the corrupt political class.

Unfortunately, the coup did not succeed in the East, Kano in the North, and some other parts of the South giving justification for the opposition against the coup as tribally motivated pogrom.

Considering, that most of the Majors that participated in the coup plot were also from the Southern part of the country, it made the accusation look real. In a seemingly ethnocentric Central Government (going by the composition of lead actors), it was easy to accuse the coup plotters of tribalism.

The Northern region, had more victims among the politicians that were killed in the coup attempt than any other regions. Was it providential that the President Dr Nnamdi Azikiwe (a leading politician from the South), was out of the country at the time of the coup plot?

The perception, that the coup was motivated by a nobler act than tribe falls on its face, when the mysterious coincidence of Azikiwe absence from the shores of Nigeria is juxtaposed with the composition of the executors of the coup. However, Ojukwu's resistance from Kano against the coup despite being of the same tribal extraction as the coup plotters, stands as a counterpoise to the argument to stigmatize the coup as a tribal initiative.

After a long impasse, with the coup plotters' threatening to march down to Lagos (the seat of power) a compromise was reached with the coup plotters. Major General Aguyi Ironsi, was chosen by the army hierarchy to head the Federal government and he asked the coup leaders to join the new government.

On their arrival in Lagos, Major Chukwuma Nzegwu and his fellow collaborators were arrested and sent to jail in the Eastern part of the country. It was a strategic move to save them from reprisal killing in any northern state prison, and keeping them in the West was inexpedient and an option those in power felt rather uncomfortable with being too close for comfort.

Meanwhile, Ironsi tried to calm the situation with a few strategic moves one of which was the appointment of Governors for the three regions from their own ethnic origin. He also kept the three regional structure of the country, thus in the North he appointed a prince from Katsina Lt Colonel Hassan Usman Katsina, for the Western region Lt Colonel Adekunle Fajuyi and Lt Colonel Emeka Odumegu Ojukwu for the Eastern region.

In May of the same year, there was massive genocide committed against the Igbo community and other people from Eastern region through-out most of the cities in the North of Nigeria. The massacre were perpetrated by northern civilians with the "blessing" of Nigerian army (dominated mostly by people from the north). The genocide, precipitated an exodus of people of Eastern region residing in the north to migrate home to the east.

General Ironsi was unable to condemn the massacre openly because, he was heading an army dominated by people of northern origin. He was afraid to commission a judicial investigation, with the intention of finding and bringing to justice the perpetrators of the mindless massacre for fear of being accused of tribalism.

Meanwhile, Gen. Ironsi embarked on a nation-wide tour of each region to promote his union government and to calm frayed nerves. On July 29 1966, on his way back to Lagos after visiting Ibadan the capital of Western region on the last stage of his tour of the country, a group of young army officers from the north led by Major Murtala Mohammed and Major T.Y. Danjuma seized power in Lagos. General Ironsi and his host Governor, Lt Colonel Fajuyi, were assassinated and this left Nigeria without a Head of State for about one week.

The fate of Nigeria, was during those seven long days being debated by the new coup leaders at the Ikeja Military Barracks with an idea of secession of the North on the cards but for the intervention of the British Ambassador in Lagos, who pointed out to the northern officers that it would be a most inexpedient option that they might live to regret.

Once the option of a breakaway was eschewed, the choice of a head of state was the next knot to untie and they discovered, that a Northern muslim leader would not be acceptable to the other regions which culminated in the choice of a compromise officer, Lieutenant Colonel Yakubu Gowon a Northern Christian.

Born on 19 October 1934 after a primary education at the St. Bartholomew's School Wusasa Zaria, Gowon attended the Government College Zaria for his secondary school education. He joined the colonial army in 1954, went to the Sandhurst military academy in England for his officer's cadet course.

He served in the Congo with the UN peace-keeping force, and was posted to the army head quarters in Lagos before the July 1966 coup. With the issue of genocide against the people from the Eastern part of the country yet to be resolved, Lt Colonel Odumegu Ojukwu who was appointed Governor of the Eastern region after the January coup, objected to Yakubu Gowon's appointment as the new Head of State.

This was the genesis of another secessionist move, this time from the East that unleashed a most horrendous human carnage in the ensuing civil war. His objection was based on the fact that he and Gowon were of the same rank coupled with his Masters degree from Oxford University in England, Ojukwu felt he was better qualified than Gowon to be appointed head of state. However since the northern anti-Igbo sentiments was one of the reasons the new coup plotters struck, they were not willing to accept his protest no matter how logical.

His suggestion of Brigadier Babafemi Ogundipe, the next most senior army officer after the assassinated General Ironsi was not accepted either by the coup plotters. A Yoruba man from the south, Brigadier Ogundipe in the early hours of July 29 1966, escaped from Lagos through Cotonou to London on a self imposed exile. Interestingly Fela's Sister, Dolu had a son (Yomi), for General Ogundipe which qualified him as a Fela brother-in-law.

In a deft political move to appease the Western region and to counter Ojukwu's objection to his quest for power, Gowon released the jailed Yoruba political leader Chief Obafemi Awolowo who was serving a fifteen year sentence for 'treasonable felony'. He also named Brigadier Ogundipe, Nigerian Ambassador to England.

Ojukwu remained obdurate, and refused to accept Gowon's leadership which he made clear at the famous Ahiara Declaration on May 27 1967. After a meeting of the Eastern Consultative Assembly which he called to advise him on measures to take, based on the issue of genocide against the people from the region.

Without one voice of dissention his nominated "Consultative Assembly" members, unanimously made a declaration to break away from the Federal Republic of Nigeria and named the seceding region The Republic of Biafra. The new republic, was backed by France, which had an eye on the oil rich region with Houphouet Boigny the President of Ivory Coast as their point-man.

The French government, sent military and material aid to the Biafra regime. They also helped evacuate Ojukwu, and many Igbo civilians away to Ivory Coast and Gabon at the end of the war. Meanwhile in a bid to weaken the cohesiveness of the Eastern region as a single enclave, Gowon promulgated a decree, dividing the original three regions into 12 states and appointed military governors on the bases of their state of origin like his military predecessor.

Awolowo was made the Commissioner for Finance and vice-chairman of the Supreme Military Council (SMC), a position equivalent to the Vice President in the Cabinet. With this appointment, the old man was thus fully rehabilitated. Awolowo used his political standing, to confer some credibility to the new military rulers. Since Awolowo couldn't rule Nigeria by being elected democratically, staying close to power albeit in a military regime, was getting close to his dream and this was the beginning of what in later years Fela would call an "Army Arrangement".

Now back to Fela, we can recall that he spent most part of the sixties and the civil war years in Nigeria searching for musical direction and identity. His major song during the war years was an appeal for Nigerian unity. A highlife jazz tune titled Viva Nigeria. Fela sermonized that "war has never been the answer to any conflict", asking Nigerians to get together as one people and unite.

The acculturation of most Africans especially before flag independence, was such that our perceptions became so westernized to the extent that Africans despised with passion their own customs and in some cases later couldn't even decipher which one was original African custom and tradition. In this acculturation, Islam and Christianity played cosmic roles. The society, had no regard for you no matter how skilful you were without western education from one of their Universities.

Fela was no exception, he had to go to England and America for his education. Talking about his trip to America in 1969 he said: "I had no previous plans for this tour. Somebody came and proposed to take me and my band to America on a tour. But the man did not have the money to sponsor the trip, to make matters worse he did not let me know about this problem of finance until all necessary publicity for the trip had been made.

I have never fallen for anybody like that in my life this was possible, because somebody very close to me at that time assured me that the man had the money to sponsor the trip. To convince me, this close associate also said he saw the man with seven thousand US dollars ($7,000) on him.

Mind you, at that time it was a lot of money. I believed him and we agreed to follow up our plans for the tour. I held a press conference, widely covered by the print media and television. Meanwhile, Geraldo Pino had started to play in Lagos gradually, pulling away the crowd attending my concerts. But the idea that I was taking my brand of highlife jazz to USA - the home of soul music, burnished my sagging image and gave some fillip to my fans base.

Another thing that helped me was the fact that on his return from Ghana, Pino did not make Lagos his operational base rather went on a nation-wide tour giving me a considerable space to burgeon. I made it out of Lagos before his return, though I almost lost the chance to go because I had opened my mouth at the press conference saying I was going to America to make some 'bread' (money). As a result, the American embassy staff in Lagos who had read the report of my press conference almost frustrated all our efforts to get visas. I had to meet with the Nigerian cultural officer, who happened to be a friend.

He gave me a letter to the US embassy, stating that our trip to the States was for 'cultural exchange'. With this letter I was issued visitor visa with which I could not work. Before our passports were handed over to me, the officer responsible for the issuance of visas demanded to see our air tickets, I turned to the promoter who accompanied me to the embassy and to my surprise there was no ticket.

It was at this point, I realised that the promoter was an irresponsible hustler desirous of exploiting me and my band". Fela was thus thrown into a dilemma. He had to produce the tickets or lose his travel opportunity. Furthermore, he was in a quandary over what he would tell an expectant nation he had earlier told that he was travelling out to make money.

It was for him an integrity issue and he weighed his options on the next way out of the predicament. With the publicity of the US trip, cancellation was not an option. He said to himself that it would cast a slur on the integrity of his person and the band which had begun to enjoy wide acceptability, to say the trip was cancelled because there was no money to buy air tickets? "All these were happening on Monday and we were supposed to leave on Thursday.

Fela and the Koola Lobitos the struggling days.
Picture copy from Anikulapo-Kuti collection

Fela left on trumpet with his group Koola Lobitos.
Picture copy from Anikulapo-Kuti collection

We left the American embassy, promising to bring the tickets the following day which was a Tuesday. Tuesday came it was the same story no tickets. So on Wednesday, I had to accompany the promoter to his brother Josy Olajoyegbe (who later owned the record label JOFABRO records), to raise the loan that would cover our air fares. Finally, he admitted to his brother that he did not have the money to sponsor our trip as he had planned. Luckily, his brother came to our rescue.

Moreover, the brother as a business man, saw an opportunity to invest in what we all thought was a potentially lucrative trip. He then gave us the two thousand pounds (£2,000) required to cover our air fares. The money was in fact raised as a loan from his bank. Immediately we left the bank, we went to the airline office for our tickets and from there to the American embassy. When I got our passports, I jumped for joy because I knew there was nothing to stop us now - USA here we come.

On board the plane to the states, I met Miriam Makeba who also was going to the US to further her musical career. During a conversation with her, I told her of my intentions and she expressed her concern about the music industry and when she realised it was my first trip to the States, she offered me contact addresses of promoters and booking agents she knew.

Though she did not talk much about the exploitative nature of the music industry, I guess because she herself was not aware of how big a problem it was then. On our arrival, I went tracing one of the addresses she gave me.

I met a White American at the office who immediately asked me what he could do for me. I explained my mission and without any delays he said: "Look America is a big country and I only promote big artists like Duke Ellington, Count Bessie, Miriam Makeba, etc. Look (pointing to the wall of his office) these are the photographs of my clients, I guess you know they are all big names in this industry.

If you have a record released like any of these artistes, then we can talk business - good morning". I sat there still waiting for him to tell me more, then he repeated his 'Good Morning' before I realised he was through with me".

The American tour, lasted for the best part of ten months and it came out to be the major turning point in Fela's career. Did he get a lot of money as he earlier expected? Far from it! America humiliated him and made him look very small - the realisation of this truth, was the major turning point in his life. Back home, the rumour mills were agog in Lagos that Fela had been arrested in connection with a sex offence involving a minor in America.

But there was no truth to this claim otherwise, taking sexual advantage of a minor American girl was a grave offence, which attracted maximum penalty and there was no way Fela would have been allowed to return home if he had breached such law.

For Fela, it was the beginning of a self discovery. He arrived in the US with a nine man band, the music he played was highlife jazz - a mixture of African traditional rhythm corrupted with jazz music - hopping it would make a difference. Unfortunately, Americans were expecting an African band with some originality. Playing traditional folk music and not jazz of which they already had a surfeit.

This was the first reality that hit him coming to the US as he did, he realised that he had over-estimated his stock. The self discovery of the unsuitability of his musical export appeared frustrating, but then it was further compounded by extortionists masquerading as business promoters who easily took advantage of a man desperate to survive.

Spurred more by a desire to earn money to defray his costs and support his band, Fela signed on the principle of doctrine of necessity any type of contract without deep reflection on their larger legal implications. On top of all these, there was the problem with the American immigrations. They swooped on him and his band, hounding them on the allegation that they did not have the proper work permits.

To avoid deportation, one of the band members (the bass player) absconded. As a result, a big concert that could have given them a chance and some exposure with big names like Bing Cosby, and Frank Sinatra attending, turned out to be a near disaster as Fela had to double as a bass player alongside his regular instrument the trumpet.

Meanwhile, he got a lawyer to argue his case in court with regards to their problem with the immigration, they were issued with new visas allowing them another three months stay in the US. Their major problem was finance. Expenses far outstripped income from their live performances, the band was making an average income of about US $900 (nine hundred dollars) a week. To supplement their income from shows, members of the band had to take up factory jobs.

Remembering this period Fela said: "Things were so bad for us I could not write home to give news of our dilemma in the States. I had boasted back home before we left that I was going to America to be a winner, I least expected any form of failure. Now the reality of America dawned on me, failure was staring at me in the eyes - I could not write home to tell my family that the trip was a monumental commercial failure. My silence got so bad that people back home thought I was in jail". If there was a lesson to learn from his American experience, it is best encapsulated in Fela's own direct testimony:

"My American experience was a turning point in my way of thinking and my general approach to life. America is a great country! It is so great, that it made me jealous that we didn't have this kind of greatness in our country. I travelled thousands of kilometres across America - from New York to Los Angeles. We spent about four days and nights driving on road, with an invaluable opportunity to see America for what it is as a truly great country. Driving from one city to the other, I almost thought we were in the same city, because development was widespread and uniform and a visitor could be excused for assuming that there was no difference in the topography of one state to the other.

The biggest experience for me on this trip was my exposure to the real Black history. The knowledge was substantially different from the colonial history we were thought in school back at home in our education curriculum. This history I am talking about provided me with the background knowledge about Africa before the arrival of the Europeans. I also got to know about great Africans such as Marcus Garvey, Kwame Nkrumah, Malcolm X, the Black Panther Party and many other authentic African activists by a girl I met and later lived with called Sandra Smith. I think I am a great person and I am sure, that every African who knows the true history of his/her heritage should think of himself/herself as great person.

It is the only way to think if one is to get out of the psychological brainwashing of the Black people by the colonial authorities. When you think of yourself as a great person, you will not accept second-rate things. I realised from my American trip that most Africans, do not really know about their life.

We have been thought that everything from overseas is better than our own natural things at home. We are not aware that what we see from these overseas countries could have originally gone overseas from our shores. It was during my trip that I found out this basic line of thought. For an example, I would have continued playing music like the English man, like my other counterparts who attended music schools in England.

During my days in England studying music, we were made to believe that only the English music could be called classic. Jazz and other traditional African style of music were not regarded as such. It was in America I found out the contrary.

Many African ex-graduates of European music schools preferred to play what they call "African Symphony" to European audience. When such Africans were asked why they were not acknowledged back home playing so well as they did, in responds these Africans claimed that the standard of music they performed was too advanced for the ken of their audience back home to comprehend.

These colonial oriented Africans lacked the sobriety of mind to admit the truth, that they had not adapted their acquired western musical education to their environment. Rather, they went about repeating stereotype propaganda and untruths about Africa - saying Africa being a jungle the people were incapable of comprehending symphonies and other classics".

From this firsthand account of his experiences in the United States, it would be incorrect to assume it was his grim economic challenges that changed his line of thought. Rather, the size of America itself and the fact that a country the size of a continent could come together as one country, bearing in mind that those opposed to African unity used the size of the continent to justify their opposition.

Front cover album design Afrodisiac

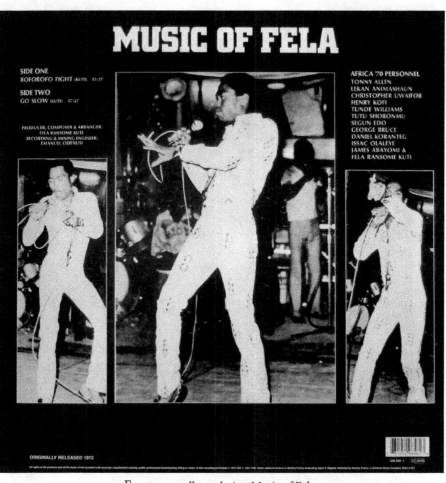

Front cover album design Music of Fela

VIVA NIGERIA! VIVA AFRICA!

Viva Nigeria is about the Biafra civil war in Nigeria as mentioned earlier. Fela was calling on Nigerians, to unite and resolve their differences in more amicable ways than through war. On January 15, 1970 General Philip Efiong Commander of the Biafra Army, surrendered to the Federal Forces. Ojukwu meanwhile had gone on a self imposed exile in Ivory Coast that would last until 1983 with the collaboration of France.

Meanwhile, Fela returned to Nigeria from America two months after the war ended - a completely changed man in ideological focus from the man who left the shores of Nigeria ten months earlier. It was not only his ideological orientation that changed, his music too had changed from highlife jazz to Afrobeat and the spirit of the new Fela could be seen in his way of dressing. Gone was the old short-sleeve shirts, in its place were clothes made from animal skins. He also changed the name of his band, from Koola Lobitos to Nigeria 70 and later Africa 70 as his ideology became more Pan African.

One might ask what has changed in the music? First his approach to music was no longer in the classic format of the student from Trinity College. Recollecting how the change came about, he said he was rehearsing with his band in Los Angeles when someone offered him a "joint" (marijuana), and until then Fela forebade any of his musicians from taking marijuana.

After smoking the "joint" according to Fela, he felt a kind of deep 'high' that enhanced his concentration taking him back to his roots in Abeokuta with all those "Sakara rhythms" and beats. To better understand this evolution in Fela's music we would need to talk a little about the kind of music that shaped Fela's musical evolution in his growing-up days in Abeokuta. Apart from highlife music, Abeokuta like most urban Yoruba cities was rich in traditional African music before the infiltration and influence on African urban city music.

The common denominator among the various groups of people that constitute the Federation of Nigeria was the shared cultural heritage, be it among the Igbo, Hausa, or Yoruba. A common streak amongst the peoples is that the naming of a child for example called for celebration.

Similarly, weddings, deaths, the award of chieftaincy titles, and similar occasions were celebrated with traditional music and musicians with the heavy rhythms of the talking drum and other types of drums and percussive instruments. Praise singers or griots, add their historic insights to the meaning of the ceremony by either singing in praise of, or recounting the historical prowess of the lineage of those present at the ceremony.

Though the instruments played by the musicians varied at each ceremony, the 'Talking Drum' is common in all the musical instruments in most of the regions. The talking drum known as 'Iya Ilu' 'mother of Drums' by the Yorubas and 'Kalangu' by the Hausas, history of this musical instrument would however show that it had been a common feature in the musical repertoire from time immemorial not only for entertainment but also as an instrument of communication. Before the invention of the telephone technology, the 'talking drum' used to serve as a means of communication in various communities.

In Yoruba land played by 'Onilu Oba' (the Oba's drummer), it was used in the same manner as bard (rhymester) to convey messages from the king to his subjects. Despite the presence of Bata Drums, congas, or Latin percussion as they are known in the Diaspora Yoruba music (places like Haiti, Cuba or Brazil) where they tend to deify the Bata Drum the important role of the Iya Ilu is invaluable. It leads the rhythm and other percussion follows. Be it traditional 'Apala' music, which serves as the root or the base of Yoruba urban dance music or its derivatives 'juju' or Fuji 'music', the talking drum sets the pace or could be described as the heart of the rhythm.

'Apala' music, sometimes called 'Sakara' music, because of the leading role of the sakara drum – a round hand-drum made from cow or goat skin. Firmly secured or attached to a pot-head top, has an emission of sound akin to the talking drum and could mimic the Iya Ilu (mother drum). The sakara drum is played with the fingers putting pressure on the skin, to change tones like the strings of the 'mother drum' pulled or released to change tones and sounds. As the evolution of apala (sakara) music is known to have influenced both juju and fuji in the present day Yoruba urban music, the same could be true of its influence on Diaspora Yoruba music - particularly in the rumba, salsa and samba music.

The Bata-Drum called the same name, conga-drums, or Latin-percussion, the samba-drums called bembe by the Yoruba, and other instruments feature prominently in apala music. Same as in samba, rumba, and salsa music like its Diaspora derivatives. The heart of apala music is percussion and the call and response vocal style of the musicians add beauty and rhythmical value to the music.

Today, the music has transformed into what is called juju or fuji music with the introduction of electric instruments. Another derivative that has remained close to the original apala is fuji music. Fuji music, has its origin in the Muslim fasting rites (the Ramadan).

Young folks in each area play drums and different percussive instruments around their communities, and sing to rouse Islamic faithfuls to perform their religious obligation of fasting during the fasting period. At the end of the fast, in keeping with the requirements of their religion, Moslems slaughter goats to mark the end of fasting.

Commonly called 'Aji Were' these young folks re-group on the eve of the end of Ramadan fast, holding duels with the goats in open grazing fields and participating in musical contests as part of the ceremony. Most of the pioneers of this Moslem-fast musical contest have become popular fuji artistes, with their record sales both official and pirated selling by the millions showing a widespread acceptance in the Nigerian population estimated at over 150 million. Although they chose to call it apala or sakara or by other names this genre of music, is like a ritualistic feature at all ceremonies.

The pioneers of apala music in Nigeria like Yusuf Olatunji alias 'Baba Legba', and Haruna Ishola alias 'Baba Gani agba', were highly successful in terms of financial rewards and testimonies of their successes could be seen in their vast estates and musical dynasties. Particularly in the Yoruba area of Nigeria musicians like late Ayinla Omowura, Sikiru Ayinde Barrister, Kolington Ayinla, and present-day popular traditional music stars remain popular because apala or sakara music are part of the Yoruba heritage.

The same could be said of juju music made popular by King Sunny Ade, Orlando Owoh, Ebenezer obey, and a host of others. However, the heavy percussion of apala music is the core of juju music.

From the foregoing, one could clearly trace the genesis of Afrobeat to ubiquitous apala music which had been in vogue in the childhood days of Fela. Fela only adapted the short repetitive phrases of the talking drum into the voice of his bass, and rhythm guitars in order to produce the great rhythmic melodies that formed the heart of Afrobeat music.

Unlike jazz, reggae, funk, or blues, that all give accent to individual instrument and personal solo contributions to enrich the overall music, afrobeat is a tight and harmonious work. A team work, with each instrument designated or assigned short repetitive phrases that makes–up the overall music.

On his arrival from America, Fela changed his venue of play from Kakadu night club to Surulere night club - he called the new club AFRO SPOT. His first appearance at the Afro Spot, was a pointer to the difficult task he had ahead of him. According to him, he greeted the audience with the Black Power salute - the clenched fist symbol, but there was no corresponding response from the crowd who did not know the significance of the clenched fist salute.

Subsequent shows after the first musical appearance had a low crowd turn out. This was understandable, because his music had changed considerably from what his fans were used to. Gone were his old highlife jazz, while the heart of his new style of play was the bass guitar, playing a steady rhythm with other accompanying instruments playing short intersectional phrases in a call and answer manner.

The concept though common in African music, was new to his fans who thought he was copying the American musical ensemble having just returned from America. However, Fela persisted, and continued to play this musical notes out of conviction that it was the right and proper direction to success.

Fela's younger brother Beko, at a point suggested that since Geraldo Pino's concerts were always jammed with crowd, he should again invite the latter to play alongside his band to bring the crowd to Afro Spot.

For Fela this was the last straw, judging by the fact that before his departure to America he invited Pino and was spurned. It was a moment to decide either to continue in his old style of music or persevere to change - Fela resolved to discountenance Beko's entreaties, to invite Geraldo Pino to join him in concert. He was prepared to die unknown than be humiliated again.

Daunting challenges, accompanied the year 1970 for Fela and his new genre of music Afrobeat. It was a period when series of tours, by commercially successful artistes were invited to the Nigerian musical space thus making the acceptance of Fela's music more herculean. Some of the notable names on parade were James Brown (god-father of soul), Chubby Checker (Mr Twist), and the sweet scintillating voice of Millicent Small.

There were new groups emerging on the Nigerian music scene all 'soul' oriented. Groups like Orlando Julius, Joni Hastrup's Clusters International, Tunji Oyelana and the Benders, and Jimi Solanke who was playing some kind of Yoruba rock 'n role. Fela playing Afrobeat was obviously different , but was still contending with acceptability in the Nigerian musical space. To support his ever-growing number of dependants, he took residence and continued to play with his band Nigeria 70 at the Afro Spot, where he had entered into a long lease with the proprietor Chief S.B. Bakare a prominent Lagos business man.

Meanwhile, he continued to play his Afrobeat working hard on different gimmicks to attract the crowd to his concerts. He also made an album titled Wayo (which means trick in Hausa language) recorded and released on EMI's (Her Master's Voice) label. Like all the other songs of the period, they were all recorded and released as 45 rmp's with the same record company. Songs with titles like "Abiyara," talking about his fear for his friend whom he did not want to covet his wife. "Mo re'gberun Mile" (walking five thousand miles) for his lover a kind of labour of love and "Eko" which we dilated on earlier.

The records released, were not rewarded with phenomenal commercial success. From Fela's stand point, he did not know what kind of message he could string together that would resonate with the fans in spite of finding a unique musical direction.

He wanted to stop singing about love and romance, which characterised his highlife jazz era. Gradually an ideological predilection towards Pan African concept was unfolding, but still not too truculent in this formative stage. However after a practice session at the Afro Spot, the idea occurred to him to sing about a social issue. He came up with the idea to sing about 'greed' he called this song Jeun Ko Ku (a glutton).

To his surprise, the crowd at this rehearsal responded positively to the music. Subsequent performance of the song brought the same appreciative response from the public, when he finally recorded the song on vinyl with EMI, it turned out to be a hit and his much awaited musical break came with this album. From then on there was no turning back. He tried to write songs on social issues or things concerning people and their environment.

There was this incident, at the Afro Spot not long after the success of Jeun Ko Ku. Fela arrived at the club to find an Alhaji (a name for Muslim faithful worshippers who performed the holy pilgrimage to Mecca in Saudi Arabia), who insisted he would not pay to enter the club as required by all patrons.

Fela was curious, to know why the man in question wanted to come into the concert without paying the mandatory fee to watch him play. If the said Alhaji could pay his way through to Saudi Arabia as a pillar of the tenets of Islam, paying to see a concert shouldn't pose any problem. Perhaps disoriented by some intake of alcohol, the man in question challenged Fela to fisticuffs pushing Fela to engage him in a duel and yelling: "Who are you?" The Alhaji, was slapped by young guys who felt aghast by his sheer effrontery and disrespect for Fela.

Apprehensive of more vicious attack, he took to his heels running as fast as his legs could carry him. Fela later composed a song, to share his experience with his fans with the title WHO ARE YOU? In the lyrics, he narrated his experience with the Alhaji and how the man got ruffled for his insolence. Meanwhile, Fela's Pan Africanist philosophy, was getting better articulation and vociferous. To demonstrate this, he changed the name of his club from Afro Spot to AFRICA SHRINE. The reason he gave for the change was that his music was no longer dedicated to entertain, but to spread a message that would make the wretched of the earth liberate themselves from both colonialism and its offshoot neo-colonialism.

The Shrine, would thus serve as the citadel of learning to explain his new ideology. Fela went further to explain, that the Shrine should be regarded more as a venerable place of worship than a relaxation and entertainment centre. This proclamation, irked existing religious communities who feared that his new doctrine would pervert the nation's Youth. Some of these religious fanatics, went to the extent of sending hired thugs to disrupt shows at the Shrine.

On several occasions the Shrine in full swing would suddenly halt abruptly due to unprovoked attacks, broken bottles and stones will be flying into the crowded dance hall causing the crowd to scurry in safety flights. The architectural design of the venue, made it vulnerable for such external attacks being an open roof arena.

These attacks continued relentlessly for some time but when Fela fought back, he was seen as the aggressor without looking back at the innumerable unprovoked attacks on the shrine. After one of such attacks, knowing that most of the culprits came from houses in the neighbourhood, Fela decided to carry the fight to the houses in the area.

During the attack with Fela's newly recruited protective squad, a notorious leader of the traducers of the shrine hitherto identified was bundled and brought to Fela's residence at 14A Agege Motor Road. It was a measure, Fela was sure would deter further assault on the shrine as the henchman was stripped bare and given what in the Shrine lingo was known as 'GB'(general beating). He was later set-free with a stern warning to cease further acts of aggression on the shrine.

But to the consternation of Fela, and other members of the commune these attacks did not abate. After another of such attacks, Fela chose to attack the neighbouring houses again. This time leading the attack personally, he shouted at the top of his voice to everyone that was around: "If you don't want us here you too must understand that you have no right to be here. We all belong to this country, from now on I am declaring war against all of you. If you won't let us conduct our business in peace then you too won't have peace".

From then on whenever they attacked, Fela's boys took their revenge on the neighbouring houses.

Bottles, stones, sticks, etc, were among the weapons freely used in this war of survival as far as Fela was concerned. It became obvious from the persistent attacks, that the culprits wanted Fela to pay protection money in order to stop the attacks. However, Fela who had made up his mind never to pay any protection money to anyone chose to employ more muscles to make his point.

With his "army," after almost a year of running battles he finally succeeded in putting a stop to the attacks. His band and organisation, was growing with the introduction of female dancers led by Dele Johnson (the beautiful dancers) as they were called.

Meanwhile Fela's 14A Agege Motor road residence, was beginning to attract all kinds of fans and hanger-on's. This was becoming a problem for his immediate family as they could no longer have their privacy. Remi, her mother and the three kids could no longer have the house to themselves and Fela as things used to be. As a compromise, he decided to rent an apartment for them in Ikate area of Suru-Lere.

He could afford it this time, because he was beginning to make some money. Bearing in mind that he had some tunes like 'Jeun Koku", "Alujon Jon Jon Ki Jon, Na Fight, doing well in the market. Coupled with this new financial buoyancy on the part of Fela, was the fact the Nigerian economy was upbeat too at that point in time due largely to influx of Petro-dollar from Nigeria's crude oil exports.

Another aspect of Fela that would later manifest itself started at about this time - his ability to use music to provoke violence among his audience. Fogo Fogo (meaning in Yoruba language "break bottle"), is an example of how he could incite his audience to violence. Whenever he performed the song live, the public seemed to react violently against each other breaking bottles. He never said they should attack each other but the fans took recourse to violent acts of breaking bottles. Femi his son, also provoked similar reactions from his audience with his song "Shé Wéré" in the New Africa Shrine. From my understanding, there was no specific instruction to push people to react violently in the song, but it just elicited spontaneous violence. The first time Fela played Fogo Fogo at the University of Ibadan "Havana Night", the students attacked each other with bottles.

Towards the end of his life, he wrote another song that would provoke violent reaction from his Nigerian listeners titled "CLEAR ROAD FOR JAGA JAGA". We shall discus this aspect of Fela in subsequent chapter.

At the start of 1971, Fela became emboldened and no longer kept secret his extra marital relationships with innumerable girlfriends. He like many other men, engaged in this pastime of flings outside the marital vows hitherto covertly sought their pleasures outside their homes. Some of these girls included his dancers who even moved in with him. Fela rationalized the relationship with his dancers, as being in line with a sincere desire in him to burnish the dignity of the girls whom society despised as dregs and unfit for marriage. Fela's failure, to communicate with his family and ostensibly brief them on his ordeal in America did not resonate well with his wife Remi. There was so much anxiety in her chest back home, coupled with all sorts of stories flowing in about her husband from the United States. It was reasonably believed, that Remi was under immense pressure from her family to file a suit for divorce.

Remi as she admitted years after, contemplated filling for divorce on Fela"s return back to Nigeria. I hope her children will publish like I said earlier, her memoirs one day and the truth of this matter would be perfectly clear. She would remain the only one, who could talk authoritatively about her relationship with Fela at this period and all the pressure on her to divorce him. Knowing that some of his musicians, squealed on his extra marital affairs to Remi during their ten month stay in America, Fela on his return admitted he was in a relationship with Sandra to Remi.

He also had to admit the existence of another girlfriend Iyamari – native of Cotonou in Benin Republic with whom he had a son named Kunle in 1971. Meanwhile with the success of "Jeun Ko Ku," his record company EMI, wanted him to return to the studio to record new materials. They proposed to record him with the eight-track studio in the Lagos port area of Apapa. Fela refused threatening to cancel his recording contract with the company, if they did not bring in more modern recording facilities into the country. EMI management in Nigeria at that time deliberated on what to do.

With Jeun Ko Ku still basking in huge market success, they were hamstrung to insist on recording Fela on their old and near obsolete studio equipment. As a compromise, they proposed to take Fela and his band to the EMI Abbey Road record studio in London (made famous by The Beetles), to do the recording promising to up-date their Lagos studio in the future. The "LONDON SCENE" album was recorded on this trip, it was a collection of short songs contrary to if compared to the one-song lengthy vinyl that characterised his later works.

It could be said, with all certainty that Afrobeat was born in this epoch. Fela shared the ideological disposition of the likes of Marcus Garvey, Malcolm X and Black Panthers, at this period in his life's evolution but still was at sea on what the message of his music should be. Limited to take on social issues such as J 'EHIN J' EHIN (gnashing of teeth), NA POI (graphic oral sex) or EGBE MI O (carry me) and FIGHT TO FINISH - an indication however that he was getting ready to combat the system.

ALU JON JON KI JON, the first song in the 'London Scene' collection is a traditional moonlight tale made into a song. Yoruba follore, makes constant references to relationship between the human and the animal world. He sang in line with this myth, how a great famine ravaged the entire world and as a means of survival it was required that all animals and human elements in the world, would have to sacrifice their mothers to provide food for all and collectively cooked for the benefit of all. When it came to the turn of the dog, the other animals discovered that he had secretly hidden away his mother in heaven before it was his turn to make the sacrifice. Alu Jon Jon Ki Jon, the other animals chorused after the dog, treating him as a selfish and dishonest comrade.

EKO ILE, is about the popular adage 'no place like home'. JE'NWI TEMI (DON'T GAG ME), is the first of Fela's attacks at the Nigeria powers that be - a strong message that he was not one to be gagged. The Yoruba language song, sent an early warning to those in power that not even the threat of jail could stifle his voice. It says: even if you jail me? You cannot shut my mouth! I will open my mouth like basket! You cannot shut my mouth!' He goes on to stress that the truth is bitter, but it remains what it is 'truth'. Hence, he will not stop talking and singing about the truth. OPEN AND CLOSE, represents a lesson in choreography and how best to dance to the new Afrobeat music with African vitality.

SWEGBE AND PAKO, sang in 'broken-English' was to encourage perfection and rear thorough professionals. It was meant to celebrate competence and disparage incompetence. According to Fela, a carpenter who does not know his trade is 'Swegbe'. A tailor who sews like someone in the carpentry trade is another 'Swegbe'. A doctor acting like a lawyer is 'Swegbe' same with a lawyer trying to act like a doctor.

On the other hand, a carpenter competent at his work is 'Pako' ditto the tailor, lawyer and doctor. The message of the song is that if you are in a position of responsibility, you need to exhibit professionalism and demonstrable competence to earn the soubriquet 'Pako'. On the other hand, if you do it perfunctorily you are 'Swegbe'. "If you are good you are Pako and if you are bad you are Swegbe".

GBAGADA GBAGADA! GBOGODO GBOGODO! Is another folk song celebrating the gallantry of the Egbas, in their resistance against the colonial forces and their agents on the coasts of West Africa. The Egba war with the British colonial forces, was led by Adubi a renowned Egba war General. Fela starts the song by calling on his listeners to sing along the words of the folklore, "Gbagada Gbagada Gbogodo Gbogodo" a verbal essence of the sound of thumping feet in a commotion.

With pride the Egba people went to war against the attacking colonial British forces. The Egba forces sought to liberate themselves and secure the future of their people from the invading British forces "Oo! Oo! Oya ooo! Eni omo wun oya ka'lo oo!" This is a clarion call, to join forces for the love of their vulnerable children and the need to bequeath an unfettered future to them.

Fela's London trip also afforded him the opportunity to re-unite with his old school friend J.K.Braimah, whom he hadn't seen since graduating from Trinity College.

Fela on getting to London, launched a broad network of connections to fish out JK on arrival in addition to his main mission to do the EMI recordings. Not a few of their old mutual friends, tried in vain to dissuade him from reconnecting with JK - with tales of big time drug dealer spurned around the neck of this old time ally J.K. Braimah. Fela discountenanced the advice and went in search of J.K Braimah.

Finally re-united, Fela found out that JK never succeeded in obtaining any degree or diploma despite his long sojourn in England. His friend he painfully realized, took recourse to deal in drugs to earn a living after all things had failed him.

That was a clear demonstration that Fela fearlessly stays with his friends no matter the threat and was capable of showing great empathy. Fela had compassion on JK, and sought to rehabilitate him by bringing him back home with him to Nigeria. He offered JK appointment as Director of Public Relations in his organisation.

Fela knew he needed someone with JK's wisdom to deal with some situations back home. JK accepted his friend's offer and thus he returned to Lagos.

Fela and JK re-united eating in Kalakuta.
Picture by Femi Bankole Osunla Africa 70 Photo Agency

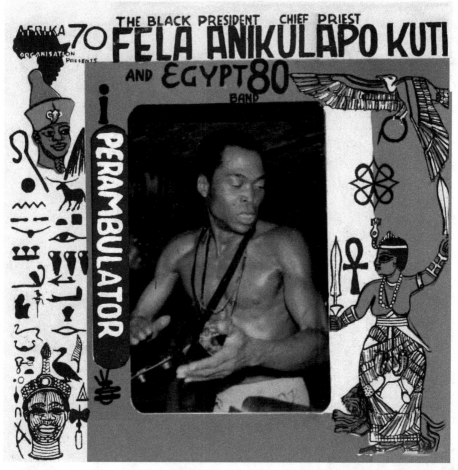

Front cover album design of Perambulator with Fela's designated titles: Chief Priest, Black President, King.

CHIEF PRIEST SAY

The first three years of the 70's would witness an explosion of Afrobeat in Nigeria, and the most parts of West Africa felt the vibrations – as far as Ghana to the West and Cameroon to the East. For Fela, it was the beginning of a creative period dishing out hit records one after the other.

Though most of the titles were not direct attacks on the system as he later did, they touched on the daily lives of the people with songs like 'LET'S START' what we've come into the room to do, telling it as it is - graphic explicit sex. It was another superlative, rendition in Yoruba language and spiced with some broken English explanations.

Fela calls on his partner in the room to get on with it 'don't play the innocent. Let's start! Take off your clothes! Let's start he admonishes his partner. The recording had Ginger Baker of the former English pop group 'Cream', playing live as guest drummer on some tracks like Let's Start in place of Tony Allen the regular drum player in Fela's Africa 70 band at that time. The album titled 'Live with Ginger Baker,' was recorded in the sixteen track studio Ginger Baker sold to Polygram Nigeria in 1972.

Ginger who had known Fela during his student days at the Trinity College in England, was having problems with drugs (heroin and cocaine) his band the Cream had just broken up. According to Fela, Ginger was looking for a place where he could get away from it all (chill-out). He chose to drive across the Sahara desert with a mobile recording studio. He arrived in Lagos and was brought to then - Afro Spot, where Fela and his band performed regularly. Remi, reminisced on some idiosyncrasies of Ginger Baker during his sojourn with Fela a few years after.

Ginger Baker she said, in the tropical climate of Lagos used to dress-up in long boots with his long hair totally stoned from marijuana. According to her, "he used to just sit in a corner in Fela's living room and the kids (Yeni, Femi and Sola) would come to me and ask: "Mummy does it talk?" Different as he was from most Africans around, Fela's kids referred to him as "it" instead of "he". Ginger would later use his friendship with Fela, to try and record some traditional rhythms for Paul McCartney (ex Beetle) who was doing the project for a computer programming of music for synthesizers.

Fela objected to McCartney recording the artist on a buy-out basis, he demanded that the local musicians be paid according to international standards. Obstructed in Nigeria, Paul McCartney went to Ghana where he got his way through the musician union who did not see the financial advantage of being paid as Fela had demanded for the Nigerian local musicians.

EGBE MI O, in Yoruba language means "Carry Me". In this song, Fela is singing about the different kinds of things that happen to you while you dance. How you could go into trance while dancing. How in a state of musical trance, the traditional beads women wear under their skirt break without them noticing. How a man's hat would fall off his head, while dancing without him noticing. All kinds of things happen to you doing the dance - but you are not alone "be ke iwo nikan ko". Fela ends this track, with a general chorus calling everybody to sing together with the band "Egbe Mi O" carry me like one in a trance.

BLACK MAN'S CRY is about identity, "I am Black and proud." Fela asks in Yoruba: "Who says Black is not beautiful?" Bring that person out let me see! There is nothing as beautiful as the black skin! Look at me! Look at me very well! There is nothing as beautiful as the black skin! Look at me very well! Composed at the era of "I am Black and Proud," he tried with the song to rid the black mind of inferiority complex, addressing in particular Africans who use chemical products to bleach their skin or Africans who feel inferior to the White folks.

YE YE DEY SMELL, is about people getting what they deserve - reaping what they sow. If you flirt with another person's wife, you shouldn't feel bad if people do the same to you. Literally meaning bullshit stinks, it implies that if you give people bullshit you should get reciprocal treatment too.

In order to draw the crowd to the Shrine, Fela took-out paid classified adverts in the government owned Daily Times with a heading: CHIEF PRIEST SAY. Referring to himself as the Chief Priest of the Shrine, he made highly critical political statements in his classified adverts. Most of the criticisms were usually directed, at the government and their mis-management of the economy. These paid adverts and their scathing remarks, against those in authority soon endeared Fela to the student populace. Various student union movements leaders , enhanced their own popularity on campus with the invitation of Fela.

This was followed by a rabid clamour for Fela on virtually all campuses of institutions of higher learning, student unions were competing with each other to invite Fela and Africa 70 to their respective campuses.

It was not just students who wanted to see this new phenomenon called Fela. General (then a Colonel) Ignatius Kutu Achampong President of Ghana, invited Fela and the Africa 70 to perform at the Christiansburg Castle (the official residence of the Ghanaian Head of State). In attendance at the event were all his ministers, diplomats and important dignitaries from all-over Ghana. Fela's burgeoning fame, was equally celebrated at home.

The civilian Administrator of Eastern Nigeria Mr Ukpabi Asika, joined the growing list of fans when he invited Fela and his group to perform at the Government House in Enugu - a welcome departure from when only the likes of Geraldo Pino and Rex Lawson, earned invitations to play and entertain troops during the war.

The band was lodged at the Hotel President with all expenses paid and free drinks in tow etc. "Asika Go Pay" was the slogan among Africa 70 personnel on this trip, meaning the administrator was going to pick all the bills irrespective of the facility utilized. About this time, Fela was invited to join the National Association of Patriotic Writers and Artists (NAPWA), an association that comprised journalists, intellectuals, and student activists.

Demanding for a social change and democracy in Nigeria, NAPWA had among its members people like Kanmi Ishola Osobu (Fela made famous 'peoples lawyer'), Rasheed Gbadamosi a business man who later became consultant and adviser to successive Nigerian regimes, Segun Osoba who later became the Governor of Ogun State during the second civilian government, Naiwu Osahon a writer, Musician-Drummer Bayo Martins among others.

With all these activities, it got to a point where government dissatisfaction with Fela was no longer a secret. The Chief Priest Say adverts, were causing a lot of people in government circles some anxiety and discomfort. Those who had business with various government agencies, for fear of reprisals from government started having a rethink about their relationship with Fela.

Some resolved to sever relationship while others became tepid. A principal "friend" if one could consider him as such, who reconsidered his relationship with Fela on account of his fear that his business would hurt, was Chief S.B. Bakare (the proprietor of Suru-Lere night club re-named Afro Spot by Fela). As a businessman, he enjoyed a lot of patronage from various government agencies and he did not want to lose the patronage by allowing the use of his building as a base by Fela to launch his now famous tirades against government.

Fela's numerous brawls with the police started in Chief Bakare's club which was Fela's base, and also he had issues with the club over control of proceeds from sale of drinks which had substantially grown in turnover in geometric proportions with Fela's fame.

Earlier, you would recall, that I explained that Fela had entered into a long lease arrangement with the proprietor of Suru-Lere night-club renamed Afro Spot. In the contract with Fela, since his crowd pulling music was responsible for the huge leap in the sale of drinks, concession was granted to Fela to take only proceeds from the gate fees while Chief S.B. Bakare took those of proceeds from drinks in addition to rent.

As a sign of goodwill, Fela however could buy drinks on credit and there was no ceiling on the amount of drinks he could possibly buy on credit and settle the bills at the end of every month. At this period, Fela was drinking heavily and entertaining friends with drinks from the credit facility. For some time the arrangement worked. However, default in settlement of credit surfaced and this was the convenient excuse needed by Chief Bakare to evict Fela from his property and save his neck from his business relationship with government hurting due largely from perceiving Chief Bakare as having provided a comfort zone from which Fela's biting tirades which at this time Government barely tolerated.

Fela's penchant for biting tirades, at its officials and activities instead was getting sharper and popular with the people. Whenever Fela asked to be served drinks, the bar man declined on account of a new unwritten order on credit squeeze in the face of mounting debts and default on the part of Fela. When Fela questioned whose authority the credit ceiling derived from the Manager, he feigned ignorance and denied ever giving such instructions.

Each time Fela came to entertain, the same instruction would have been issued to deny Fela credit and the Manager would make himself unavailable to avoid confrontation with Fela or have cause to reverse the order since he had earlier denied knowledge of any existing directive to deny Fela credit. As soon as Fela returns to perform, the manager would issue the same no credit order to the bar man, and thereafter disappear from the club's vicinity to avoid being confronted by Fela. When Fela saw through this recurring plot, he seized the initiative and walked straight to the bar himself to pick his choice of drinks.

The situation heightened the tension in the club, and continued for some time until one Tuesday evening. Fela's advance party, arrived at the Afro Spot to prepare the place for the day's show and on their arrival they found the place sealed and policemen were on guard. Ostensibly surprised, the advance party of Fela sought to find out from the Manager who himself was standing with the Policemen what was amiss and the manager told them they could not go inside. At this time since there was no mobile telephone communication, one of the advance team members went back home to inform Fela of the unfolding development.

An obviously miffed Fela retorted "Who says I cannot play? He got dressed, and headed for the club with the informant. Meanwhile, the unusual development had attracted a huge crowd around the venue obviously expecting a showdown. It must also be emphasized that amongst the huge crowd, were predominantly those who had come to watch the scheduled show which was being threatened by the police lock-out.

Fela riding on the back of the supportive huge crowd, could not be stopped after all from going in to perform his legitimate business for the day. However, the police as a soft landing for their inability to cow Fela instructed him to report at the police station after the concert. At the station later, the Management of Surulere night-club wanted the police to arrest and detains him for an alleged breach of contract.

The police officer on duty, one Police Constable popularly called 'Baba Ibadan' who incidentally was a Fela fan declined the request. The police officer made it clear that there was no available fact on ground to warrant such action, and educated the Club's Management that the issues at stake were civil matters requiring the adjudication of the court.

Fela was consequently released by the police but the management of Surulere night-club, did not relent in their scheme to arrest Fela and kick him out of the club. The Police Constable who refused to pervert the law, was reported to his superiors who could not fault his decision and commended him instead for taking the right decision. Fela sought protection thereafter from the courts, to stem the incessant harassment from the club's management and disruption of his legitimate business.

The suit succeeded, and as such halted further harassment from the police at the Afro Spot. If Chief S.B. Bakare's schemes to oust Fela from his property were premised on a desire to protect his relationship and thriving business with government, another businessman Chief Kanu saw in Fela a profound business opportunity. Chief Kanu who owned a night club situated about fifty meters from Fela's 14 A Agege motor road residence, made a proposal to Fela to move his Afro Spot to Empire Club.

This provided Fela the opportunity to create a base in the heart of the Lagos ghetto. He moved from the middle class enclave in Surulere, to where the oppressed masses resided around Moshalasi and coupled with the fact that at this time, Fela was no longer the struggling artiste searching for identity or direction for his music but a fully developed musical identity.

This time around, Fela had gained substantial financial independence and no longer the perpetually broke man who turned for soft loan at every turn of event from his mother. The Fela that was moving his base to Agege Motor Road, was already on his way to stardom a phenomenal one at that. He was not a "one" hit record wonder either at this point in his life, his name was reverberating not only in West Africa but all over the continent.

By this time, Lady and Shakara, were already being sold officially and pirated all-over Africa. Earlier, I explained how Fela despised African Ladies whose values were tainted by western values which was the inspiration for the recording of "LADY." Rather than understand this concept, his unrelenting critics saw Fela as being anti feminists.

SHAKARA sang in Pidgin English, (another block buster) was Fela's scathing criticism of people on track of empty boasts. He decried loud mouth braggarts who can talk more and deliver short on action. Fela as a social critic, used this song to ginger Africans to stand up for their legitimate rights. With songs like this and those already mentioned in previous chapters, the Fela that moved to Moshalashi was aware he had become a musical icon.

This time, he also stopped playing the trumpet following the departure of his erstwhile brilliant tenor sax player Igo Chiko who left the Africa 70. He played most of the tenor sax solos on all Fela's albums until end of the year 1973. Igo Chiko in spite of his manifest musical talent, had a big alcohol problem and several times he would go on stage drunk and lacked the required discipline for the business.

Unfortunately Igo Chiko, had a huge ego also and believed he was indispensable. Whenever Fela as band Leader called him to caution, Igo Chiko would put-down his sax in full glare of the audience and he would pick-up Fela's trumpet and play a few notes. Knowing Fela didn't play the sax, he would challenge him to do the same with the saxophone.

This went on for some time, until Fela couldn't take it anymore and he decided to fire him. Without a tenor sax player and convinced of the beauty the voice of the saxophone adds to afrobeat, Fela took-up the challenge of playing the alto sax and the result of his first attempt at playing the sax is the beautiful and brilliant solo on Gentleman album. One could hear Fela approach alto sax like a trumpet player, all the time searching for high notes on the sax like he did as a trumpet player (listen to songs like Funky horn and Witchcraft).

Front cover album design Shakara

Front cover album design Alagbon Close

ALAGBON CLOSE

The reader will re-call that since his return to Nigeria from London as a student in 1963, 14A Agege Motor Road had remained his residence where he lived with his wife, mother-in-law and children. The house belonged to his mother and had always served as the Kuti family Lagos home for ages while they lived in Abeokuta. Bringing the Shrine to a distance of about fifty metres from his home was like bringing his business home.

Agege Motor Road is situated at the strategic junction that leads to Ikorodu road and Western Avenue - the two avenues that connects Lagos Island with the mainland before the construction of the 3rd, Mainland Bridge by the Babangida regime.

Driving through Lagos City to or from Lagos Island, one is obliged to drive through either of the two avenues and Fela's house was strategically located at the junction of the two avenues. Over the years the Kuti family witnessed the evolution of the area from a quiet Lagos suburb, into the big ghetto it became re-known for with its swinging night life and prostitution business.

Prior to Fela entering into a long lease and the installation of Africa Shrine in the premises of the Empire Hotel owned by Chief Kanu, the venue was noted to host most of the travelling bands visiting Lagos town. Moreover Moshalashi, Idi-Oro, and Mushin areas of the Lagos mainland controlled a remarkable amount of what went on in the nightlife of the city this time around. Western Hotel, Lido night-club and Empire Hotel were venues that featured live bands regularly and they were all situated around Fela's home area.

Another institution that was located in the area good for business was the Lagos Garrison Organisation band, a Nigerian Army band based in the Abalty Barracks some five hundred metres behind the new Shrine. The presence of the army barracks in the neighbourhood, was good because most of the soldiers frequented the prostitutes and drank from the many illegal bars that were installed all over the small alley ways that dotted the area. Urban migration, a phenomenal problem in Nigeria that started to manifest itself at the end of Biafra war, brought along to the big cities like Lagos young able-bodied men and single women some still in their teenage years.

Some of these single women already mothers of one or more kids, widowed from the war and without any source of income took to prostitution for a living. With its economic potentials and advantages, houses located next to hotels and bars were always attractive for such women - it served as work place and home. With this urban social evolution, came a cultural explosion with Fela and his Africa 70 organisation at its head.

His popularity, taking residence and performing regularly (four times a week) at the Shrine, brought with him to the area an unprecedented economic boom. For those who came from near and far, everything was in place to amuse and keep them busy till dawn. Not too expensive assorted food, drinks, music and prostitutes to spend the end of the long night with. The area had changed with time, transforming from a quiet suburb into big-time red-light district.

Another problem emanating from the civil war and urban migration is that Nigeria, like most other African nations before independence was an agrarian society. Traditionally, agriculture had for ages been the live-wire of the African economy. Majority of the citizens earn their living from the farms and animal husbandry. Even during colonial times and some years after independence, school's long holidays were planned and organised to coincide with farm harvest periods to enable students give extra-hands to their parents and guardians. Apart from basic food crops planted by the farmers, groundnut pyramids were regular features of northern Nigeria after each annual harvest from the local groundnut farmers. It is the same story south of the country with cocoa as the product.

99% of Nigerian population have not benefited from the so-called oil-boom. Most of the rivers and faming lands in the oil producing areas are polluted and inexploitable for agriculture. The cocoa farms the Western parts of Nigeria are noted for are getting extinct. Groundnut pyramids that the North is known for, has disappeared to be replaced by able body men who should be working on farms doing money exchange.

At independence, the nation's political founding fathers inept and pre-occupied with feeding their personal ambitions neglected the agriculture industry. Prior to independence, Nigeria produced a great part of her food requirement. The civilian government, failed to take advantage of this traditional sauce of gross national product transforming it into an economic industry that would have given employment to millions of the citizens. It is same story with the successive military dictators who seized power from them. To the politicians "Noise for Vendor Mouth", was Fela's description of their attempt at shaping a country's destiny.

In the song NOISE FOR VENDOR MOUTH, he was responding as the reader will shortly realise, to people who considered him a "hooligan" and "hemp smoker." Indifferent to their name calling, for him people in Kalakuta were really a bunch of hard working citizens, trying to survive in a society riddled with corruption and mismanagement. For him, Africa 70 Organisation constitutes what can be described as a form of artistic and social rebellion. Considering that the music profession, not until recently had not been accorded the professional recognition it deserves in most modern day African society. To be a musician or dancer, is like being regarded as a beggar and for a woman to be a professional dancer she was looked down on as a loose woman, prostitute and a never do well.

Most Nigerian youths, who wanted to be professional musicians or dancers, found themselves in trouble with strict parents and guardians who share this negative view of the artist. As a result, these youths run away from home in order to realise their professional dreams. For such youths, Fela's Kalakuta republic became the attraction as they became aware that such negative views of the artist were not entertained there. Fela concludes in the song Noise for vendor mouth, that the real hooligans are the politicians and those in authority who resort to political infighting and gangster-like actions or military coup d'état in order to resolve constitutional issues. He considers their criticisms as nothing but the noise made by street vendors to sell their wares.

Like his civilian and military predecessors, General Yakubu Gowon's regime was inept and corrupt so much that Fela called them: MR. GRAMATICALO-GYLISATION - IS THE BOSS. The song is critical of the education system in Africa - which he calls a poor imitation of the Western education system. The man who speaks better English gets paid more. Fela sang: «the better oyinbo you talk, the more bread you go get! School cert! Nah grade four bread!' (Meaning, school certificate education qualification rated grade four salary scale) BA! (Bachelor of Arts), na grade three bread!', 'MSc! (Master of Science), nah grade two bread!' 'PhD! (Doctor of Science), nah grade one bread!"

He went further to explain how Africans are graded and oriented towards Western values. According to him, first thing we are given in the morning - newspapers! The brainwash starts from the 'Big' English words used in the newspapers "the oyinbo (English) wey dey inside, na riddle for labourer man! Inside the paper! Jargonism dey (that one nah Latin" (meaning there is a lot of Latin jargon in the newspapers). Fela considers all these as irrelevant issue that has no bearing towards alleviating the sufferings of the poor man on the street.

Then the leaders blame the poor man's problems on "ignorance" and "delinquency." Fela asks "who be delinquent? Na them delinquent! Who be delinquent? The oyinbo talker delinquent!" Meaning who is delinquent? The Mr. English speaker is the one who is delinquent - referring to the leadership ruling most African countries.

In 1970, Nigeria emerged from the Biafra civil war with the largest standing army in black Africa, with no debts and careering along on at least two million barrels of sulphur-low oil pumped daily into the world oil market. With such daily income there was no justified reason for the millions of unemployed Nigerians milling around our urban centres hustling for a living, judiciously managed, Nigeria could feed her millions of population and sister countries.

Corruption is the only reason, in-order to enrich them the military regime of Gen. Yakubu Gowon embarked on prestigious ventures as solution to solve the mounting economic problems of the nation - building suspended highway networks to "decongest" the Lagos traffic, constructing a national theatre, importation of food all in order to take the ten percent cuts from all the deals.

Scandals and accusation of corruption became the hall mark of the regime, this corrupt practice was epitomised by the placement of an order worth 20 million United States dollars, for the importation of cement from Europe. The regime paid two-way transport charges to the shipping companies, who were not attracted to bring the cement to Nigerian shores only to return empty because the country was not exporting anything of interest to the shipping companies.

The cost of this senseless importation of cement, was more than enough to develop the Nigerian cement industry which would in turn provide jobs for the unemployed. More people openly denounced the military regime like Fela was known to do. Intellectuals from the universities and student union leaders, that once approved of the regime started to openly criticise the government. In the end, General Gowon had to promise a hand over of power to a democratically elected civilian government in 1976.

However, he did not remain in power long enough to keep his promise as we shall see in the chapter ahead. The advent of oil boom and the massive migrations of Nigeria's young working force from the villages, forced an erstwhile nation that fed her population to look outside her frontiers for means to feed her citizens. The abandonment of the farms, for the old and retired in search of the "golden fleece" in the cities changed the way of life of the people. Before, people who paid visits to their folks in the villages returned to the city with food, this time around it is the city folks who take food to the villages.

Instead of the authorities investing the oil money in building infrastructures necessary to ameliorate the living conditions in the villages – roads, hospitals, dispensaries, schools, electricity and pipe-born water, etc. Successive governments, neglected these social infrastructures that could entice the younger generation to stay in the villages. Instead, they embarked on building prestigious projects and organising events.

The result is that Nigerian big cities, like those of other so called independent African nations became massive markets for the west. Radios, cars, television, air-conditioners, construction materials, food and all kinds of machinery, anything and everything are imported by those in government and their middlemen who grow fat off the sweat, blood, and tears of their fellow country men and women.

With these development, immigrants to the big cities take-up residence in ghettos and make-shift homes with few jobs available, their only options were prostitution, illegal bars and other related professions. Like earlier explained, red-light districts are the best areas to carry-out such trades.

Later, Fela who only provided an atmosphere for these young folks to earn some kind of living, was criticised as "a social pervert who used his popularity to corrupt young girls socialising them into lifestyles that espoused the subversion of family values". These critics failed to realise, that what Fela was doing was providing for many destitute children who were not cared for by their parents or guardians.

Some of these children could no longer communicate with their elders, forcing them to leave their respective homes for places like Fela's. Instead of recognising and probably emulate his example, spending his money to keep these young folks off the streets they accuse him of abducting teenagers.

Forgetting that for as long as Fela lived and there are constant immigration of able bodied men and women to the cities, there were more and more going to his house because he fed them. Since they are in the habit of looking outside Africa for solutions to African problems, Nigerian government should emulate European governments and register every child so that when anything goes wrong they can trace them.

The situation as it is where these young folks arrive in Fela's house, without any identity other than what they tell Fela they are how could he find out their respective identity. Fela should be thanked, by the government for helping them to do their job. Meanwhile not minding their criticisms, he continued to make highly critical statements of government in his classified adverts issues as those mentioned earlier.

The bold nature of the classified adverts, plus his satiric lyric made Fela a folk hero in the ghetto community, but for those in government this was no good news if we bear in mind that Fela's popularity was growing by the day and there were lots of youths attracted to him. Children of the rich who previously were living away from the ghetto started to troupe to Fela, attracted by the music or the culture of rebellion. The 30th April 1974, Fela was attending to some guest in his house suddenly some policemen walked into the living room demanding that every one should subject them to on the spot search, they produced a signed warrant by a high court judge authorising the search and they went through the house searching every room, until they were satisfied they had what they came looking for.

After the search, Fela was arrested along with other persons found with him in the house. The police claimed they recovered some weed suspected to be "Indian Hemp" from the house, and all the arrested persons from the house were taken to the Criminal Investigation Department (CID) at Alagbon Close on the Lagos Island. At the CID headquarter Fela was detained in a cell named KALAKUTA by previous occupants, and he was latter charged to court for possession of prohibited substance suspected to be "Indian Hemp" and "abduction" of juveniles.

The last charge was included, because of teenagers arrested along from the house. After his release from police custody, Fela would chronicle police methods of torture in the song titled ALAGBON CLOSE. It was also the beginning of Fela using visual art designs to illustrate his message on album covers 'Alagbon Close' album cover, was the first of the series from the artist Ghariokwu Lemi - one of the pioneers of visual illustrations in Nigeria.

Ghariokwu Lemi my friend who introduced me to Fela did a great job with the album covers. On the Alagbon Close album cover, he tried to illustrate the message of police brutality in Alagbon CID jails and how Fela came-out of their jail still strong.

Painted originally in poster colour, Lemi decrypted a scenario that had a rocky background with Fela's Kalakuta Republic home standing solidly on the left and an Alagbon CID jailhouse in the last stage of decay with a broken chain. Half part of the chain still attached to the left wrist of a dancing Fela triumphant over a capsized police patrol boat tipped over by an enormous whale. His friend from the National Association of Patriotic Writers and Artists (NAPWA), Kanmi Isola Osobu a trial lawyer offered to defend Fela.

Osobu appeared before the judge, and he pleaded that since "the charges against Fela under the Nigerian law was a bail-able offence" he demanded the judge, to grant Fela his freedom pending the period it took to prosecute the case. Despite objection from the police lawyer the judge granted Fela bail pending subsequent court hearing of the case.

Another member of NAPWA and President of the musician association, the drummer Bayo Martins signed the bail bond for Fela's release.

One of many Nigerian Police raids on Kalakuta.
Picture Femi Bankole Osunla Africa 70 Photo Agency

Meanwhile, with all the publicity the case generated among the Nigerian press there was a huge crowd waiting outside the courtroom, and immediately after Fela was granted bail he stepped out of the court room into the hands of a huge crowd who carried him and his lawyer Kanmi Oshobu, shoulder high dancing through Lagos streets from the Apapa court house to his residence - a distance of about twelve kilometers.

The female members arrested along with Fela, were however ordered by the judge to be detained in a juvenile home pending the determination of their respective ages. Fela's position regarding the juvenile charges was that he was not contesting the fact that some of the female members of his household were by law underage however, he had never gone to induce them away from their respective homes rather they all came to him of their free will. Most of the parents and guardians of some of the girls, on hearing of the police raid went to the CID headquarters to identify their wards. But most of them returned home disappointed as the girls refused to be identified with the names given by their parents.

Even in cases of physical identification, they all refused to answer to the names giving different names to the police. Like earlier mentioned in a society where there is no national identity card, how could the police ever think of making any legitimate identification of any of the arrested? Another point the government failed to look was that Fela was providing for many of these so-called delinquents, who without places like his probably would have ended-up as destitute or prostitutes. Some of them as children, were not cared for by their parents or guardians.

Others as we have seen, came from so-called respectable homes with "white" Christian values as education background. With the changing times, some of the children found it difficult to communicate with their parents a kind of generation clash, forcing them to leave their respective homes for places like Fela's. Instead of recognising and probably emulate his example spending his money to keep these young folks off the streets, they accuse him of abducting teenagers.

Forgetting most of the youths around Fela had problems with their parents or guardians hence they chose to seek refuge around the musician, who did not question them why or how they chose to leave their respective homes.

Moreover, he let them do whatever pleases them as long as they did not disturb the next person. After he was released from police detention, he named his house KALAKUTA REPUBLIC - after the police cell he was detained in at the CID quarters in Alagbon Close.

He also erected a ten foot high barbed wire fence, to prevent anymore unexpected raids - a new innovation to an erstwhile quiet Lagos family home. Prior to the police raid Fela's home had it's door always open to friends for ages, now security guards were placed at the entry persons coming into the house needed to be identified and cleared before entry – a complete departure from the past.

Meanwhile, it was obvious to the police that they could not make the charges against Fela stick since the latter had made it public that his house was open to everyone. As a public place, anybody could have come to his home with the weed suspected to be "Indian Hemp."

As such, the onus was on the police to find the owner of the illegal substance allegedly found in his home. The media coverage of the arrest and court appearance of Fela, plus his heroic return home made it imperative that the police had to act again if they want to convict Fela in a law court.

Back cover album design Alagbon Close

Prior to the police raid, Fela's home had it's door always open to friends for ages now security guards were placed at the entry, persons coming into the house needed to be identified and cleared before entry – a complete departure from the past. Photo by Femi Bankole Osunla Africa 70 Photo Agency

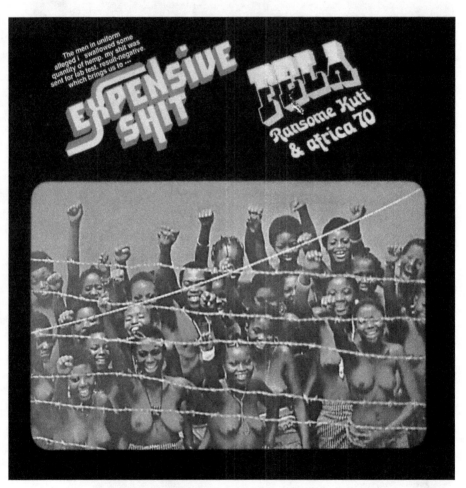

Front cover album design Expensive Shit

EXPENSIVE SHIT

One week after his return home the police struck again at about 5.00 am, three trucks - loaded with armed police men forced their way into the house tearing down the wired fence and like previous raids, everybody was searched and since Fela was expecting the raid from information he got from police friends the house had been cleaned of any marijuana. He calmly led the police men into his bed room for them to carry out their search, knowing that his room was clean of any "grass". Fela did not suspect, that the police in their desperate attempt to put him in jail will try to plant evidence in his bed room.

They searched the room thoroughly and finally when it was obvious that there was nothing to hold him on, one of the police men suddenly moved to a table where Fela kept his mail, he pretended to look through the mail again then he came up with an envelope containing some substance suspected to be marijuana. Fela who had personally cleared the table before he went to bed, realised that the police came prepared and in such a situation he realised that he had to try and out-think his foes.

He asked the most senior of the police men in his room, if he could be allowed to examine the alleged exhibit. The over confident officer readily agreed for Fela to examine the content of the envelope, in compliance with the law that allows an accused to examine such exhibits before it was sealed in an evidence bag. Pretending to examine the weed according to Fela he emptied the content of the envelope into his palm, and swiftly poured the grass into his mouth in full view of the police men who were too stunned to act.

Capitalising on their shock and slow responds, Fela walked over to the bedside table and drank from a whisky bottle washing the weed down his stomach and he then fell on his bed saying to them "Carry Me".

He was carried to the Police CID Alagbon Close headquarter again, this time he was the only person arrested from the house. Fela was detained on a floating cell anchored on the Lagos Lagoon behind the police headquarters. Like his Kalakuta cell the floating cell was called TIMBUKTU (the floating boat that never reaches its destination) by previous inmates, and in their attempt to extract the contents of his bowels the police tried unsuccessfully to make him excrete.

He was taken to the military hospital on Awolowo Road in Ikoyi in-order to 'flush' his stomach but, Fela refused to co-operate telling the medical doctor he was going to break down the place before he could be made to go through the stomach flush. In the end they took him back to his cell in Alagbon Close and this time again, they used force on him in order to make him co-operate but Fela refused to comply.

In the end, he was locked up among other inmates. Fela who had anticipated the possibility of the police attempting to 'flush' his stomach, had requested his mother to bring him vegetable soup with the hope that a mixture of vegetable and the marijuana would be difficult to determine the difference in a laboratory test.

On his return from the hospital, she was waiting with the vegetable soup which he was allowed to eat and late in the night his cell mates showed him a disused toilet where he secretly used the toilet three times during the night. In order for the police not to suspect, when they asked him in the morning to excrete again, he refused to comply and again physical force was applied but Fela did not give in.

Finally in-order to avoid prolonging the pain he told them he was ready to excrete and according to him, there was great excitement from all the police present as they all were searching for a chamber-pot to collect his shit. After voiding himself of the 'famous' expensive shit the contents of his bowels was carried away in a chamber-pot and sent to the police forensic laboratory for analyses, the police would later arranged him before a Lagos magistrate for possession of "weeds suspected to be Indian hemp" and possession of "dangerous drug" and like the previous time was granted bail by the presiding judge.

Defiant as ever, Fela continued to perform regularly at the Shrine where he kept his audience returning every time he played, to listen to his 'yabbis' and accounts of his experience in the hands of the police. He stopped between songs to tell stories of his detention to the public in details and episode by episode. On the musical level one couldn't understand how, he had the time to think of his legal defence and write new songs narratinghis experiences. Fela would again write the episode into another hit song titled EXPENSIVE SHIT.

This time the album design was more a provocation from Fela as the cover had Fela posing with his women around him, all naked from waist up and him in his habitual underpants. The parents and guardians of most of the girls were shocked, and outraged to see their daughters exposed half naked on an album cover.

Meanwhile, four of the girls arrested during the April 30th raid whose ages have been determined by their respective parents or guardians were released, but the girls refused to go back home with their family members claiming to want to live with Fela as a choice. While the case was pending, the court ordered the four girls to report to the police every day as a condition for their temporary release from the juvenile home.

For all these cases he was being prosecuted Fela had a good defence team headed by Kanmi Ishola Osobu, a relatively unknown trial lawyer who suddenly became famous thanks to the police and the never stopping charges against Fela. Many known law firms in Nigeria were envious of the sudden celebrity statue accorded Kanmi in the press, and it was clear that most legal luminaries would have paid anything to represent Fela in court for the publicity it generated. It turned his lawyer into instant hero, "People's Lawyer" Kanmi was called.

Meanwhile Fela was billed to perform in Cameroon with all these people detained, he had to embark on the three-week tour with just the four female members and in terms of public responds the tour was a big success. Everywhere they performed in Cameroon – Douala and Yaoundé were jammed with crowd. The daughter of the Cameroun president Ahmadu Ahijo, who was the guest of honour at the Yaoundé stadium concert, got a rude shock from Fela as she was supposed to present Fela with a bounty of flowers, instead of descending right to the field where the stage was erected, she preferred to invite Fela to the presidential stand high-up in the Presidential gallery, but Fela refused to walk all that distance to receive the flowers and the president's daughter waited in vain for Fela.

Apart from this incidence, it almost seemed a trouble free three week tour however as Fela and his entourage relaxed in their hotel rooms on the last day of the tour suddenly, the Nigerian police struck again without warning this time across the frontier in a Cameroon hotel.

Their reason for the cross-frontier raid, was to arrest the four female members of the group who did not report daily to the police as instructed in their condition for bail. Luckily one of the four girls escaped arrest after the police had left, the group chose to return immediately to Lagos.

Back to familiar grounds, Fela found to his surprise that the girls detained at the juvenile welfare home had escaped and they were all waiting for him in Kalakuta, according to them they were tired of the promises from the welfare home staff that they would soon be released so they hatched a plan to escape. They all had agreed to move late in the night by jumping over the eleven-foot high wall surrounding the home, come zero hour all but one of the girls left the home taking some mattresses with them to use as landing pads.

Luckily for them, a table had been left outside in the compound of the home and they carried this table to the edge of the wall, the tallest of them climbed the table and threw the mattresses over the wall. They all helped each other to scale over the wall, and with the cover of the night they found their way to Kalakuta.

To preempt any possible attack by the police on Kalakuta with the pretext that they came to apprehend the escapees, Fela instructed his lawyer Kanmi Ishola Oshobu to file a motion in a Lagos court asking the police to produce the detained girls. During the hearings of the motion in court, the police tried to get a court order for them to be able to go into Kalakuta in search of the "missing" girls, but Fela's lawyer argued against this request citing previous attacks by the police on Kalakuta as a violation of Fela's individual rights. The police request was turned down by the presiding judge and by the end of the trial, the police could produce only four girls - the one who refused to escape with the others and the three arrested in Cameroon during Fela's tour.

Since there was no reason for the four girls to remain in detention the court ordered them to be released and like the previous attack, Fela continued to talk openly in the press and during his shows at the Shrine about all these experiences to an ever increasing public. He called the police and their army bosses dumb and the regime of Yakubu Gowon was proclaimed publicly by Fela as incompetent.

He denounced them as corrupt, arbitrary and inept agents of neo-colonialism in Africa. We have to remember that with time the endemic corruption has extended throughout the rank and files of both the army and the police, sometimes during periods that could be described as 'scarce kobo' (lean periods before pay-day), soldiers and police men have been seen threatening innocent civilian motorist or road users with imagined offences in order to extort money.

Men in military and police uniforms have on several occasions engaged in armed robberies, and to save face successive military regimes in Nigeria claim that the men involved in these criminal acts were impostures dressed in military uniforms to give the military a bad name. To curb the actions of these "impostures", Nigerian army authority outlawed the use of the 'olive green' colour on civilian vehicles but despite this law cases of armed robbery were on the increase on Nigerian roads, and in most cases the victims claim that their attackers were dressed in military uniforms.

There were cases of military men, implicated in gun and ammunition sale to so-called criminals, the soldiers and police see that their commanders are living well with their political appointments, while they are not getting any benefits they thus result to criminal activities to supplement their meagre salaries.

Meanwhile Fela's open criticisms of the government continued despite their attacks, he openly sang songs such as "DON'T GAG ME" to inform the military that their arrests and threats won't stop him. His popularity was growing by the day and there were lots of youths attracted to him.

Children of the rich who previously were living away from the ghetto started to troupe to Fela, and as earlier mentioned this was no good news for the elite with their Christian values. They saw Fela's life style, as too bohemian for their liking and felt they had to do something about it. They however tried to use the excuse, of Fela's open admittance of marijuana use as excuse to go into Kalakuta.

Back cover album design Expensive Shit

Front cover album design Kalakuta Show

KALAKUTA SHOW

Despite the hostile attitude of the government towards Fela, some of the children of the rich - those privileged youths, started to defy their parents choosing to hang out around Fela and his growing empire. One of such youths was Folake Ladeinde (named Folake Kalakuta Show by her peas after the song Fela wrote to describe the attack on his house in November 1974). The daughter of a prominent Lagos lawyer, she left her parents cool Ikoyi home after returning late from an outing with her friends.

Folake, afraid for the beating that she anticipated from her strict father whenever she violated any of his laid-down rules, chose to return to Fela's house to spend the night with a girl from her neighbourhood. The girl in question had left her parents home a couple of years earlier, and for more than three months there was no news from her.

Meanwhile Folake was living in his house, and had been presented by her ex-neighbour to Fela as someone who was looking for the opportunity to dance as a professional. Like those before her, she was admitted and asked to join the new dancers during rehearsals. On her first attempt to dance in public at the Shrine, she ran into another neighbour living on her street as she attempted to climb into one of the many dancing cages strategically placed around the dance floor. Shocked at seeing someone close from home in the public, she summoned courage to put-up her best for the show at hand, and she also did her best to avoid this neighbour on her way back stage after her dance.

This neighbour of Folake who had on previous occasions attempted to date her, went back to his area with the news of seeing her among Fela's girls and when the news got to her parents they invited him to their house and Folake's parents asked him to help them 'kidnap' the girl from Fela's commune.

An old admirer who thought he might finally have his way with Folake if they succeed in kidnapping her from the commune, voluntarily offered to go along with her parents on their 'kidnap' bid. On the appointed date, waiting patiently at the entrance to the Shrine just before the start of Sunday afternoon jump, this neighbour of Folake surveyed all the women coming into the venue from Fela's Kalakuta.

Finally, there she was coming in company of her other neighbour who had presented her to Fela and without any attempt to hide, the neighbour called-out to the two girls who didn't want to stop at first but changed their minds at the final moment. Feeling nothing to be ashamed of about being Fela dancers, particularly from an old admirer whom they were not aware was hip enough to visit Fela's area.

The big 'area brother' (as the two girls came to address him) invited them to have a drink with him in one of the many illegal bars around the Shrine, and pretending that it might be difficult to have some quiet time like this with them once the band starts to perform, the two girls agreed to have a drink with him knowing they had sometime before they started to work. Unsuspecting his motive, the two girls tried to install themselves in the bar when suddenly a car stopped right in front of the illegal bar and Folake's father emerged from the car asking her sternly to get into the waiting car. She refused talking back sternly at her father.

Grabbing Folake by the wrists an action that provoked the young girl to raise her voice and cry for help from the 'Area Boys', she shouted for help from members of Fela's organisation across the street. Instead of the learned lawyer to calmly explain who he was to the boys who came to his daughter's rescue, he continued to drag Folake towards the waiting car. Moreover as someone used to being obeyed he talked to the boys with disdain and contempt, telling them to run-back to their mothers instead of acting like delinquents.

The boys who by now had had enough of his tantrums, snatched Folake away from him with some hard slaps to the side of his face to the bargain. Folake's neighbour who came on the "kidnap" mission with her father, sensed the situation was getting out of hand and in-order to avoid it degenerating into bigger problems for them, managed to drag and convinced the lawyer to abandon their mission.

Vexed and with a feeling of humiliation, he returned to his Ikoyi residence deciding to use the law. As a close friend of the then Inspector General of Police (IGP) Mr Sunday Adewusi, Folake's father called the IGP narrating his humiliation and woes in the hands of those he called "Fela's thugs".

The IGP promised Folake's father that he would do something about it, and he also asked the lawyer to keep in touch to identify his daughter whenever his men were able to arrest all of the delinquent kids living with Fela.

November 23, 1974, the police aware that up till then they have been unsuccessful in their attempts to hold Fela directly responsible, for any of the alleged crimes finally attacked his house again. Three truck loads of Nigerian anti-riot police squad armed to the teeth with guns, batons, tear-gas, axes and cutlasses - like Fela sang in the album Kalakuta Show, held-up traffic for hours around Moshalashi area. They cut down the wired fence and beat-up the inhabitants of Kalakuta - forcibly arresting and pushing them into the waiting police vehicles. Fela was seriously wounded from the beating he received, and was admitted to the Lagos University Teaching Hospital for treatment from injuries he sustained from the police attack.

He came out of the hospital with 18 stitches on his head and a broken arm, and his older brother Olikoye Ransome-Kuti a paediatric professor at the hospital remarked on seeing Fela: "those who did these to you wanted to kill you". The reader will recall that this was the period the author had the privilege of meeting with Fela, and getting to know him as explained in the preface of this volume. Fela came-out-of the hospital, and immediately continued his routine of performing four times a week at the Shrine despite his injuries. Undaunted by the brutal attack and the injuries he sustained, he continued to perform and publicly denounced police and army brutality in the country.

Shortly after, he released Kalakuta Show album with the sleeve (cover) an oil painting originally painted on canvas designed by Ghariokwu Lemi. It was complete with an artistic recreation of the police attack on the house, pictures of Fela with his scalp wounds were also displayed on the album cover and his lawyer who happened to pass by Fela's house also got beat during the attack causing him to sing: "look lawyer! Him dey run! Dem go beat him lawyer! Look lawyer him de run!" Despite the persistent attacks, Fela became more politically vocal criticising the endemic corruption in the Nigerian system and calling attention to the abject poverty majority of the population is living in.

Stressing in songs like NO BREAD that the military leadership is unsympathetic towards the plight of the people they profess to govern, Fela claimed that even if the Gowon regime officially authorise an increment in workers salaries like they did with Udoji Awards the solution is not in salary increments.

For him the solution is in an African oriented economy, that will jointly exploit to the benefit of all African people, the collective natural riches of the continent. 'No Bread' message was addressed to the average man on the street, the African, and Africans throughout the Diaspora, with all the sarcasm he could muster and singing in Pidgin English, Fela calls the average man who has been for so long exploited to look closely at himself.

'Look you! You stand for ground your leg dey shakes!' 'Nah your legs weak ground no dey shake!'(Meaning your legs are responsible for your shaking and not the ground - because they are weak and tired from long sufferings), '....you sit down like you don reach gbi! Eyes dey role like thief him eyes... hunger dey show him power! You no get power to fight - No buredi (No Bread).

The average man accepts all the short-falls of the system without protesting against it. Fela concludes, that Africa the home of the black man, is rich with all the natural and mineral resources necessary to develop the continent into a world economic power. However, it is only in Africa that man still carries the shit of the world on his head. Fela stresses the fact that everything overseas came from Africa.

In conclusion, he says the average man should stand firm now and say "Enough to No Bread" (No Money) 'I don tire hen! No Buredi!' (Meaning we are tired of your grants and aid packages we are tired of No Bread – no money). The album cover designed by Ghariokwu Lemi, is an elaborate visual artwork of the ills in Nigerian society, another oil paint illustrating a mix of social ills plaguing Africa. Like Fela sang in "No Bread", Lemi tried to capture Fela's message of an impending economic doom in Nigeria despite the oil boom ('Mr Inflation is in town').

Messages like these did not go well with the Gowon government and using the police to do their repressive dirty works, the regime tried everything to send Fela to jail using the "law." The reader has to bear in mind that under the law in force in Nigeria at that time, one could be put in prison for ten years for being found in possession of a "joint" (marijuana).

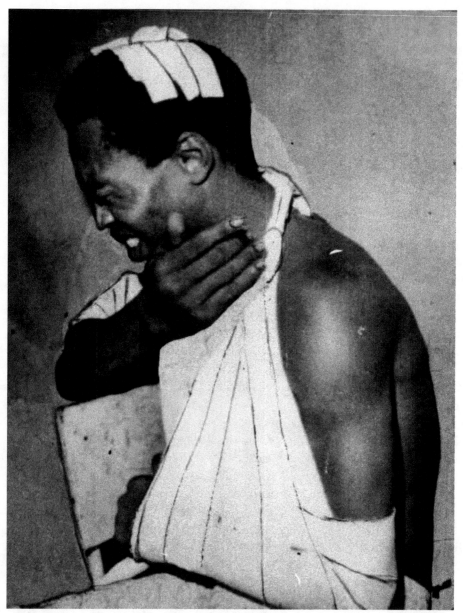
Fela came out of the hospital with 18 stitches on his head and a broken arm, and his older brother Olikoye Ransome-Kuti a paediatric professor at the hospital remarked on seeing Fela: "those who did these to you wanted to kill you".

In later years, the Nigerian police would be blamed by the army authority, for an alleged "levity" with which accusation of "crimes" against Fela was treated. What crimes if one may ask? The relentless police harassment Fela was constantly subjected to, should be considered as "levity" by the authority bent on circumventing the law to continue their repressive acts. Despite the attacks, Fela's popularity kept growing and in terms of music, he was releasing hit after hits using the attacks on him as the base to condemn police and army brutality.

Student union movements of Nigeria's higher institutions, were contesting with each other to host Fela and the Africa 70. In solidarity with the students, he kept his fees at the minimal – judging from the prevailing economic situation in the country. The authority did not like this public support for an artist they considered as "professing a counter culture" and there were cases where the police were prepared to bend the law in order to incriminate Fela.

For example, apart from the 'Expensive Shit' case where they tried to plant evidence in order to convict him, there was this case from his invitation to perform at the Kwara State Polytechnic in Ilorin where the police went out of the way to try and arrests him. The Nigerian police authority, aware that wherever Fela performed there was bound to be marijuana around, were looking for ways to arrest him for possession of marijuana.

Previous attempts at arresting him in Kalakuta so far had not produced any direct implication, hence they took the decision to attack this time while the band was on road outside their Lagos base. To have concrete reason to invite Fela to the police station, Bayo Matins Fela's friend and member of NAPWA who stood bail for him in the Alagbon Close Case, was forced by the police in Lagos to accompany them to Ilorin with the objective of renouncing his previously signed bail bond for Fela. All these were happening, without Bayo being aware of the police plan.

Fela's concert at the Polytechnic was incident free, with the students dancing to Afrobeat music till the 'wee hours' of the morning.

However, the next day the police struck as the instrument truck of the group tried to leave Ilorin town for Lagos. A special police unit mounted a roadblock along the Ilorin–Lagos road and they stopped Fela's road-managers travelling in the instrument truck while searching the vehicles, the police men claimed they found some illegal "weed" suspected to be Indian hemp in the vehicle.

The vehicle was impounded and while they were organising to drive the arrested persons in the vehicle to the police station, 'Show Boy' one of Fela's boys arrested escaped by jumping behind a trailer truck moving into the city from the opposite direction.

He went straight to Kwara State hotel and alerted Fela of the police raid plus the arrests of the advance team heading to Lagos. Fela in-turn immediately ordered other members of the group to move out of their hotel rooms before the police came, warning each member to make sure they had nothing incriminating on them.

Shortly after as anticipated, the police arrived at the hotel and they invited Fela to come with them to identify the vehicle and members of his organisation arrested earlier. Insisting on driving along with the police in his car with the police in escort, Fela and the rest of us in his entourage headed to the Kwara State Police headquarters in Ilorin where all the arrested were taken.

On our arrival the police without discussing the incidence of the truck impounded earlier, presented Bayo Martins to Fela and they claimed that for personal reasons, the drummer would like to withdraw the bail bond he had signed for Fela's release from police detention during the Alagbon Close case. Suspecting a trap, Fela asked Bayo Martins why he couldn't wait until he got back to Lagos before he withdrew his bail bond, and in reply Bayo said he was always willing to stand bail for Fela, and that in this case the police forced him to accompany them to Ilorin without informing him of their intention.

Thinking of a way to escape and knowing by law that the police could not hold him until the document was signed, Fela asked Bayo Martins to withold signing until he could return to check-out from his hotel room.

Bayo Matins an activist in his own right realised what the Police was up to, he refused to cancel his bail bond until Fela's request was granted.

Waiting in the car while Fela went into the police station were some of his women and the YAP boys, he narrated to us all that had transpired with Bayo inside the police station when he came back to the car where were waiting. Fela returned to the hotel, promising the police he would be back in a few minutes.

The police let us go without escort, because they were assured that they had men watching the Ilorin–Lagos road in case he attempted to escape. Fela on the other hand, decided to escape driving as fast as he could out of town and taking back roads that led-out of town.

Aware that the police were waiting on the Ilorin–Lagos road, Fela took the Ilorin–Offa road which to any road user is a deviation and much longer way to get to Lagos. I guess the police never imagined that Fela in an attempt to escape would take a longer rout out of town. This way he avoided the police, and instead of heading for Lagos directly Fela drove first to his mother's house in Abeokuta, from where he sent word out to his lawyer Kanmi Osobu.

Knowing they could come looking for him in Abeokuta, he drove same night to Agege a Lagos suburb and we spent the night in an obscure hotel until Fela was able to contact his lawyer again. Unfortunately, Fela's performance that day at the Shrine had to be cancelled with the crowd waiting as other members who were not arrested in Ilorin came back with the news of the police raid.

The following day, Kanmi Isola-Osobu filed a law suit at the Lagos High court against the Inspector General of Police and the Kwara State Commissioner of police for harassment and intimidation and he named Bayo Matins as witness which further put the police in a dilemma.

From his engagements with the National Association of Patriotic Artists and Writers (NAPWA), it was clear to the police that Bayo Martins would not betray Fela despite their intimidation – hence their dilemma.

Whatever the police had in mind before the attempted arrest of Fela in Ilorin failed, his escape and also the crowd waiting at the Shrine for him to perform made the press catch on to the scoop.

The following day, the press was full of Fela's brush again with the police in Ilorin.

His musical instruments seized by the Kwara State police took some time before they were returned. Meanwhile, Gowon and his police brutality were all swept out of power in a bloodless military coup in July 1975, headed by Murtala Mohammed the Comissioner for Communication of the regime.

General Murtala Muhammed, in his own way, tried to give the Nigerian nation a sense of accountbility when he attempted to stop the endemic corruption that was the system. We shall discus this in the coming chapter.

Young African Pioneers (YAP) Care-Taker Committee members, sitting to the right of the lady in red behind Fela in the court yard of Kalakuta. Picture by Jean Jacque Mandel.

Young African Pioneers (YAP) Care-Taker Committee members, presented to the Shrine public by Fela at the launching of the movement. From left: not visible Fela, Mabinuori Kayode Idowu, Ghariokwu Lemi and Duro Ikujemiyo.
Picture taken by Femi Bankole Osunla - Africa 70 photo Agency.

YOUNG AFRICAN PIONEERS (YAP)

I guess it will be appropriate at this point to explain how those of us around Fela came to be addressed as YAP BOYS, particularly since as earlier mentioned, it was the period where the author was newly presented and integrated into the Fela entourage. However, before I proceed it will be necessary to clarify a point here regarding the idea behind Kalakuta.

As a "Republic" Kalakuta was not Fela's idea of a pan-African republic. Fela's personality, Kalakuta and the Africa 70 Organisation, constituted what could be described as a form of artistic and social rebellion but not an idea of a pan-African republic. The person and actions of Fela and members of Kalakuta Republic for a long time had become cause for controversy among the Nigerian public, there are those who see Kalakuta as a negative influence and those who see the contrary.

This should come as no surprise, if we take into account that throughout African history, griots and musicians have played a great role in the transmission of history. Musically from his album released in 1973 titled Confusion, with his Pan-African solution - critical of what transpires as government on the continent, to his Army Arrangement album released in the '80's – a narrative of how the military institution have high-jacked the people's clamour for freedom and democracy, every song of Fela Anikulapo-Kuti from his Africa 70 to Egypt 80 works are narratives of Nigeria's 20th and 21st Century contemporary history.

January 15, 1966 saw Nigerians from all works of life trooping to the streets to welcome the first ever military coup d'état in the country, their jubilation stemmed from the aspiration that the military will deliver them from the persistent wave of political gangstarism - burning down of homes of those considered as opponent, a common scene in the Northern and Southern parts of the country.

The climate of insecurity which was the order of the day in the Nigerian contemporary politics of the early sixties, paved the way for the arrival of the military in the political arena and haven tasted power they are finding it hard to relinquish it thus prompting Fela to sing 'Army Arrangement'. His 'EVERYTHING SCATTER' album, is another perfect example of his historic insight into why there is constant clash between the people and those who govern them:

"Them go say, bring me the Fela people, make I lock and charge am for court! Then I shut him big mouth for am! And I hang-am to mosquito! That is how this country be! That is why everything dey Scatter! Scater! No wonder re-re dey run!" Singing the song in the manner of a story teller with some history behind it, Fela presented the Nigerian society like passengers in a moving public bus driving past Kalakuta Republic, a passenger in the bus representing the establishment view makes a remark condemning Fela and members of Kalakuta as 'hooligans', 'hemp smokers', 'prostitutes' and 'political non - starters'.

Another passenger who like countless of Fela's teaming admirers see him as 'Black President', Chief Priest, Mystic man (Abami in Yoruba language), challenges the establishment man. Meanwhile the debate spreads among all the other passengers in the bus dividing them evenly - those echoing government opinion of Fela and those against, at the end a big commotion in the bus and like in all conflicts Everything Scatter.

Successive military regimes in Nigeria, in their attempt to silence Fela's bold criticisms have labelled him all sorts of names including trouble shooter. Fela however would not relent in his criticism of the corruption and colonial mentality of the establishment, the end result is what he described as Everything Scatter. As mentioned earlier, with the Nigerian urban social evolution came a cultural explosion with Fela and his Africa 70 organisation at its head.

To understand this explosion, we need to look at the attitude of the educated elite and their so called Christian values that has been the way of life in Nigeria since the installation of colonial administration, particularly their point of view regarding professions such as music, art and sports.

Not until recently, the music profession like those of other forms of art and sports were not recognised as stable professions in the Nigerian colonial oriented society. If you are not a lawyer, doctor, or working in the administration, you were never accorded the professional recognition merited in most modern day African society. To be a musician or dancer, is like being regarded as a beggar and for a woman to be a professional singer, or dancer, she was looked down on as a loose woman or prostitute and a never do well.

Most Nigerian youths who wanted to be professional musicians, dancers, and those who wanted careers in sports, found themselves in trouble with strict parents and guardians who share these negative views of the artist. As a result the youths run away from home inorder to realise their professional dreams, and like mentioned earlier for such youths, Fela's Kalakuta republic became the attraction as they became aware that such negative views of the artists were not entertained there.

Somehow most of these youths, find work within Fela's organisation and if they do not loose their direction from their new found freedom they end up playing whatever instrument or skill they manage to learn.

Two examples of such youths are Oghene Kologbo and 'Show Boy', the evolution of the two would be perfect example to buttress this point because they were the youngest members living in Kalakuta then. Kologbo arrived in Kalakuta at about the age of twelve years, he learnt to play the guitar from Fela's house and ended-up playing the instrument in the band. Though Kologbo would desert the band in later years, we shall discus this when we talk about the break-up of Africa 70 band.

The second was known to everyone as 'Show Boy', he got his name from his acts as an acrobat and fire-dancer. He came from Porto Novo in Republic of Benin, with a dance group when he was only thirteen years old and he decided to stay in Fela's home after getting the chance to perform in the Shrine with the dance troupe doing acrobatic shows and fire-dancing to entertain the audience before the band went on stage and running errands while learning to play the bass guitar.

'Show Boy' got discouraged learning to play the bass because Kologbo with whom they started learning, knew how to play his instrument faster and started to play in Fela's band before him. Discourage, he left the organisation after a careless incidence on his part that cost him an eye.

Because of constant shortages of electric power supply in Nigeria, Fela mounted an electrical generator outside his home to supply electricity regularly to the house and stored around the generator were Jerry-cans used for buying petrol to run the generators.

'Show Boy' was looking for an empty Jerry-can to buy water (another commodity in regular short-supply), without thinking of the consequence and with a burning 'joint' in his mouth he peeped into the Jerry-can to verify if it was empty. Unfortunately for him the Jerry-can was earlier used to store petrol and unexpectedly, flame leapt-out of the jerry-can from the close contact of his burning 'joint' and it consumed a part of his face.

Luckily Beko (Fela's brother), was running a private clinic situated in-front of the house, 'Show Boy' was rushed there for first-aid treatment before he was taken to the hospital. This incidence and his not making progress from learning the bass guitar, pushed him to depart Fela's organisation not long after. He later worked briefly with a Nigerian magician called Professor Peller and shortly after quitting Peller, he joined the navy as a civilian learning how to repair musical instruments.

From his handling of various instruments at the Naval base, he came to learn how to play the saxophone and he returned to Fela's group in 1985 playing the baritone sax and has remained in the group even after Fela's passing. There were others like Okoli who came to Fela's area running errands until he became Fela's valet. He was responsible for cleaning Fela's room and also taking messages from Fela to each woman whose turn it was to share his bed. Fela had this unspoken, arrangement with his women where messages were transmitted between his valet and the respective woman he desired to share his bed.

Only Remi was not invited in this manner, because she had her arrangement where messages were relayed through the 'kids' (Yeni, Femi and Sola). She usually sent written notes to Fela to ask when to come over, and she often sent along with the note newspaper cuttings of items from the numerous foreign journals in English she had read that she considered important for Fela's information.

Remi was never invited like the other women since she no-longer lived in Kalakuta, but her children visited their father daily. Soon as school was over Yeni, Femi, and Sola, were usually picked–up in one of Fela's chain of cars from their respective schools and brought to Kalakuta. It was during occasions such as this that Femi started to learn how to drive a car. They spent most of their time in the house with their school friends, playing around or listening to their father as he held court.

Asked if he felt treated differently as a son, in comparison with his two sisters and other Fela children? Femi said: "He only started to have kids from other women in 1971, by this time we first three kids were already teenagers. From my mother's side, we were treated equally until his final days when I had started to earn my own money and then he started to make a little difference between the three of us.

For him my two other sisters were not earning as much as me so he did more financially for them than me, however we used to laugh over-it because I was aware that it was nothing against me. He was only trying to say I have a career that is going well for me, there was no point in him giving me anything anymore.

However, with regards to his other children I wouldn't know how he treated them. I was no longer living with him when he had them Moreover, I was only coming to visit with my two other sisters and his household didn't like us. Why? I don't know.

No one of them gave reasons for not liking us, but we could feel they didn't like us and we had problems with them as a result of this. For Fela he was too liberal to feel concerned about things like this. Fela was probably trying to tell us that if he was rich, he would give us everything when he allowed me at the age of 12 to drive his car. I think it was more his manner of showing affection. He was a very liberal man, not only towards us his children he was liberal to everybody that had close contact with him".

Another evidence of his liberal approach to life to buttress Femi's earlier claim, despite the fact that Fela had bank accounts he was in the habit of keeping cash under his mattress. The reader will note as mentioned earlier, that he played with his group four times a week and with his growing number of dependants he needed regular cash to meet the needs of all these people around him.

Okoli (the valet) like most people around Fela were employed without any reference a standing policy with Fela. Meanwhile; Okoli usually helped himself from the money under Fela's mattress, spending the money on drinks in bars in Kalakuta area.

He had the habit of preferring to drink whisky instead of water with a meal - claiming "whisky sweet, fanta (an orange drink) bitter". Okoli spent money so recklessly that Fela realised only too late that it was the money from his bedroom that the guy was spending. Okoli, I believe was tempted from the big amount of money he saw regularly in Fela's room and hatched plans to steal a large sum from the stock before he ran away from Kalakuta.

He was apprehended a few days after he made his move in a hotel where he was staying with a prostitute and was dragged back to the house, he was beating on Fela's orders by boys in the house but from his reckless spending, he had spent most of the money he stole and was admitted back to the organisation doing menial jobs.

Fela allowed all kinds of people around him. I guess he did this believing like his father, that there is no one that cannot be reformed given the opportunity. He usually trusted people for whatever they were until such person proved to be the contrary. He gave everyone he came in contact with, the opportunity to prove them before making any judgement of the person. Talking about opportunity, there were guys like Lat Darrassin a professional boxer who ended-up in Fela's organisation as a bouncer and body-guard. Before and during his involvement with the Africa 70 organisation, he was for many years the Lagos state heavy weight boxing champion.

Lat Darrassin, encouraged by Fela to continue his boxing career while working with the organization, won the Nigerian boxing heavy weight title against the former champion Abraham "Assassin" Tonika at the sports hall of the National Stadium Suru-Lere in 1975 and 1976. On both occasions, with massive support from his Lagos public lead by Kalakuta Area boys dressed in special T-shirts with the inscription "Africa 70 Show Boy Lat Darrassing," boldly printed with his picture on it.

Thousands of such T-shirts, were distributed for free to fans of Darrassin during his many title fights and Fela attended some of the fights to mobilize public support for Darrasing. Apart from musicians, 'bouncers' and body-guards, others were employed and paid to do menial jobs like 'Tunde Roller' who got so named, from rolling thousands of 'joints' for Fela and his numerous guests who visited Kalakuta daily. Fela at this time had stopped drinking alcohol because of liver problems, thus he chose to entertain guests in his house with marijuana.

Rounds of all-ready rolled 'joints', were usually passed around sitting guests on Fela's orders. There were others in the organization, that were employed to train the boys in martial arts, and the women dance. For many years, Ogunde (called 'teacher') one of the sons of the famous Nigerian dramatist Chief Herbert Ogunde was teaching Africa 70 women dance choreography. He also played the role of "Iku" the death masquerade that appears on stage, reciting spiritual incantations in Yoruba language during Fela's Saturday night shows.

The reader will recall that since Fela changed the name of his 'club' from Afro Spot to Africa Shrine, he regularly interrupted as part of what he called 'Comprehensive Show', his performance at the Shrine to render homage or worship the departed souls of African ancestors in the struggle. Great Africans and those from the African Diaspora such as Malcolm X, Marcus Garvey, Patrice Lumumba, Kwame Nkrumah and his revered mother Funmilayo. All these people had their images carved in wood, and placed on alters made special at the Shrine.

Concerning the women in Kalakuta, they were either employed as dancers, singers and disc jockeys (DJ's). The DJ's were responsible for music played on the hi-fi stereo set in Kalakuta. Since his house was situated in the heart of the Lagos ghetto, household inhabitants shared many discomforts with the ordinary populace such as water and power shortages, cramped conditions and poor sanitation, the women slept twelve to a room in bunk beds. Fela was planning to re-build the house around 1975/1976. I remember him talking about an architectural design with the 'black power' clenched fist as a model.

He was waiting to make more money, saying he was on his way to become a millionaire. The female inhabitants of Kalakuta were mostly of different backgrounds like the boys, some from rich parents like Folake Kalakuta Show mentioned earlier and Bukola Adedipe, the daughter of a Lagos Judge. This group of people constitutes a category of people around Fela. They like the musicians were members of the Africa 70 Organisation. They were all on the pay role and got paid every week.

The other group of people around Fela, were mostly friends who either were ex-school mates or people whom he shared some teenage experiences with. The latter group of people, did not work directly with the organisation. They were mostly men and a few women who had their respective professions - doctors, accountants, lawyers, musicians, writers, etc. However, some of his lawyer friends did work with him during Fela's several trials in the Nigerian courts.

People like Kanmi Ishola–Osobu (people's lawyer), and Wole Kuboye, a corporate lawyer who played the role of Fela's father in his film 'Black President' because of his big physical build like Fela's father. Wole Kuboye, was also known to all in Kalakuta as "Feelings Lawyer," because of his artistic streak and beautiful baritone voice.

He loved to sing and he knew all of Fela's songs by heart. He usually sang Fela's part on stage, at the Shrine whenever Fela was detained and the Shrine opened to the public. There were others like Bayo Matins, Wole Bucknor, Tunde Kuboye (feelings lawyer's younger brother who later married Fela's niece Frances).

Also JK (Jimoh Kanbi), who had the position of director of public relations, Steve Udah was Fela's press attaché, Ekow Oduro, a Ghanaian poet and film maker - he directed the never released epic film produced by Fela titled 'Black President. There were also people like Abdulrahaman Dusty Johnson, a Nigerian who grew up in London during the hippie era. He returned to Nigeria in the 70's and was the manager of the group "T-Fire" and Suru-Lere Night Club respectively, after Fela had left the club for Empire Club renamed Africa Shrine.

There were musicians like Joni Hastrup, Tee Mac, Segun Bucknor, Jimi Solanke, journalist Linsay Barret, Tunde Harrison, and a host of others. Dusty Johnson was one of those friends critical of Fela's Africanism concept, saying we wanted to take the country back to savagery with our ideology. We YAP boys, used to get into arguments with him over such positions. Particularly his mix of Islamic and English name which we considered as double colonialism. He had a friend with whom they hung out in Kalakuta named Michael Vidal.

To us (YAP Boys), these guys (particularly Dusty), were considered as yuppies that profited with the liberty in Kalakuta, to use drugs (cocaine and heroin) which they brought with them.

Some of these friends shared his ideological believes and participated in his various political activities. However others like Dusty, did not give a damn what he was talking about. They were only concerned about the free flow of drugs around Fela.

Talking about drugs (cocaine, heroine and LSD), a lot of these drugs were coming into Nigeria around this period. Fela, who did not approve of hard drug use but tolerated it among his friends exposed us (YAP Boys) to drugs. He insisted on us having a taste of them saying "they are not good for you, but I want you to have personal experience of them to understand why I consider them not good". According to him, he did not want us to fall victim to those friends who could encourage or influence us in that direction.

Thanks to his advice, I never touched any of those drugs despite my coming in contact with them in the cause of my involvement with musicians and artists who use them. There was this incidence in Zurich, where I was invited backstage with Roy Ayers and his musicians after a concert at the Karffloitten. This was many years after my departure from Fela's organisation and I was resident in Switzerland. It was a pleasure to see Roy in concert since the 1979 tour in Nigeria with Fela.

After the concert was over, one of Roy's musicians came to inform him that "snow was falling" (meaning there was cocaine available in the musicians dressing room). Roy asked me along, and I saw this large stash of "coke" on the table and the musicians sniffing lines of them. Roy proposed me some which I declined and he remarked that I was a smart guy. I told him thanks to Fela I don't use the stuff.

Going back to the story of the different groups around Fela, It was in this group of friends that I and my two other colleagues Ghariokwu Lemi and Duro Ikujenyo became classified as we got close enough to Fela and the decision making body around him.

Towards the end of 1975, when he officially dropped "Ransome" from his name and he took on 'Anikulapo,' despite the decree by the military regime banning any form of political activities in Nigeria, we felt the need to organise and mobilise the Nigerian public to stand up and resist the draconian military dictatorship.

To this end, we launched the Young African Pioneers Movement (YAP). As part of its professed aim and objective, we stated that the YAP movement was a non-political organization, out to spread economic and cultural awareness among Africans and Africans in the Diaspora.

As a result of our visible dedication and understanding of Fela's political views, Lemi, Duro, and I were appointed Care -Taker Committee members of YAP. The three of us were responsible for the day to day running of the movement. We were in charge of the YAP office based in the Shrine, we registered members and started to use this platform to mobilise youths who frequented the Shrine towards African values and the ideology of Pan-Africanism. Like other friends of Fela, the three of us had our separate professions.

Lemi apart from his artistic designs was working with the Nigerian Federal Ministry of Works as a clerical officer, and he was still resident with his parents while he did the art designs for Fela's album sleeves. Same with Duro, who was working with the Federal Ministry of Trade at the same time, he took private music lessons as part of his desire to be a professional musician majoring in piano. In later years Duro would play in Fela's band. Duro too was living with his parents in the same building as Lemi's parents. For me, I was working as a sales representative with the United African Company (what irony) a British trading subsidiary in Nigeria.

I had moved to Lagos from Zaria where I used to reside with my mother. I decided and I managed to convince my mother, to allow me to work for one year before going to the university to sturdy philosophy or history. As chance would have it, I was lodged at an uncle's who resided down the street from Lemi and Duro. Shortly before the launching of YAP, I felt the need to defy the dress code from my employer requiring every sales representative to wear neck ties to work. It was not long before my boss noticed this change in my mode of dressing to work, and he sent me an official query demanding why I chose to defy the official dress code.

Convinced of the authenticity of the African way of life as Fela sang in GENTLEMAN, I was determined to contest this dress code. In the song, Fela explained that the concept of Pan Africanism is about identity, the idea of Africans and Africans in the Diaspora to be proud and seen as African personalities.

The practice where Africans dress in western suits and ties in a temperature more than 30 degrees hot is considered as stupid. "Gentleman" in the street terms is the equivalent of an Uncle Tom, an African who prefers western mannerisms and values to original African traditional ways of life. A gentleman is also a black person, who turns the other cheek in a passive protest against oppression.

In my responds to the query sent me by my employer, I explained that the wearing of a neck tie in the hot tropical climate of Nigeria is un-African and uncomfortable in work places. I went further to explain that the wearing of a neck tie, had no contribution whatsoever to my productivity as a sales representative. I was aware that I stood the risk of being sacked from my job, but I preferred to be sacked from the job than compromise my convictions in view of my newly found identity as an African personality and Pan-Africanist.

When Fela was informed of my confrontation with the UAC management, he made it clear to me that he was proud of me as a man who would stand up for his believes but as a realistic leader, he wanted to know if I had other plans in mind for an alternative job in the event that I got sacked from the UAC.

I made him understand that my desire was to become a writer and since most of the higher institution of learning in Nigeria, are colonial oriented I was not prepared to attend any of such schools in order to learn how to write. I went further to explain that I was determined to read wide, covering every discipline in order to broaden the scope of my knowledge and to write as much as possible whenever the situation permitted me.

Meanwhile in order for my employers to understand the nature of my resolve vis à vis wearing of the neck tie to work, and with Fela's reputation as the champion of a new and authentic Africa, we agreed that he should pay me a visit at work. Before this decision to visit me in my work place, it is important to note that after my boss received my reply to his query, I was suspended from work pending the decision of the UAC manage ment. However, I was obliged during this suspension period to report at the office twice everyday. I guess my boss because of my track record in office as an efficient sales representative, wanted to give me the chance to comply with his dress code directive and to show some remorse.

Unfortunately, I was not prepared to concede this to them and Fela's visit to my work place made this point clear. For us, this was more of a resolve not to compromise our belief in the African personality. My employers saw it differently, for the UAC management I was setting a precedence which had to be curbed before it spread through-out the establishment, and as expected I lost my job and this was why I came to work full time with the Young African Pioneers and later after the burning down of Kalakuta the Africa 70 Organisation.

For my two other friends, they voluntarily resigned their appointments in order to devote their attentions to their respective professions, and the work of the Young African Pioneers Movement. Thus we became known, as YAP Boys within the organisation.

Meanwhile, as part of the movement's attempts to educate the average man on the streets, we launched a weekly news letter called YAP NEWS. We were printing and distributing for free, eighty-thousand copies of the YAP NEWS. It was no secret that Fela in his capacity as founder and financier of the Young African Pioneer movement bought a $40,000 (US) printing machine for the publication of the YAP NEWS. We were still printing the copies of the news letter with private printers, pending the installation of our new printing machine before the Nigerian Army attack on February 18, 1977.

Fortunately, the printing machine was not yet installed in Kalakuta as earlier planned before the army burnt down the house. We printed the news letter, from private printing houses and Fela financed the publications. The news letter carried on the front page of every issue: THE NEWS OTHER NEWSPAPERS CAN'T PRINT WE CAN PRINT.

Most of the views expressed in the articles published in the news letter, were very critical of the military dictatorship in Nigeria. This should not come as a surprise, in view of Fela's strong criticisms of the military in songs such as ZOMBIE - a song he portrays the military and their orientation as zombie. Fela in his life time as the reader must have noticed was never 'a good bed-fellow' of the military institution. As a political activist, he believed the army should operate under the mandate of a civil government. If national interest compels the armed forces to intervene in government, the army is obliged to hand over power to a new civil government elected by the people and enjoying their mandate.

To do otherwise, is to usurp power particularly since a soldier's duty is not to seek a political mandate. It is not the duty of the army to rule or govern, because it has no political mandate and its duty is not to seek political mandate. Normally, the duty of the armed forces is to defend and support the civil government – not to overthrow it or usurp the duties of any branch of the government. The army can only operate under the mandate of the civil government.

If national interest compels the armed forces to intervene then immediately after such intervention, they must hand over to a new civil government elected by the people and enjoying the mandate of the people under a constitution accepted by the people.

Since the departure of the former colonial powers in Nigeria and equally in most other parts of Africa, the army with the co-operation of the educated elite and corrupt political class has clung to power. For example under Gowon, with the participation of Chief Obafemi Awolowo in his government, likely oppositions to the military were reduced to nothing. The political "chief" brought intellectuals and the educated elites to support the military administration.

Gowon regime, rewarded them with appointments but reduced their likely effectiveness. Offering them positions, where their capacity to influence the public would be minimised. We shall talk more on this issue the chapters ahead.

Like all Fela's direct attacks on the military, YAP NEWS carried issues openly critical of Nigerian military ruler's solutions to daily problems of our society. For an example, in one of its publications we condemned the policy where traffic offenders were subjected by army personnel directing traffic to physical punishments by the road sides. YAP NEWS, from the African cultural standpoint saw this act as a debasement of the African personality.

Most of the views expressed in the various publications, were written by me with contributions from Fela and my two other colleagues in the Care-Taker committee of the movement. I remember how Fela used to encourage me to write, to the displeasure of some of his friends older than we YAP boys. I wrote an article titled "Youths Demand the removal of Colonel Tarfa," with regards to the horse-whip solution the Colonel chose to resolve the Lagos traffic congestion in 1976.

The article was pretty long, and I mentioned the history of the army as representing Nigeria's colonial institution. However Steve Udah the Africa 70 organisation press attaché, was not happy with the "preferential treatment" he claimed Fela accorded us (YAP Boys). He re-wrote the article cutting out all the history of colonial army I had stressed. When Fela was presented the edited version, he turned to me asking why I let Steve re-write what he considered a well explicit article.

I replied that Steve was claiming to know more about writing than I did hence my compromise. Fela was furious with me, saying if I was not capable to defend my works then who would. From then on, I wrote most of the texts we published in the News letter.

CROSS EXAMINATION OF THE AFRICAN COLONIAL SOLDIER, is another song Fela performed live around this time in which he was critical of the "African neo-colonial military institution." Putting them on trial before the "peoples court" Fela sang: "Calling you all African people! This is an African court!" Assuming the role of a prosecutor in the audience were the Young African Pioneers representing the 'people', and Fela questioned the 'imagined' African colonial soldier before the peoples' court saying: "Where were you trained?" The soldier replies "I can't remember!" "I put it to you, you were trained overseas!" Again the soldier replies "I can't remember".

He continues prosecution saying: "Your uniform is foreign!" "Sometime ago our people fought for independence! I put it to you! You did not fight along with the people! Your colonial masters used you!" To kill and torture our people!" To all these questions and observations, the colonial African soldier always replied either "I can't remember or I don't know". Fela after presenting the case against the accused concluding his prosecution, he invited the people to comment and in unison they pronounced the verdict: "You are guilty".

All the opinion published in YAP news, would later anger the government of General Olusegun Obasanjo who took over power after General Mohammed was assassinated in February of 1976. Meanwhile it will be appropriate to discus Fela's relation regarding the regime of General Mohammed.

Front cover album design Confusion

Front cover album design Zombie

Carved ivory mask of Queen Idia of ancient Benin Kingdom, the bronze copy was used as the symbol of FESTAC '77. Most of these African legacies, are presently kept in European and European-American museums and private collections.

SECOND WORLD BLACK FESTIVAL OF ARTS AND CULTURE (FESTAC '77)

Between July 1975 and February 1976, the repressive military and police machine against Fela was on a "seize-fire" thanks to the appointment of M.D.Yussuf as the new Inspector general of Police (IGP). He admitted in a conversation with Fela that before his appointment as the IGP, there were times he attended Shrine sessions disguised to find out what went on.

M.D. Yussuf was a pragmatic and rear police officers who like Fela, never judged a person unless he had proof to so judge that person and from his admission to Fela it was clear that thanks to him Mohammed regime dealt with Fela differently from previous military regimes. Fela was convinced that the IGP must have been pivotal to the regime trying to ameliorate, the military relationship with Fela and the Kalakuta community.

M.D's first notice of Fela according to him, was in the early 70's shortly after the civil war when he was the head of security in Eastern Nigeria posted to Enugu. He was at the concert during Fela's performance at the Government House in Enugu. The reader, will recall that Fela was invited by the then Administrator of Eastern Nigeria Mr Upabi Asika to perform with his group Africa 70 at the government house Enugu. The new IGP claimed he followed Fela's career closely, like those of other Nigerians who interested the security agency.

MD was said to compile dossiers on "who was who" in Nigeria, something that gave him leverage over most of his associates. He was aware of what went on in the Shrine and he made it known to the new regime. With his information, he was obliged to caution the new administration to go easy with Fela from his personal experience of what transpired in the Shrine.

Respected by his pears in the Supreme Military Council (SMC the ruling body that governed Nigeria), I guess he must have been instrumental to Mohammed's attitude of appearing in public places disguised as he was reputed to do to find out situation of things himself.

General Mohammed shortly after he took power, embarked on a mass retirement of various senior members of the Federal government ministries.

All those corrupt 'super permanent secretaries' who abused their positions, he "fired" on the spot and any state governor accused of any form of corruption. In order to mobilise the people behind his regime, the law which hitherto condemned people to ten years in prison for possession of "Indian Hemp" was reduced with a decree to six months with an option of fine.

This move would largely endear him to the Nigerian public and the press, the latter started to write about "Ramatism" as an ideology - an allusion to proclaiming the new Head of State's approach and style of rule as a new ideology for Nigeria.

"Ramatism" was coined, from the middle name of the head of state Murtala Ramat Mohammed. Dressed in civilian clothes, Mohammed entered post offices to buy stamps but to his surprise he was told to go and look for change, something that should have been done by the person selling the stamps.

Rebuffed at every 'counter' for not having the right change to purchase a stamp, he retraced his step to the first 'counter' identified himself to the stamp seller and 'fired' the culprit on the spot.

Mohammed with moves such as recounted above, seemed to respond to messages from Fela's songs like POWER SHOW. In this song, he condemned the rich as professing a culture where everyone is using his or her position to exploit instead of serving the people. How in post offices 'tellers' manning public counters, feel no obligations to their customers he sang:

"I open my eyes I see for my land!
Nah wrong show oh! (Chorus)
Everywhere you dey!
Everywhere you go!
Everybody wan't do power show!
Nah wrong show oh! (Chorus)
You reach boarder, immigration officer dey!
Him go bluff you!
Yes! (Chorus)
Close him pen!
Yes! (Chorus)
Some go tidy dem table!

Yes! (Chorus)
Before him go know say you dey there!
If you no talk quick!
Yes! (Chorus)
Him go go for shit!
Yes! (Chorus)
Him go shit come back!
Yes! (Chorus)
And you talk to am!
Yes! (Chorus)
Him go shout for you!
Him go say you no go cross today!
Nah that time dem go start dem Power Show!
Nah wrong show oh! (Chorus)
Go Post Office nah the same!
Dem go bluff you!
Yes! (Chorus)
Comb him hair!
Yes! (Chorus)
Him go say no change…."

Ordering customers around or refusing to offer services because the customer did not have the right change to buy a stamp, tellers who performed their duties in this manner were targets of General Mohammed.

His regime seemed to take seriously issues raised by Fela in this song. The period also was one of the most productive musical eras of Fela, we shall discus this later. Meanwhile let's go back to General Mohammed and his actions. He announced plans to move the federal capital from Lagos to Abuja, and he also appointed a new constitution drafting committee to draw out a new constitution that would guide the new civilian regime he hoped to install in power by October 1979.

Keeping with the general public opinion on foreign policy, Mohammed regime vigorously backed Augustino Neto's Popular Movement for the Liberation of Angola (MPLA) during the country's civil war. He openly identified with the liberation struggle in South Africa, a clear departure from Gowon who was considered a stooge of the British government.

The British government not wanting to be seen as abandoning their former ally, offered political asylum to the deposed General under the pretext that Gowon was pursuing academic studies in University of Warwick in England.

Mohammed distinguished his regime as anti American by calling on America and other foreign powers to stop their meddling in what he called the internal affairs of African nations, his regime seemed to give the Nigerian nation a sense of accountability.

People like Fela at this period were calling the attention of those in government, to the need for an authentic national ideology such as Pan Africanism in order to give Nigerian people some sense of direction but no one would listen.

Published in his Chief Priest Say pre-paid adverts in leading Nigerian journals, Fela said: "Our country needs an authentic revolutionary ideology to progress e.g. Nkrumaism otherwise we shall always loose our heavy leaders and valuable property too".

To put pressure on the government for an ideological direction for the nation, publications in the YAP News called on the government to propose a national ideology based on the concept of Pan Africanism in the new constitution for the nation. Mohammad regime did not interfere with Fela despite the criticisms of his regime by Fela and publications in the YAP News. In his no-nonsense manner to get things done, Mohammed overlooked the deep rooted influence welded by the forcibly retired civil service personnel - this mistake eventually cost him his life.

Mohammed, who approved of capital punishment for crimes such as armed robbery, failed to do the same with the discredited and corrupt members of the previous regime, the tribunals set up by his administration to try civil servants found to have corruptly enriched them-selves did not use the same standard as those condemned for armed robbery.

People who had plunged the Nigerian economy into disaster, were left with trivial penalties while the poor who were forced to commit petty-crimes in-order to survive, were heavily sanctioned by public executions at the Lagos Barbeach. Fela considered the Mohammed regime as full of 'double standards'.

The role he played in the previous administration justify this opinion of him by Fela. As Commissioner for Communications in the Gowon administration, he was responsible for the award of almost a billion dollars contract to ITT to install a functioning communication network for the country. Twenty years after, Nigeria still does not have a functioning telephone system and "everything is UPSIDE DOWN like Fela sang in the song with the same title.

Mohammed's anti-American stands shortly after he took power, boiled down to double standards too, particularly since he remained friends with Moshood Abiola the chairman for ITT middle-East and Africa, with whom he signed the telephone deal when he was Commissioner for Communication. Abiola's ITT never delivered despite receiving all the contract fees.

Moreover, this was happening soon after the widely publicised alleged ITT's involvement in the assassination of Salvador Alliende in Chile. Fela who had read the book: 'The Sovereign State - Secrete History of ITT by Anthony Samson, would later condemn the multi-national company in his song International Thief Thief (ITT).

Fela in the song International Thief Thief (ITT), condemns the diabolical role of multi-national corporations and their local collaborators in the politics of African states, calling them International thieves that should be fought with all strength and vigour.

Their method is usually the standard practice world-wide, they employ a local citizen who in turn warms his way up the ladders of power by bribing and arse-licking Fela stressed in the song. Departing from his habitual satirical reference to individuals in power, Fela in ITT named the local collaborators of such multi nationals: "like Obasanjo and Abiola! International Thief! Thief!"

Mohammed was assassinated while caught in a Lagos traffic jam on February 13 1976, his assassination was said to be the hand-work of disgruntled influential Nigerians who were forced out of their former posts by the regime. I hope one day in the spirit of finding the truth, archives of coup d'état trials and condemnations would be open to public, for I believe that a lot of political murders were committed and justified by coup plots charges by various military regimes in power in Nigeria.

Mohammed was succeeded by the number two man in the regime General Olusegun Obasanjo, refereed to in the ITT song by Fela as an "international thief thief". During the rule of Gen. Mohammed, Fela was named member of Nigeria's National Participation Committee for FESTAC '77. It would be appropriate at this juncture to give a background on the World Festival of Arts and Culture that gave birth to this festival.

The decision to hold the 1st World Black Festival of Arts and Culture in Dakar from 1–24 April 1966, emanated from the resolutions taken at the 2nd World Congress of Black Writers and Artists held at the Capitol in Rome from 26th, March to 1st, April 1959, with the theme "Unity of the African Negro Culture" in responds to the wave of nationalism and a black identity crises that was blowing across the world like a wind.

At the Congress in Rome, it was suggested that with all pragmatism the next world meeting should be held alongside an international festival with rhythms, dances, theatre, poetry and plastic arts. However, the independence of Ghana one year earlier to the Rome Congress, added a disturbing political dimension for colonialist observing the declarations of delegates to the meeting in Rome.

Kwame Nkrumah, Ghana's first elected President's encouragement to other nationalist movements in Africa to breakaway from their colonial domination with the declaration: "the Independence of Ghana is meaningless unless linked with the independence of all African states" lead to the politicisation of the proposed Dakar festival.

Also, the 1st International Africanist Congress held in Accra Ghana between 11th to 18th December 1962, helped underline the intentions of Pan Africanist to use the festival of arts and culture as a rallying moment for African thinkers and writers who through their respective publications, affirmed Africa's strong contributions to civilisation and the need for unity on the continent.

The publication of "Challenge of The Congo" a blatant denunciation of the role of the United Nation with regards to the political crises in Congo, and "Africa Must Unite" by Kwame Nkrumah clearly indicated the intention of Pan Africanist like him to use gatherings of black intellectuals and artists as a political rallying point and subsequent publications from Nkrumah such as: "Neo-colonialism Last Stage of Imperialism in Africa" prompted a wave of reactions from the imperialist (notably France and United States of America).

The French government headed by General Charles De Gaulle, in-order to dissuade other Francophone states from following the Pan African path chosen by Sekou Toure in Guinea, encouraged Senghor and Aimé Césaire to press the idea of "negritude" as a concept for people of African origin in the new developing world. A political ally of Kwame Nkrumah, Sekou Toure was the only one with courage among the ex-French colonies, to demand total independence from France in 1959.

The imperialist and colonialist lead by the US however, saw the Pan African movement as a dangerous obstacle to their manoeuvres in Africa hence the encouragement of a wave of military coup d'état beginning with Mobutu in Congo in 1963, Togo in 1965, Nigeria followed in January 1966, closely followed by Ghana in February 1966 before the 1st World Black Festival of Arts and Culture was held in Senegal in April 1966.

Despite the coup in the countries mentioned above, the 1st World Black Festival of Arts and Culture, took place in Dakar with 37 nations and communities from five continents represented. Apart from the colloquium dominated by the 'Negritude" theme championed by the President of Senegal Leopold Senghor, the three week gathering had people like Duke Ellington, Johnny Hodges, Cat Anderson, Ray Naces, Harry Carney and Langton Hughes participating.

There were others like the Nigerian play-write Wole Soyinka, the Brazilian Clementina de Jesus and Josephine Baker present in Dakar. At the end of the meeting in Senegal, the next festival was previewed for 1975 in Nigeria with the theme 'Colloquium on Black Civilisation and Culture' as the focal point.

However the political climate in Nigeria in 1975, was not conducive for such gathering as the Gowon's regime was toppled and the new Mohammed regime decided to postpone the meeting in Lagos until January 1977. Unfortunately General Mohammed too was assassinated in a coup in February 1976, and his successor General Obasanjo pledged to continue Mohammed's policies and respect all engagements agreed to by his predecessor hence the hosting of the festival in February 1977.

Professor Chike Onwunchi a member of the Nigerian FESTAC secretariat, was first to contact Fela asking him to join the Nigerian national participation committee - a preparative body, to decide the scope of Nigeria's participation. It is not clear, if the initiative to invite Fela came from the respected professor or the presence of M.D. Yussuf in government particularly since Professor Onwunchi too spoke highly of Yussuf to Fela.

The first and only meeting of the committee that Fela attended, was held at the Bagauda Lake Hotel in Kano in 1976, Fela was accompanied on this trip by JK, Ekow Oduro (the Ghanaian poet who directed the film 'Black President') and the YAP Boys. Unlike all the other invited members of the committee whose charges were paid by the FESTAC secretariat, Fela chose to pay for himself and his large entourage.

Also present at the meeting were the crème of Nigeria's academic and intellectual community people like: Dr. Ekpo Eyo, Professor Ben Nwowu, Professor Wole Soyinka to name a few. Session after session for four days, the meeting was turning around in circles without concrete issues discussed. Those of us who accompanied Fela were allowed like other members of the public, to observe the proceedings from the public gallery and we took notes and observed the participants for discussion with Fela after.

General I.B.M. Haruna, Commissioner for Information in the new Obasanjo regime and the committee's chairman, instead of discussing specific issues linked with Nigerian participation, took pleasure in explaining how during his travels all over the continent representatives of each country made comments about their pride in Fela's Afrobeat music. He particularly mentioned Guinea how he was officially received at a state reception in Conakry with Fela's music.

Fela however was determined to make the committee move and he put forward a nine point proposal which if adopted, would have made Nigeria's participation more meaningful than the cheap display of traditional dances that was the heart of the Lagos festival in 1977.

Unfortunately the Chairman of the committee rejected the proposal saying: "the government had already planned and decided what was to be done, the committee meeting was just a formality and Fela was only invited to participate in the committee deliberations in-order to find out how much he would charge to perform".

Shocked at the reply of General I.B.M.Haruna, Fela addressed the gathering of people saying he did not come all the way from Lagos to be a "rubber stamp". According to him in his address to the assembled members, he affirmed that he thought the idea of the Kano gathering was to map-out a meaningful programme of participation for Nigeria in FESTAC '77.

Despite Fela's insistence to be heard during the meeting, there was not one of the so-called intellectuals or academicians present who was prepared to support Fela's position, they all were content to be invited to participate in the committee meeting and hoping to be rewarded with appointments in the government or sign some lucrative contracts.

A kind of compensation that reduces their likely effectiveness as earlier mentioned, and the new regime took the queue from Gowon who offered positions to likely dissidents to silence them. With Fela's passionate appeal to the gathering, General I.B.M. Haruna had to adjourn the session according to him "to let tempers cool". But Fela insisted on continuing the debate, he called-out to Professor Ben Nwowu seated a few paces away hopping the sculptor would speak in favour of an open debate to discus his proposals.

"Professor Ben Nwowu please" Fela called out to the Professor, but to his surprise Ben Nwowu walked out of the conference hall with others like Wole Soyinka doing the same not wanting to be identified with Fela. Professor Wole Soyinka in a different context, I believe would be quick to admit publicly "Fela is my cousin" and here in a situation important for the future of our people, he kept mute playing the "YES" game.

In terms of age, all those participating in the Kano meeting were of the same generation as Fela but as we can see, he was the only one from that generation who did not compromise his beliefs. He was one, to resist material gains for his liberty of speech.

The policy, by successive regimes to reward prominent political activists with appointments, but reduce their likely effectiveness caught up with most of the so-called Nigerian intellectuals. Tai Solarin an atheist and educationist who had brushes with the Gowon regime over his convictions, also compromised later when he joined the Babagida administration. Same with Wole Soyinka who later became Commissioner for Traffic - a glorified traffic warden. Kanmi Ishola-Osobu, Fela made famous lawyer also compromised as we shall see.

With the army in power, dignity of labour which was the bastion of Nigerian traditional values was reduced to "arse licking" - they systematically eroded the pride of the individual contribution to society known in Yoruba as "Owo igbe kii run" meaning "shit money don't smell shit". For generations, most Africans are content to follow in the foot-path of their ancestors even if the labour is not dignifying, all these values are gradually being eroded or lost to an army imposed corrupt culture.

Today "shit money don't smell" concept of life, is being replaced by new expressions like "egunje no spoil nothing" meaning, "kick-backs don't spoil our fraternity". Traditional African value of service to humanity, is systematically replaced by new corrupt ways. As a sculpture, Professor Ben Nwowu's works deserved their professional recognition without him arse-liking, same can be said with Wole Soyinka as a playwright with his "Kongi's Harvest".

Since he couldn't convince the "arse lickers" present to discus the merits and de-merits of his nine point proposals to the committee, Fela resigned his membership and he made it public stating to the Nigerian press that he did not see any objective in the festival organisation except that some people were trying to make money out of a sham.

To better inform the public on the reasons why he resigned his membrship, Fela also printed in the YAP News his nine point propositions to the national participation committee.

The proposals were:

1. The aim of the festival as a whole should be to redirect the thinking of the common man.

2. Specifically, the festival should attempt to re-educate the common man in Nigeria and Africa about the role of colonisation on African history and religion.

3. The festival should aim to rid the present generation of the imposed influence of foreign cultures. The festival should provide African history books which are written from an African (rather than colonial) perspective, which due to imperialist manoeuvres are not easily available in Africa.

4. To achieve a solid unity among the black race based on a strong foundation of African unity, an effective communication system should emerge from the festival. The idea is to have in Africa a common monetary system and lingua-franca such as Pidgin English, Swahili or Hausa geographically wide-spoken on the continent. Also to open-up highways, air, sea and rail links throughout the continent. And the interchange of radio and television programmes.

5. Efforts must be made to encourage all Nigerians to participate in the festival. That financial incentives and encouragement should be given to artists to encourage them to participate and perform at their best.

6. All directors responsible for various sections of events, should be given opportunities to use their positions to bring about policies that will enhance the future development of cultural institutions in the country i.e. theatres for film, performance space and art galleries.

7. The activities of the festival and the ideas behind them, should be channelled through the education curriculum in the country to benefit future generations.

8. Mini-festivals should be held all over the country, to select the types of artistes to represent the country and those selected should be provided with necessary instruments and equipment to perform. In the face of this, the sum of 5 million Naira (approximately 7 million U.S. Dollars in 1977) voted by the Federal Government of Nigeria to host the festival was inadequate to support a meaningful participation.

9. The composition of the committee itself, drawn from outside the circle of working artists makes Nigeria's participation in a festival of this nature a huge joke. (Fela argued that a soldier who does not know the professional problems faced by artists, cannot effectively represent the needs of artists to the committee.)

These suggestions were ignored, with the exception of point N° 8 which specified that the money voted by the government was not enough to fund a festival of that magnitude.

Today, if one looks at the education system and programs on Nigerian television all oriented towards Western values, one can see Fela's point about developing programs that emphasised African rather than Western values and having them reflected in the educational curriculum to benefit future generations.

Also his song CONFUSION explains clearly point N° 4 of his proposal to the committee: "to achieve a solid unity among the black race based on a strong foundation of African unity, an effective communication system should emerge from the festival".

In the song, Fela draws an analogy with three African men selling by the road side, and the reality of the monetary system of the respective countries linked to the colonial economy. For specifics he mentioned how the three men were paid in pounds, dollars and French money 'the francs'.

He sang:

"Them be three men wey sell for roadside yeah!
Them three speak different language yeah!
One white man come pay them money oh!
He pay them for pounds! Dollars! And French money oh!
For the thing wey him buy from them oh!
E remain for them to share am oh!
Me I say nah confusion be that oh…!"

Literally translated:
"There are three men selling their wears by the road-side!
The three speak different languages!
One White, comes and pays them for
Things he bought from the three!
He paid them in Pounds, Dollars and French money!
Now it is time for the three to share the money! Fela says:
That is the Confusion in their situation…"

In 1962 President Kwame Nkrumah of Ghana, championed a group of newly independent African nations in a demand for the formation of a United States of Africa with one monetary system for the continent, one defence system etc.

As a convinced Pan Africanist, Fela describes the non-existence of a United States of Africa and a sole monetary system for the continent as Confusion. Sung in his characteristic satiric and sarcastic manner, he compares what transpires as 'government' in Africa to a cross-road in Lagos, popularly called 'Ojuelegba Confusion Centre' a cross-road with a permanent traffic jam.

It is hard to tell today if probably it was the big media coverage of Fela's resignation from the FESTAC committee, or YAP News publication and distribution to the public of Fela's proposals, or an advice from the Inspector General of Police M.D. Yussuf or all these issues together, would lead to an invitation from the Head of State General Obasanjo. Shortly after the massive media coverage of Fela's resignation from the committee, a Nigerian army Captain visited Fela on a Friday night at the Shrine.

He claimed to come with a verbal invitation, for Fela to visit the Head of State General Olusegun Obasanjo with all those 'Black books' Fela was appt to quote from. The Captain wanted to know when Fela could be free to visit the state house bringing along his books.

Soon as we YAP boys got wind of the man's mission, we stationed boys to watch him until he left Kalakuta area. The army Captain, was reported to have left in a black official Mercedes Benz car with the licence plate number SHQ 4, an indication that he came from the Supreme Headquarters the seat of power. After Shrine was over, Fela called a meeting of his close associates in Kalakuta and we all agreed (YAP Boys and Fela) to honour the invitation.

It is important to digress a little here, because people who did not know him have criticised Fela for not listening to advice. This invitation by Obasanjo, is an example of how decisions were taken around Fela.

Convinced that there was a possibility that the Obasanjo regime could be interested in listening to Fela for a change, we wanted to honor the invitation. And to show that the decision was not only his to make, Fela informed the army Captain to come back in a week's time.

Fela wanted to hear from his lawyer Kanmi, and he also sent JK to take an appointment with M.D Yusuff as he wanted to verify from the IGP if he was aware of the invitation from the Head of State. Kanmi Osobu was not in Lagos, but the IGP was able to accommodate Fela even at a short notice. As usual, we Yap Boys, JK and some of Fela's women accompanied him to this meeting with M.D.Yusssuf.

The rendezvous was at the official residence of the Inspector General of Police on Awolowo Road Ikoyi. Like in previous visits, M.D. Yussuf welcomed everyone in Fela's entourage in his living room, offering traditional Hausa-Fulani sweets to Fela whom he was aware "had sweet-tooth" habits.

The IGP claimed the sweets were made especially by his mother, who sent them regularly to him in Lagos. After the pleasantries, Fela and the IGP retired to a corner a little far away from all of us present to discus the issue at hand. They both returned a little while after to join us and shortly after, we bade the IGP farewell.

On our way to the Shrine in the car, Fela told us the IGP did not say if he was aware or not of Obasanjo's invitation but insisted that Fela should honour the invitation. Saying it will be an opportunity for the Head of State, to discover what he called the "undiscovered" intellectual aspect of Fela by those in power.

Kanmi Isola-Osobu arrived two days after this meeting with the IGP, and when told of Obasanjo's invitation and the advice of YAP Boys to honour the invitation, Kanmi was furious with Fela saying: "we were going to walk into the enemy territory without an official invitation".

He added further that the government could turn-around to accuse Fela of a coup attempt. Kanmi demanded from Fela if he could explain away, his presence in the State House faced with such accusation.

At this point, we YAP Boys intervened saying we cannot out-of fear fail to pass the message given the opportunity that the invitation provided. But Kanmi made it clear that even if we accompanied Fela, it would be him as our lawyer who would be obliged to go to court to get all of us out of jail if we were arrested.

He called our determination to accompany Fela on an un-official invitation to Doddan Barracks suicidal. When Fela mentioned that he had been to the IGP to seek his advice, Kanmi demanded if the IGP confirmed knowledge of the invitation and Fela repeated that M.D.Yussuf did not indicate which ever way but he only advised that he should honour the invitation.

Kanmi was insistent saying "if the IGP was not aware of the invitation of a decedent like Fela to the seat of power, for him he could smell a rat". His point was, if the head of security in the country was not informed of a visit of someone the like of Fela's to the seat of power there must be something in the cooking. With nothing more to say to his "legal" arguments, we agreed not to attend without an official invitation.

The army Captain returned as promised one week after, and Fela politely asked him to return with an official invitation if the Head of State wanted him to visit. Fela did not see the IGP for sometime after this incidence but after the army burnt down Kalakuta, Fela went again to see M.D.Yussuf and the first thing the IGP asked Fela was why did he refused to see the Head of State? This was in reference, to the invitation from General Obasanjo. In his reply, Fela explained to the IGP that people have accused him of not listening to advice stressing further, that he did not respond to the invitation based on his lawyer's advice.

M.D. Yussuf was furious with this advice from Fela's lawyer, asking what kind of friends and advisers are his lawyers? The IGP told Fela he was surprised that Kanmi would advice not to go to the head of state, when at the same time he (Kanmi) had applied to be a judge of the Federal court. This piece of information was shocking to Fela, his lawyer's application to be named as a judge could not be the reason why Kanmi adviced not to honour the Head of State's invitation.

Fela was convinced that the only reason why Kanmi would advice him not to honour the invitation from the Head of State, was to keep him at loggerheads with the government. Thus provoking the government to react violently towards Fela at the same time, giving his lawyers work to do and the publicity that accompanied his defence.

The author is also convinced about this position based on subsequent representation of Fela by another lawyer Tunji Braithwaite, who also used Fela for the publicity that came with it. We shall discus this in the chapter ahead. That was the last we heard of the invitation to Doddan barracks and the army Captain that brought the message, until we deposited a coffin at the seat of power a sign of protest to the out-going regime in 1979.

However before we talk about the events around Fela during FESTAC, it will be appropriate to refer us back to the three years of his musical career leading to FESTAC'77.

Like I mentioned earlier, the period was one of the most artistically productive eras of Fela's musical career - he was at his zenith. A writer in the New York Times published about the same period described him as: "musically he is James Brown, Bob Dylan and Mick Jagger all rolled into one. Politically, he is Stockely Carmichael, H. Rap Brown and Hue P. Newton all rolled into one".

Fela to those who knew him, was neither musically a Miles Davis nor politically an African Che Guevara, he was however what one could describe as a personified answer to colonialism. By the year 1976 in Nigeria, he had become a phenomenon releasing albums on a monthly basis (twelve albums a year) and during his live performances he had the habit of regularly playing un-recorded songs. Fela was thus obliged, to write new songs to meet the demands at his public performances.

His relationship with record companies had changed drastically and with his successive hits, Fela was no longer signed exclusively with any record company he licensed each album to the highest bidder. Polygram, Decca, and EMI were competing to have the latest record from Fela whose album sales (official and pirated copies) were in the millions. In-order to have exclusivity, DECCA records proposed him a twelve album a year deal.

Financially this contract made him start to openly talk about being on his way to becoming a millionaire, and it gave him the means to finance his 'epic' film Black President.

The three years preceding FESTAC '77, were really productive musical years for Fela. He wrote songs covering all social and political issues, and the messages they carried as we shall discover, were predictions of things to come on the African continent – making him "the man who sang about tomorrow" - a musical Nostradamus.

Songs such as:

PANSA PANSA, was Fela's most defiant statement to the Nigerian military rulers that he was for real in his determination to champion the cause of Pan Africanism. Mid 1976 when Fela started to play this track live, musically he was at his Zenith - extremely popular in Africa and politically his message was beginning to get across. Youths in Nigeria were beginning to identify with the Fela ideals and registering en-mass, at the Africa Shrine head-quarters of the new grass-root movement Fela inaugurated and called Young African Pioneers (YAP).

Economically, it was the peak of the oil-boom and Nigeria as a country never had it better, careering along on at least two million barrels of sulphur-low oil pumped daily into the world market. Fela had just signed a twelve album a year deal with DECCA records, the record industry was booming and people were buying records, with the boom on government level it was corruption galore. Despite persistent denunciations and criticisms from Fela in his songs and public declarations, corruption in the highest echelon of government continued and it constantly brought him in open confrontation with the military rulers. Alagbon Close! No Bread! Monkey Banana! Zombie! Go Slow! Kalakuta Show!

The release of all these songs angered the military establishment in Nigeria and most times prompted attacks on Fela and Kalakuta republic residents. For Fela however despite all the repression, he felt that 'as long as Africa is suffering! No freedom! No justice! No happiness! They will hear PANSA PANSA (Meaning those in power will hear more and more from him).

The song MATTRESS, is Fela's sarcastic answer to those who accused him of not being concerned about the issue of unequal status of the sexes and feminism. Though it may be interpreted more as disrespect compeering, a woman with the mattress humans sleep on top. This answer if we look closely is in no way any disrespect to the WOMAN, rather Fela was emphasising that everybody and everything has its role in every society.

African women have always made the decisions in African traditional homes, hence today's African woman doesn't need 'feminist cause' to be in-charge. Despite critics claim that he arbitrarily upheld and attributed his views to several traditions, it would be appropriate to affirm that several issues from the African custom and traditional stand-point are counterpoise to Western modern traditions and unfortunately the domination of the world with Western culture from Fela's point of view impedes most people to see this reality. The world cannot be uniformly the same, the diversification of cultures is one of the riches of human society.

Take polygamy for an example, Fela has been criticised for openly endorsing polygamy, how could a man who campaigns against the unequal status of sexes and racism endorse a male domination? Fela's justification for polygamy, apart from the traditional re-population from slavery of African society is the polygamous nature of man. Man is polygamous by nature. In Christian dominated societies where polygamy is not tolerated, the men marry officially with one woman but keep mistresses. African men are more honest in their approach, by keeping all the women in the know and under one roof in the spirit of family unity.

The woman is not made to be polygamous because before the invention of the pill and preservatives, a woman after a natural act of making love with a man has at least twenty-five days of waiting for her menstrual circle to be sure she was not pregnant – this was not the case with her male partner. Songs like Mattress from Fela may not help change his 'macho' image, but we have to try to understand from an artistic point that he is only making comparisons and no way disrespect to women.

WHO NO KNOW GO KNOW, is a clarion call to all Africans and the African Diaspora to heed the calls of all the leaders of the African struggle for emancipation. Saying for many years Kwame Nkrumah was shouting for togetherness (Unity), we let him die without heeding his call. Sekou Toure shouted we didn't listen and even Idi Amin as head of Organisation of African Unity, shouted we did not listen. Fela concludes by saying who does not know today, will come to realise one day that 'Nah Blackman go fight for Blackman.' Only a black man can truly fight to save black folks.

MISTER FOLLOW FOLLOW, is talking about those who allow themselves to be led blindly by others or by ideology foreign to their respective environments. Fela's believe is that nobody can live in isolation, people learn from each other in-order to progress. In Follow-Follow, Fela sings about those who follow with their eyes wide-open and those who follow with their eyes close, saying if you have to follow, it is better to follow with your eyes and ears open. For if you follow blindly you will always remain in the dark (ignorance). 'If you dey follow-follow them book! Na inside cupboard you go quench! Cockroach dey! Rat dey! Na inside darkness you go dey!' In conclusion if you have to follow those books his advice is that you should read with some sense, see with your eyes and hear with your ears.

MONKEY BANANA is Fela's advice to those who want to work for the Nigerian status quo without social security, health insurance, job security, to think twice before slaving for nothing. In his habitual manner of putting-down the Nigerian elite, he sings of the popular English expression of 'a fool at forty is a fool forever' - implying like the popular adage "life begins for a man at forty". Fela says, he will not advice his brother to wait until forty before the man realises he has been making a fool of his life. Twenty, for him is the limit to make a fool of one's life after that, a man is supposed to know how to take his destiny in his hands. He sings: "....book sense different from belle sense!" Meaning the reality of hunger is not always the way the elite like to project it, how can majority of the people continue to live below poverty line despite the much publicised oil-boom? The Nigerian 'elite' who profit from the oil-boom, encourage the younger generation to be optimistic hopping one day the living standards of the average conscientious worker will improve.

But Fela advises the contrary in this song, saying corruption and mismanagement of Nigerian economy is responsible for the poor state of the social order. Calling on the worker to stop slaving for nothing, he compares the worker to a monkey that can only be enticed to dance if you offer it the banana and he concludes by singing: "Before I jump like monkey! Give me banana!"

Ghariokwu Lemi's JOHNY JUST DROP (JJD) album sleeve design, and the message written behind are very explicit of Fela's message in this song. Lemi wrote: "In the hot baking sun, he is the only African in suit and tie, he is the youngster in faded jeans, and he is also the one in high 'guaranteed' platform shoes. He is the alien in his own country – his motherland." Johny Just Drop, is talking about Africans who travel abroad only to return home with new values and mannerisms. Since the advent of colonialism in Africa, the education system left Black people with an inferior perception of their culture. Those who are Western educated, are in the habit of repeating untruths about African traditions and heritage because the discipline to think and act big has not yet become a part of Africa's present day academic and intellectual traditions.

For example those trained in the use of English, Spanish, German, French or Portuguese languages, will argue forcefully that those are international languages in which alone science and technology can be intelligently studied. If this is true one wonders how the ancient Black Egyptians, built the pyramids or how the guild of craftsmen in Benin and other parts of the continent created the works of art produced over many centuries. In JJD, Fela is reminding Africans travelling abroad in search of greener pastures, to be proud of their original cultural values - those inherent values the JJD 'educated' elite have been brainwashed to despise.

Fela says UNNECESSARY BEGGING in area (ghetto) rules, is not done and it is not necessary. Traditionally in the ghetto, if you give your word people believe you for such words until you do otherwise. African ghetto thoughts and deeds are the traditional way of life of the people, they are based on age long believe that 'words are like eggs when they drop they cannot be retrieved' and this brings us to the way we are governed in Africa sings Fela.

Front cover album design Johny Just Drop (JJD)

Front cover album design Gentleman

According to him the people in this "spirit of trust" believe in our governments, the people enter into an agreement with the government to provide (the people) good houses, good roads, buoyant economy. What do the people get? No government, corruption at the highest level of power, injustice, etc.

To make the plight of the people even more hopeless leaders of thought who should know better, intellectuals and academics instead of being on the people's side, speak-out in the defence of those in government by preaching patience. They try to justify the mismanagement of African lives as 'problems of young democracies' but, Fela say this is Unnecessary Begging. He called on those in power to beware of the day the people will revolt against this situation, it will be a day to render accounts and there will be no room for any Unnecessary Begging.

In IKOYI BLINDNESS, Fela defines mental blindness as the case of a person who with his eyes wide-open, misses his direction and keeps
turning round in circles without ever getting to his destination.
He sang:
"You miss road! You miss road!
When you miss road you no go reach!
You no go reach where you dey go!
Because that no be the road oh!
No be the road wey you go take! (Chorus)
One man wey I know him be lawyer!
Him want buy the thing for him work!
Him go buy the thing them call hammer!
Wetin lawyer go take hammer do?
Him no go reach where him dey go!
Because that no be the road!
No be the road wey him for take! (Chorus)
One man wey I know him be music!
Him want buy the thing for him work!
Him go buy the thing them call spanner!
Wetin music go take Spanner do?
Him no go reach where him dey go!
Because that no be the road!

No be the road wey him for take! (Chorus)
These two of my friends them different from the man!
Them different from the man wey no see road at all!
Wey no see road at all him go stand near river!
Nah shallow him go drop oh!
Shallow! Shallow! Him go drop oh! (Chorus)
Make you help me tell the man wey dey stay for Ikoyi!
From Alagbon close to Atlantic Ocean!
Wey them no see road at all them go stand near river!
Them no see us for Mushin at all at all!
Them no see us for Ajegunle at all at all!
Maroko nko them no see at all
Wey them no see us for Kalakuta at all!
Nah shallow him go drop oh!
Shallow! Shallow! Him go drop oh! (Chorus)."

The message of the song is directed at the Nigerian elite who choose wrong professions, because it provides them status in the society than job satisfaction. Fela explains that in the elite search for 'job satisfaction', some of them make the necessary efforts to find the right path - pointing to the example of a lawyer who instead of buying law books chooses hammer as his trade tool or a musician who chooses spanner as his trade tool. Fela says there is still some hope for such people if they could channel their way of thinking towards their environment.

"Them use them sense them change them spanner and hammer! Them miss road them find road again oh! Hen! Hen! Hen! However, there are those who not only are in the wrong professions but they are also blind to this fact – a kind of mental blindness. Warning that if they don't make the necessary efforts they will fall deeper into the abyss of mental blindness. According to Fela, their wrong choice of profession renders them blind to the sufferings of their fellow country men who live in the ghettos like Mushin, Ajegunle, Somolu, Maroko and even Kalakuta. In their state of mental blindness, they feel secure locking all these problems away from their Ikoyi residential area.

Warning those social-climbers who feel comfortable to replace the colonialist in their Ikoyi residential area that they will be worse off than a blind man going to stay near a river - they will fall shallow into more 'Ikoyi mental' Blindness.

Elites, who see the status quo and stepping into the shoes of former colonial administrators as a sign of moving up in society - forgetting that majority of their folks are still struggling in the ghettos, such people must realise that they are worse off than a blind person living next to a river. Ghariokwu Lemi in his Ikoyi Blindness album cover-design, depicts the afflictions of the rich Nigerian elite in purely graphic terms. Modelling for the oil paint on canvas, Duro Ikujenyo appeared as an overdressed and puffed-up lawyer scrambling away from his roots in the Lagos ghetto with his eyes blindfolded. The message of Ikoyi Blindness, is also to warn the Nigerian rich that they cannot run away from the realities of ghetto life. They can either work towards changing the situation, or fall into an allusion of escaping ghetto life by locking themselves away in rich residential areas.

EXCUSE O, is about natural human reactions to situations we confront in our daily endeavours. If you walk into a bar ask and pay for a drink and you happen to recognise a friend in the bar, you take time off your table to chat with this friend. While you are at it, another man walks over to your table and drinks your glass of beer, of course you turn round and find him drinking your beer your reaction will be: Excuse O! Same for the person who goes to withdraw five Naira (exchanged for the equivalent of US $7 at that time), takes public transport in the bus, the person finds another man trying to pick his pocket the obvious reaction is: Excuse O! For the man who dates a woman for the first time the situation is even more serious particularly since on their first date, he takes the woman to a swimming pool, after which they had lunch, from lunch to cinema, from cinema to dinner. After dinner, the man again invites her to have a dance at the Shrine (Fela's Club) - sitting at a table after ordering drinks another man comes to excuse his partner for a dance he does not object to the first, the second he consents to grudgingly. A third dance? That is enough Mr. Excuse O, will be the reaction from the man who had invested so-much for him to let another man take his woman away from him.

Fela in SENSE WISENESS, is singing about the state of alienation from the society of the educated elite. According to him, after their education in Western ways and mannerisms the educated elite in Africa try to distant themselves from the ghetto. Sense Wiseness is his sarcastic way of saying "book sense is different from street sense". The song starts with 'You are student! You've been to grammar school (or college). Graduate with a MA (Master of Arts degree). MSc (Master of Science) and PhD (Doctorate) you go for London! You Go for New York! You come for Lagos? You start to miss your road! One boy for Mushin (ghetto) Him hustle you! For Ajegunle (another ghetto area) you no get mouth! For Jankara (big ghetto market) your money lost! In conclusion, Fela sings that all your travels in those foreign cities are not enough to see you through the realities of the world, if you learn things from other parts of the world don't forget your roots and the only way to keep abreast of things is to always identify with your roots he advises.

ROFOROFO FIGHT is about human intolerance towards each other, issues that could be resolved amicably usually end up in fist-fights that sometimes finish in a bloody or muddy manner. Dramatising the scenario that ensues before a fight particularly in a muddy place, Fela says it usually starts with words like "You dey craze! (Are you crazy?) I no craze! (I am not crazy) Get away! Who are you?" These are two people who could quietly resolve their differences screaming and yelling at each other, unfortunately for both of them the area where the argument is taking place is full with mud (roforofo in Yoruba). Meanwhile, the dispute draws the attention of people passing-bye and before you know it the gathering turns into a big crowd within seconds. "If you dey among the crowd wey dey look!" Meaning: "if you are among the crowd standing by looking, and "your friend dey among the two wey dey yap!" (And your friend is among the two arguing). Tell am make him no fight oh!' Meaning, if you are in the crowd watching and your friend is one of the two disputing, please advice your friend not to fight. However, because of human egos instead of heeding the advice and walk away quietly they both feel disrespected and shamed. To settle scores, they choose physical combat to resolve their dispute and in the end a muddy fight follows.

After tempers have cooled, on-lockers and eye-witness of the dispute couldn't differentiate the one from the other, both of them look like twins. They won't get any sympathy from the people looking too "you don tell am before make him no fight! Roforofo dey for there!" You have told him not to fight because there is mud all over the place.

"The rights to the land belong to all" sings Fela in DON'T MAKE GARAN GANRAN (BIG MAN) FOR ME. We are all sons and daughters of the land, he advice the rich and highly placed Nigerians who frequently try to lord it over the poor - Ganran Ganran in Yoruba language is reserved for an egoist, a self centred person full of himself. Warning those in power to know the limit, Fela says "if you bring your big-manism close to me, heavens will fall" (to ba se ganran ganran si mi orun a woo!) We all know if heavens fall, it will fall on every one he concludes.

Sandra Izsidore (nee Smith), the African American woman who stood by Fela and also brought him in contact with the ideas of true Black history and resistant movements during his transformation period in the United States, came back to visit a highly popular and successful Fela in Nigeria in 1976. UPSIDE DOWN was written by Fela to portray a worldly travelled African who searches in the dictionary and discovers the definition of upside down - a perfect description of the African situation. 'I have travelled widely all over the world like any professor!' Fela makes Sandra sing. 'The things I have seen, I will like to talk about upside-up and downside-down, in overseas everything is organise. Their system organise! They have their own names! But back home in Africa, everything is 'head for down, yansh for up! Everything is disorganized! Meaning back home, everything is totally disorganised - Upside Down!

GO SLOW, is about the crawling Lagos traffic-jam that symbolise the confusion that reigns in Nigeria. Fela compares the traffic situation with a person in jail he says, 'you have to be a man in life' (to be courageous) this is a natural instinct in man, but when caught in a Lagos traffic all your aspirations and confidence as a man will wither away. You feel suddenly incapacitated like a man in jail or how would you feel, driving on a Lagos road and suddenly everything seems to be in a stand-still.

There is a lorry in your front that is not moving, and to your left a taxi cab also blocked, to your right a tipper-truck and behind you 'molues' passenger bus all incapacitated, while above you a helicopter is flying. To complete the picture of you in a prison on the Lagos road, Fela sings that all these are happening to you in the hot tropical Lagos climate. Lagosians used to the crawling traffic call it "Go Slow".

QUESTION JAM ANSWER, is another song about human nature. Fela sang: "When question drop for mouth! Answer go run after am! When question jam answer for road? Another thing will happen." He says when people pose questions to the other, they definitely expect to get answers in return and the answer could be something we never expect. This does not erase the fact that for every question there is always an answer, if you pose questions such as "Why did you step on my leg? Didn't you see my leg on the ground?" These are questions that needed answers, you shouldn't be surprised if the person in front of you replies "Why did you put your leg in my way? Don't you see me coming? It is a song to those who like to pose questions to always bear in mind, that they may not get the answers they expect to their questions whenever they decide to ask.

TROUBLE SLEEP YANGA WAKE AM, an expression in Pidgin English which literally translated means 'toying with a loaded gun' or 'playing with fire'. It is a song talking about the limit to human endurance. Mr. Trouble is lying quietly and Mr. Provocation (yanga) goes to play around him, what else could he be looking for except palaver (trouble). A good example of such trouble-shooting according to Fela in this song, a man who has just got out of prison he goes about desperately looking for work in-order to avoid what led him to jail. While at it, a police man stops and charges the man for wandering Fela asks: what else could the police man be looking for but trouble? It is like when a cat is asleep and a rat goes to bite its tail or a tenant who has just lost his job sitting quietly thinking of where his next meal will come from, his landlord comes knocking demanding his rent from the un-employed tenant. Of cause he will get trouble bigger than the rent he came to collect. Trouble Sleep Yanga Wake Am simply means there is a limit to any human endurance.

Front cover album design Upside Down

From 1884–1885, colonial powers met in Berlin to divide and share Africa among themselves. With this Balkanisation, artificial boarders were created to separate African people. After independence, most of the nations still adhere to and respect the artificial frontiers created from colonial times. CUSTOM CHECK POINT is Fela's criticism of the system that still respects these artificial boundaries separating African people.

Tracing the cultural, linguistic and traditional unity of African people to a common origin, Fela describes the men of Custom and Excise charged with the duty to police African frontiers to see themselves first as humans who have been put in place to do the dirty works of those who want to keep Africans apart. He advises them to pack-up and allow our people to travel freely among sister nations. Cut down the barriers! Custom she kia kia kia! Asking them to hurry-up and get out of the way.

Daily life in the African ghettos could be hell on earth as the Lagos ghetto life signifies. Constant shortages of clean drinking water, electricity supply are interrupted regularly, no functioning public transport system etc. In ORIGINAL SUFFER HEAD, Fela states that Africa possesses two-thirds of the world's natural resources and he asks why a people with such riches would sit back and watch her population wither away in poverty.

Original Suffer Head is calling on African people to rise and fight the malady that is keeping them down poverty-lane. According to him, "before we all can je'fa - head oh! We must be ready to fight for am!" Meaning "before we all can enjoy we must be ready to fight for it".

The practice where Black people use all kinds of chemical products, to lighten their skin in order to appear close to the White colour is called YELLOW FEVER by Fela. Describing such psychological and mental-block as a sickness or malady, he compares the lack of pride in the black identity (their skin colour) as sickness like jaundice, malaria or influenza. He calls on Africans who bleach their skin, to realise that it makes them look uglier than their desired beauty.

In every society or gathering of people there is always one person who tries to assert their difference even if all assembled agreed to a collective decision. In an attempt to be noticed Fela sings, as laud-mouth braggart they try to disrupt such assembly for personal reason or just to be noticed. Such person Fela considers in this song as OPPOSITE PEOPLE.

As we can see from the above summary, the three or four years before 1977 were really productive years for Fela musically, he gradually was progressing from satirical songs to bold and unequivocal attacks on the establishment and those that represented them, songs like: I No Get Eyes for Back, He Miss Road, Equalization of Trouser and Pants and Ikoyi Mentality Versus Mushing Mentality, were written by Fela to show the state of cultural alienation of the Nigerian elites towards their people and environment.

His disregard towards the establishment and those that represents them, couldn't be more affirmed than the way he did in 'I no get eyes for back'. There were also songs like NNG (Nigeria Natural Grass) that he never recorded, talking about the natural qualities of marijuana. One major factor that motivated Fela to compose and write so many songs, was his standing policy of never playing live, songs already released. Whenever fans ask him to play popular hits already released, his answer was: «if you want to listen to such and such song, go buy the record».

Front cover album design Original Suffer Head

Front cover album design 'Yellow Fever'

Front cover album design Ikoyi Blindness

Front cover album design Unknown Soldier

UNKNOWN SOLDIER

To the unsuspecting mind this song's title represents a homage to military 'heroes', in keeping with world-wide trend of erecting statues in memory of soldiers who lost their lives in wars.

While Fela in his lifetime cannot be described as 'a good bed-fellow' of military orientation and approach in a civil society, his song Unknown Soldier has nothing to do with homage to the memories of fallen soldiers. Rather, Fela wrote the song as a result of a controversy that 'rocked' the military regime of General Obasanjo in February 1977.

It will be necessary at this point to recount the events that preceded this final confrontation between Fela and the Obasanjo regime. As explained in the preceding chapter, Fela's musical out-put in the years before FESTAC were highly productive. He was at the peak of his popularity hence between January 26 and 12th, February 1977 the official celebration of FESTAC '77, the Nigerian authorities in an attempt to isolate him discouraged other participating artists from visiting Fela and the Africa Shrine where he performed with his band Africa 70.

Despite this official discouragement, the American delegation to the festival held an unofficial 'mini-festival' at the Shrine with artists like Steve Wonder performing. There were other artist who appeared during the four times a week performance of Fela at the Shrine - musicians like the pianist Randy Weston, Lester Bowie of the Chicago Arts Assembly, Huge Masakela, Manu Dibango, the London based Afro-Rock group Osibisa and many others – poets, writers and journalists both from the participating nations and the international press.

In an attempt to show appreciation for this gesture of solidarity and at the invitation of Steve Wonder, Fela and some members of his organisation (some of his women, YAP Boys and friends) paid Stevie a visit at the Mainland Hotel Ebute Meta Lagos where he was lodged. At the hotel, a Nigerian army major in charge of security insisted he was under orders to prevent Fela from visiting members of the foreign delegation. Angered that the army authorities were depriving him of his rights, Fela began to argue with the soldiers insisting on his liberty to move freely in the country as a fundamental right.

In what looked at first glance an odd turn of events, Louis Farrakhan the leader of the Nation of Islam also a guest at the Mainland Hotel approached the audience which had gathered around Fela and the soldiers in the hotel lobby. A.J. Saffi (a.k.a. A.J.Moore) an African American, who migrated to Nigeria in 1976 from the United State claiming persecution for his involvement in the Detroit riots and being a member of the Black Panther Party was in Fela's entourage.

He recognised Farrakhan as he approached and greeted him with a clear American accent "Salaam Allekum". Louis Farrakhan replied: "Are you close to the brother? Tell him to watch-out because the word within Nigerian government circles is that something has to be done to stop the brother.

They are concerned about his growing influence on the Nigerian youths who dress the way he does and smokes what he smokes". Yet it should not come as a surprise that the African American Moslem leader, should have accurate "insider information" from government circles.

Farrakhan was known to hobnob with various Nigerian regimes a relationship that culminated in the re-naming of "Eleke Crescent", the street where the American and other embassies in Lagos are located to "Louis Farrakhan Crescent" during the tenure of the late Nigerian military dictator General Sanni Abacha (1993–1998).

With regards to the mention of a Muslim leader, please bear in mind that during his lifetime Fela considered Islam and Christianity to be the major instruments used to enslave and colonise Africans and the Diaspora Africa in places such as in America, Brazil and other parts of the Caribbean.

Permit a short digression here like he sang in the song titled SUFFERING AND SMILING, we can see that confrontation with police and military was not the sole combat Fela had to face in his active militancy as the song explains.

Christianity and Islam, playing on the spiritual nature of the African traditional society have been the major instruments used to exploit and colonise African people. In Suffering and Smiling, Fela highlights the ambiguity of the Christian and Muslim doctrine of "suffering in this world in exchange for a 'glorious' place in heaven."

Fela points to the opulence and rich life of the Pope and his Episcopal followers as examples of people not suffering in this world and waiting to go to heaven to enjoy: "Archbishop na miliki! Pope na enjoyment! Imam na gbaladun!" he sang.

Fela questions why Africans would believe in a Jesus, whose blue eyes and blond hair disqualify him as a Black man's god-head same with Mohammed and his Arab looks. Though today Louis Farrakhan Crescent, has since the death of Abacha been reverted to its old name the significance (insider information) of the Nation of Islam leader's advice cannot be questioned even if he was not saying something new to A.J. Saffi.

Driving out of the parking area of the Mainland Hotel on his way back to perform at the Shrine, A.J. mentioned the conversation between him and Louis Farrakhan however Fela's reaction was "the Muslim leader was not telling us something new".

It should be noted, that Fela couldn't have his way to see Stevie Wonder despite the Mainland Hotel verbal duel with the Nigerian security agent. Concerning Nation of Islam, Fela had more respect for Malcolm X than he did Louis Farrakhan even if the former equally started-out as a Moslem. Unfortunately, Malcolm X was assassinated before he could put together his Organisation of African and African American Unity movement.

For us in the Pan-African movement, any African or African American who professes to be a Moslem, is substituting a form of "slavery" with another considering, that the propagators of Islam in Africa committed as much genocide in Africa as their Christian counterparts.

From all indications, the "seize-fire" that hitherto reigned between the army and Fela was about to erupt. To confirm Louis Farrakhan's "insider" information, precisely one week after the end of FESTAC on 18th February 1977, about one thousand armed members of the Nigerian army invaded Fela's Kalakuta Republic rapping the women, beating and arresting every-one within sight and finally burning down the house.

The author was a witness to the attack and I infact escaped being trapped in Fela's house by air's breath.

I had gone to the house to present the estimated cost to Fela for the construction of space behind his house to install the newly purchased YAP News printing machine. The reader will recall that I mentioned that it was no secret, that Fela invested $40,000 (US) for a printing machine to publish YAP news. We had agreed to install the machine in Kalakuta, and I was delegated to find-out the cost of preparing a small area behind his house to install the machine.

As usual at about that time (10:30 am), Fela was in bed and I had to go speak with him through his bedroom window. He asked me to come back later in the day as he had just gone to bed. Since I had other appointments at the YAP office situated in the Shrine a few meters away, I left the house with the idea to return in a few hours.

While at it in the YAP office, I was not aware of the following incidence, we only got wind of trouble a short while after and it all started with an alleged traffic offence from one of Fela's drivers. A military police officer directing traffic at the 'famous' Ojuelegba junction, forcibly dragged one of Fela's drivers out of the car he was travelling in beating and kicking him for an alleged traffic contravention.

The driver's passenger unable to interfere for fear of being subjected to the same brutal treatment, rushed to Kalakuta area about five hundred meters from the scene to call for aid from 'area boys' in-order to rescue the driver from his aggressor. Armed with sticks, and other weapons the mobilised Kalakuta 'area boys,' rushed to the scene only to find the badly beaten driver abandoned at the road side - his soldier aggressor had disappeared just before they arrived. The injured driver was driven to Kalakuta and Fela was immediately informed.

He got out of bed to see the state with which the boy was, and gave instructions to those around to take the injured driver to the hospital. While at it, an army Captain arrives asking Fela to release the boy to him. According to the military officer, he wanted to question the driver on an 'alleged' obstruction of an army officer from performing his duties. Fela refused telling the Captain that a military barracks was not what the injured driver needed. The man was badly in need of medical attention, and it was clear he was not going to get the medical attention in an army barracks. Moreover, there was the possibility of more beating inflicted on the man.

He told the Captain that he had instructed some boys to take the wounded driver to the hospital, if they needed to take actions against the wounded driver it was best they went to make an official complaint to the police.

Unable to get Fela to release the driver, the army Captain instructed the soldiers that accompanied him not to let anyone out of the house living behind about a dozen armed soldiers. It was during this impasse that a young guy came running to inform us at the YAP office, screaming that soldiers had surrounded Fela's house. We YAP boys and other prospective members in the Shrine, rushed to see what was going on and we were informed of the incidence narrated above by members of Kalakuta speaking to us behind the barbed wire fence.

Meanwhile some more army reinforcement arrived all armed, they surrounded the house at the same time dispersing the gathered crowd. With the crowd and the neighbours forcibly evacuated, the entire area within a radius of two hundred meters was occupied by the invading soldiers who waited menacingly. They waited for almost two hours after the area was evacuated, not letting anyone out of the house an indication that the soldiers were waiting for instructions from high-up the military hierarchy. Those of us earlier standing outside the house, ran back to the Shrine securely locking the main-door at the entry behind us.

It is sad it was not the era of smart-phones, web-cam, and video cameras, we would have shot a vividly brutal "movie". With our position on the balcony of the Shrine out of the occupying army view, we watched helplessly from the distance as the soldiers waited for instructions to attack the house. While all these was going-on, Beko (Fela's younger brother) arrives insisting on being let into his Junction Road Clinic situated in the premises of the occupied Kalakuta. He was let in, after long insistence from him to the invading soldiers.

After their long wait, an official army Mercedes Benz car arrived in front of the house and though the occupant was not visible from where we were, however from the way the soldiers who surrounded the car stood at attention, it was clear the occupant must have been a high ranking officer and definitely more high in rank than Major Daudu who led the military attack.

While members of the Nigerian Army soldiers were setting on fire cars, vehicles and trucks around Fela's Kalakuta Republic, others arrive in confisticated civilian trucks to join their colleagues in the attack.
Picture by Femi Bankole Osunla Africa 70 Photo Agency

Shortly after the car left, the army attacked the house. Initially, the house was not possible to penetrate by the invaders because Fela had electrified the barbered wire fence that surrounded the building to prevent attacks such as the on going.

The soldiers were forced to hold their onslaught sending armed soldier to Idi-Oro, to force the Nigerian Electric Power Authority (NEPA) to turn-off general power supply to the area. With power turned off, the invaders cut down the fence beating and kicking every one at sight. They looted everything of value, and raped some of the women like an army of occupation. Fela who usually had large amounts of money under his mattress, claimed he saw soldiers struggling between them to stuff their uniform with wards of Naira (Nigeria' currency).

Fela's 77 year old mother, was thrown down from the first floor balcony of the house and the shock plus trauma she suffered from this attack, kept her in the hospital until her death a year after. Fela's pets, a family of four German Shepherds named Wokolo (meaning 'go find penis), Jokotobo (sit next to pussy), Gbangba lobo (widely open pussy) and Ido n'dun (clitoris is sweet), were burnt in the inferno that engulfed the house. A French speaking snake-charmer who wanted to discus the possibility of presenting his acts with Fela at the Shrine, was trapped in the house along with everyone he was beaten and lost a finger and his snakes in the inferno.

Fela, A.J. Saffi, and some few guys were the last to get out of the burning house. They managed to cross the fence separating Fela's compound, into his Lebanese neighbour's house where they were all later arrested. One of Fela's body guards who tried to prevent his arrest, was bayoneted in the stomach and was dragged through the streets with his intestine falling out of his stomach. Segun Alagbara (Segun-strong man in Yoruba), was forced to push his intestine back by holding his bloodied hands over the wound in his stomach.

Fela was paraded naked on the street with the soldiers taunting and teasing him on their way to the near-bye Abalty barracks. With Fela in their hands and the house on fire, the army moved into Kalakuta area getting drunk from the many abandoned illegal bars that dotted the area. Looting, and stuffing their pockets with all the abandoned marijuana and everything of value.

At almost night fall, they finally lifted their siege living behind them SORROW TEARS AND BLOOD (STB), like Fela sang in the song with the same title. Fear, one factor that has kept black people in bondage for so long is addressed in the song Sorrows Tears and Blood. Fela underlines how people using family bonds as justification for their non involvement in the struggle. Fela states that individual fears will not make the fight for progress, freedom, happiness and injustice disappear. For as long as there is fear, police and army brutality will always be a part of our daily lives leaving in its wake, Sorrows Tears, and Blood.

Returning to the Kalakuta attack, dispersed like sheep without shepherd we YAP Boys were forced to go searching for Kanmi Ishola-Osobu in his legal chambers situated along Herbert Macaulay Street in Ebute Meta- Lagos. Scaling the fence at the rear of the Shrine, we joined the flow of civilians forced by the invading army to raise their hands in sign of 'surrender' as we trooped pass the ruins of Kalakuta. In front of "Peoples Chambers" as Kanmi called his office, it took the three of us several moments of insistent knocking on his office door before he let us in.

All the windows were firmly locked - I believe he must have been lying down on the rugged floor in the dark, this was the impression he gave us on entering his office he resumed the same position after. Thanks to our spotting his car parked in a street corner, we suspected that Kanmi was around hence our persistent knocking on his office door.

We asked him, if he was aware of the army attack on Kalakuta to which he replied: "Who in Lagos today can go not aware of such attack?" We then asked him what he intended to do and in reply, Kanmi said he was waiting to find-out where the attack came from before deciding on his next line of action. Since in the decision making process around Fela, older folks like Kanmi usually considered the contribution of YAP care-taker committee members as motivated by youthful exuberance, with what we have just witnessed it was clear we had to act.

Hence we asked him why he was waiting to find-out where the attack came from before acting. It was clear that members of the Nigerian army were responsible. We told Kanmi that since it was week-end, he should prepare a motion to be filed before a high court first thing on Monday asking the Chief of Staff Nigerian army to produce Fela and the other arrested members of his entourage.

Feeling lord upon, Kanmi reacted in an aggressive manner to our proposal telling us we couldn't tell him how to do his job. He went on to ask where we were when the attack was going on. We told him we were hidden on the balcony of the Shrine watching the whole scene. Kanmi then attacked us saying that if we really loved Fela so much, why didn't we try to prevent the army from attacking the house and to this we answered that YAP didn't have an 'army'. If we had one, we probably would have taken up arms against them - a kind of organised urban militia could easily take-out a Nigerian army reputed for their record of indiscipline.

Gowon and his military successors refused military training for the National Youth Service (NYSC) scheme, out of the fear of arming radical students against an undisciplined Nigerian army. Unfortunately at this time when we were publishing monthly, and distributing for free 80,000 copies of YAP NEWS, we didn't have Facebook, twitters, and all the social networks available today. Maybe if we had, the more than 40,000 civilians standing and watching while 1,000 Nigerian Army soldiers were burning down in broad-day-light Fela's Kalakuta Republic would have reacted differently.

Fela infact gave instructions, to his road managers to mount a public address system on the balcony of the house to enable him speak to the public gathered watching. The attacking soldiers, prevented the attempt to communicate with the crowd by cutting power supply to the area. Attempts by members of Kalakuta, to re-install power supply by switching on an electric generator inside the compound, was foiled by the attacking army soldiers, who threw stones and sticks at them from across the barbed wire fence.

Social networks would probably have paved the way for and encouraged the masses watching, to overcome years of fear and apathy, to take-on the soldiers or take to the streets like the case with Arab streets demonstrating and calling for change today. Moreover, the concept of YAP was not that of an armed resistance rather we were out to educate Nigerian masses on their rights and how to fight for these rights within a constitutional framework. We couldn't convince Kanmi to file the motion demanding the army to produce and free Fela.

The three of us in the end left him alone in his office heading for the house of Wole Kuboye (Feelings lawyer). It was only years after that we became aware of the reason behind the "cold–feet" developed by Kanmi. As a result of his earlier application for the post of a high court Judge, he didn't want to be seen as antagonistic towards the regime, this prevented him from moving against the army authority in court.

Meanwhile on arrival at "Feelings Lawyer's," we found other Kalakuta residents who escaped the inferno re-grouping. To Feelings lawyer, we narrated our experience with Kanmi and he however told us he was unable to file legally any motion as a corporate lawyer. He promised, to contact the two Kuti brothers (Koye and Beko) on what line of action to pursue. We informed him that Beko was also arrested with Fela as he went into the house before the attack started.

With nothing more to do at Wole Kuboye's, the three of us decided to visit a YAP member named Ejebba resident at "Abule Chair" (chair village in Yoruba), a ghetto area near Ikeja known for production of cane chairs. We wanted a place where we could work without being disturbed since our source of finance to print the YAP News was temporarily out of circulation we had to decide what possible means to pass our message to the public.

Ejebba welcomed the three of us and earlier on our way, we had decided to post hand-written posters in strategic places all over Lagos, so we asked him if we could use his house as a temporary operational base. He agreed and we mapped out our line of action with our limited financial resources.

Luckily Lemi knew a printer friend who could give us poster-size papers, we were aware also that very few printers would agree to print the messages we wanted to put across, afraid of possible reprisals from the army.

Hence, we collected the poster-size papers he was able to give us and we went to work hand-writing messages like: "1000 soldiers attacked Fela's house! What barbarism!", "Today it is Fela tomorrow it could be you!" "Army are paid with public money to protect not to destroy us", were the kind of messages that were hand-written on the thousands of posters we produced.

We signed all the posters on behalf of YAP and for days we were holed-up in Ejebba's little room, we worked through out the night and early every morning, we pasted the finished posters on moving buses and on public walls all over Lagos city. We also made sure, to send one of us everyday to Feelings Lawyer's house to follow developments.

During one of such visit, Wole Kuboye informed us that he had spoken with Koye who informed him that a lawyer named Tunji Braithwaite had been engaged by the Kuti family to make contact with the army authorities. Meanwhile the military regime was shaken by the outpour of public sympathy for Fela and his clan, soldiers tried to stop newspapers from carrying the news of the attack and they impounded printed copies of both Punch and Daily Sketch publications that carried news of the attack.

Government owned Daily Times which did not print any news of the attack, hastily came out with a government induced explanation that "the soldiers had gone to Kalakuta to make a legitimate arrest". To justify why Fela was still being detained 27 days after the burning down of his house, the army using the police charged him to court for 'possession' of firearms. It was the first time since the attack Fela would appear in public, the army authority wanted to keep him in custody for fear of his ability to mobilise public behind him. We got wind of Fela's appearance in court through Wole Kuboye, who kept in-touch with the older Kuti brother.

Appearing before a Lagos high court judge in Fela's defence his new lawyer Tunji Braithwaite, pointed to the fact that the alleged gun seemed to be the only object in Kalakuta that was not burnt in the inferno.

Demanding that Fela should be released, he mentioned to the judge that from his state (with multiple fracture to his left leg), Fela needed his freedom to pick-up what was left of his life and organisation. The presiding judge granted Fela bail as requested by his lawyer despite the opposition from government prosecutor, but the police promptly arrested him again outside the court room this time, he was detained under a special state security decree not open to challenge in any court of law in Nigeria.

While still in the court room before his re-arrest, we were able to fill him in with news of what had transpired since the attack, he also told us he was informed by his older brother regarding Kanmi and his 'cold-feet'. He assured us that his brother Koye, had assured him of the competence of his new lawyer Tunji Braithwaite. Fela also wanted to know if anything, in the house survived the inferno particularly the sound track of his film Black President.

We informed him that the soldiers prevented even fire fighters from approaching the burning house and for the first time, those of us present saw Fela shed tears - he had invested a lot of money on the film Black President as we shall talk more about this later. Meanwhile, to calm the public out-cry for the Army attack, a tribunal was appointed to investigate the cause of the Nigerian Army attack. Headed by a high court judge Justice Agu Anyan and an Air Force Officer Wing Commander Abdulahi, the tribunal listened for several days to testimonies from both civilians and army personnel.

Contrary to what the Obasanjo regime (1976-1979) would have people believe, there is no doubt that Fela's refusal to participate in the FESTAC sham, the sea of black power salutes that surrounded him wherever he went in Nigeria, and his uncompromising bold lyrics condemning government's corruption, plus his financing and publishing of YAP NEWS were the true reasons behind the Nigerian army attack.

The official justification given for the attack by the army, was that they went to Kalakuta to arrest some members who after a fight with a military corporal for traffic violation, burnt down the motor cycle the corporal was riding and escaped into Fela's Kalakuta republic.

Major Daudu who led the attack on Kalakuta, claimed that on arrival to execute the arrest, he found that the wired fence around the house was electrified hence he instructed that power supply to the area be cut. The army major, added he was surprised that Fela re-installed power supply by switching on an electric generator and he claimed that it was the generator that short-circuited setting the house ablaze.

This excuse by the army was rendered useless by eye-witness accounts from members of the public, who came forward to testify that they saw the army attack and set the house on fire.

The electric generator which the army claimed short-circuited, was mounted on a mobile truck parked outside Kalakuta gate, there was no member of Kalakuta who had access to the truck while the soldiers surrounded the house.

The tribunal sat regularly for weeks hearing testimonies from more than one hundred and eighty-three witnesses (both military and civilian) among them were state fire fighters, who claimed that the attacking soldiers prevented them from fighting the fire when they arrived at the scene.

There were also members of the public, who claimed they saw soldiers carrying Jerry-cans presumably containing inflammable substance poured on the parked vehicles in front of the house to start the fire and pictures were tendered to prove this.

Although the proceedings of the tribunal was supposed to be in theory public, a New York Times correspondent John Danton, covering the proceedings was forcibly evicted by Nigerian security agents and he was deported the following day from the country.

Finally the tribunal submitted its findings in a report to the Lagos State government, the report said among other things that "the fire was started unintentionally by an exasperated and Unknown Soldier". To apportion blame the report blamed the Lagos State police command, for the "levity" with which they treated allegations of "crimes" reported against Fela. What crimes if one may ask?

The tribunal recommended that since there was no hope that Kalakuta inhabitants could co-exist peacefully with soldiers in the neighbouring Abalti barracks, it suggested moving either the barrack or Fela from the area, it also condemned Fela for using the word "Republic" to describe his house in defiance of the constitution and it went on to suggest that the government should stop Fela from calling his house as such.

Finally, the tribunal recommended that the Young African Pioneer (YAP) movement, be proscribed and its activities investigated by law enforcement agents. The Lagos State government in their acceptance of the tribunal recommendations concluded in a paper dubbed as "white paper report", with the remarked that: "the government wishes to point out that no individual no matter how powerful or popular, can set himself above the laws of the land.

Fela and members of Africa 70 Organization waiting for member of the Anya Tribunal outside the ruins of his Kalakuta residence.
Photo by Femi Bankole Osunla, Africa 70 Photo Agency.

Major Daudu (in military uniform above) explains to members of the Anya tribunal, how soldiers on his orders attacked Kalakuta.
Picture by Femi Bankole Osunla Africa 70 Photo Agency

Fela carried on the shoulders of two members of his Organization, conducts members of the tribunal around the ruins of Kalakuta. The tribunal Chairman, Justice Agwu Anya in dark glasses and Wing Commander Abdulahi in traditional dress and dark glasses.
Picture by Femi Bankole Osunla Africa 70 Photo Agency

Government will not allow or tolerate the existence of a situation which is capable of undermining the very basis of civilised society."

From the manner the government report was worded, one would have thought they were directed at an army General planning secession or a Coup d'état rather than Fela whose only weapon was music. His 1978 hit "Unknown Soldier," best explains his position vis-à-vis the tribunal findings and the Government position as expressed in their so-called "White Paper report".

He classified the tribunal members as "government instruments of magic." His use of the word "Republic" to describe his house, does not defy the constitution as the constitution was suspended by successive military regimes ruling with decrees in place of the constitution.

With no home and Shrine to perform but determined to keep the pressure on, Fela and the remaining members of his entourage took residence at the Cross Road Hotel situated on Ikorodu Road about five hundred meters away from the ruins of his burnt house. When I say "Fela and the remaining members" this is to show the psychological impact, of the army attack and how it scared away many members of the organization.

To keep the pressure on the Obasanjo regime, we placed a coffin on the balcony of the burnt house with a banner inscribed boldly with the words: "THIS IS THE SPOT WHERE JUSTICE WAS MURDERED". For about a year after the "war" on Kalakuta, people driving or walking pass the ruins were confronted with this symbol of defiance.

In an attempt to get justice in the Lagos High Court, Fela on behalf of himself, the Kuti Family, and the Africa 70 organisation, sued the Nigerian army Chief of Staff and some top ranking officers from the Abalty barracks claiming 25 million Naira (exchanged for about 35 million United States Dollars in 1977) as damages.

The proceedings of the case would trail in the court for almost a year, we will discus this in the chapter ahead when we talk about the role of his new lawyer Tunji Braithwaite.

Fela testified before the Anya tribunal that his financing and publishing of YAP NEWS were the true reasons behind the Nigerian army attack.

Meanwhile, Fela was prevented from making any further public concerts as armed police men were posted to prevent or disperse people from any venue advertising a Fela appearance. In order to be able to get some more advance royalty from Decca Records the company with which he had signed a twelve album a year deal, Fela went into the studio to record more albums that would complete his part of the deal.

He recorded songs like "No agreement" mentioned in the early chapter of this book and on the flip side, Fela added an instrumental piece titled "Dog Eat Dog" with Lester Bowie as guest playing trumpet solo. The later a member of the American delegation to FESTAC'77, remained for a short while in Lagos after the other members of the Chicago Arts Assembly had returned to the US.

Determine to perform live, Fela reached an agreement with the proprietor of Cross Road Hotel Chief Adeniyi, to erect a stage in the court-yard of the hotel and he took adverts in leading newspapers to publicise his shows. He also kept the place alive with his band for about seven months, Lester Bowie and Huge Masakela appeared as guest performers during these shows at the Cross Road Hotel.

On the political front, a delegation from the African National Congress (ANC) representing South Africa's liberation movements in exile present in Nigeria for FESTAC also visited Fela at the Cross Road Hotel, the ANC delegation was headed by Tabo Mbeki the successor of Nelson Mandela as President of post-apartheid South Africa.

Fela's sojourn at the Cross Road hotel, was also the period when Jimmy Cliff was put in jail in Nigeria arrested over a 'breach of contract' allegation by a Nigerian business man Ado Ibrahim. Jimmy had the presence of mind to send word to Fela to come to his aid and despite his personal set-backs, Fela was able to settle the Jamaican musician's problems with Nigerian law enforcement agents.

Jimmy Cliff would latter sing the event into a song in one of his many albums. After about seven months of playing in the Cross Road hotel, during which he finished work on the twelve albums required of him with his contract with Decca, Fela decided to move his organisation to Ghana.

Fela in warm handshake with African National Congress (ANC) delegation headed by Tabo Mbeki on a solidarity visit to the Cross Road Hotel.
Picture by Femi Bankole Osunla for Africa 70 photo agency.

Moving to Ghana, was necessitated by the burning in the Kalakuta inferno of the sound track of his film BLACK PRESIDENT. Principle shooting of this film had been completed during the week preceding the army attack, and Ghana film Industry crew responsible for shooting the film had departed Lagos with the film rushes the day before leaving behind the sound track because Fela needed to do some over-dubs.

Unfortunately, the recorded dialogues mostly done add-lib was burnt along with everything in the house. Since the band could not perform anywhere in Nigeria without police or army disrupting the concert, Fela moved to Ghana taking residence at the Hotel President in Tudu area in Accra, and to supplement the income of his organisation, the Africa 70 performed regular shows at the NAPOLEON CLUB owned by his long-time Lebanese friend Faisal Helwani and APOLLO THEATRE in Accra.

Weeks before Fela's arrival in Ghana, during an all Ghana University student's demonstration against measures taken by the Achenpong military government, the students were heard chanting the lyrics of Fela's ZOMBIE. It was therefore no surprise when the Ghana security learnt of a meeting held in an Accra hotel, between Fela and leaders of all Ghana University Students Union. At the meeting, Fela advised the students from pitching unarmed students against armed military or police personnel. The resent clash that prompted the meeting was reported to be brutal with female members of the protesting students, allegedly raped by the policemen sent to their campuses to disperse the demonstration.

Fela made it clear to the student leaders, that it was useless to peach unarmed students against armed and undisciplined colonially trained army or police men. He advised that instead of such clashes, the students should peacefully close down and vacates their campuses until their demands were met by the authorities.

Heeding Fela's advice, the following day after the meeting all Ghana universities were closed down by the students who were demanding the stepping down of the country's military president as the only condition to re-open the universities. Ghana security agents couldn't take actions against Fela immediately, since they only learnt of his meeting with the student leaders long after the effect.

Fela and Africa 70 dancers doing the Comprehensive Show at the Apollo Theatre in Ghana.
Picture by Femi Bankole Osunla Africa 70 Photo Agency

Taking residence at the Hotel President in Tudu area in Accra and to supplement the income of his organisation, Fela and the Africa 70 performed regular shows at the NAPOLEON CLUB owned by his long-time Lebanese friend Faisal Helwani and APOLLO THEATRE in Accra. Above is the publicity for one of his concerts at the Apollo Theatre in Ghana.
Photo by Femi Bankole Osunla Africa 70 Photo Agency.

However to their credit all Ghana universities remained closed for more than eight months, until General Achenpong was replaced in a "palace coup" by his N° 2 in the administration General Akuffo.

From this narrative the reader can see that Fela in most African country was seen, as a folk hero among the majority of the population. Afrobeat music is identified with among the poor populations of African cities, not only as an artistic creation but also a form of mass expression. Loudspeakers and cassette players blast afrobeat music in all the slum areas of Africa's urban centres. It has become more explosive because of its appeal to the teenage offerings of the "African" elite.

For the first time, slum dwellers and the children of society's privileged are coming together in a highly charged educative cultural experience. It is a music that reflects the pace of the struggle in some of the world's worst slum. Fela provided a focal point around which social forces can rally and find expression.

This was what prompted the burning down of Kalakuta Republic. Nigeria's military leaders, hated and feared not so much of Fela as a person but of his influence on the wretched of the earth that listen to and identify with his music. Therefore, the anti Fela reaction from Gen. Achenpong's military regime did not come as a surprise. It was clear that the military regime in Ghana, will not approve of the re-activation of the concept of Pan–Africanism in Ghana after Kwame Nkrumah.

A Lebanese shop owner across the street from Hotel President, provided the Ghanaian authority the excuse to kick him out of Ghana. Fela was practising his saxophone in his hotel room, when he saw the Lebanese shop owner across the street dipping a bowl into the open drainage and pouring its content at the African women selling fruits outside his shop. At this point, Fela asked a member of his organisation to go and tell the Lebanese man to stop debasing and being disrespectful to the African women.

The Lebanese man's reaction was "who is Fela to tell me what to do in front of my shop?" When told of the man's reaction, Fela quickly got dressed and went down accompanied by members of his organisation.

To the shock of everyone, the Lebanese man stopped pouring the dirty water at the women when confronted by Fela, he also apologised to the women saying everything was "cool". Unfortunately, the following morning Fela found out that the Lebanese man had sent all the women away, saying they could not sell their fruits in front of his shop anymore.

Since there was no way to contact the affected women, Fela gave money to Ghanaian female members of his organisation to purchase fruits and set up shop in front of the Lebanese man's shop. It came out from investigation that the Lebanese man had inherited the shop business from his father, and most of the women selling fruits in front of the shop knew him as a boy. Why should he be allowed to kick the women away just like that, was Fela's question? Hence his decision to send female members of his organisation, to set-up shop in front of the Lebanese man's shop.

Eventually, the police was called in by the Lebanese man in order to get Fela's women away from his shop front. Fela joined the women as soon as he noticed the police arrive and within minutes, there was a crowd gathering. An inspector of police who led the troop to the scene tried to justify the action of the Lebanese man, but in the end he got ridiculed by Fela and people gathered.

Pandemonium ensued and in the end Fela and members of his organisation, were arrested and later charged to a special tribunal for "actions likeable to bring breach of the peace". He was represented before the tribunal by his lawyer friend in Ghana George Gardner, and all the accused persons were granted bail by the tribunal.

Meanwhile, Fela returned to Nigeria with members of his organisation to mark the first anniversary of the burning down of Kalakuta Republic. As part of the programme commemorating the anniversary, series of shows were organised through-out the country and to round-up the commemoration Fela got married to 27 female members of his organisation in a traditional ceremony held at a Lagos hotel where he was temporarily staying two days after the original date planned.

The marriage earlier slated for 20th, February 1978 at his lawyer's chambers, was cancelled at the last moment with all the participants and press present. His lawyer Tunji Briathwaite who had consented to the event to take-place in his office despite being aware of Fela's marriage in England to Remi, succumbed to pressure from Nigerian authorities with their Christian values - he claimed the marriage was immoral and against social norms. According to him, Fela could be charged with bigamy and it was his place as a lawyer to advice him against such act.

Fela would later arrange the marriage to take place at his temporary hotel residence in Anthony Village area of the Lagos mainland. He publicly declared that he was waiting for the judge that would charge him for bigamy, aware that most of the Nigerian elite have extra marital affairs thus making them incompetent to morally judge him.

Returning to Accra after the celebration, Fela was refused entry into Ghana by the immigration authority despite the latter insisting on entry to attend his next rendezvous with the tribunal. He was subsequently informed that the case had been withdrawn from the tribunal, after a long wait at the Kotoka Airport, Fela and members of his organisation later returned to Nigeria on the next available flight.

Like Kanmi Osobu before him who profited with the publicity that came with his representations of Fela in court, Tunji Braithwaite despite his 'moral' claim was an opportunist. A lawyer without professional scruples, Tunji had no respect for the client/advocate confidentiality. As a lawyer, he had all the time before everyone was assembled for the marriage, to air his objection instead of waiting till the last minute when everyone including members of the press was gathered.

In our opinion (Fela and organization members), the only justification to cancel the marriage from holding in his office was to get cheap publicity and he confirmed this opinion after Fela's death with his 'Sunday Punch' newspaper of August 10, 1997 interview, captioned "How I Disrupted Fela's Wedding – Tunji Braithwaite". The marriage incidence and two other issues led to Fela parting ways with Tunji Braithwaite.

The reader will recall that Fela shortly after the burning down of Kalakuta, sued the Chief of Staff Nigerian army and other high ranking officers from the Abalty barracks whom he held responsible for the destruction of his house. Being Fela's lawyer, the Nigerian army authority contacted Tunji through Colonel Ibrahim Badamosi Babangida (who later ruled Nigeria from 1985–1992).

Fela and some of us (his close associates), were visiting Tunji at his Victoria Island home when Babangida arrived proposing a settlement out of court. Tunji however did not want Fela to meet with Babangida saying it was better that he handled the matter from a lawyer's point, hence we all left through the back door of his "Beulah Court Mansion" in Victoria Island.

Basking in the publicity that went with each court appearance, Tunji Braithwaite turned down the settlement offered by Colonel Babangida and to Fela he later said the army sensed they were going to loose the case in court hence their search for a settlement advising Fela not to accept.

Before the settlement move by the army, Fela kept on stressing to Tunji that he should prosecute the case from a political angle, claiming that his political influence on the masses was the reason behind the army attack on his Kalakuta republic commune.

However, Tunji refused to stress the political aspect of the case in court saying it was a constitutional issue. Come judgement day before Justice Lateef Dosumu, the case was thrown out of court by the presiding judge. A law that claimed: "the crown can do no wrong" abrogated since the early 40's in England, was used as grounds to throw out the case claiming in this case that "government can do no wrong".

At a meeting in Tunji's office after the court judgement, the lawyer would break-down shedding tears and blaming himself before us that he should have listened to Fela's views over-looking the political aspect of the case. He tried to reassure Fela he was sure it was a constitutional issue. Fela told him, he was surprised to hear a lawyer claim constitutional issue in this case aware, that the constitution had been suspended by the army who ruled by decrees.

Meanwhile the army authority as part of transition to civil rule programme lifted the ban on political activities in the country.

From left: Fela, Beko and Tunji Braithwaite outside the Lagos High Court Premises. Picture by Femi Bankole Osunla Africa 70 Photo Agency.

Tunji Braithwaite who had never expressed his ambition to go into politics, suddenly invited Fela to accompany him to a meeting of 'Committee of Friends'. This committee would later transform into a political party named the Unity Party of Nigeria (UPN) lead by Chief Obafemi Awolowo.

At the meeting according to Fela, all those present were discussing positions instead of an ideological direction for the proposed party, and he added that it was only at the meeting that he discovered that Tunji wanted to become Governor of Lagos State.

He also discovered that Tunji Braithwaite, had assured his colleagues at the meeting that Fela was going to support his campaign if nominated as UPN candidate for Lagos State Governorship. Fela left the gathering after he realised what game his lawyer was playing, Tunji had never discussed his political interest with Fela prior to the meeting let alone solicit Fela for his campaigns.

With his ace gone and without any plausible grounds for support within the UPN for the post of Governor, Tunji Braithwaite quitted the committee of friends that preferred as candidate Lateef Jankande an old political associate of Chief Awolowo. Tunji would later form his own political party shortly after, and called it Nigerian Advance Party (NAP) and he also presented himself as the presidential candidate of the party.

Fela on the other hand, launched his own political party called the Movement of the People (MOP) and despite his poor financial state, he was able to rally volunteers who proposed and vacated their homes, transforming them into offices for MOP in-order for the party to meet the requirements of the Nigerian electoral commission laws.

However like Fela later sang in Army Arrangement, Obasanjo's military regime wanted a civilian regime that would continue their corrupt system hence, all the radical parties capable of making a change were technically eliminated from presenting candidates for the federal elections in 1979.

In ARMY ARRANGEMENT he sang:
"....election story nko! Obasanjo plan am very well.
The same old politicians! Wey rule Nigeria before!

The same old politicians! Wey steal Nigeria before!
All of them dey there now!"

Army Arrangement is about Nigeria's attempt in 1979, at a transition to 'democracy' after more than a decade of military rule. In 1970 Nigeria emerged from a three year Biafra civil war with the largest standing army in black Africa, no financial debts careering along on at least two million barrels of sulphur-low oil pumped daily into the world market. With such revenue invested prudently in the Nigerian economy like earlier explained in previous chapter, there is no reason for any Nigerian to live below the poverty line.

However with persistent scandals of corruption as the standard in every administration since independence, the army lost all credibility to effect any change especially since the arrival of the military in the political arena created the illusion of a peaceful 'democratic' participation in government with the daily running of government carried out by civilians who reported to military bosses.

Fela in this song calls on the people to be bold enough, to criticise the government because fear of the man with the gun, would not put an end to the sufferings of the masses who eventually pay for government mismanagement. Pointing to the foreign exchange scandal, that prompted the military regime to arrest highly placed Nigerians, most of them were tried and sentenced to jail terms ranging from five years to fifteen.

But with the change from military to civil rule, most of the jailed socialites were released by the new administration - a previewed scenario by the departing Obasanjo military regime Fela accuses.

Turning to the election issue how the military manipulated the country, eliminating the young political movements like the Movement of the People (MOP) that were calling for a change in the system. Fela pointed to the fact that the military handed power to the same elite politicians, who prompted the army to seize power earlier.

Concluding that it is an arrangement from the ex-colonial rulers, who put the military in place to do their dirty works and he says the whole political maneuver is an Army Arrangement.

FELA MOVES TO JK'S

All the events mentioned above, were happening during a considerably difficult time for Fela, deported from Ghana he couldn't afford to lodge his large entourage in hotels anymore as he used to do since the burning down of his house, and financially at this point in his struggle against the Army authority's persecutions - he was in a mess.

The film that could have given him some income if completed, was abandoned as a result of his deportation from Ghana, and venues were hesitant to welcome Fela and his entourage to perform with the Obasanjo regime responsible for his persecution still in power.

Fela was not planning to move Kalakuta to Ikeja before the burning down of his house. In fact his Agege Motor Road residence as earlier explained, was strategically placed and he had plans to transform the building. We discussed the possibility of Lemi doing some artistic designs, like the clenched Black-fist in glass as possible architectural designs. All these were ideas and plans for the future, he never thought that a government would burn down his house the way Obasanjo's regime did.

Before the Kalakuta attack, Fela had bought a piece of Land from the father of his long-time drummer Tony Allen. Pa Allen owned two plots, one he had built on where he was residing with his family, and the other one he sold to Fela both situated on Gbemisola Street in Ikeja. At this time, Ikeja Area was an immediate suburb of Lagos mainland, not the Capital of Lagos State that it later became.

With no where else to go, JK his long time friend proposed to house Fela and his large entourage in his three bed-room apartment located on Atinuke Olabanji Crescent in Ikeja. JK was living in this house with his Italian girl friend Cerelina and their dog 'Jamba'. It must have been difficult for Cerelina to accept this sudden brutal transformation of their home into a new Kalakuta commune and not long after Fela moved in with the couple, Cerelina got separated from JK. For many years since his return to Nigeria in 1971, Fela was paying JK's apartment rent and paying him a salary as public relation director for Africa 70 Organisation.

Immediately Fela and his community moved into JK's apartment, most of the occupants from the other apartments started to evacuate the building for fear that Fela could provoke another attack from the government. The vacated apartment were re-occupied by members of Fela's entourage with an agreement to continue to pay the rents. The building owned by Mr. Adesanya, an old school friend of JK's from Ijebu Ode Grammar school, consisted of six three bed-room apartments. As earlier explained regarding living conditions in the burnt down Kalakuta where inhabitants, shared many discomforts with the ordinary populace: water and power shortages, cramped conditions - the women slept twelve to a room in bunk beds.

This time around, it was more discomfort as there were no place to install bunk beds, the living room in JK's doubled as sleeping space at nights and general living room during the day - the women had mattresses placed on the living room floor most times and Fela received visitors with some of the mattress serving as seating space. The boys from the organization squatted in the other vacated apartments and those who could build make-shift homes, squirted across the street on an un-occupied land.

The situation was made more uncomfortable, by the immigration of young men and women who joined the group from Ghana. Ghana's economy like those of other countries where the military seized power, was on the downward trend with a lot of 'brain drains' and terrible shortages of basic commodities like soap, detergents, tooth pastes, etc. Professionals of all sorts, were leaving the country in search of greener pastures. Like in Nigeria, the elite and intellectual class in Ghana helped provide legitimacy to military rule because they directly profited from the situation.

Years after the mismanagement of the economy, the end result is mass migration of able bodied men and women needed for the development of the country who abandon their homeland in search of greener pastures. With the advantage of the oil boom, Nigeria became the attraction to would-be immigrants from the neighbouring countries like Ghana.

George Gardner Fela's lawyer in Ghana, Kwesi Yope one of the student leaders Fela held meeting with during the Ghana student boycott, both moved to Nigeria and they were among those that moved to JK's house with Fela.

Immediately Fela and his community moved into JK's apartment, most of the occupants from the other apartments started to evacuate the building for fear that Fela could provoke another attack from the government.
Photo by Femi Bankole Osunla Africa 70 Photo Agency.

Meanwhile, we YAP boys, were squatting in a flat occupied by one of Fela's Ghanaian girl friends who abandoned the apartment after Kalakuta was destroyed. Fela had paid one year's rent in advance for apartment, before the burning of Kalakuta. Like most people around Fela, the army attack on Kalakuta put fear in a lot of them so much that these associates abandoned him after.

Ayesuwa the girl who was occupying the apartment, returned to Ghana and we took-over the vacated apartment and remained there until Fela couldn't afford to pay the rent after which we moved in with him in JK's. With no income to feed his large entourage, he couldn't even pay the rent for his immediate family. Remi, her mother and the three children (Yeni, Femi and Sola), had to abandon their Ikate flat and they also moved in at JK's. It was so difficult that to feed the group, Fela had to go to his old friends to ask for money - friends like Dapo Tejuosho, Victor Akan, mentioned in the early chapters.

It will be appropriate at this point to discus Fela's relation with record companies EMI, Polygram, and Decca particularly since ZOMBIE was used during the Anya tribunal by the army to justify the burning down of Kalakuta. Fela was accused, by some of these record companies based in Nigeria as difficult to deal with.

Concretely there was nothing any of these companies did to help advance the financial blockade Fela was experiencing from the hands of the Obasanjo regime and to make things worse, all the companies were holding back from releasing any new albums from him for fear of reprisals from the military government.

Take Decca for example in 1975, the company a subsidiary of Decca Records in England approached Fela through it's managing director a British named John Boot, the reader will recall that this was the peak of the oil boom and the record industry was in an economic boom.

John Boot as Managing Director, was impressed by the sales from 'Yellow Fever' earlier licensed to his company by Fela. He was regularly visiting Fela at the Shrine whenever he performed, and at home in order to convince him to enter into a long term contract with Decca. At this period Fela's musical out-put was at it's zenith, and as earlier stated he was releasing in the Nigerian market an album every month.

He objected to any restrictions on him by record companies, preferring to sell his album to the highest bidder without any exclusivity. To avoid any competition from other companies, John Boot proposed to do a twelve album a year deal with Fela paying a huge advance royalty on the twelve albums. Decca was represented legally by Chief H.O. Davies one of those lawyers that considered Fela difficult to deal with, and to protect the company in case of any breach of contract Chief Davies, advised Decca management to include a penalty clause in the contract in the event that Fela failed to honour his part of the deal.

A sum of 250,000 Naira (about $350,000 at that time), was fixed as penalty for default from any of the parties involved in the deal. Thanks to the advance royalty paid to Fela on the twelve albums, he was able to start work on the film Black President at the same time he went into the studio to record most of the albums required of him and what was left of the recordings the reader will recall he finished shortly after his house was burnt down by the Nigerian Army in 1977.

After the burning down of Kalakuta, Obasanjo's regime attempted to investigate Fela's source of finance and contrarily to what the regime expected, they discovered that all Fela's income came from his record deals and not from any foreign "leftist" government. In their attempt to strangle him financially, the army authority used M.K.O. Abiola the largest shareholder of the company and a bosom friend of Obasanjo and his predecessor General Mohammed to do their dirty work.

Most of the record companies had developed 'cold feet' towards Fela since the burning down of Kalakuta. Non of them wanted to release any new album from Fela for fear of the army authority. Fela was insisting on DECCA paying a fine for the delay in honoring their contract. John Boot put the blame of the delay on one Chief Abiola whom he described as the largest share-holder of his company.

At this time, Fela did not know who Chief Abiola was, hence he did not take John Boot seriously. He would only start to take the Decca Managing Director seriously, when the latter on his way to the airport stopped at Fela's new home in Ikeja to say 'good bye'. John Boot had just been 'fired' by Abiola and replaced by a German named Mr. Orgus because Boot would not re-negotiate DECCA's contract with Fela.

Shortly after, the new DECCA boss Mr Orgus without taking into consideration the penalty clause in the Decca contract with Fela, unilaterally cancelled the company's engagements saying Fela could buy back his deal if he was not pleased. This was the position, Abiola expected John Boot to adhere to, but the former refused causing him to be sacked as Managing Director. All attempts by Fela to make the new Decca Managing Director to see reason failed, Orgus with the backing of Abiola insisted on Fela going to court if he was not pleased.

Faced with the option of going to a government controlled court with a judiciary known for its lack of independence, Fela contacted the Inspector General of Police M.D.Yussuf to see what the IGP could do to save the situation. Claiming neutrality in a civil case, M.D.Yussuf told Fela he couldn't help but the IGP however advised that Fela should take into consideration the law in his attempt to get re-dress. With no other option left, Fela and his entourage took-over and squatted the company's head-quarters in Lagos - he claimed to "Dogo" (means sitting-in in Yoruba) in Decca until the company was prepared to settle.

The new managing director of Decca contacted M.K.O. Abiola, who in turn called the Pedro Area Police Station to try and dislodge Fela and his entourage from the company premises. He claimed that Fela forced his way into the building another false allegation on the part of Abiola, because we had planned the take-over of Decca with the intention of avoiding any violence. Dressed in suit like a potential customer, I was sent ahead of the others as a decoy to distract the security at the entrance of the company.

On my arrival, I claimed to the security officer at the gate that I had an appointment with the new Managing Director, and while one of them was trying to verify this with the director's secretary, Fela arrives with the other members of our organization - we immediately stationed guys with the company's security men preventing them from alerting their boss.

Peacefully without violence five of us accompanied Fela to the director's office, while the rest of our entourage took strategic positions in the building. Mr Orgus who previously refused to have an appointment with Fela to discus the dispute, decided to ignore our presence in his office pretending to be busy typing on his private typewriter - the Decca boss ignored our presence totally.

While Fela and those of us with him sat across the table waiting for Orgus to react, the company MD continued to write with his typewriter. As I was sitting next to Fela placing me directly in front of Mr Orgus, I chose to place my feet on his typewriter a move that caused the Decca MD to finaly react.

Suddenly he stood-up, he was red all-over his face blushing from rage and without saying a word to us, he pulled out the sheets of paper from his typewriter grabbed his bunch of keys on the table and worked-out of the building with other staff members of DECCA following suit. With the building deserted by the company's staff, every office space was immediately occupied by Fela's entourage and shortly after a truck load of anti-riot police was drafted to the building.

The police, were surprised to see that there was no sign of violence contrarily to what the Decca management had claimed. The Commissioner of police that lead the team, demanded why Fela chose to occupy the company's premises and in reply, Fela told him he was waiting for the company to pay him the money owed.

As a solution, the Commissioner delegated two police men to stand watch at the company's entrance, he also asked Fela to a meeting with Abiola at the Pedro police station the following day to see ways of resolving the impasse.

Accompanied by the author to the meeting held at the Pedro police station, Fela accused Abiola of being responsible for his troubles with the record company, he based his accusations on information from the 'fired' Decca managing director Mr Boot. Fela also stressed that though he was not in possession of written proofs to support his accusation, he swore (a Yoruba tradition) on the grave of his mother that he was sure Abiola had things to do with his troubles in Decca. Abiola in- turn, denied any involvement with decisions of the Decca management.

Claiming he was only an ordinary share holder he said: "I don't know anything about your prob-lems with De-cca! I sw-ear by the grave of m-y mother too that I have no-thing to do with De-cca decisions..!" Abiola stuttered.

To impress those present at the meeting how dearly he loved and respected his late mother, Abiola narrated the story of how his mother missed his first paycheque to convince Fela that he had nothing to do with the latter's problems with the record company.

Confronted with claim and counter-claim, the Commissioner of police decided that it was best both parties resolve the problem according to the dictates of the contract that explicitly demanded an arbitration in case of a dispute between the two parties. Fela proposed Gani Fawehinmi (a popular Lagos lawyer) as his representative for the arbitration, while Abiola played for time saying it was up to Decca to decide who would represent the company.

Since there was no immediate solution to the dispute, Fela returned to the occupied company's premises and on our way back we discussed Abiola's early denials and I suggested that it would be interesting to look in the Managing Director's files.

Since Fela was occupying his office, I asked his permission to go in there as soon as we got back. Yoruba custom forbids people raised with such tradition to swear with the souls of their departed except if telling the truth, looking through written correspondence between Abiola and Decca MD's (Boot and Orgus) to my surprise, several correspondence from Abiola written on ITT letter-head were in the file. The man was an abominable liar, for him to swear the way he did as the correspondence in the DECCA MD's files would reveal.

In the public relations war that ensued between Decca management and Fela, we made public these letters to prove that Abiola was a lying bastard swearing the way he did with his dead mother to prove he had nothing to do with Fela's problems. The letters were explicit, Abiola assured Mr Orgus that with his connection in government, Fela could go to hell if he was not satisfied with the position of the new Decca management.

Despite his government connection, Abiola couldn't get Fela to quit the company's premises and out of desperation he hired thugs to storm the building with the hope of dislodging the occupants. We were very few to defend the company's three-story building but as luck would have it, some of the thugs sent to attack came to warn Fela and they asked for money to dissuade the others from carrying out their mission.

But Fela told them to go to hell, saying if he could face Nigeria army attack there was no group of thugs that could scare him. Meanwhile most of the bodyguards and bouncers the likes of Darrasin, Segun Alagbara, Yemi "Roy" Smith, Gbenga, all those glamorous "roadies' (road managers) from kalakuta days had deserted the organisation after the violent experience in the Kalakuta Nigerian Army attack.

Left to defend the building were a few YAP boys, his wives and a few new immigrants from Ghana who had just joined the organisation. Fela still had his band Africa 70 intact, but the group couldn't perform and the musicians didn't live with him. Fortunately for us within DECCA premises, there were several crates of empty soft drinks staked in a pile behind the office complex. Soon as the thugs left, we went to work preparing our defence.

Most of the empty bottles were strategically placed on all the balconies in the building. The attackers arrived in combi mini-buses and unaware of our prepared state of defence. As the leading bus came to a halt in-front of the main entrance, the attackers were met with fierce resistance from Fela's entourage. We showered the leading combi-bus with bottles breaking the wind-screen. Fela's queens were throwing bottles at the attackers from the balconies of the building, while the boys attacked below - thus the attackers were forced to rush out of the immobilised vehicles dispersing in different directions.

This was the cause of Fela's dispute, with Abiola and the multinational company he represented in Nigeria – International Telephone and Telegraph (ITT, International Thief Thief - apology Fela). Fela still had his band Africa 70 intact but the group couldn't perform and the musicians didn't live with him. Meanwhile, Fela couldn't rehearse his group and at the same time, there was no progress on the case.

It was during this occupation that George Gruntzs, one of the directors of the Berlin Jazz festival visited Lagos to negotiate Fela's appearance for the 1978 Berlin Jazz festival previewed for November of the same year. For seventy-eight days, Fela and his entourage occupied the company premises and since calling rehearsals in the occupied premises was not possible for fear of being attacked while rehearsal was going-on, we had to abandon the occupation to allow Fela rehearse the band for the concert in Berlin.

After his return from Berlin, Fela found-out that his occupation of Decca had dealt the company a big blow economically to the extent that the company was in a mess and they were forced to close down the "occupied" Anthony village office reducing its staff to less than half. Orgus the company's MD, would shortly after depart paving the way for an Abiola stooge Mr. Akinbolu to take over. Our occupation also paved the way, to a rapid demise of the company in Nigeria - reduced from a subsidiary of its parent company to just a record label called 'Afrodisia'.

Fela did not let Abiola get away with his meddling in the company's affair, we deposited ten buckets of human faeces (shit) in Abiola's home in Ikeja early 1979 prompting the song "You Give Me Shit! I Give You Shit!" In the song YOU GIVE ME SHIT I GIVE YOU SHIT, Fela is addressing Africans and the Diaspora to stop playing 'the second-fiddle' in life. Using a discussion between him and a European businessman to make his point, he sang "hear the discussion between European and myself."

According to Fela, the European in an attempt to show how important and well connected he is in Africa, talks of having so many companies with a lot of black people working for him. The European also claims to be a friend to many African heads of state, and how he was at a dinner last night with the president of Nigeria.

To make the European tell more, Fela said he offered the man the last 'joint' (marijuana) in his pocket - the smoke further let-loose the European's tongue. After his long narrative, Fela decided to ask if in Europe and America any black man could have the same opportunity as he does in Africa? If black people own companies in Europe like he does in Africa?

Fela also asked him, if it is easy for black people to get invited to dinner with any European or American leader? He told the European that negritude and colonial mentality, are responsible for the cause of African inferiority complex. For Fela, it is the problem of leadership in Africa where Africans don't like to do things for their own folks. He says he feels vexed that Africans in the twentieth century are still slaves of the system.

For him, it is time to stand firm, anybody that gives us shit! He go get shit! Like Abiola him get! He go get shit! Ten buckets full of shit! He go get shit!

With regards to EMI, most of Fela's early career recordings were done with the EMI Nigeria a subsidiary of EMI United Kingdom. While Fela was signed to its Nigerian subsidiary, EMI Nigeria systematically authorised her parent company in England to release in the European market most of Fela's works without paying royalties for the foreign releases.

Whenever Fela demanded to be paid for the overseas releases, EMI regional director at that time, Michael West later replaced by Mr. Plumley usually claimed that the records were not doing well in the market, a claim that Fela judged ridiculous if one takes into account the number of albums released.

The company had released twelve of Fela's albums in the international market, the last a double album. For an artist whose works were not doing well, releasing twelve albums is not convincing from a marketing point of view. Fela confronted EMI management with this argument, demanding that if his records were not selling as the company claims, what was the interest of the company in releasing twelve albums particularly the last a double album?

To calm Fela, Michael West and later Plumley authorised an advance of 30,000 Naira (about $45,000) to Fela as royalty. Since EMI was not ready to discuss in detail an international contract with Fela, whenever he needed money he went after the company's management demanding payment for his back catalogues.

There was the case of a visit in Nigeria by Mr. Plumley who had promised to pay some money to Fela on a previous visit. However when the latter arrived at the company's office in Lagos, Fela was told that Plumley had gone home. Fela drove to the official residence of the company regional director only to find a security guard at the entrance, after some inquiry of the director's where-about the security guard informed Fela that the director was away to the airport.

We headed to the Ikeja airport in search of Plumley and enquiries at the departure counter, proved helpful as the EMI boss had checked in earlier but was hiding somewhere around the airport vicinity.

Fela decided we should comb the parking area to see if he was in the car. Bingo! Plumley, was waiting for his flight in his car when one of us who accompanied Fela spotted him.

He tried to escape seeing Fela heading towards his parked car and without wasting time, Fela shouted "Ole! Ole!"(Thief! Thief! in Yoruba) as the EMI Director tried to escape.

In Nigeria, one could get lynched easily with a cry of thief! Within minutes of the cry «thief» you have people running after the alleged thief with sticks, batons and sometimes used tyres to burn the victim alive. With the aid of people who had assembled at the shout of thief by Fela, the EMI director was apprehended and the police was called in.

Plumley and Fela ended-up at the Ikeja Airport police station, the EMI boss was obliged to sign a check worth 25,000 Naira (about $35,000), and promising to settle the problem with Fela before he was allowed to leave the police station by the police.

Polygram, the last of the major record companies in Nigeria, couldn't accuse Fela of acquiring the reputation of being difficult to deal with, as Fela was at the zenith of his career when the company appeared on the scene. He was no longer the unknown artist that could be ripped-off and dictated to in the industry.

Fela did not subscribe to restrictions placed upon his musical out-put by the record companies, and Polygram Nigeria respected all these criteria as a result they had a good working relation. Apart from the licence fee paid to Fela in 1976 as advance royalty for the release of ZOMBIE, Polygram Nigeria did not move a finger to help him during the period of persecutions from the Nigerian military regime. But the overall busness relationship was cordial. Fela never had any cause to quarrel with the company.

Fela at home in Kalakuta.
Picture by Femi Bankole Osunla Africa 70 Photo Agency

Picture above front row left, (ID and right J.K. with plastered eye) and all arrested persons, stepping out of the famous police truck named Black Maria. Photo by Femi Bankole Osunla, was used in the album design of Coffin For Head of State.

Front cover album design Coffin for Head of State

COFFIN FOR HEAD OF STATE

Every opportunity he had, Fela never failed to try and make the African personality standpoint clear to his audience even if it creates controvercy. Ninety-five years after the notorious scramble for Africa between 1884-1885, the city of Berlin became another focus for Europeans on African issues at the annual Berlin Jazz Festival in 1978. Writing about the festival several months after the event Hannes Schmidt wrote:

"For many years, the Berlin Jazz Festival in the city of West Berlin has been one of the major events in the field of improvised music. The inner tension of jazz music is expressed in various counter poles and contrasts, such as tradition and progress the documentation of historical styles of music and the latest information on the current stage of development of modern jazz and the confrontation between the 'fathers' and the 'rebels'. The boundaries have become fluid between the trends in style and the various forms of folk music. The word 'JAZZ' features as a collective term for everything that has developed from Afro-American music.

One of the highlights of the autumn 1978 festival in Berlin was music from Africa. This return 'back to the roots of jazz', is in step with a new movement among Africa's black musicians. Political motivations and cultural interest are two important reasons why they are focusing their attention on Africa and on traditional African music and folklore, hitherto which are sectors that have virtually remained the domain of music ethnologist. But almost wholly neglected in the USA and Europe has been the contemporary music of Africa's cities, the urban phenomenon of a type of 'city folklore', which in turn has been influenced partly by Western and Caribbean popular music.

In this phenomenon, we can observe the process of cultural feed-back a development which is said to have become personified in the last few years in the figure of a musician extremely popular in Africa - Fela Anikulapo-Kuti from Lagos Nigeria.

Jazz enthusiasts in the Federal Republic of Germany, have got to know him through a T.V. portrait and his recordings. But none had experienced him in perperson i.e. live in concert in this country.

He is held to be the leading exponent of new and politically explosive African urban folklore music. His rare concerts attract hundreds of thousands in Africa and in Nigeria, Kuti and his retinue have long been an important political phenomenon. Kuti has founded his own political party the Movement of the People (M.O.P.), stands as a candidate in the presidential elections and is committed to Nkrumah's Pan-African nationalism.

As the champion of the poor and under-privileged, he stands as a figure with which people from this social stratum can identify themselves. Accordingly the organisers of the Jazz Festival the Swiss George Gruntz and the German R. Schutte-Bahrenberg, are proud to be able to present this self assured African 'eccentric' and his group for the first time in a representative setting in Europe in the Berlin Philharmonic hall".

As we begin to read the various reports, one can observe that the responds of the audience and the German press at the festival were mixed for different reasons. B. Holger Krusamann writing in the Jeue Ruhe Zeitung/Neue Rhein Zeitung, described Fela as "the most colourful personality of the festival who revealed how wide the gap is between cultural philosophy in Europe and Africa". Continuing the critic wrote: "He was booed for being a potentate and misunderstood as a musician. He does not care about the rules of musical composition or the issue of feminism.

He is the first musician in post-colonial Africa who had the strength to break the bounds of his continent. With the help of his music - a combination of traditional African music with jazz/rock elements, Fela Kuti has become a cult figure in black Africa. What he has to say is revolutionary, his impact dangerous for the regime in Nigeria. It was reported in Berlin that the Nigerian Army had taken advantage of his two weeks absence to raid and burn down Kuti's village for the second time in two years.

Kuti came over from the metropolis of Lagos with an ensemble comprising about 70 performers, among them 27 female dancers and accompanying vocalists all of them married to the maestro.This fact alone, was enough to totally confuse a number of European critics. How? They asked could a man like Kuti who campaigns against the unequal status of the sexes and racism, at the same time travel and live like a monarch and feudal master - with harem and servants.

The organisers of the Jazz Festival the Swiss George Gruntz and the German R. Schutte-Bahrenberg, presenting Fela and members of his organization to the German press.
Photo by Femi Bankole Osunla Africa 70 Photo Agency.

His answer several traditions which he arbitrarily upholds, he views as a counterpoise to western colonial civilisation and its persistent influence".

Rudolph Ganz, wrote in the Frankfurter Rundschan: "Musically, he presented a long drawn-out and rather uninteresting show, related to the old commercial soul music which becomes embarrassing when he puts aside his saxophone for the electric organ (unfortunately something he does quite often)". In the Frankfurtter Algemeine Zeitun (FAZ), Ulrich Olshausen described Fela's music as: "unfortunately very western, namely a variation of the most primitive disco music with a faint African undertone received by Berlin audience with boos and calls of No disco and No Travolta!"

Some other critics were of the opinion that: "the only musician at this year's (1978) festival to record 'the magnificent power of African music from a deep understanding of its 'traditions' was the red-hairdo Briton the drummer Ginger Baker, who has lived for many years in Nigeria.

He took the stage after Kuti and demonstrated drive and poly-rhythmic solos with the virtuosity of a complete percussion ensemble, and was demonstratively acclaimed with thunderous applause". Finally another critic pointed out that: "…one of black continent's greatest musicians is currently living in Berlin, the xylophonist Kakraba Lobi from Ghana, who has a teaching post in Berlin.

He could have easily been engaged and would certainly not have involved the same expense as Kuti's DM. 250,000 ($100,000), and he would have performed with more African soul and art than all the other musicians at the festival".

For any critic to say: "…the only musician at the festival to record the magnificent power of African music from a deep understanding of its traditions was a red hairdo Briton the drummer Ginger baker….", is an absolute display of the ignorance of the western world about the concepts and traditions of African music.

Though Ginger Baker lived in Nigeria for some time, one wonders what standards or criteria the critic put into consideration to come to such conclusion. What if one may ask, does Ginger Baker know about African music? How can he know more than the Africans who naturally have the rhythm born in them?

It is like saying, Fela has a deep understanding of Chinese music more than the Chinese who naturally grew up with their music.

The reason for black prominence in jazz music, is that jazz has its roots in African music and African Americans have produced the greatest in Jazz music because of their historic link with black Africa. Also to be noted, is the fact that Ginger Baker's musical career at this period was on the downward trend, he only used his friendship with Fela to get invited to perform at the festival. He assured the festival organisers that he was going to play with Fela without informing Fela in advance.

When Fela learnt about this, he refused to include the red hair-do Briton in his package and as a compromise, Fela authorised Tony Allen and one percussion player from his group Ado Netty to back Ginger during his show. The later would later propose some recording deals for Tony Allen inviting him to London after the festival paving the way for the eventual break-up of Africa 70. But before we go into details, it is important to talk about Fela's performance.

Addressing the booing crowd in Berlin during his appearance at the festival Fela said: "I want you to scream and shout more because the more you shout the more you convince me that you wish Afrobeat was German music. Unfortunately, it is an authentic African music a product from the African musical archives..."

Fela was more than just a musician he was to use the words of a critic: "...the first musician in post-colonial Africa who had the strength to break the bounds of his continent... 'BUT HE IS FANTASTIC', was the heading of the article written by Holger Krussman and published in DES TAGESSPIEGEL.

Written months after the festival, the article according to the author is a portrait from the distance of Fela he wrote: "Pardon me you want to write a story about Fela Kuti after all these time? Let him and his 27 women stay where they came from.

He cannot play the piano, he is a poor saxophonist and a jazz festival is not the right place for him. It is good, that he has made a fool of himself over European Television - so we all know it.

This colleague of mine was there of his own opinion, just as much as the young man at the stage entry who in the third of the much disputed concert in early jazz day's history, shook his 20 year old head and said: "Will have to kill him or he will never stop". I write about Fela because I never thought that this could be possible. What? That a young man talks about killing somebody just because a concert lasts longer than expected?

No, the crux of the matter is that somebody now in Berlin in his own way, does things and in so doing gets the people so excited - Fela Anikulapo-Kuti is that somebody. What has he done? Fela came with plenty headed clan, took quarters in the Hotels Plaza and Kempiski with his entourage and his 27 wives, residing on two floors in the manner of one who knows that he has become a political factor in his home country Nigeria.

Fela knows how he attracts the people everywhere he goes and he astonishes them. Ueremy Steig says 'He plays a horrible saxophone man, but he is fantastic'. Fela insisted that one of his wives who was to be sent to the hospital after a malaria attack should be treated by an African doctor. He also found out that the Nigerian army had taken the opportunity of his European trip to destroy his burnt house (for the second time within two years).

Who is still saying that this man is no political factor? Despite his unusual style and his defence, plus the vague information about his origin and his music - not one of his records has been officially released yet in Germany. As a result of these, the expectations of the public in the end were so over-stretched that the bow broke. Kuti was booed by the Berlin public as a ruler and misunderstood as a musician. It was not Fela's ability as an instrumentalist that brought him to Berlin, as was the case of Dollar Brand.

The festival programme director George Gruntz said: 'my finger moved as if to show him to play something else than these poor tars there below, but just this would have been disastrous. Then it would not have been Fela anymore as Jeremy Smith'. Fela, the natty dread was in a limbo because he neither liked to be the Mozart of jazz, nor a leftist black man.

For the jazz fans, he was a shabby pop-star and entertainer mixture. For those who think politically, he himself as a despotic leader could not fit into the well established picture of the third world.

For the women, he was the chauvinist who commanded his 27 women.

George Gruntz did not call him a jazz musician, but the most important representative of new and undiscovered African city folklore. This is the point! Fela is neither a Miles Davis nor an African Che Guevera, nor yet a remnant found in the bush - he is a product of African history. Fela is not only the product but also the personified search for an answer to colonialism.

He is by the way, the first in post colonial Africa who had the power to come over the shores of his continent without the diversion through an American career - like Miriam Makeba or Dollar Brand".

From its controversial outcome, it is clear that very little is known in the western world about Africa. The reaction of the German press convinced us further that until African history are written by Africans, from an African perspective, a lot of misunderstanding of the African personality stand-point will remain unclear to the average western mind.

Musically, Berlin jazz festival was Fela's "breaking of the boundaries" and from my personal observation of the event during the festival, Fela's meeting with Abdulahi Ibrahim (Dollar Brand) and Miriam Makeba back stage at the Berlin Philharmonic was very cordial, particularly Miriam who was living at that time in exile in Guinea.

For the first time in post-colonial Africa, a musician would break international despite him being based in his homeland. The trip would also signal the end of the band Africa 70 and its foundation members. Those musicians learnt on the job at the start of Fela's professional career and they helped expressed his musical feelings. Without him speaking out with words, members of that group understood every Fela body movement.

From their long stay with him, they were the few musicians that felt and could interpret his un-spoken jests on stage. Fela never was able to build another band as tight after he disbanded the Africa 70. The break-up of the band started long before Berlin, for some time before the burning down of Kalakuta some of the musicians led by Tony Allen were not satisfied with their salaries because they felt they were being underpaid.

Whenever members of the band tried to go on strike, some of them refused to participate suggesting sending Tony to resolve the problem with Fela. But Tony like other members of the band couldn't complain directly to Fela because, they always received extra allowance from him whenever they needed money plus the fact that some of them were having secret affairs with some of the women Fela was sleeping with.

Moreover, certain jealousies existed among the band members particularly between Tony Allen and his immediate deputy Lekan Animasaun. As a result, Fela was always in the know of the maneuvers from members of the band before Tony brought the matter up.

The matter reached a climax, after some members of other less-popular groups such as those of Ebenezer Obey and Sunny Ade, were seen driving cars bought for them by their respective band leaders. Members of Africa 70 however, could not compare their situations with those of the Juju bands mentioned earlier because unlike Ebenezer Obey and Sunny Ade, Fela was responsible for all the composition and arrangement of his music.

While rehearsing new songs, he used the tonic sol-fa on his piano to explain notes to his musicians. That was why all the credits went to Fela as indicated on all his albums. People like me and others who knew the details of how Fela composed and arranged his music, were shocked to read in interviews where ex-members of Africa 70 like Tony were quoted as claiming the contrary.

Knowing Tony Allen the way I do, I am sure he would deny ever saying he wrote the drum beats in Afrobeat as he was "alleged" to have claimed in the press. How many times during rehearsals, Fela would hum out the drum pattern he wanted for a new song to TonyAllen and other drummers after Tony left the group. There is no doubt that Tony must have added his feelings to the beat, but the concept and overall rhythm were written and arranged by Fela as credited in all his album covers. Another important point was that Fela encouraged, his musicians to compose their proper songs and he helped arranged the songs in groovy Afrobeat patterns.

He also helped to produce the albums – it was the case with Tony Allen and the album "Jealousy" released on Sound Workshop label in 1976, same with Lekan Animashaun and the album "She Rere".

From Fela's standpoint, he preferred to help his musicians advance professionally than buying them cheap cars like some of the musicians wanted. After Fela's death, even people who didn't play with him have also tried to take credit for the creation of Afrobeat. Orlando Julius (O.J), a Nigerian musician who migrated to the United States at about the time Fela made his musical break in Nigeria was reported to have claimed being the originator of Afrobeat.

At the time Fela so named his music, bands like OJ's were playing soul as Orlando Julius sang in one of his early albums: "...eyin ero to duro! Ati eyin to'nmbo lona! A tun gbe ijo tuntun de! Soul lowa tun laiye! Meaning: "...all people standing bye and those coming on the way! We have brought a new dance! Soul is the new thing in life!"

All the popular bands at that time, were all following the soul music trend while Fela was planting the seeds of afrobeat music. Another issue that inflamed Africa 70 band members was Fela's $40,000 investment in the printing machine for YAP News. The musicians were grumbling that he spent money on 'politics' more than he spent for the band that was bringing in the money.

For the musicians, bringing YAP members along on tours like the Berlin Jazz festival was not necessary, money spent on our air tickets could have been given to them. They made a big fuss over this issue in Berlin so much, that Fela in order to satisfy their demands chose to lodge all the musicians in the five star Hotel Kempiski where they eventually ran-up enormous bar bills paid by Fela.

The sad thing about the musician's position is that when Fela gave them the opportunity to learn to read and write music, they never took the lessons seriously. The reader would recall how at the beginning of Koola Lobitos, I explained how Fela used to try and teach his band members to read and write music. They never took the lessons seriously, the opportunity that would have given them the independence and possibility to play music as professionals, were thrown away as a result of their individual laziness.

The opportunity he gave his band, was not taken seriously despite the fact that there were no music schools available in Nigeria. Since their departure from the band, most of them couldn't use their respective wealth of experience to become great musicians like the case of ex - Miles Davis or James Brown band members.

John Coltrane, Herbie Hancock, Maceo Parker, and Marcus Miller, all these great musician played alongside Miles Davis and James Brown respectively. Somewhere in their respective careers, they benefited from the musical wealth of experience of their ex-boss. These great musicians mentioned above have kept alive the spirit of funk, jazz and soul - can we say the same with ex-Africa 70 members with regards to afrobeat?

Who among the many musicians who performed alongside Fela, could lay claim to be professional musician like ex-members of Miles Davies and James Brown bands? Apart from Femi who after leaving his father's band, went ahead to create his own brand of afrobeat with his group –The Positive Force. Most ex-members of Fela's band soon as they departed Africa 70 end up in musical obscurity. One reason for this is laziness on the part of most of the musicians and afrobeat by arrangement, is a collective music that does not give room to individual creativity within the music like the case is in Jazz and Funk.

All Afrobeat musician does, is memorise pre-arranged short phrases that he plays all through the duration of a musical piece with stops or acceleration of rhythms as indicated by the arranger. Respective member of the group in each piece of Afrobeat music, are allotted short phrases which does not give room for the individual to express his or her dexterity. Another default of the musicians is that after each concert, most of them pack-up their respective instruments without further practice until the next concert. With this attitude towards the music, when they leave the band they are lost because they only know how to play short phrases on their respective instruments.

Take for example jazz and the evolution of the music, Miles Davies performed with Charlie 'Bird' Parker he did not learn to play jazz by packing- up his instrument until the next concert, rather he worked on his personal voice to become the all time great musician he was. Today Miles has a legacy of producing great musicians like John Coltrane, Herbie Hancock, and Marcus Miler to name a few. These musicians have also paid their dues in the industry they took time to learn the music, lived the music and sacrificed for it.

I am looking forward to the day when ex-Africa 70 musicians would add their wealth of experience to the Afrobeat legacy of Fela. I remember as early as 1995 when I just took residence in Paris, I used to encourage Tony Allen during his concerts to play Afrobeat and to do Fela covers.

His reaction to my advice was negative. Now with the explosion of the phenomenon that was Fela, and his creation of the brand of music everyone wants to jump on the bandwaggon. Everyone wants to claim being a part of the creation. As a YAP member, I guess I am not in the best position to criticise Fela's musicians who considered us as people who profited from his money. They believe because he financed YAP News, and we were seen regularly in his company he must be spending more for us privately.

One thing the musicians overlook, is that our constant presence beside Fela left us vulnerable too whenever he was attacked and jailed. How many of them went to jail with Fela for their believe in the struggle like some of us from YAP did? Disillusioned in Berlin because Fela did not spend the big part of his DM. 250,000 ($100,000) fee paid for his appearance at the festival, most of the band members were not looking forward to return to Lagos and the persecution from the Nigerian army authority after the trip to Berlin.

Tony Allen claimed he was invited by Ginger Baker to do some recordings in London, Oghene Kologbo, the youngest member of Kalakuta who learnt to play the guitar in Fela's house would later be influenced by the bad feelings from the senior members of the band to run away in Berlin.

After his departure from the group, Kologbo ended up playing music with different groups in Germany. Apart from Tony Allen, there were eight members of the group that ran away in Berlin. Since most of the band members behind the scene, were always grumbling about being under-paid Fela decided to disband the group Africa 70.

He told the musicians who returned to Lagos with him, that they had to re-apply if they wanted to be part of his new group. The new group he named Egypt 80, and appointed Lekan Animasaun the new leader. From the Africa 70 group, apart from Animasaun and the guitarist Okalue Ojeah (nicknamed Las Palmas), all the other members that returned to Lagos from the Berlin trip refused to re-apply.

Tony Allen, who left for London with the pretext that he was invited to do some recordings with Ginger Baker returned a few weeks later to Lagos. Unfortunately for him, Fela had replaced him with Lekan Animasaun as bandleader.

Meanwhile, Fela on his return back to Nigeria after the trip to Germany accompanied by members of his organisation and the Young African Pioneers, visited the site of the dispersed Kalakuta commune and realised that General Obasanjo's military regime had seized the opportunity of our absence from the country, to forcibly evacuate the inhabitants of the area breaking down their homes and what was left of the Kuti family house. A population of more than five thousand people, were forced to evacuate their homes without alternative provisions or compensation.

The reader will recall that shortly after Obasanjo's army regime burnt down Kalakuta in 1977 as a sign of protest, Fela and members of the Young African Pioneers placed a coffin (not his mother's) on the balcony of the ruins of Kalakuta Republic with a banner stating: "This Is The Spot Where Justice Was Murdered". People walking or driving-pass the ruins, saw this symbolic protest as a defiance of the military regime and on our return to Lagos from Berlin, we found the coffin placed on the debris of the demolished buildings.

Asked by members of the press present, what he intended to do with the coffin? Fela replied: "on or before 1st October 1979, we will deposit this coffin at the state house Doddan Barracks as a parting gift to the Obasanjo regime whom we hold responsible for this barbaric act". Keeping this promise on September 30, 1979, accompanied by members of his organisation, the Young African pioneers, and the public whom he described as Movement of the People (MOP) in the song Coffin for Head of State, we deposited the coffin despite security put in place all along the route to prevent us from getting to the seat of power.

On the eve, Fela and members of his organisation had performed in the Shrine till the early hours of the morning, we all were just going to bed at about six a.m. when the security men were taking positions all over the route that led to Lagos Island where Doddan Barracks is located.

We did not start our match with the coffin until late afternoon, and by this time most of the soldiers posted along the route to prevent us from getting to the State House, were tired from controlling the millions of vehicles on Lagos streets.

After waiting in the burning hot sun for hours looking-out for Fela and causing a lengthy traffic jam, the soldiers relaxed their vigil.

This was the opportunity that Fela seized when he arrived at the checkpoint, as the soldier manning the post was not expecting Fela to drive the 'Nissan' bus that we were travelling in. By the time he realised who was behind the wheels, Fela had accelerated and the soldiers had to hastily force a taxi cab driving behind us to abandon its passengers by the roadside and to pursue Fela and his entourage.

It was a hot chase on the Eko Bridge as the taxi tried to catch-up with us. We managed to shake-off the taxi by a last minute deviation Fela made sending the taxi driver in the other direction. On our arrival at the State House entrance, the security men at the gate were not alerted of our impending "visit". I guess the army authority, must have assumed that they had sufficient security men in place to prevent us from getting close to the seat of power.

Fortunately for us, as Fela drove into Doddan Barrack entrance a security officer dressed in civil clothes was just coming out of the main entrance, and when the man realised who it was behind the wheels he was too surprised that he forgot to close the gate behind him in his haste to alert others of Fela's presence.

We took the opportunity of this confusion to quickly carry the coffin into the State House courtyard, where we deposited it and walked back into our waiting buses. It took us less than five minutes to do this and return to our respective seats in the two buses. Picture of this memorable event was captured by Femi Bankole Osunla for Africa 70 photo agency and used on the album cover of Coffin for Head of State.

A few minutes after however, there was this sound of the military horn (called biggle) calling all the military in the adjacent barracks to assemble. Those on duty and the rest that were off-duty, were hastily gathered and armoured ferrets with heavy machine guns hastily took position between the coffin and us in the waiting busses outside the gate.

There were soldiers who recognised Fela, and were menacing us saying we had the guts to come that far? Promising us it would be our end for disrespecting the military institution, while there were others among them that were pro-Fela calming the aggressive soldiers: "Fela na our man!"

"Fela is our man" they shouted to their aggressive colleagues.

The army Captain who was sent by Obasanjo to verbally invite Fela for a meeting with the then Head of State, before the burning down of Kalakuta was one of those pro-Fela soldiers who openly declared support for and placed himself protectively between Fela and his aggressors. Not long after, Fela was taken away by the army Captain and some of his pro-Fela colleagues, this gave the aggressive soldiers remaining to take-out their frustrations on the rests of us in the two buses.

We were frog-matched and beating into waiting prison cells at the Brigade of Guards (presidential guards) headquarters near bye. We were all (including Fela), later transferred to Onikan Police Station on Awolowo road Ikoyi, where we were detained for two days until the official handing over of power from Obasanjo to Shehu Shagari had been completed.

With a civilian government in power, Fela and 56 other members arrested were charge to court for action likeable to bring the breach of the peace and the presiding judge in the case Mr. Fela Young granted all of us bail and we were released. Picture of all arrested persons, stepping out of the famous police truck named Black Maria also taken by Femi Osunla, was used in the album design of Coffin For Head of State. Coffin for Head of State was a parting gift from Fela, to a corrupt and dictatorial regime.

After handing over to a civilian regime, General Obasanjo would later try to give an impression of him internationaly as a democrat. However his track record in the military and as Head of State can only fool those who overlook this period of his rule in Nigeria.

Also as part of a survival move after our return from Germany, broke without means to continue to finace his organization, Fela sent an emissary to Miriam Makeba in Guinea. The South African singer, had proposed to Fela at their meeting back-stage in Berlin to contact her if there was anything she could do for him in his struggle.

Returning to Nigeria after Berlin, the militlary government had begun their transition to civil rule programme. The decade long ban on politics was finally lifted and people could "freely" make political alliances.

Fela was 'broke' despite the US $100,000 he was paid for the Berlin concerts. He had spent a large part of the fee paid him for his appearance at the festival, to cover expenses during the two week trip and he couldn't afford to pay salaries of members of his organisation anymore. Members of his entourage for example had to eat from a collective pot, no money to buy cars and he had to hire public transport if we needed to travel.

Gone were the days when he could print and distribute for free the YAP News. Added to our problems this time around in keeping with government regulations, we needed a licence to import newsprint. Since YAP as a movement had been proscribed by the departing military regime, we could not afford to continued to print YAP news even with a new name. It was certain we never could get the necessary permit to publish.

Meanwhile, the printing machine paid for by Fela before the burning down of Kalakuta, was temporarily stored in the basement of the building he was still constructing on Gbemisola Street in Ikeja. While in Ghana, Fela had an arrangement with Tunji Braithwaite to build on the land he bought from Tony Allen's father, and his lawyer's construction company had only built the basement while the going was good with Fela.

But work stopped on the site after their separation of ways. With all these accumulated problems enumerated earlier, Fela couldn't keep on financing his political movements, so we decided to look for support outside.

Fela sent Steve Udah, his press attaché to contact Miriam Makeba in Conakry in order to ask what she could do for us. During the transition from military to civil rule, since YAP was proscribed by the military regime behind the so-called transition, we decided to name our political party Movement of the People (MOP).

With more than fifty-thousand people in attendance at a rally during the launching of the movement held at the Tafawa Balewa Square on the Lagos Island, a signal was sent to the military regime that Fela was not "done" yet. Though most Nigerian intellectuals, academics, and elites of the era did not take him seriously, Fela was really popular in Nigeria. Anywhere he went in public accompanied most times by a huge entourage, people could be seen with their clenched fists salute in the air shouting his name "Fela Baba!

Fela, the Black President!" Permit a quick digression to give two examples here, during a 1974 Jimmy Cliff concert at the National Stadium Suru-Lere, Fela accompanied by his large entourage walked into the presidential stand at the stadium, and soon as he was spotted, the crowd rushed towards him with their fist clenched in the Black Power salute.

He was carried shoulder high to the centre of the field, doing a tour of honour around the stadium before heading to the centre where the crowd milling around the Jamaican star deserted the stage area to join in the celebration with Fela on the people's shoulder. The second incidence I would like to site took place in the same stadium in 1975 during the finals of the African Cup of Champion Club, a football(soccer) match between the Hafia Club of Guinea and the Enugu Rangers of Nigeria.

General Yakubu Gowon (the then Head of State), was in the Presidential stand and shortly before the march was to commence Fela walked into the presidential stand. The uproar of the public shouting Fela's name, momentarily drew the public attention towards him forcing the huge crowd to stand-up including Gowon to try and have a glimpse of Fela.

Despite this huge public appeal, most of the Nigerian elite try to overlook this phenomenal aspect of the man. Some people close to Fela like Steve Udah, whom one can describe as a product of the Nigerian neo-colonial system did not take Fela seriously. They are people with white Christian values, who still look down on some aspects of their traditions as primitive in comparison to 'modern' western mannerisms.

With his journalistic background Steve couldn't understand, why Fela would prefer my not too classic approach to writing scripts for example to his Nigerian standard journalism style. From Steve's point of view, YAP News should be presented in the same manner as other leading Nigerian newspapers: 'Daily Times', 'New Nigerian', 'Punch', etc.

As a result, he couldn't see the essence in our attempt at not being poor imitations of the 'New York Times, London Daily Mirror, or the France Soir' like other so-called leading Nigerian News papers tend to look.

For him YAP News media-outlook, should be presented like the medias mentioned above if we want to be taken seriously. But Fela and we YAP boys consider this attitude as a "house-slave" syndrome, a process where success is measured by how much assimilated the person is in 'modern' Western mannerisms. Take for example intellectuals like Wole Soyinka who unwittingly concede that Africans are "savages" by saying: "I prefer to show my Tigre-tude than negritude".

Statements such as this does not take into consideration facts of history, that states without any doubts that while Europe was still being inhabited by a roaming band of barbarians, a wonderful civilisation was flourishing along the banks of the Nile and Great Lake region. I believe that some of these intellectuals are aware of this information, but are too far gone in the neo-colonial system to accept them as facts of our history.

It is a house-slave mentality or syndrome. Steve Udah would drink large quantities of beer, because society accepts it as a form of socialisation, but if you smoke a joint within the same setting to him you are anti-social. I guess he was the wrong person to send on the mission to Guinea. Instead of sending Steve Udah, maybe Ekow or JK would have manage to get in touch with Miriam Makeba instead of being deported on the next available plane to Lagos as Steve was.

He spoke no word in French, and as he admitted to Fela he arrived in Conakry announcing to the immigration officer on duty that he was on a mission to see Miriam Makeba adding he was Fela's Press Attaché. A little discretion is required in such situation, particularly in a closed state as that of Guinea.

For a closed country like Guinea it was too much show–off. Steve was refused entry and was sent back to Lagos on the next available flight. Not long after this failed trip by Steve, the Guinea Ambassador in Nigeria contacted Fela inviting him to meet with President Ahmed Sekou Toure at the Embassy situated on Victoria Island during the president's state visit to Nigeria.

However, the Obasanjo regime would do everything to make the meeting impossible. Fela was waiting at the Guinean Embassy in Victoria Island as earlier arranged with the Ambassador, who had gone to the airport to receive the visiting head of state.

Kwame Toure (Stockley Carmichael) pictured sitting second from right during one of his visits to Fela sitting right.
Picture by Femi Bankole Osunla Africa 70 Photo Agency

Many years after my departure from Fela's Organization, I met Miriam Makeba in Zurich and we talked about Fela and our attempt to contact her in Guinea.
She ended our discussion with this beautiful authograph below.

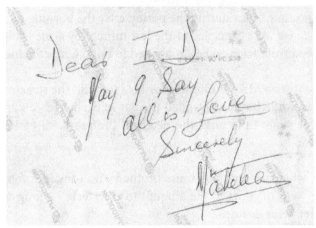

The Nigerian Government despite being aware of other engagements at the Embassy awaiting President Sekou Toure, used state protocol to keep the visiting President from living the state reception. Suspecting that the Nigerian authority might be blocking this meeting, Fela drove to the State House along Marina road where the reception for the visiting Head of State was taking place, but he was prevented by State security agents from gate-crashing the "party". He returned to his Ikeja home after a mission impossible.

However, since the President of Guinea's visit to Nigeria was short he delegated Kwame Toure (Stockley Carmichael) on exile in Guinean and in the Presidential entourage, to see Fela explaining why they couldn't meet. Kwame Toure would later explain that protocol, was the reason why the meeting with the President of Guinea couldn't take place. He visited Fela on several occasions after - whenever he passed through Lagos and he discussed with us ways of collaboration with his All African Peoples Revolutionary Party.

THE IKEJA AFRICA SHRINE

From Afro Spot (formerly Suru-Lere Night Club), to the first Africa Shrine (formerly Empire Club) situated fifty meters away from his burnt down Kalakuta Republic home - the history of the 'Shrine' continues. Shortly after his return from the Berlin tour, Mike Binite an architect friend and concert promoter proposed to Fela to use a parcel of land belonging to his (Binite) family on Pepple Street in Ikeja to construct a new Shrine.

Mike Binite had tried unsuccessfully to organise concerts featuring Fela in different venues around Lagos during the period after the burning down of Kalakuta, but the shows were cancelled at the last minute by armed soldiers. With money borrowed from friends, Fela managed to build a new Shrine in Ikeja.

His arrangement with Mike Binite was for Fela to build the structure and take all the gate fees, while Binite controlled the bar in exchange - an arrangement that worked for some time until the death of the patriarch of Binite family many years later.

The land was 'willed' to another Binite brother who wanted it for something else hence, he went to court in the attempt to evict Fela - a long process that lasted until after Fela's death.

Meanwhile, Fela and his new musical out-fit named Egypt 80, continued to perform as resident band in the new Shrine and despite two years of lay-off, harrowing and anguish from the departed military regimes, he was able to stage a come-back making Ikeja his base.

The transition to civil rule had just taken place 1st, October 1979. General Obasanjo handed over the reigns of power to Shehu Shagari, who contested the elections on the platform of National Party of Nigeria (NPN) the party from the Hausa north. Obafemi Awolowo's Unity Party of Nigeria (UPN) won the election in Yoruba dominated west, while Dr. Nnamdi Azikiwe's Nigerian Peoples Party (NPP) won in the Igbo dominated east. Like the situation at independence with the first civilian government, Shagari had to reach-out to NPP to be able to form a government with federal representation.

After thirteen years of military rule (or better misrule), Nigeria has come full circle from where it left off. The reader would see why Fela called this an Army Arrangement. The political founding fathers of the country were kicked out in 1966 for their regional and corrupt politics, replaced by successive military regimes, that plunged the country into three and half years of civil war and later they divided the Federation into twelve states. Now in 1979, a new democratically elected civilian regime is put in place to replace the army, all the registered parties formed again along the old three-region federation style of the 60's.

All the academics and intellectuals who had served under various military administrations (state or federal), became members of or supporters of the new political formations prompting another song from Fela critical of the transition to civil rule titled: JUST LIKE THAT. A song that is a call to arms from him, to all Africans to rise up and do something about the political, economic, social and cultural retrogression, that has plagued the continent since independence. For more than three decades of independence there is glaring mismanagement of people's lives, corruption in the highest echelon of government, and all these carried out with impunity 'Just Like That' Fela sang.

Using the Nigerian experience as an example of the 'lack of maintenance culture' in Africa's present day neo-colonial administration he sang: "White man ruled us for many years we had electricity constantly, our leaders take over, No electricity in town-Just Like That!"

Fela explains, that the attempt to transplant 'Western style democracy' in African society is the cause of all the problems. Instead of heeding Nkrumah's call for African Unity, Nigeria's political founding fathers like most African leaders at independence, chose the option of fashioning the constitutions of their respective countries after those of the departing colonial 'masters'. The ambiguity of such decisions, can be seen in the poor imitation we make of our attempt at 'Western style democracy'.

Persistent political gangster-like way of governing, military coups, and sometimes wars, are means used to enforce the already compromised constitutions. Fela sings about another example of enforcing a fragile constitution, according to him in 1966 Nigeria fought a civil war to keep the country ONE and in the name of "unity" General Gowon the military head of state, divided Nigeria into twelve administrative regions. Subsequent military administrations, have further divided these regions to 19 and later 36 states - Just Like That he exclaim.

Fela adds that if the idea of the civil war was to keep the country ONE, sub-dividing Nigeria into more regions would separate rather than unite the country. Turning to the position of traditional rulers in the mess called government, he sang: "...nothing good for town to give the youth good examples! How our traditional ruler they do! Them come make youths look-up to Europe and USA! In those places them don loose them common sense! Na the number of Nuclear weapons you get na him give you power pass! Right now! Fight now! Suffer must stop! Just LikeThat!"

Translated: "there is nothing in town to give the youth's good examples, the traditional rulers who as custodians of tradition are supposed to show the way but because of their new acquired values, they make the youths of Africa look-up to Europe and the USA" for cultural inspirstion. Fela says in those places too, they have lost their common sense because it is the number of nuclear weapons and guns you have that determines how strong you are. In conclusion, he calls on the people to fight now for a better society and to put an end to their sufferings.

From all indications, Fela's message was not destined for the Africans shores alone as thing were turning around him. Shortly after the change in Nigeria to a civilian administration, he was invited with his band to headline the annual Italian Communist Party Festival - DE UNITA.

He was billed to perform with his band Egypt 80 in key Italian cities - an opportunity to internationalise his struggle. The festival would have afforded him the opportunity to link his Pan-Africa struggle back home, with the International Communist Workers struggle and this international setting I believe, would have enhanced his political standing.

Considering again, the "insiders" warning from Louis Farrakhan earlier mentioned in the events that led to the Nigerian Army attack on Kalakuta, an international political statue for Fela would not go well with any Nigerian government - the new civilian regime inclusive.

Fela was convinced the Nigerian governement in collaboration with American Central Intelligence Agency (CIA), tried to set-him-up with marijuana traffic in-order to discredit him politically as a "drug trafficker". The role played by Susan Findlay, an African-American helped convinced him of the CIA theory.

Susan Findlay got acquainted with Fela and members of his organisation through Lindsay Barrett, a Jamaican born naturalised Nigerian journalist with whom she had a close relationship. Lindsay wrote stories for various Nigerian newspapers as freelance journalist, and he frequented Fela's shrine regularly during FESTAC in company of Susan who had a "daughter" with him – this was her claim.

They kept regular visits to the new Shrine in Ikeja after Kalakuta was burnt down and even after her separation from Lindsay Barrett, Susan kept friendly relation with some of Fela's wives occasionally leaving her toddler daughter with some of the women when she needed to go shopping.

As a policy within the Africa 70 Organization, non-members of the organisation have regularly accompanied Fela and his group during their numerous travels within and outside Nigeria. This invitation to Italy, was no exception as various fans who could afford the air ticket were officially listed with air Italia the airline reserved to take the group to Milan the first stop during the Communist party festival tour.

Soon as she got wind of the coming tour, Susan demanded from Fela if she could travel with the group and I was asked by him to include her name on the list.

One week before the departure date of the group for Italy, Susan Findlay informed some of Fela's wives that she wanted to rush to the United States to leave her young daughter in her mother's care in-order to give her more freedom during the month's long tour. Also to show gratitude to some of Fela's wives with whom she had established close relationship particularly those who occasionally helped her with her daughter, she promised to bring-back nice suitcases that they could travel to Italy with.

The day before our departure for Italy, Susan Findlay returned to Lagos with seven suitcases and she invited seven of Fela's wives to her residence to hand-over the suitcases as she had earlier promised.

All these was happening among friends and un-known to the women, the suitcases were pre-lined in the interior with forty-three point five (43.5) kilos of marijuana. To enhance easy displacement of luggage and personnel with seventy people travelling, Sami Ojomo the Shrine manager was delegated the duty of checking-in the luggage of all members and getting all the necessary boarding passes.

He was at the airport on time, and had checked-in more than seventy suitcases belonging to the travelling members of the organisation. Not long after, Fela's valet arrived at the airport asking Ojomo to retrieve the suitcase containing Fela's shoes, according to the valet there was a specific pare of shoes Fela had chosen to wear during the voyage which he (the valet) had erroneously packed with other shoes.

Ojomo who was aware that Fela was running late before departure time, told the valet the entire luggage had been checked-in and he sent him (the valet) back with the message that Fela should hurry-up because he was delaying the plane's departure.

With Nigeria's communication system in a mess like he indicated in his song 'Upside Down', there was no way to communicate this to Fela by phone hence the valet had to rush back home in a taxi with the message - an exercise that would take the best part of an hour in the crawling Lagos traffic. Meanwhile, after waiting for more than an hour for Fela and his entourage, the Air Italia airline pilot left with the entire checked-in luggage of the group unaccompanied.

When Fela finally arrived at the airport, the airline's agents at the airport couldn't do anything for us as the flight was the last of flights scheduled for Europe from Lagos for that day. We all had to go searching, for another airline carrier that could take the large group at a short notice. Finally we managed to arrange something for the next morning with KLM, a flight to Amsterdam with connection later in the day to Milan.

Next morning, we were all at the airport on time including Fela, and since we didn't have any luggage it was relatively easy to handle travel arrangements for the seventy passengers from Africa 70 Organisation.

On our arrival in Amsterdam, we could only secure fifty-six seats on the next and last flight to Milan for that day. The airline agents, assured us that the fourteen remaining passengers could travel on the first available flight the next day.

Meanwhile, Fela chose to remain behind with the last group which included me and as he accompanied the fifty-six members in transit to the boarding gate where they were to take their flight, he asked me to contact the Italian organisers to inform them of the impending arrival of our advance party.

From the moment we missed our flight in Lagos, we didn't have the time to call our Italian agents because of the running around we had to do to secure seats on another flight at short notice. Moreover we got back to our Ikeja residence so late that day, as a result I couldn't go to NITEL office to call the organisers in Italy.

Remember that we didn't have phone at home, because of all the corruption in high places that prevents basic services from being made available to the masses. Another reason why we didn't call was that we assumed Egidio Pastori, one of those responsible for our trip in Italy would be at the airport to meet us and it was useless to call his home hence we had previewed calling him from Amsterdam.

Soon as I got through to him on the phone, he recognised my voice and he asked me where I was calling from? I replied Amsterdam and his next statement was: "Don't come to Italy! The police have discovered 43.5 kilos of marijuana in your group's luggage".

I quickly hung-up telling him I would call back. I didn't have time to explain to him that fifty-six members of the organization were about to board the transit flight to Milan, I had to hurry to the boarding gate to stop them from taking the flight. At the boarding gate, all the passengers were aboard except JK who was having a last briefing from Fela, I broke in on their conversation giving them the bad news.

Fela immediately decided against letting those members aboard to leave, and we informed the nearest air hostess of our decision, insisting we all preferred to travel as a group. In return, the air hostess cautioned us that we might have difficulty in getting seats next day for all of us together and to drive the point home, she insisted the airline wouldn't be responsible for the accommodation of the fifty-six in Amsterdam if we refused to take the offered seats.

Meanwhile, Fela had gone aboard asking all Africa 70 members to descend, and we immediately organised transport to take us to the nearest hotel. We checked into the Hotel Okura International close to the airport. At the hotel, we were able to cover our hotel expenses totalling five thousand Naira (exchanged for about US $7,000) in cash.

At this point, I will like to digress a little because all through this volume I have been stating the value of the Nigerian currency in comparison to the America Dollar. During this period until the devaluation of the Naira in 1985, the Nigerian currency was stronger than the American Dollar in the world foreign exchange market.

Since the devaluation and the introduction of austerity measures in Nigeria in the 80's by successive military regimes and kept in place till now, very few Nigerian citizens can afford to feed themselves with the basic staple food - same goes for other African population.

The mismanagement of the Nigerian economy by succesive regimes paved the way for the devaluation and all the austerity measures that have lead to cuts in all social services almost inexistent in our society. Excuse the digression, as it is important for the reader to see how the powers that be have conspired to keep Africa and her people down.

Returning to the story of Fela and the attempt to sabotage our trip to Italy, at a meeting hurriedly organised in Fela's hotel room, we started to question every travelling member of the organisation to find-out who had taken marijuana with them.

The questioning was done by Fela and JK, with the YAP boys in attendance. During our investigation, one of Fela's wives who had the knowledge that Susan had given suitcases to some of his wives raised the question about the possibility of the suitcases containing marijuana. The women she gave suitcases, were called-in a second time for questionings and all of them admitted being given suitcases but to their knowledge the cases were empty when she handed them to each recipient. At this point, we had to call-in Susan and Fela asked her if she had some marijuana in her suitcase to which she answered in the affirmative.

Fela asked how much quantity and she replied "a little!" He again asked her if it was true she gave suitcases to some of his wives and if they contained "a little" marijuana like hers? At this point she admitted lining the inside of eight suitcases with marijuana. She also claimed she had the intention of collecting back the suitcases from the seven women in Italy, with the hope of buying them new suitcases after selling the 'weed'.

During our interrogation we found-out she had gone the previous week to the United States, one of us in the room asked her if she was paid to set-up Fela, but she denied it vehemently claiming she worked alone. We asked her if her trip to America, was connected with a re-call by her CIA handlers for briefings. She denied this too, saying she went to leave her toddler daughter in her mother's care. Though it was clear to us she was not telling us all she knew, we had problems dealing with the situation. Her origin did not permit Fela to hand her freely to white police whom he considered could treat her in a racist manner.

Despite the trouble she had created for Fela and the rest of the group, her African origin did not permit Fela to hand her freely to white police whom he considered could treat her in a racist manner. Susan on the other hand, wanted to be handed over to the Italian police - saying she was ready to admit ownership of all the suitcases.

Apart from the need for an official investigation, Fela still felt he couldn't hand her over to the police. Meanwhile, he decided that we needed to contact our press friends in Amsterdam to make the Italian police aware that he voluntarily chose to continue his journey to Italy knowing from Amsterdam of their alleged "discovery."

A press conference, was hastily organised at the Amsterdam Schipol Airport for early next morning before our scheduled flight to Milan. Addressing the assembled journalist at the airport departure lounge, Fela claimed knowledge of the 'alleged marijuana burst' stressing he was on his way to confront the Italian authorities regarding this. The press statement, destined for world-wide release would coincide with the departure from Amsterdam of fifty-six members of our group for Milan.

Fela had instructed JK at the head of the group, to inform the Italian police that he was on his way with the last batch of fourteen passengers that included himself, Susan, and the YAP boys. We arrived in Milan, two hours after the arrival of JK and other members of our advance party. We all went towards immigration booth like every passenger on board the flight from Amsterdam, some immigration officials called-out to members of Fela's entourage to step aside from other passengers indicating a pre-arranged reception area a little away from other in-coming passengers.

An English speaking Italian immigration officer, collected all fourteen passports and he instructed us to proceed to identify our luggage that had arrived two days earlier. Fela speaking on behalf of all fourteen, told the immigration officer that he was aware of their alleged "discovery" but before he would authorise any member of his organisation to identify any luggage, he would like the following to be present:
1. The pilot of the Air Italia flight from Lagos.
2. The airline crew aboard the plane.
3. All the immigration officers who carried out the search on the unaccompanied baggage.

Since it was impossible to assemble all these people within the time limit, the Italian police and Immigration authorities were faced with a dilemma. All fourteen passengers, were allowed to join other members of the group who had arrived earlier while they deliberated answer to Fela's request.

Untill now everything seems to go according to the law but as we realised shortly after the plane touched down, Fela's judgement of the Italian police of possible racist attitude was not out of place. Complains from most of his wives from treatments they received from the police and immigration confirmed this position.

Those of them who wanted to use the toilet, were body-searched before being authorised and those who refused the body-search were ordered to use the toilet with the door open. Fela made a big fuss about this to the Italian officers, and he claimed his queens should be treated with some respect. Already compromised by the search on the unaccompanied luggage, they were unable to intimidate Fela.

The police and immigration officers were thus forced on the defensive. Unable to arrest any member of the group, particularly since they couldn't force us to identify our luggage and with valid entry permits the Italian authorities were obliged to let us in. Waiting outside in the arrival hall, were about two hundred journalist and photographers who had got news of our intended arrival in Milan from Fela's earlier press conference in Amsterdam.

This helped fuel their curiosity, as the consensus from the Italian print media was no-show after a widely covered press release from the police the day before said that: "following the discovery of 43.5 kilos of marijuana in the luggage of the musician Fela Kuti, his appearance at this year's Communist Party Festival is very doubtful".

The news of his arrival in Milan, inflamed the entire Italian press as flash bulbs were going-off in quick successions when Fela and his entourage stepped into the arrival hall. Some members of the organising committee of the tour, quickly piloted us into waiting buses and this would provoke a chain of car chase from the journalist and unmarked police cars that followed us around.

We had missed the Milan concert scheduled for the day before, so we headed for Napoli where we were billed to appear that night. It was a fantastic concert in an open air stadium with about twenty-five thousand people in attendance.

With the group's luggage still in the hands of the immigration authority, Fela and members of the band had to perform with the same suites and clothes they had been travelling in. However, this did not alter the impact of the music on the audience.

Napoli, reminded us a lot of Lagos a sea side city with clothe-lines hanging out in public view like we do in Lagos. Also the public was extremely warm, dancing to the vibrating rhythm of afrobeat music and people from the public offered for free, marijuana to members of the group during and after the concert.

With a big reputation for the good quality of Nigeria grass (marijuana) in Italy, the consensus from the public was that it was sad that 43.5 kilos of good 'weed' from Nigeria should be seized by the police. Our attempts to assure them, that we didn't try to export marijuana seem not to sink in.

During his performance, Fela in his habitual 'yabbis' tried to assure the public that 43.5 kilos of grass was not his idea of marijuana traffic. According to him, if he would go into such traffic he would rather have cargo plane loads and not suitcases as he was alleged to by the police. This drew loud ovation from the public, and it was a beautiful concert with positive reviews in the press the following day. The group, returned to Milan the following day to do a hastily organised concert in the suburb of Milan. It was organised to replace the previously cancelled concert.

Organised in a sporting complex, the crowd was warm with same reaction as in Napoli - they all expressed regrets at the seizure of what they assumed to be the group's supply of weed. Like in Napoli, more marijuana were offered to members of the group and we returned to the hotel in Milan after the concert with something to smoke for those in the group who smoke.

Unknown to members of the group, plain clothe Italian anti-drug squad had checked into all the vacated rooms, leaving members of Fela's organisation and the police as the only guests in the hotel. At about seven a.m. the following morning, armed with the rooming list from the hotel management the police knocked violently on all the doors from members of Africa 70 shouting "Policia". I quickly got dressed telling the police in English, that he should wait a minute for my girl-friend to dress-up before I opened the door.

This gave us time to flush down the toilet, the little weed we brought back from the concert the night before. Clean at last, I opened the door of my hotel room a few meters away from Fela's.

My partner and I were asked for our passports and we were immediately ordered to step-out in the hotel corridor while one of the plain-cloth policemen went into the room to do a quick search. While he was at it, I saw Fela standing naked at the entrance of his hotel room in a conversation with other plain-clothe men. He wouldn't let them into his room, claiming he had one of his wives in there trying to get dressed.

One of the men who identified himself as Joe and was speaking with an American accent, insisted in fluent English that Fela should get dressed and accompany them to the police station.

Infuriated by his aggressive and arrogant manner, Fela remarked that he had never in his life walked into any police station, adding that if they wanted him to go with them they would have to carry him. In an attempt at more intimidation, Joe threatened to knock Fela's teeth-in if he did not co-operate with the police.

Rather than being intimidated the plain clothe police man's remark infuriated Fela, forcing him to observe that he thought the Italian law was based on some kind of modern civilisation. He threatened that if the police lay their hands on him, the Italian government would pay a heavy compensation from the courts.

At a signal from one of the plain-clothe men four of them rushed Fela who remained naked at the entrance to his room, they wrapped a towel from the hotel around him and they half dragged half carried him out into a waiting car. All the other members of the group, were marched with the police closely watching into waiting cars.

The operation involved fifty-six police cars, as we were all driven to the Central police Station in Milan. Still wrapped in a hotel towel Fela was detained in a closed glass porto-cabin and some of the police men around, were seen trying with some gesticulation, to persuade him to put-on the clothes they recovered earlier from his room after their search.

Despite the presence of a lawyer claiming to have been recommended to represent Fela by the party, we felt that the Communist party was starting to distant themselves from Fela. This lawyer would later approach Fela, trying like the police men to persuade him to dress-up.

Convinced finaly to put on his dress, the lawyer accompanied Fela to the prison for preliminary investigations and audition before an Italian magistrate who held Fela as leader of the group responsible for all the suitcases and what they contained. He ordered, that Fela should be detained in the prison until members of the group complied with the baggage identification required by the Italian immigration.

With no other option, the lawyer returned to the police station with the instruction for members of the group to proceed to the airport to identify their luggage.

He insisted that it was the only condition that Fela would be allowed out. We were all driven to Milan Feumicino Airport where we identified our luggage. Susan Findlay, claimed the eight suitcases in question and she was immediately arrested by the police. All other members of Fela's entourage, were released and we were handed back our passports.

If we hadn't turned-up late at the Lagos airport, we would all probably have been arrested and while we are in jail Susan would be free with the intervention from the American embassy on her behalf. Thanks to Fela's valet and all that shoe business, we probably would have remained in the dark as to who planted the marijuana in the group's luggage.

Since the Communist Party was taking their distance from Fela, most of the other shows we were scheduled to perform were cancelled and we were reduced to live at the mercy of hastily organised charity. Without the means to pay our bills, we couldn't return to the hotel and we were subsequently lodged in student's hostels where we were obliged to vacate our rooms at 8 a.m. every morning. With little to do but wait while investigation was on, we were obliged to stay-out the day in the nearby Milan central park. Meanwhile, the Italian authority contacted the American Embassy and a lawyer was sent to Milan to represent Susan.

According to information from the lawyer that represented Fela, she pleaded guilty to trafficking but made a plea-bargain to be deported from Italy because she had a little daughter waiting for her in the United States. She was in detention for about three weeks before she was finally deported to the US.

Fela was shortly after her arrest released with a signed statement from the Italian Justice Ministry, completely absolving him and members of his entourage with drug trafficking.

But the political damage was done already, as none of the left-wing leaning Italian politicians wanted to be associated with Fela. With no money to pay hotel bills, some lodging was found in an old castle not too far from Florence for all members of the group. The irony of our stay in this castle was our discovery of black faces painted on the wall of the main hall a testimony to the ancient proprietors of the castle.

The castle is another confirmation of the African presence in Rome before and during the "glorious" Roman Empire. Just before the group returned to Lagos, Fela was presented to a journalist from London New Musical Express Vivien Goldman. She did an interview that was published in the magazine, and also presented Martin Meissonier a young French citizen, who would later propose to organise a tour in France for Fela after this trip in Italy.

On our return flight back to Lagos in what looked like coincidence, Fela was sitting next to a Lagos State Commissioner of Police who claimed he was returning to Lagos from vacation in Italy. Coincidence or not, there was no doubt of an international conspiracy to sabotage Fela's tour in Italy. He returned to his Ikeja base, playing his usual four times a week gigs.

Tuesday nights he called "LADIES NIGHT" and all women went in for free and Friday nights was "YABBIS NIGHT", during these shows Fela openly named and criticised members of government and their policies.

Saturday night "COMPREHENSIVE SHOW" he performed with his band dressed up in uniform and he usually took time off during the show, to worship the departed souls of African ancestors in the struggle.

"Sunday JUMP" designed to reach out to the young who cannot go out all night, an afternoon affair that starts at four in the evening till ten p.m. The construction of his new shrine in Ikeja and his tour to Italy promised a new horizon for Fela, but the system would not let it be as we have seen. While Berlin was a controversial tour, Italy that could have given him international political standing was sabotaged.

Towards the end of 1979, Daily Times of Nigeria through their leisure services department, organised a nation wide Nigerian tour with Fela headlining for Roy Ayers and his 'Ubiquitous'. Despite the tour being financially a disaster, in terms of media attention and public turn-out it was a big success. At the end of the tour, Fela and Roy recorded a joint album titled "MUSIC OF MANY COLOURS".

On the "B" side of this album, Roy Ayers did a song titled "2000 Black". The African American vibraphone player expressed the hope that by the time the year 2000 comes around he hoped that Africa would be free and unite.

Africa Centre of the world was Fela's contribution on the "A" side, a song about Africa being the cradle of today's civilisation. Recorded, twenty-one years after he left the Nigerian shores to study music at London Trinity College of Music. Fela in this song, tried to project what he called the ignorance of the Western world about Africa and her history.

According to him, Englishmen who were not aware of the ape-like origin of man used to come-over to him to find-out if he got a tail like apes and monkeys. For him, it is only ignorance that could be the reason for such dumb questions. He points to Africa's place at the centre of the world map as not by accident rather because Africans were the first people on earth. Territory has been man's major reason for going to war, if Africans occupy the best area in the world with good climate and fertile soil this cannot be archived by accident.

Africans must have been the strongest people on earth, to occupy the centre of the world he affirmed. The question that needed to be asked is "Were African ancestors ruling themselves before the White man and the Arabs came?" Before "white" standards and values became the nom and yard-stick to judge a civilised person in the name of an education?

Fela sings in this song, that Africans have been subjected to various diversions and irrelevancies knowing more of the colonial education to the detriment of our traditional values and education. He also sang about the effects of religion on the mentality of Africans in the song "SHUFFERING & SHMILING "(Suffering and Smiling):

"Suffer suffer for world!
(Chorus)   Amen!
Enjoy for Heaven!
(Chorus)   Amen!
Christians go dey yap 'In Spiritum Heavinus'
(Chorus)   Amen!
Moslems go dey call 'Allah wa Akbar'
(Chorus)   Amen!
Open your eyes everywhere
Archbishop Nah miliki (miliki in Yoruba means – to have a good time)
Pope Nah enjoyment
Imam Nah gbaladun (in Yoruba – to enjoy)
(Chorus) Archbishop dey enjoy
(Chorus) Pope self dey enjoy
(Chorus) Imam self dey enjoy
(Chorus) My brother wetin you say
My sister wetin you go hear?
Archbishop dey for London
Pope dey for Rome
Imam dey for Mecca
My people them go dey follow Bishop
(Chorus) Amen!
Them go follow Pope
(Chorus) Amen!
Them go 'juba' (Yoruba-'bow to') Imam
(Chorus) Amen!
Them go go for London
(Chorus) Amen!
Them go go for Rome

Fela and Roy Ayers at the Eldorado Cinema concert in Kano.
Photo by Femi Bankole Osunla Africa 70 Photo Agency

(Chorus) Amen!
Them go go for Mecca
(Chorus) Amen!
Them go carry all the money
(Chorus) Amen!
Them go 'juba' Bishop
(Chorus) Amen!
'Juba' Pope
(Chorus) Amen!
Them go start to yab themselves
(Chorus) Amen!
In spiritum Heavinus
(Chorus) Amen!
Allah uh!
(Chorus) Amen!
Every day for house
Every day for road
Every day for bus
Every day for work
My people!
Everyday my people dey inside bus
(Chorus) Suffering and Smiling
Forty-nine sitting Ninety-nine standing
(Chorus) Suffering and Smiling
Them go pack themselves inside like sardine
(Chorus) Suffering and Smiling
Them dey faint them dey wake like Cock
(Chorus) Suffering and Smiling
Them go reach house water no dey
(Chorus) Suffering and Smiling
Them go reach bed power no dey
(Chorus) Suffering and Smiling
Them go reach road go-slow go come
(Chorus) Suffering and Smiling
Them go reach road police go slap
(Chorus) Suffering and Smiling

Them go reach road army go whip
(Chorus)Suffering and Smiling
Them go look pocket money no dey
(Chorus) Suffering and Smiling
Everyday nah the same thing
(Chorus) Suffering and Smiling
Suffer suffer for world!
(Chorus)   Amen!
Enjoy for Heaven!
(Chorus)   Amen!
Christians go dey yab 'In Spiritum Heavinus'
(Chorus) Amen!
Moslems go dey call 'Allah wa Akbar'
(Chorus) Amen!
How many many you go make?
(Chorus) Many! Many!

With a song like Suffering and Smiling, Fela was able to respond to the question: "Were African ancestors ruling themselves before the White man and the Arabs came?" All-over Nigeria during the tour with Roy Ayers, wherever he played the song there was this positive aspect from the public (both Christian and Moslem) that they identified with.

The tour was a success in the sense that Fela re-established his popularity with the public, despite the attempts by the military regime to "kill" his following among the people. Kano was the only city on the tour, where there was violence from the local community against Fela.

Noted for its anti-Western ideas and ideals, the political and religious leadership in Kano have regularly demonstrated their hostility towards Western Christian values and its inherent attitudes. The same double standards prevalent in White Anglo-Saxon protestant (wasp) values, are also common in the Islamic interpretation of what is required of a true Moslem.

That do what I say and not what I do syndrome. Most of them participate and practice what they condemn as Western influence - alcohol, extra-marital sex in private while they condemn it publicly.

For many years, different concerts featuring bands both international and local have been disrupted in Kano in the name of preservation of Islamic values in the city. Miriam Makeba, Kool and The Gang, Third World, have been advertised to perform in venues in Kano only for the concert to be cancelled because of Moslem "extremist" who are opposed to the concert happening.

Like their Saudi Arabia counterparts who condemn the use of alcohol in public but use alcohol in private, many prominent Kano political and religious leaders have demonstrated this double standard for many years. Fela's presence therefore in Kano and his well publicised condemnation of the double standards of religious leaders, was a big test to his popularity outside Lagos.

Eldorado Cinema, the venue reserved for the Daily Times sponsored Fela-Roy Ayers concert in Kano would serve as the base to put this popularity into test. Open-roof venues are common in Africa because of the hot tropical climate, but at the same time this architectural design makes such venues vulnerable from external attack from those intent on distrupting activities inside. The stage was set, and the cinema hall was packed with people anxious to see Fela and Roy perform.

Shortly after Roy started to perform, broken bottles, stones, were flying into the crowded cinema hall from young Moslem activist opposed to what they termed Western corruption of an Islamic society, causing the crowd to scurry in safety flights.

The news of this attack reached Fela in the hotel and Fela who had the habit of driving his cars, hastily moved into the 'Nissan' bus with all his entourage and drove quickly in a convoy of buses that had accompanied us from Lagos. We numbered about a thousand men.

Armed with specially prepared weapons known in Kalakuta as "Mau Mau weapon"- a piece of wood, specially crafted with a thing handle and a round head about an arms length, crowned with nails with their caps cut-off to give point sharp heads. On our arrival in-front of the Eldorado cinema, all the boys who accompanied Fela, filed out forming a circle round the cinema hall. With the "Mau Mau weapons," we went after the young extremist attempting to disrupt the concert - it was a war.

They were all chased away from the Eldorado Cinema vicinity, and were kept away within a distance of about two hundred meters radios from the venue. It was no 'cinema' as Kano City street–hoods met their match and even superiors as they would admit calling Fela and his people "manafiki" meaning "evil" in Hausa language.

Alhaji Mahmood Dantata a Kano prince, popularly known as «Govementi or Government» because of his powerful influence in the city and reputed to be the 'don' behind the extremist, when informed of the fight-back from Fela and his entourage personally came and invited Fela and his group to perform at his West African Pilgrims Association (WAPA) House club at the heart of Kano ancient city to make peace.

This invitation was symbolic because it signified, Fela's acceptance and respect from the Moslem North, despite his open condemnation of the influence of Islam and Christianity.

For Fela's son Femi, the trip to Kano served as double "baptism," he started to play the alto-saxophone in his father's band and the clash with the extremist in Kano provided the young Kuti the possibility to prove to his father how much street-wise he had become at sixteen.

Femi, who had chosen to quit school earlier in the year following his inability to make the right grades required to promote him to the fifth and final year chose to play music as a professional. I remember accompanying Fela with the young Femi, to his school principal at Igbobi College. He (principal), was firm on his position not to promote Femi into the next class because the young man didn't have the necessary grade.

According to the school principal, if he promote's Femi to the fifth class with his low grades it would oblige him to do the same with the other students with much higher grades than Femi.

Judging from the way Fela accepted the position of the school principal without any coment for or against, it was clear that he accompanied his son more as a gest to give pleasure to the young man than actually using his popularity to influence the school principal.

On our way back home, faced with the reality of Femi's poor marks at school, Fela in his liberal manner asked Femi if he wanted to repeat his class as the principal suggested.

The young man said he did not want to repeat his class, insisting on wanting to play music professionally. On our arrival at home Fela gave him an alto saxophone, but he had to learn the hard way by practically teaching himself the instrument. Femi spent most of 1979, learning to play the alto sax and the tour with Roy Ayers finally gave him the opportunity to play in his father's band.

He was also on the front-line, resisting with Kalakuta «army» against the Islamic fanatics that tried to disrupt the Fela / Roy show at the Eldorado Cinema in Kano - a big platform for the young Femi to prove to his father how much street-wise he had become at sixteen.

Back cover album design Coffin For Head of State

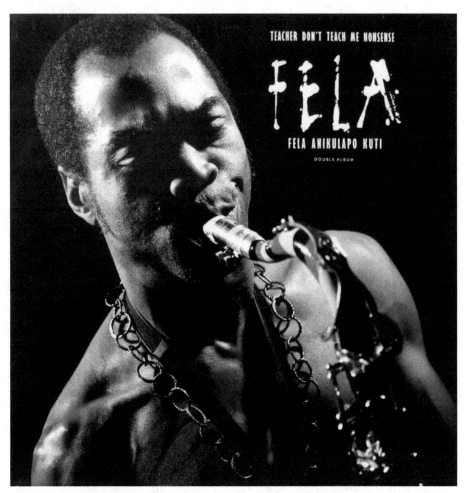

Front cover album design Teacher Don't Teach Me Nonsense

TEACHER, DON'T TEACH ME NONSENSE.

Fela, in the song 'Teacher Don't Teach Me Nonsense' explains the role of the teacher in any society with the concept that 'all the things we consider as problematic and all the good things we accept from life begin with what we are taught. According to him, the individual teaching begins when we are children and our respective mothers are our teachers. When we become of school age, our teacher is the school-teacher and at the university the lecturers and professors are our teachers.

After university when we start to work, government becomes the individual's teacher promting him to ask: "Who is government's teacher? Culture and Tradition - says Fela. As for him this should be the order of things everywhere in the world. However, in this song it is the problem side of teacher and student that is of interest to Fela.

He states that everywhere else in this world except Africa, it is the respective culture and tradition of that country that guides the government how to rule their people. Going for specifics Fela mentions France, Germany, England, Korea, Japan, Syria, Jordan, Iran, and he affirms that it is the culture of those countries that shapes and guides their respective government decisions. In short, it is the culture and traditions of the countries mentioned, that serves as teacher to their respective governments.

Turning his attention to Africa and her problems which he already sang about: corruption, inflation, mismanagement, authority stealing, electoral fraud, etc. The latest addition to the problems which even makes him laugh is austerity. Fela say's if you ask him why 'austerity' makes him laugh - the answer is that it is beyond crying.

Government representatives, steals money from the country and the same government is introducing austerity measures in the society, forcing the poor people to pay for their greed and calling it 'austerity measures' this is funny if to say the least. He then went on to ask who taught African 'leaders' to rule the way they do today? He answers: 'Na the oyinbo' meaning in Yoruba language: 'it is them white folks' referring to ex-colonial rulers of each country. To justify his claim, he say's - let's take electoral fraud which is a true test of our democracy.

Many African leaders, rig-elections with impunity and their respective ex-colonial rulers say nothing against this form of 'democracy'. While the same 'white folks' are quick to claim credit for Africa's 'civilisation' which Fela disputes in this song. Is this democracy he asks? Mentioning other problems like the ever growing gap between the rich and the poor bearing in mind, that the rich are the same rulers who are stealing the country's wealth and plunging the society into poverty. Fela asks is this democracy or dem-all-crazy?

In conclusion as an African personality Fela says he is not in the same league, as those who believe in dem-all-crazy calling on the Western powers who claim to be Africa's teacher not to teach him nonsense - Teacher Don't Teach Me Nonsense.

It will be appropriate at this point, to discus Fela's intellectual abilities exposed as far back as 1974 to the author from my regular attendance of his Shrine concerts as I explained in the preface of this volume. Those sessions opened my mind to the vastness and richness of the African cultural endowment and accorded Fela's music in my heart a place beyond mere music to a profoundly authentic educational theme. It was almost like an apotheosis, a supreme or ideal example of the kind of wisdom that must propel a society. It motivated me to abandon the project of going to study philosophy or history in a Nigerian University. This aspect of him has not been projected by those who try to sell his image since his demise.

After the burning down of Kalakuta, for the first time the student community was beginning to take Fela seriously as the only dissenting voice against military rule. While a great majority of the academic and intellectual communities were struggling for jobs and posts offered by the regimes, Fela stood-out as one of the few successful citizens that turned down personal gains to advocate true democracy African style. Like the case of the Student Union movements in Ghana in 1978, Nigeria's Student Unions were clamouring to have Fela talk on their campuses.

His participation in a symposium organised by the economic student society of University of Ife (UNIFE), can serve as an example of how the intellectual and elite class in Nigeria looked down on Fela despite his comments and criticisms of those in power and his popularity among the student community.

At this particular symposium while other participants were being introduced as "Professor this or that", when it came to Fela's turn the students who had heard of Fela's previous participation in lectures and symposiums of this kind demanded the moderator Professor Adejuwon, then Deputy Vice Chancellor of UNIFE and Dean of the faculty of Social Sciences to equally address Fela as a "Professor".

Claiming not to be aware of Fela being awarded such title, Professor Adejuwon turned towards Fela to ask if Fela was nominated 'Professor' from any University. In reply, Fela said it was the "peoples wish" and at the end of the debate the learned professor admitted that Fela deserved a Professorship.

During the 1980-1981 academic session alone, Fela took part in more than sixty lectures and symposiums in different Nigerian institutions of higher learning - an attestation to the impact of his message. For a clearer insight into his deep drinking from the waters of Africa's authentic history, below is a transcript of the lecture he delivered at the University of Ife Nigeria on the "THE ESSENCE OF CULTURE IN DEVELOPMENT".

Talking to the students at the University's crowded theatre he said: "Dr. Kwame Nkrumah the father of Pan - Africanism says to all black people all over the world that "Until all foreign institutions and cultures are removed from the African land, that is when the African genius will be born and African personality will find its expression".

Africa was in the fore-front of world's adventure and the black pharaohs who built the pyramids and had obsession for the world of the dead, contributed to the advancement of material civilisation. These great African pioneers of civilisation as we know it today taught the Greeks, several things which they would otherwise not have known - but the history of Africa has changed since.

As we can see in Africa today the discipline required to think and act big, has not yet become a part of our academic and intellectual traditions. The emphasis on our cultural heritage has to a large extent excluded the study of these heritages, and their development as vehicles of thought and agent of civilisation.

We are in the habit of repeating untruths about African languages for example because they suit our mental laziness.

Those of us who have been trained in the use of English, French, Spanish or German languages, will argue forcefully that those are international languages in which alone science and technology can be intelligently studied, if this is so I wander how the ancient Egyptians built the pyramids. The African colonial / neo-colonial situation, can partly be compared with the present-day situation among Germans.

Before the Second World War the whole of Germany was one nation. During these period Germans could manufacture rockets and other high powered technology. But today thirty-four years, after East Germany became colonised by Soviet Union and West Germany by the Allied forces, Germans have lost their ability and independence to produce high powered technology. If the situation, is allowed to continue into the next century Germans may even loose their ability to produce cars.

Africa, like Germany is going down everyday because we fail to heed the call to unite. If the European Jews can fight for an arid piece of desert, the Irish for a small emerald Island, the British for a barren Island of misery, Protestant Anglo-Saxon Americans for their stolen Indian empire, why should the black man(African, African Caribbean, African American) not fight for the richest piece of real estate on the planet earth?

Many of you who watched the film 'ROOTS' by Alex Haley, must have seen Kunta Kinte resist when he was about to be given the name TOBY - that was the kind of African minds in 1742 we are talking about. Please let us not quote dates for nothing or because we know dates, quoting dates in this context is for us to give our minds food for thought by visualising what these dates represent in our life time - to enable us to align with time.

Since Nigeria's so-called independence in 1960 nineteen years have gone bye, think back what you have done in nineteen years. For me it is a long period in my life and I guess it is for all of you out there. If they send any of us to jail for a year, we will surely realise that it is a long wasted period in ones life.

We all belong to one generation, the next generation will follow us and at the rate we are going, we may not know about the generation before us. Think about the generation that lived in 1600 and compare the time difference to our generation today.

The generations 1700 or 1800, think back to all these years and compare your present day sufferings with those of the generation before you.

If in 1978 Nigerian army can shoot to kill protesting student and get away with it within international community, what is happening to our people in this generation is a child's play compared to what black people went through three hundred years ago. In 1742, we had proud Africans like Kunta Kinte who would not take a white man's name, he was flogged to the point where he almost died but he proudly refused to be called Toby".

"Do you know why?"

Noooo! (The students replied).

"According to the estimation of Africa's natural riches, every black man should be millionaires why are we so poor today? Why is the black man carrying the 'shit' of the world? It is time for us to investigate. For more than 300 years, the African population was stagnated by slavery. According to "liberal writers" 50 million able-bodied Africans were forcibly taken to Europe and the Americas.

On the other hand however, more authentic African writers are claiming that more than 200 million Africans were taken out of the African shores, half of those taken perished at the bottom of the sea during passage. Able bodied African men and women, including teenagers between the ages of fifteen to forty years old.

Contrary to Western writer's opinion, at the beginning there was no slave trade in Africa. What we had was kidnapping, rampage, devastation. Even in Alex Haley's film 'ROOTS' you saw how Kunta Kinte got kidnapped. The trade and auctions were done in Europe, the Americas, and the West Indies.

However, at the later stages of slavery when the plundering and devastation of the African continent was at its peak, it is plausible to think that some African Chiefs took part in the trade. Africans were pressured to do things they would normally not have done.

Take me Fela for example, I never would beg anybody for money but last December I had to go beg my friends for money.

You all are aware that since my house was burnt one year ago, I have been prevented by the same people who burnt my house to work and earn my living. I have had to find, different ways to keep my organisation going. Same can be said of the African situation during slavery. After slavery was abolished, the generation of Africans who lived in that era had other kinds of pressure to contend with for example, if you did not have an English name it was difficult to find work within the society.

Have you stopped to think why most so called rich families in our society today have English names? Williams, Doherty, Braithwaite, Johnson and Ransome are not African names. Even my grand father too had to add Ransome to his Kuti name. Ransome-Kuti can you beat that? My father was Israel Oludotun Ransome-Kuti. The "Israel" he seldom used but the 'Ransome' he kept for status sake. Our society since the advent of colonialism has come to see status from a material point of view. The more visible material you have, the more enhanced your position is in the society.

Materialism, gives you more prominence in society than what the individual can contribute towards the advancement of man. We have been made to believe that you can only get your point across with status (importance). To publicly speak against the Christian or Moslem institution in Africa is like committing social suicide.

For more than four or five generations, African people have been brainwashed into thinking that their salvation in life depends on their embracing Islam or Christianity. Africans can only progress when we realise that Islam and Christianity, were responsible for the division and hatred in the African society today.

White liberal writers and their brainwashed African stooges, claim that the coming of Christianity in Africa saved her from savagery. More evidence are abound today proving that from the beginning to the end, slave trade was a denial of any standards except those of profit and loss. A black man, was worth exactly what his flesh would bring to his white owner in the market. If his flesh would bring nothing, he was tossed overboard as if he were a horse with a broken leg. Bishop Las Casas (the bishop of Chiapas in Mexico) in 1517, stood before the throne of Charles V. of Spain and begged his 'majesty' to import Africans as slaves to work the plantations and mines.

Reverends and Priests, who profess coming to Africa to save us from savagery participated in this beastly exploitation and degradation of man by man. One of the most remarkable slavers and curious personality of the eighteenth century Captain (later Reverend) John Newton, who wrote the famous hymn: "How sweet the name of Jesus sounds..." while waiting for a slave coffle on the coast, was one of the most famous eccentrics of the Anglo-Saxon society of the era.

The religious justification for slavery which claimed that "African were heathens, whose souls must be saved" has given way to new racial justification that condemns all black people to a further bondage. Using texts from the bible which claims that "Negroes were children of Ham" whose father Noah had his famous: "cursed be Canaan a servant shall he be unto his brethren" (Genesis 9:25).

Please let us put some thought into what we are taught in school. A father goes and get drunk, he strips himself naked and his son finds him naked and told his other brothers - who is to blame? "

"The Father" shouts the audience.

"The father of course! But the bible wants us to believe the child is to blame for seeing his father's nakedness. If Christianity sees black people like this, what is the black man doing embracing the religion? Most Christians of the slave era, were of the opinion that it might be wrong to enslave fellow Christians, but Africans were not human beings therefore could not become Christians.

One 'pious' lady said when asked if her African maid was to be baptised: "You might as well baptise my black bitch". Bishop Berkley put the same words into philosophical language when he said: "Negroes are creatures of another species that had no right to be included or admitted to the sacrament".

An Introduction to Benin Art and Technology by Philip J.C. Dark says: "The story of Benin and its treasures used to conjure up in the western minds visions of human sacrifices, crucifixion pits with decomposing bodies a veritable city of blood. But such visions, were for those at the end of the last century and for the first fourteen years of this one when Benin was 'rediscovered' by Europeans.

The world was still being explored and gobbled up by imaginative Europeans with an eye for glory on the one hand, and for natural resources and markets on the other. But the quest for domination and control, led to the West's own special brand of mass murder and agony. The fame of Benin, rests on the works of traditional arts produced over the last 600-700 years by guild of craftsmen who lived in Benin City". African people were the first on earth and the first to develop technology.

The Whiteman, is not a superior human being as they would want us to believe. Most of the things they know were taught to them by black teachers. When was electricity invented? Towards the end of last century of course, electricity was not invented by the Whiteman because he is superior in sense to the black man.

Far from it, electricity was invented after they had slave money to invest in research programmes. The slave trade made the industrial revolution possible in Europe and America. At the same time, it set the wheel of progress on the reverse in Africa.

While they plundered and devastated the African continent they were investing the gains in Europe and the Americas. In 1897, the British went to Benin Kingdom on what they called "punitive expedition".

They demolished the beautiful houses killed as many as were in sight, the beautiful city which Africans today could look up to proudly and point to our architectural achievements of the era were destroyed. Benin City was not the only African city subjected to such punitive devastation, everywhere the Whiteman set his foot on the continent they ruined, plundered and devastated.

Cecil Rhodes (after whom Rhodesia was named), King Leopold II of Belgium (who also managed the whole of Congo as his personal estate), Captain 'Lord' Lugard, all these three men were responsible for the murder of several millions of Africans - they committed a type of genocide in Africa that was never equalled by Adolph Hitler and his fellow Nazis at the height of their massacre of European Jews.

If we are not aware of these facts of history, it is because most books available to us on African history are written from Western or Arabian points of view. And as you must have seen, Africans are projected as primitive in order to continue the domination of the continent and its people.

How can Africa be considered uncivilised when it is known by every European historian of the ancient times, that Africans who ruled most European kingdoms and empires as late in history as 711 C.E (Christ Era) introduced the common bath to their European subjects beginning with Spain southern France and Portugal.

Stanley Lane-Poole's book "THE MOORS IN SPAIN" explains how European of Spain, demanded that the indigenous Africans from Morocco (called Moors) give up bathing he wrote: "The misguided Spaniards knew not what they were doing, the infidels were ordered to abandon their native and picturesque costumes to assume the hats and breaches of the Christians, to give up bathing and adopt the dirt of the conquerors, to renounce their language their customs ceremonies and even their names".

A History Of The Atlantic Slave Trade also states that: "The first white man to reach Benin Kingdom, was a Portuguese Roy de Sequira in 1472, before Sequira was ushered into the King's presence he and his party were taken to a caravanserai and carefully washed"(See Black Cargoes by Daniel P. Manyx). Up until 10th century, European Anglo-Saxons were regarded as barbarians living outside the walls of Rome as slaves. This includes the period, when the indigenous African Septimus Severus and his son Caracalla were emperors of the Roman Empire.

During this period, Africa had a university in Timbuktu where students came to seek knowledge from different parts of the world. The propagation of a so-called 'Western civilisation,' is responsible for the no attempt being made to find out why southern Europeans are generally dark skinned. Spain for instance, was captured by General Tarikh (an African) in 711 CE. He was the first Moor to capture part of the Iberian peninsular.

These black skinned Africans and brown skinned Asians over the years, inter-bred and amalgamated sexually with most of the white skinned European population they met with along the Iberian peninsular. Another amazing phenomenon, about the African Moors in Spain is that it is stated that no less than three million African Moors, were banished between the fall of Grenada and the first decade of the seventeenth century.

However, these African Moors extended their rule for two hundred years in Grenada when in other areas of Spain the Asian (Arab) Moors, have been driven out by the Christian Spaniards around 1285 CE. The African Moors, first to enter and conquer Spain in 711 CE were the last to leave in 1485 CE. As you can see from this information I am passing across to you students today, you will realise that the African continent is no recent discovery.

While Europe was the home of wandering barbarians, one of the most wonderful civilisation on record, had begun to work its destiny on the bank of the Nile River (See the History Of Nations, vol. 18 p.1, 1906). The findings of crude tools weapons and other evidence of man amidst the fossilised bones of long-extinct animals, and the growing sophistication of archaeologists and biologist have come a long way to discredit false propaganda about Africa.

Charles Darwin, in 1859 published in "THE ORIGIN OF SPECIES" that human beings had evolved from some lower form of life. However by implying that man was related to apes, Darwin incurred the derision and wrath of several perpetuators of a so-called Western civilisation. "Descended from apes?" Exclaimed the wife of the Bishop of Worcester when she heard the news in 1860. "Let us hope it is not true, but if it is let us pray that it will not become generally known".

Her prayers were not heard, because more and more archaeologists went in search of fossils to prove man's origin from some lower form of life. Prominent among these were the couple Dr. Louis S.B. Leaky and Mary Leaky, who discovered along the Oldduvai George Lake in Tanganyika (Tanzania) an ape-like human skull and jaw bone dating back to 1,750,000 and 3.75 million years old respectively.

With these discoveries, Africa's claim to the cradled of world civilisation is no doubt proven. Another proof was found in Johannesburg South Africa on 7th February 1970, when South African archaeologists reported the discovery of the world's oldest mine.

The mine said to be in an iron ore rich mountain in the neighbouring Swaziland, is said to be 43,000 years old according to radio-carbon dating.

The opinion "out of Africa comes something new" has always been commonly shared by ancient Greeks whom European writers have chosen to call "Greek Philosophers". However, historic facts available today are pointing to the fact that the Greeks were not the authors of what is acclaimed by western writers as Greek Philosophy. The black people of North Africa who today are called Egyptians, were the authors of the philosophical thoughts credited to the Greeks.

George G.M. James, in the introduction of his book STOLEN LEGACY said: "The term Greek philosophy to begin with is a misnomer, for there is no such philosophy in existence. The ancient Egyptians had developed a very complex religious system called the mysteries, which was also the first system of salvation.

It regarded the human body as a prison house of the soul which could be liberated from its bodily impediments through the disciplines of art and sciences, thus advancing from the level of a mortal to that of a God. This was the notion of the 'summon bonum' or greatest good, to which all men were expected to aspire to and it also became the basis of all ethical concepts in the society.

The Egyptian mystery system, was also a secret order whose membership was gained through initiation and pledge to secrecy. Teachings were graded and delivered orally, to the Neophytes under circumstances of secrecy. Also developed by the Egyptians, were secret system of writing and its teachings forbid initiates from writing down what they learnt. However, after nearly five thousand years of prohibitions against the Greeks, they were permitted to enter Egypt for the purpose of their education, this was first through the Persian invasion and later through the invasion of Alexander 'the great'.

From the sixth century BC (before Christ) therefore to the death of Aristotle (322 BC), the Greeks made the best of their chance to learn all they could about Egyptian culture. Most students received instructions directly from black Egyptian priests.

However after the invasion of Alexander 'the great,' Egyptian royal temples and libraries were plundered and pillaged. Aristotle's school converted the library in Alexandria into a research centre. There is no wander then that the production of the unusually large number of books ascribed to Aristotle, has proved a physical impossibility for any single man within a life time.

The history of Aristotle's scholarship, has done him far more harm than good since it carefully avoids any statements relating to his visit to Egypt either on his own account or in company of Alexander 'the great' when he invaded Egypt. This silence of history, at once throws doubts upon the life and achievements of Aristotle. He is said to have spent twenty years, under the tutorship of Plato who is regarded as a philosopher yet he graduated as the greatest of scientists of antiquity.

Two questions might be asked:

(a) how Plato could teach Aristotle what he himself did not know, and
(b) why should Aristotle spend twenty years under a teacher from whom he could learn nothing?

These parts of their history sounds incredible again and in order to avoid suspicion over the extraordinary number of books ascribed to Aristotle, history tells us that Alexander 'the great' gave him a large sum of money to get the books. Here again the history sounds incredible and three statements must be made:

(a) In order to purchase books on science, they must have been in circulation so as to enable Aristotle secure them.

(b) If the books were in circulation before Aristotle purchased them and since he is not supposed to have visited Egypt at all, then the books in question must have been circulated among Greeks philosophers.

(c) If circulated among Greek philosophers, then we would expect the subject matter of such books to have been known before Aristotle's time and consequently he could not be credited either with the production of them or introducing any new ideas of science.

Another point of considerable interest to be accounted for, was the attitude of the Athenian government towards the so-called Greek philosophy which it regarded as foreign in origin and treated it accordingly. Only a brief study of history, is necessary to show that Greek philosophers were undesirable citizens, who throughout the period of their investigations, were victims of relentless persecution at the hands of the Athenian government.

Anaxagoras was imprisoned and later exiled, Socrates was executed, Plato was sold into slavery, and Aristotle was indicted and exiled while the earliest of them all Pythagoras, was expelled from Croton to Italy. Can we imagine the Greeks, making such an about turn as to claim the very teachings which they had at first persecuted and openly rejected?

Certainly, they knew they were usurping what they had never produced, and as we enter step by step into our study, the greater we discover evidence which leads us to the conclusion that Greek philosophy, is STOLEN EGYPTIAN PHILOSOPHY.

We can at once see how easy it was for an ambitious and even envious nation, to claim a body of unwritten knowledge which would make them great in the eyes of the primitive world. The absurdity however, is easily recognised when we remember that the Greek language was used to translate several systems of teachings which the Greeks couldn't succeed in claiming.

Such were translations of Hebrew Scriptures into Greek called the Septuagint and the translation of the Christian gospel "Acts and the Epistles" in Greek, still called the Greek New Testament. It is only the unwritten philosophy of the Egyptians translated into Greek, that has met with such an unhappy fate - a legacy stolen by the Greeks (see Stolen Legacy by George G. James).

Here is a brief chronology of the history, of ancient indigenous Africans of the Great Lake region and along the 4,100 miles Nile river valley. They were forced to migrate to their present regions, as a result of several bloody battles against foreign invaders in Africa.

4,100 BC: This was the period of the first Solar Calendar ever made by man it had 365, 1/4 days to one year. Three seasons of four months each and it was introduced by the indigenous Africans of the Nile valley descendants of whom have migrated east, west, north, and south of the African continent.

2,780 BC: Beginning of the Great Pyramid age. The period began with most ancient of the truly great pyramids, built during the reign of Pharaoh Djoser around the third dynasty. Imhotep, was Chief architect and builder of this project - the step Pyramid of Sakhara (Saggara).

The stone used in the building of this structure, was taken from quarries which were opened up earlier by indigenous Africans at the eastern most point of North Africa and kept in service by following Pharaohs from C.3200 to at least 2780 BC (see Black Man Of The Nile, by Yosef Ben-Jochannan).

2,686 BC: The Grand Lodge of Luxor was built, at Danderah by Pharaoh Khufu during the third dynasty. This area was part of Ta-Nehisi, when the Great Lodge presently called 'Temple of the city of Thebes' was built. Moreover, the original structure was 2,000 feet long and 1,000 feet wide at its base. Its oblong shape is presently copied by all secret societies, mosques and churches based upon Masonic principles. Also, the fundamental basis for the rituals of Free Masonry, were taught and established in Luxor and most of the 20th Century western secret societies were established by indigenous Africans. The ancients, including the Greeks and Romans visited this Grand Lodge, to obtain the highest degree in human learning. Here they were introduced to philosophy, law, religion, science, engineering, mathematics, astronomy, astrology, medicine, history and other disciplines of the seven liberal arts. Even King Solomon of Israel, Moses of the Hebrew (Haribu religion), Jesus Christ and others of ancient world had visited this Grand Lodge for their education in the Mysteries of the Osirica - see G.G.M. James, Stolen Legacy and Black Man of the Nile, by Yosef Ben-Jochannan, and also The Destruction of Black Civilisation by Chancellor Williams. Luxor however was destroyed by fire - burnt to the ground in C.548 BC by foreigners, who were jealous of the indigenous Africans knowledge of the mystery taught in Osiricas which included all of the mentioned disciplines.

2,340 BC: Four different expeditions of Egyptian Pharaohs who left Egypt for visit to Nubia, Meroe, Itiopi, and Puanit - all of them to the south of Egypt. These visits, further adds proof to the fact that the whole of Africa had commercial, social, and even sexual contacts, with each other for thousands of years before the arrival of the westerners.

2,300 BC: Imhotep of Egypt became known, to the ancients as God of medicine. This indigenous African was the first medical man (physician) known to mankind, even preceding those mentioned in the five Books of Moses (Old Testament). The Greeks, Romans, Chaldians, Babylonians, Sumerians and others of the ancient world, learned their basic medicine from this African man - Imhotep.

He was also Grand Vizier, Prime Minister, Architect, Poet, and holder of many other positions during his life time while he served his Pharaoh Djoser. Imhotep was known to the Greeks as 'Prince of Peace,' over two thousand years before the Christian Jesus Christ was born or long before he was given the said title. Imhotep lived more than 2,000 years before the European "father" of medicine - Hippocrates of Greece was born, yet in their attempt to propagate a so-called White supremacy, Western 'educators' continue to teach and proclaim Hippocrates as the father of medicine.

2,300 BC: The oldest and first known records of a journey from Elephantine (Aswan), to Ta Nehishi (Nubia), to Memphis in Ta-Merry (Egypt), dealt with Pharaoh Mennere's ambassador, the son of the ritual priest named Iris trip to the kingdom of Yam. The purpose of the trip, was to establish a highway between both cities. Here again, the false propaganda of the western world about the so-called 'Natural Semites,' from the 'Nubian Negroes,' are exposed as nothing but a racist and separatist hypothesis that has no foundation in facts of history. The second journey of Pharaoh Mennere's ambassador on the Elephantine road from Isthet to Msklem, then to Tereres and back to Isthet, was a trip that totalled eight months duration (See H.J. Breasted's Ancient Records of Egypt and Yosef Ben-Jochannan's Black Man of the Nile).

1,490 BC: Amenhotep IV, otherwise known as Akhennaten (Ikhanaten) was born. He was known to the ancients of his time and after as the 'Religious Pharaoh'. This was way back, in the hundreds of years before the proclaimed birth of Jesus Christ. Akhenaten taught his followers about a Trinitarian God. He called his God - the Virtues or God in Three Virtues. The virtues were broken down into Love and Body of life. But he was not much of a politician or administrator neither was he a forceful man. It was during his reign in the history of Ta–Merry (Egypt) when a powerful leader was most needed, Egypt did suffer defeat from foreign invaders. Akhaneten made Egypt militarily weak, and started her down the way to her eventual downfall. This was the beginning, of the decline of the most 'Fearful Power' of her time. Akhaneten had actually reduced the army of Egypt to a mere police force, thus allowing her enemies to constantly invade her border towns and other out-posts. As a result, Egypt's trade was cut to mere trickle, her treasury was almost broke and her generals were in total disunity.

700 BC: The world's first religious principle was substantiated. It was verified, when a slab of basalt was unearthed in Egypt bearing an inscription with Cushitic script, relating to a treatise on the moral concept of right and wrong. King Ori in the year C. 3,758 BC declared that they are 'Moral Forces Of God' (The Sun God Ra).

670 BC: Ionians and Carians were recruited for the first time to serve in Egyptian armies. During this period, Greeks were used as translators in matters related to Europeans in Egypt. From this contact, they began receiving their first light into the Mysteries of African philosophy and other aspects of the seven liberal arts. This experience has been the basis for what was later called "Greek Philosophy" by European writers. There is no record of anything describing Greek arrival in Egypt and Nubia, or their arrival in Ionia where they studied under African (Egyptian) teachers brought into Ionia (then an Egyptian colony). However, Greeks were later brought into Egypt as students in the Mystery system to sturdy the Osirica's mysteries. All the works they studied, were of the genius of the indigenous Africans of the Nile Valley including those defined by Herodotus and Count Volney as: 'The Colchains, Ethiopians and Egyptians have thick lips, broad nose, woolly (kinky) hair and they are burnt of skin'.

600 BC: Pharaoh Neku II (Nechu or Necho), commissioned a fellow African to sail (circumnavigate) the entire continent of Africa. The name of the African navigator, was Hano (Hanno) a native of Khart-Haddas (Cartage). This historic fact, disproves the western scholars claim that "Vasco da Gama, was the first to sail around the coast of the southern tip of Africa". It is to be noted that the Portuguese, the first of the western Europeans at Monomo-Tapa (South Africa) of whom Vasco da Gama was one were not the first people there. They (the Portuguese) too, wrote about the 'Kaffir Sailors and Pilots,' they met around the coast of the southern tip of Africa in their ship logs. The first of the Portuguese at Monomo-Tapa was Captain Bartholomew Dias in C. 1488 CE (Christ Era). This fact of history is in contradiction to the claims of white racist (English, Boers, Indo Christian, etc.), that when the white man arrived in South Africa, there were no Africans there except the Hotentos and Bushmen. Such western scholars have conveniently forgotten, that they arrived in South Africa in the latter part of the 17th Century Christ Era. This was more than 100 years after the arrival of the Portuguese, who met there Africans called Bantus or Kaffir (See Black Man of the Nile, by Y. Ben-Jochannan).

525 BC: The genius of Greek enlightenment into the 'seven liberal arts' as did in the field of science, law, engineering, medicine, etc., came about during many periods of their sojourn in Egypt. But mostly during this period, when for the first time, immigration regulations barring them from Egypt was lifted by the Persians who attacked Egypt in 1675 BC. This relaxation of immigration laws allowed the Greeks to settle in the town of Naacrates, where they met with thousands of other foreigners from Asia. This took place during the reign of Pharaoh Amasis. In Naacrates, the Greeks were for the first time introduced into the full secret of the Egyptian (African) Mystery System or fraternal brotherhood. Thus, they began their first contact in philosophy, and other disciplines which they had been introduced to before by other much indirect means. All of their teachers up to the rank of Chief Priest, were indigenous Africans from the Nile river valley and the Great Lakes region. From this beginning, the Greeks began to copy and otherwise aped the Nile valley African concepts and teachings at their settlements. Most of them taking the same back to Greece where they returned frequently (See Plutarch History, G.G.M. James' Stolen Legacy, Yosef Ben-Jochannan's Africa, Mother of Western Civilization).

500 BC: Herodotus the father of European history established through his own writings that the basis of Greek high culture (western civilisation), were copied from the teachings of the Africans of the Nile river valleys and the Great Lake region. This revelation by Herodotus, has caused most European and European-American historians and other educators to establish their own colour and racial distinction for each group of nations of the ancient Africans contrary to what Herodotus reported in his book "THE HISTORIES". These so-called "authorities on African history", begin their works by trying to separate indigenous Africans into 'Africans North of the Sahara' and 'Africans South of the Sahara'. They further create new and separate races for Ethiopia, Egypt, Nubia (Sudan), and other north and east African nations through the biblical mythology created by the Hebrews (Jews and Christians of Europe and the Americas). Hence we have today such characters as: Bantus, Hamites, Semites, Nilotics, Pygmies, Bushman, Hottentots, Negroes, Nemites, Caucasians, etc., in order to sustain their claims of "separate" people apart from Africans existed on the African continent. More also, for more than six thousand years after the historic recordings in hundreds of tombs (Pyramids, etc.), of numerous Pharaohs and Kings - long before the period relating to Herodotus birth, the ancient indigenous Africans along the Nile valley and Great Lakes region recorded their history on the inside and outside of their temples and other

structures many of whose works have survived the ages of time to substantiate the above mentioned facts revealed. Most of these African legacies, are presently kept in European and European-American museums and private collections.

430 BC: Herodotus the Ionian of Greek citizenship arrived at Elephantine (modern Aswan) in Upper Egypt. He wrote details of this journey in his book The Histories.

345 BC: The Khart-Haddans (called Carthaginians by Europeans and European-American writers), established an embassy in Rome. Many western writers and historians, claim that it was at Fort Vail which is located a few miles from Rome. They based their contention upon the fact that Etruscans (friends of the Khart-Haddans), were already expelled from Rome in approximately C.510 BC or one hundred and sixty-five years before the establishment of the embassy.

332 BC: Alexander (the great) of Macedonia, entered Egypt under military power. This conquest, initiated the European control in the Eastern limits of North Africa for the first time. Aristotle, the so-called "Greek Philosopher" and many of his fellow Greek cohorts shortly thereafter, ransacked the archives of Egypt especially that of the Grand Lodge of Luxor (Thebes). They stole what they understood, and burned-down much of what they could not decode or decipher (see G.G.M. James' Stolen Legacy and Blackman of the Nile by Yosef Ben-Jochannan).

323 BC: Alexander II died in Egypt, his vast conquered empire was divided among his top generals all of whom refused to recognise the authority of King Phillip III (Alexander's brother in Macedonia).

306 BC: General Sotar, Alexandra's best general to whom Alexander assigned the post of Governor of Egypt declared himself Sotar I Pharaoh of all Egypt. He became the first European after Alexander in history, to sit on the throne of the 'Star of the Nile'. All the other foreign conquerors who preceded the Macedonians and Greeks were from Asia (see The Destruction of Black Civilisation by Chancellor Williams and Black Man of the Nile by Yosef Ben-Jochannan). It was during the Ptolemy I reign, the African-European (mulatto) High-Priest Manetho, became the first historian to codify Egyptian royal history based

upon 'Dynastic Classification'. He also completed a compilation of Egypt's History of Antiquity, and divided it into the first thirty of the thirty-four royal dynasties. Manetho's works have been translated by such noted historians as Josephus, Leo Africanus, and Eusebius - the latter, brought forward the most important translation of Manetho's works to-date. We have to note that Leo Africanus was an indigenous African. He was only renamed, by his god-father Pope Leo of the Roman Catholic Church, following his capture, enslavement, and conversion to Christianity. Josephus was a Hebrew (Jew).

256 BC: The African Empire of Khart-Haddas conquered finally after the defeat of the battle of Econus.

200 BC: Polybius a Greek historian and explorer, visited the same ports established by Admiral Hanno (the Carthaginian) many hundreds of years before, on the coasts of West African rivers such as the Gambia which he called Bambotus. It is interesting to note that the present-day Mande Africans, called 'Mandigos' of Gambia name for crocodile is still Bambo. This must have given Polibius, the basis for the name he used to describe the river Gambia.

260 BC: The indigenous Africans of Khart-Haddas (Cartage) were defeated at the battle of Mylae.

190 BC: Another Greek Eudoseus of Cyzicus, sailed down the east coast of Africa after leaving Arabia. He sailed around the cape of Monomotapa (renamed 'Good Hope' formally named 'Cape of Storms' by the Portuguese) with African navigators, stopping at Ngola (called Angola by the Portuguese), and the Empire of Zaire (called Congo by the Portuguese). He continued up the Ethiopian (south Atlantic) sea coast to East Africa until he returned easterly through the Pillars of Hercules (later called the 'Straight of Gibraltar') along the Mediterranean Sea back to his native Greece.

50 BC: Marcus Anthonius (Marc Antonio or Mark Anthony) captured Egypt for the Caesar (King or Emperor of Rome). There is quite a lot of confusion as to whether this date should be C.47 or 30 BC. Mark Anthony through his Caesar, forced Queen Cleopatra VIII to surrender and abdicate the throne. Egypt was made a 'province' of Rome, following the publication of a decree to that effect by Julius Caesar in Rome.

47 BC: Julius Caesar, reinstated Cleopatra VIII daughter of Ptolemy XIII (son of African-European parentage) as Queen of all Egypt. All of the Ptolemys except Ptolemy I (the former General Soter of Macedonia), were of similar African-European parentage (see Black Man of the Nile by Yosef Ben-Jochannan).

30 BC: A Roman Sentinus Flaccus, crossed the Sahara to reach the Kingdom of Niger around the region of Lake Chad. The report he gave upon his return to his native Rome, indicated that he actually saw ancient Ghana Empire. However, western historians have falsely assigned Ghana, an origin of approximately 300 A.D. in an attempt to keep all of the African nations south of the Sahara, to a history without pre-Christian origin. Flaccus followed Paulinus, another Roman who visited the northern-most reach of the Niger River in approximately C. 50 BC.

00 BC: Roman rule, continued in North Africa during the proclamation of the birth of Jesus Christ. Some historians however, relate the year one (1 BC) to the death of Jesus Christ.

From the above brief chronology, the facts points to a long period in human history of Africa being the focus of the physical development of man on earth. The whole four thousand one hundred miles Nile valley, plus the Great Lake region were the major centres of Black (African) civilisation until the fall of Khart-Haddas (Cartage) the last of the Nile valley kingdoms.

The fall of Khart-Haddas, led to the massive migration of Black people to their present day regions south of the Sahara. Another important fact that should be noted is that not all non-mixed Africans are Jet-Black in their colour of skin. There are a lot of people of African decent who lived in cool areas of the continent, with lighter skin complexion and with no trace of White blood.

The Arab (Asiatic) people who occupy North Africa, are no more native to the African land than are the Dutch and British who occupy and control the southern region of the continent.

Arab imperialism though rarely mentioned, is as devastating to the African as the European imperialism - though their strategy of brotherhood through Islam deceives people of African origin.

The story of how such an advanced civilisation was lost, is one of the most tragic in the history of mankind. The strength and determination of the African people, can be measured by how in the face of what seemed to be the forces of hell (destruction), they fought and kept alive the spirit of African traditional values.

Even within the framework of the smallest surviving states, Africans adhered to and kept alive the basic principles of the traditional African constitution and held-on to through all the passing centuries, the fundamental elements of its ancient democratic, social, and political systems.

Centuries after mulattos and Asian (Arabs) emerged as the only Egyptians, they still regard Black Africa as the chief source of the Spirituals. 'The land of the Gods' or 'the land of the Spirits', the whole of the African continent was once 'Bilad a Sudan' (the land of the Black), and not just the southern region of the Sahara desert to which Africans have been steadily pushed by foreign invaders.

Evidence from works of arts available through-out Black Africa today, points to historic links between ancient Egypt and present day Africans dating farback to centuries prior to the establishment of the old Egyptian kingdom, to the end of the Greek era and the beginning of the Roman era.

The general trend of opinion among many writers and folklore, is that the Yoruba's (of present day Nigeria), came from the east although their migration must have taken place at a very early date. This opinion finds strong support in common-held beliefs, similarity of language, religious beliefs, ideas and practices, plus survival of customs, these are parts of a chain of evidence which leads to this conclusion.

SIMILARITY OF LANGUAGE:

The West African word 'YE' which means 'to exist', is subject to many changes in the different languages of the region. 'E' sometimes becomes 'a' or 'i' or 'o' or 'u' or these vowels nasalised. Throughout all these changes, the meaning remains the same. However for the sake of convenience the root-word 'YE' will be used during this debate. The word occurs in several of the leading West African languages viz: Tshi, Ewe, Ga, Yoruba, Edo, it also does exist in Egyptian language.

Another example is the Yoruba word 'Ekuabo' which means welcome, in the Ivory Cost they say 'Akuaba' for welcome. In the Egyptian language the word 'Amon' means 'to conceal' or 'concealed'. This word exists in Yoruba with the same meaning 'fi pa mon' 'conceal it', or 'regard it as hidden or cause it to be hidden'.

Other examples are abound 'Uu' = 'Wu' 'rise up' or 'swell', 'Miri' = 'Water', in Yoruba this word is used only as an adverb – viz: 'miri-miri' 'dazzling like water'. But among the Igbo people who are neighbours of the Yoruba, the word is still used to denote water - 'miri' (see Religion of the Yoruba by Archdeacon Olumide Lucas).

SIMILARITY OF RELIGIOUS BELIEFS:

Most of the ancient Egyptian principal Gods were well known at one time or the other to the Yorubas. Among these Gods are: Osiris, Isis, Horus, Shu, Thoth, Khepera, Amon, Anu, Khosu, Khnum, Khopri, Hathor, Sakaris, Ra, Seb, the four elemental deities and others. Most of these Gods survive in name or, in attributes or in both.

Ra for instance, survives in name because the majority of the Yoruba people are no longer Sun worshipers but the word Irawo, Rara, Ra-ra, preserve the idea. The literal meaning of 'Irawo' (a star) is that which appears when Ra (the sun) has set 'wo' (means set). Also, the Yoruba expression 'Ra-ra' (not at all) or (no-no) is probably an old form of swearing by the Sun God Ra.

The word 'Amon' exist in the Yoruba language with the same meaning as it had in the language of the ancient Egyptians. The God 'Amon' was one of the Gods formerly known to the Yoruba. The Yoruba words 'Mon', 'Mimon' (which means holy or sacred), are probably derived from the name of the God Amon.

'Thoth' was the Egyptian God of truth and righteousness if the initial letters 'th' becomes 't' and the final 'th' is dropped, the word thus become 'to' (which means right, fair, or just). Other words derived from 'Thoth' are: 'o-ti-to' (truth) or (that which belongs to Thoth, right, fairness, or justice).

From the few examples mentioned above, the apparent survival of indigenous African words in both Greek and Latin languages, gives credence to the impress of African high culture on both Greek and Roman culture (civilisation).

Another obvious example is the Greek word for Egypt 'Aigupto', it is said to be derived from 'Khi-Khu-path' (the temple of the south of Ptah). So also is the Latin word 'Fere' (almost), which survives in its entire form and with the same meaning as the Yoruba word 'Fere' (almost).

In the field of plastic art, it has been argued by some West African historians that although the carved ivories, wood masks, bronze and elephant tusks, found in Ile-Ife and Benin, are indigenous to the people but the inspiration is said to come from Egypt. This conclusion is adduced from the evidence of similar works of art, found in the pyramids.

Finally, all these historic contribution of Africans to world's civilisation as I have explained during this lecture on "The Essence of Culture on Civilisation" it is for us to see ourselves in a different light.

Contrary to what western writers would have us believe, our ancestors had well defined ideas of nature, human life, existence, social relations, as well as of man himself. It is on the basis of these well defined ideas that the fundamental elements of human civilisation were developed.

For us then in this contemporary period in history, it is not enough to talk about these developments in civilisation and education, rather we must progressively translate these lofty ideas into positive actions, for our collective existence so that the Black Man must not Carry Shit again".

Ha! Ha! Ha! (Laugh from the audience).

"Don't laugh it is a serious issue for us in the black and African world, the fundamental issue in our education is the issue of relevance to our environment not rhetoric. These books I have quoted extensively during this lecture are saying the same thing.

Until when African scholars interpret their history from an African perspective, for an African reading public everywhere all over the world, then we shall have a true African history - that is the essence of culture in development. You are in a university and you are all reading wrong and irrelevant books".

Ha! Ha! Ha! (Laugh from the audience).

"Please! It is not just me Fela saying so – these books I have quoted from during this symposium are all saying it. Even the "Colloquium on Black Civilisation and Culture" says: "Universities can be degree producing factories, and as we can still see in Africa the discipline required to think and act big, has not yet become a part of our academic and intellectual traditions".

Many of you have been educated to believe that African history began with the institution of slaver, like you were made to believe the story that claims that Mungo Park 'discovered' the river Niger. If I may ask, 'he discovered the river for who?

Certainly not for the Africans who had lived along the banks of the Niger for generations. The only reason why we are not aware of these facts in our history, is because of the present day neo-colonial oriented governments in place since our so-called independence. They help perpetrate colonialism, by the use of what we call simple words which are derogative and help keep the African mind inferior.

Words such as: Dark Continent, third world, underdeveloped, non-aligned, etc. As a result, a lot of people of African origin have come to develop negative images and lack of pride in their heritage.

For your information before the advent of slavery, 15th century European technology was not superior to that of other parts of the world. Though there were certain specific features, which were highly advantageous to Europe namely shipping and guns.

This was due to their geographic situation, they had to travel across the sea in search of consumer goods hence the need for transport and guns for protection.

A significant proof that European system of production was not superior was the fact that European traders, had to make use of African and Asian consumer goods (see "How Europe Underdeveloped Africa" by Walter Rodney).

Though I don't hold any doctorate degree in economics, I can conveniently say "I have PhD common-sense". My common-sense, clearly points to the fact that Africa since independence is run by an economy based on a master/slave relationship. Take the monetary system in place in Africa since our so-called independence.

If an African intends to travel from his 'country' to any neighbouring sister country, the person is obliged to change the money of his country to that of the country he intends to visit. Is this not dumb? Why can't we have the same currency to facilitate freer and easier transactions on the continent?

On the issue of apartheid, we call conference against apartheid because we are afraid to hit the nail on the head. We don't need atomic power to depose the apartheid regime in South Africa, what we need is united minds.

Take Vietnam for example, Americans fought Vietnam for fifteen years spending ten million pounds sterling everyday on bombs. Despite all these, the Vietnamese came-out victorious - that is the type of united mind I am talking about.

Do we as Africans, have the united minds to resist ten million pounds sterling worth of bombs to defend Africa? I have said times without number that the basis of African unity can only be laid in an authentic education system, planned in a way that all school children are conscious of what goes on in Africa.

Our school children must be aware of what goes on in the liberation movements and the idea behind African unity otherwise we shall reduce the struggle to speech making.

I met Sam Nujoma the leader of the South West African Peoples Organisation (SWAPO), at the East Berlin Airport on our way back to Lagos after performing at the Berlin Jazz Festival in 1978.

One of my close associates, asked the SWAPO leader how long he envisages the struggle to go on for? Nujoma replied that the struggle will continue for a long time, our children will continue where we stop. "Aluta Continua! Vitoria Acerta! You know". Shortly after, we were asked to go aboard, so the discussion was cut short.

Aboard the Russian Illusion jet, Sam Nujoma and his three-member entourage were booked in the first class compartment while my 70 member entourage travelled in the economy class.

Resuming our conversation with Ekow Oduro who discussed with the SWAPO leader before going aboard I said it is only the African struggle that continues Chinese struggle is over, why is it the African struggle that will continue generation after generation?

Do you know why it is only the African struggle that continues? African leaders don't want to sacrifice. I pointed to the example of Sam Nujoma, if the SWAPO leader had travelled in the economy class, he could save the extra money to equip his soldiers in their trenches.

The African struggle will continue, because our leaders see the struggle in terms of travelling first-class and getting VIP treatments wherever they went. What else can we expect from the leadership of our liberation movements, judging from the prevailing situation in so-called independent African states who treat their citizens worse than the apartheid regime in South Africa.

Every year we organise conferences against apartheid in Nigeria, is the killing of nine demonstrating students by the Nigerian police force not worse than the acts of the racist regime in South Africa?

These are African police charged to protect us, at the same time killing our students like chicken. Bokassa, Mobutu, Olusegun Obasanjo and several so-called African Heads of State, condemn the racist regime in South Africa while they individually commit worse crimes than apartheid in their respective nations. In conclusion, let us go and re-read African history and the ideology of Pan-Africanist, it entails the recognition of the equality of man, it gives everyone the chance to try-out his or her individual capacity to be a better person.

We have to return to our early medical and spiritual institutions. Until when all these basic developments are attained in our society, then only can we talk about an absolute independent society.

The only reason why people see me Fela Anikulapo-Kuti, as one voice different from our so called academic and elite class, is because I base my information on authentic African history books. Most of these books claim: "You will never know where you are going, if you don't know where you are coming from." So my brothers and sisters in the African universities, when you read all those books your motto should be "teachers don't teach me nonsense".

The students and other participants applauded Fela with a standing ovation. Professor Adejuwon who had reluctantly addressed Fela as 'Professor' at the beginning of his contribution to the debate, described his submission as the most brilliant contribution on the essence of culture in development.

Concluding, the learned professor said "Fela merits his professorship". This submission, by a member of the Nigerian academic circle is very much contrary to the opinion of those in power.

Since this lecture, a great deal of changes has taken place in the world that has direct relevance to the original text and issues treated by Fela. For an example Fela made an analogy of the situation between West and East Germany, he compared the situation between the two Germanys with those of the present day African States saying if the disunity of Germany were to continue, Germans who before World War II were a leading force in technology could loose their know-how and leading position.

The Berlin wall has been broken down, the two Germanys are once again united. This development, is a pointer to the fact that Fela's "common-sense" is visionary especially if it is viewed in the context of a united Europe.

Another significant change is the fall of the apartheid regime in South Africa. Nelson Mandela has since been elected the first Black President of post-apartheid South Africa, and all the opponents of the racist regime have been liberated from prison.

However, it is important to note that the election of Mandela and the demise of the apartheid regime will be meaningless, unless it is linked with the total unity of all the independent states in Africa and the Diaspora.

This is so in the light of the fact that a united Africa both economic and political, will bring a new order to the world's political situation.

Especially since United States of America, with her North Atlantic Free Trade Agreement and the Pan-European union, constitute these two world regions into strong economic and political blocks.

For now the only thing that has changed is that, the South African blacks have the right to vote while the white South Africans control the economy.

Front cover album design Open And Close

Back cover album design Shakara

LOOK AND LAUGH

If we continue on the theme of change like those mentioned in the preceding chapter, another change since is that the author has parted ways with Fela after an association that lasted almost a decade. My decision to quit Fela and his organization, despite my strong believe in his Pan African ideals is one of the most difficult for me to make, in the light of a conversation between him (Fela) and some of us members of the organisation.

Travelling back to Lagos from University of Nigeria Nnsuka after participating in a symposium, a nostalgic conversation took place between us in the car, we were reminiscent about the good and bad times we all had shared and at a point during our conversation Fela turned and said: "ID! If you YAP Boys ever leave me..." Unfortunately, he never completed the statement beyond what is quoted above.

However, between 1981 and 1983 when it became obvious to me that our struggle was losing its direction, whenever I thought of Fela's "If you YAP Boys ever leave me..." statement, I found it difficult to "abandon ship mid-stream". It took me three years to make-up my mind to leave the organisation.

Looking back over the years, I can understand why he never completed the statement. Deep down him, he appreciated what we had all gone through but the reality of life made him see that there is never anything in life that is permanent. Everything and everyone has the right to change their points of view, it is only an imbecile that never changes.

Consistently subjected to harrowing and anguish from successive regimes, betrayed and deserted by trusted friends, exploited and used by lawyer friends considered as trusted advisers, like he sang years later in the song Underground System: "Since I de young nah to trust people I understand! Since I de grow-up to find people to trust hard!" Meaning "while growing-up to trust is what I was educated with, but since my adulthood to find people to trust is difficult".

I believe that all these let downs plus the continued combat against a repressive system, pushed Fela to adopt the "spiritual façade" in the last two decades of his life.

The "spirit" saga started shortly after the first French tour with Martin Meissonier. It started with Femi (Fela's son), who suffered a strange fever very much unlike the normal malaria fever with high temperature. His temperature was stable, but he refused to eat living from drinking water and chain-smoking (cigarettes and marijuana).

Fela was very much worried with the state of the young Kuti, particularly since people like George Gardner (Fela's Ghanaian lawyer) and Kwesi Yope (a former Ghana student's union leader), were insinuating that Femi was "going crazy".

While most of his discussions varied from coherent to non-coherent, generally Femi was insistent on reforms within his father's organisation. To convince everyone that he was in control, Femi would make people around him pound his head with punches with him not showing any sign of pain. This more than convinced George that Femi was loosing his mind.

Caught between the observations from two of his friends and the reality of Femi's demand for some kind of reform within Fela's organisation, Fela delegated the YAP boys to take turns to stay around Femi reporting back his state to his anxious father.

The young Kuti came-out of the situation, wiser and determined as we shall see but at what price? He was manipulated to marry one of his father's wives (a Ghanaian named Sewa) in responds to the "wishes and dictates of a spirit". For some time, Femi had been a target by people around Fela who wanted to manipulate the young man in order to get to Fela. This was particularly obvious with his women who after their mass marriage in 1978, not a single wife (queen) had been pregnant a challenge to their fatality and that of their husband too.

Most of them wanted to have children or be the first to be pregnant after the marriage, and they did everything to have a Kuti child. Some of them sleeping with close Kuti relations to ensure a physical resemblance if they get pregnant, while others slept with close Fela friends like JK.

It was no secret in the house that JK would return from his gambling spree in the wee-hours of the morning, walk quietly to some of Fela's wives sleeping in his living room, wake-her-upand invite the woman to his 'Renault' car parked outside for a 'quickie'.

Thanks to an incidence I personally witnessed, Femi was able to admit to his father how some of his queens were making passes at him from the age of fourteen. I remember catching the young Femi in the act sleeping behind the house with one of Fela's wives Ngozi. Instead of reporting the matter to Fela to avoid creating a wedge between father and son, I told my friend Duro Ikujenyo in the YAP leadership.

In my opinion I felt that we needed to talk to Femi about this direct instead of talking to Fela. Duro agreed with me that we should discus this with Femi, making the young man understand how negative it was the idea of sharing those women with his father. For reasons best known to Duro, he changed his mind reporting the matter direct to Fela.

I was summoned to Fela's room with Duro, Yeni, Femi and Fola (Fela's cousin) who worked as accountant with the organisation. To my surprise Fela was not angry with Femi who admitted that most of his father's wives harassed him sexually. To justify the sexual harassment from his wives, Fela claimed that after the birth of his son Kunle in 1971, he discovered from medical examination that his sperm-count was low.

According to him most of the women who shared his bed were aware of this and with his mass marriage to 27 women whose cultural and traditional backgrounds attaches' great importance to having children, as essential to the harmony and happiness in any marriage it was obvious that these women would do anything to have a child for Fela.

Unlike the impression of a harmonic and happy family displayed in public, the queens had a kind of jealousy and hostility prevalent among them. It was no secret that some of them resulted to or deployed "spiritual forces" against their mates or towards Fela to win his 'love'. Stories of 'love' portions used to prepare meals shared with Fela were abounding.

Africans believe in a third personage apart from Christ or Mohammed. Though they may not publicly admit it, whenever an African feels his job or progress threatened they usually seek refuge in a third personage from the many deities worshipped on the continent. Fela considered it as the women's attempt at wining his love, and the incidence with Femi sleeping with his women was considered by him as the attempt at having a Kuti child.

Over the years, some of the women who couldn't wait left, others changed their minds about the marriage but Fela continued his evolution in the struggle and after his release from prison in 1986, he decided to renounce the marriage with the queens that remained from his mass marriage.

While the storm in the family transpired, his relationship with the student community waxed stronger particularly, at a time when the student union movements were being deferred to by the military government. After the 1978 "Ali Must Go" student riot in Nigeria against the Obasanjo regime, the student union movement became a voice that was taken into consideration. Their leaders, were invited to participate in the new appointed civilian constitution drafting committee.

Most of the student union leaders of respective universities were known on a first name basis with Fela. Segun Okeowo, Femi Falana, Wole Olaoye, Donald Duke (who Fela nic-named Donald Duck), all visited the Shrine and had Fela debate and participated in lectures organised on their respective campus. Despite these close contact with the student community, the feedback we in the leadership of our organisation were getting, was the need for physical proof of the existence of Africa's contribution to world's civilisation as we have come to know it today.

As proof on several occasions, Fela referred to the current professional respect and recognition African Europe based traditional medical practitioners are getting from their European counterparts. He made it clear that the recognition accorded these traditional medical practitioners is not only from their professional counterparts.

He also proved to these people how the traditionalists enjoy an economic boom to the extent that some of them are millionaires. To further give proof Fela drew a parallel with Chinese medicine, how Chinese acupuncture is accepted and used in the Western world.

He also made clear to his student audience how all Europe based African traditional doctors use roots, weeds, and tree backs, to form the base of their research and cures. He emphasised that these practice in traditional medicine that has been a part of African society for ages, should be seen as evidence of our contribution to modern day civilisation.

The fact also, that these Africans can cure anything from varicose veins to the more complex heart troubles and many other maladies about which European medical specialists have a lot to learn should have been enough proof to convince the students.

However the legacies of both Christianity and Islam in Africa, plus the "intellectual" and psychological climate of the institutions left behind by colonialism has conditioned the thinking of most Africans. Bearing in mind that 'scientific truths' had been "White" for such a long time, the idea of Africa's contribution to civilisation is unacceptable to a neo-colonial people.

Take for an example the 'Negritude' movement, it was championed by "eminent" people like Leopold S. Senghor, a former president of Senegal and member of the French Academy.

He like others in the movement accepted the so called African inferiority to the White man and boldly assumed it in full view of the world. Not only that, he further went on to preach this gospel of "Negritude", by claiming "Emotion is the Negro and reason is Hellenic" (Greek). It is negative thoughts such as this that makes it difficult for people like Fela to get across, particularly coming from a president who had power behind him unlike Fela who only had his music as platform.

On the other part despite all that is stated above, the demand for physical proof of the spiritual contributions of African ancestors was not much of a surprise if one considers the fact that there is no where in Africa where there is an absolute believe in the doctrines of both Islam and Christianity as I have stated earlier with the case of Fela's wives.

Usually, Africans believe in a third personage apart from Christ or Mohammed. Though they may not publicly admit it, whenever an African feels his job or progress threatened they usually seek refuge in a third personage from the many deities worshipped on the continent. Metaphysics, far from being outdated in Africa is more and more a part of our historical sociology.

With this in mind, we at the head of our organisation consulted extensively with elders of our society but it was fruitless because most of these elders were afraid of government to come out openly to practice their metaphysical knowledge.

Fela once posed the question to a traditional medicine practitioner who regularly consults oracles, why they stopped to tell publicly secrets of ages to our people? The man answered in Yoruba "a n'mberu ijoba ni" (meaning "we are afraid of the government").

African spiritual way of life, which should be source of national guidance as the case is in other nations is taboo in our own land. It is called: "secret-cult", "voodoo", "obeah", "juju", etc. Those who are not afraid of government, prefer to keep the knowledge within their immediate family. Knowledge that was passed from generation to generation, nurtured in an atmosphere of communalism for the protection of the whole community is thus reduced to individual property.

In our search for physical proof, we by chance met with a Ghana based Nigerian business man named Alabi (also called Baba Ajilete). On a trip to Lagos from Ghana, Baba Ajilete told Fela that there is so much talk abounding about Fela's believes and search for 'spiritual powers'.

According to him, the reasons for his visit is to inform Fela of the existence of a magician endowed with spiritual powers called Professor Hindu. Among Hindu's many attributes, was the claim that he could kill and raise a man from the dead. After our extensive consultations, we found it hard to believe this claim by Baba Ajilete.

However he convinced us to allow Hindu prove himself in a performance at the Shrine. Baba Ajilete also informed us, of the existence of medicine men in his village Ajilete about 40 kilometers outside Lagos, who could make African jackets capable of stopping live bullet in its track. Fela asked Baba Ajilete to arrange for him to meet with one of such men. A few days after, we met with the medicine man and it was agreed that he would make one of those jackets for Fela.

As part of our condition to verify its authenticity, it was agreed between us and the medicine man that we bring along a gun to test the jacket. On our arrival in Lagos, since I knew that none of us in the organisation owned any gun I asked Fela if I could consult a neighbour whom I was aware owned a revolver. Fela gave me the go-ahead and I contacted Dr Fola Awosika a medical doctor, who also was doing research in pharmacy with a speciality on African herbal medicine.

He also was very much interested in the bullet-proof jacket story, when I told him the reason why I was asking to borrow his hand gun. Unfortunately due to a previous appointment scheduled, he told me he could not come with us to test the jacket on the agreed day, he however gave us the use of his revolver and when I told him that I had never shot a gun before he showed me how to load and shoot the gun.

Luckily, I did not have to shoot because, J.K. Brimah indicated that he was conversant with guns. Come test day, in the company of Baba Ajilete and some of us top members of the organisation, we arrived in the medicine man's house and he took us immediately into the forest area of Ajilete village.

We placed the prepared jacket on a dead piece of wood, and J.K. from a close range fired three shots from the revolver at the jacket, after the shots we inspected the jacket and did not find any bullet holes in it. To us, it was proof enough of its authenticity.

The medicine man told us he needed to purify the jacket before we left, and he took the jacket into his room and a few minutes after came back with the jacket rapped in a plastic bag. We paid the agreed fee and left with the jacket or what we thought was the tested jacket for Lagos.

On our arrival in Lagos before heading home, Fela suggested we stopped at his older brother Professor Koye Ransome-Kuti's house. The older Kuti brother wanted to know if we had informed Beko, when he was told the reason of our visit. Fela then informed his brother that we would stop at Beko's to possibly invite him to witness the next test.

Beko, a Western trained doctor with a bias towards African traditional medicine, insisted on bringing a gun of his choice for the next test and Fela accepted his terms. Since Beko also did not own a gun, he invited another doctor friend of his who owned one.

Dr Ore Falomo, Koye and Beko arrived at Fela's Atinuke Olabanji residence in Ikeja to carry out the next test. Two goats were purchased for this purpose and since the jacket was designed to protect a living being, our assumption was if it could protect a goat it would do the same for humans.

Without any delays, one of the goats was strapped with the jacket and Dr Ore Falomo took aim and fired a shot at the goat's head. Within seconds of the shot, the goat fell and was dead and to assert that we were doing things right, the next goat was also strapped with the jacket and again Dr Ore Falomo fired a second shot killing the second goat instantly.

The silence from all of us watching was deafening. Fela was speechless and only the tear-drops from his face told it all. The older Kuti brother Koye, had to hug him closely like a father trying to console a disillusioned child. In almost a decade of association with Fela, I only saw him shed tears three times.

The first occasion was the first day we had the opportunity to visit him in court after his house was burnt down, and he was arranged to face a trumped-up gun possession charge. In our brief conversation with him before he was re-arrested and detained under a decree not liable to challenge from any court of law, Fela inquired about the sound-track of the then just completed film 'Black President'.

When we informed him that nothing in the house survived the inferno, I saw tears drop down his face. The second time I saw Fela shed tears, was when he was informed of his mother's death and the third occasion was this day with the bullet-proof jacket. It was obvious how disappointed Fela was.

After the test, Fela made Baba Ajilete and Femi Photo (a member of our organisation) return the jacket with the dead goats to Ajilete, thus ended our liaison with Ajilete and the 'medicine man'.

Meanwhile Professor Hindu seeing the distress and disappointment his friend and manager had caused, approached and assured Fela that he was not a part of the Ajilete hoax. He also affirmed that he intended to prove this to everyone. However for him to be able to prove the existence of this mystical power, he requested Fela to have absolute trust as the only condition that his magic could work.

He added that he was going to prove himself in order to earn this confidence he requested for. Come Hindu's day at the Shrine, to his credit he went on stage just in a short pair of pants and T-shirt, unlike other magicians who perform dressed-up in specially tailored clothes with gadgets etc.

Magic, according to English dictionary definition, is "the art of producing effects by superhuman means, sorcery, enchantment, power similar to that of enchantment". While Hindu's performance cannot be called magic in any sense, it will suffice to say he did play some tricks on his audience dressed the way he did.

He conjured several gold and silver watches from no where, he reassembled shreds of fabric into skirts and a striped dress offered to a young woman in the audience. The high point of his act was the moment where he claimed to slit the throat of a man from the audience.

This act is in dispute because the victim was seated on a chair held down by four hefty looking men and Hindu, with a cutting knife in one hand and a big roll of cotton-wool in the other acted like cutting the man's throat. At the same time he was pushing the cotton-wool over the man's face.

Obviously, something was being done to put the victim to sleep, especially with the cotton-wool that could have contained some chloroform a volatile thin liquid used as an anaesthetic. Hindu's refusal, to allow the unconscious man's throat to be examined by a doctor from the audience put more doubts to his act.

The only concession he gave the doctor was that he could take samples of the blood on the cotton-wool around the victim's neck to test. Another point of dispute was the blood alleged to have come from the victim's neck. It was too small to have come from that part of a human body. Finally, the victim was "buried" in a not too shallow grave, his body was not totally covered with sand and the grave was covered with a white piece of clothe (to facilitate respiration I presume).

For the three days while the body was "buried", only Hindu and his assistant had access to the Shrine and after the victim was alleged to have been "raised" from the dead, there was no visible mark of any cut on his throat. The man said he felt like he was put to sleep, this is another testimony to some form of anaesthesia in use. Despite all these flaws in Hindu's performance, Fela seemed to accept the man as a legitimate magician especially with the turn of events in Kalakuta after Hindu's show and his departure to Ghana.

But before we get to that, Fela's argument was that Western trained doctors will be biased if allowed to examine Hindu's victim.

In a way, his argument had some grounds in view of our previous encounters with such Western trained doctors. For an example traditional African treatment for convulsion is cow urine, this violent involuntary contractions of the muscles is widely treated with cow urine. Almost every cooking place in most homes in Africa, has bottles with this medicine hanging over the fire place. Not until 1977 when the Nigerian Medical Association (NMA) published its approval in one of its bulletins, most Western trained Nigerian doctors condemned the use of cow urine to treat convulsion as unhygienic.

Hindu's acts, should have been subjected to more scrutiny just as we did with the bullet-proof jacket from Ajilete. It became more imperative, to verify Hindu's acts in view of subsequent events in Fela's house after the 'magicians' departure to his Ghana base. Shortly after Hindu left "spirit" men and women started to spring up within the organisation, most of them claimed to have been possessed by Hindu's "spirit" or that of Fela's late mother.

Randomly, people were falling into all kinds of 'spiritual trance' and making outrageous "prophecies". With these came personal witch-hunting and vendettas, if you have any 'bones to pick' with someone all you needed to do is fall into a "trance" and you could accuse the person of anything from being a spy to practising witchcraft.

Outrageous claims of clandestine involvements became the order of the day, people claiming to have been sent to the organisation for various clandestine reasons some of them even claimed to work for America's CIA. There was the case of one "spirit woman" Sewa one of Fela's wives (a Ghanaian), who manipulated Femi to marry her in responds to the "wishes and dictates of a spirit". She wanted to woo me into lending credence to her "prophecy".

During a 'trance', she claimed I was about to be possessed by spirit: "ID will soon come!" (Meaning ID is about to be possessed by spirits). In order to ascertain the truth, I tried to be objective to see if I was about to be possessed by spirit or not and despite my objective state of mind, nothing like that happened to me and I made it clear to everyone.

As a Fela confident, I also called him to caution making him aware that the whole spiritual transformation thing could be a hoax. To avoid making him look gullible in the presence of everyone as the leader of our organisation, I called Fela into his room several times to try and impress this point to him without others being there. I even went as far as saying that the whole spiritual transformation he thought he was experiencing could be psychological. Unfortunately after one of such private talks, Fela chose to come out of the room to tell those present what I had told him.

For me it was OK because it made my position clear to everyone and to make matters worse, Fela chose to give me the name: "ID Mr. Psychology". This was his explanation for why I did not believe in his 'spiritual transformation' thus, the "spirit saga" gained more legitimacy and those who did not believe had to leave the organisation or join in the game.

There was the case of two of Fela's wives (Alake and Adejonwo), whose turn it was to prepare the day's meal for Fela. Usually, such meals were prepared for him as well as those of us friends and top members of the organisation including Femi his son.

I remember that I ate the meal along with four others including Fela but the following day Fela woke up with a stomach upset and Sewa (the spirit woman), accused Alake and Adejonwo of practising witchcraft with Fela's food. They on their part denied this, but they were given some time to think things over before judgement was passed on them. Since I also ate the food, I was consulted by the two women and on my part I made it clear that I enjoyed the meal and like the three others who ate it I did not have any stomach upset like Fela. Unfortunately, my assurance was not good enough to alleviate their fear so they chose to go to Beko with tales of the turn of events in Fela's house.

I was invited along with the two women to Beko's and he in-turn, invited us to accompany him to the older Kuti brother Koye. After our respective explanation of the turn of events in Kalakuta to Koye and Beko, it was decided that the two women would travel to Ghana to bring Hindu to verify the claim of Sewa who said she derived her 'spiritual vision' from Hindu.

To the reader Beko's sanction of this trip might sound out of place, if one bears in mind the fact that he was an atheist and a Western trained medical doctor.

I presume he encouraged them to go and bring Hindu, based on the fact that he knew that only Hindu could say convincingly to Fela if Sewa (the spirit woman) was right or wrong. On their arrival in Ghana after telling Hindu of the turn of events in Fela's house since the 'magician' departure, he denied any knowledge of Sewa's claims and according to the two women who went to invite him from Ghana, he would like to return with them to affirm this and as a result Alake and Adejonwo invited Hindu back to Lagos to clear the air.

The two women, in their excitement to take credit for exposing Sewa's spiritual claims as false contrarily to their agreement with Koye and Beko at their departure for Ghana, chose to take Hindu straight to Fela's home and Sewa who was surprised to see Hindu return started to explain her role to Hindu in a Ghana native language that was not widely spoken by most of the people around. Fela who in other situation as this, would have questioned openly the magician as to what Sewa was saying this time let her brief the Ghanaian without stopping her.

Contrary to what he said to the women in Ghana after Sewa's explanation of events in Kalakuta since he went back, the 'magician' claimed she was seeing 'visions' through his power. The "spirit saga" thus gained credibility, Alake and Adejonwo were punished for their troubles in bringing Hindu from Ghana.

With a hind-sight, I considered as facade Fela's so-called 'spiritual transformation' because we have to remember that he was not getting any younger and after his numerous loss of property and beatings from the army and police, he was getting tired from always being in the fore-front while others sat back. This was one reason, why I felt Hindu gave Fela the needed facade to "Look and Laugh" as he later sang to justify what was going-on around him.

Meanwhile, Fela was preparing to embark on his second Europe tour with his group. The tour was organised from France, by Martin Messioniere the young tour agent whom we met a year earlier during our troubles in Italy in the company of The New Musical Express journalist Vivien Goldman.

As expected in an atmosphere full with superstitions, all kinds of "prophecies" were being foretold especially regarding the outcome of the coming tour.

Almost everyone was trying to out-do the other with their "spiritual prophecies". Like the saying goes "if you cannot beat them you join them" Adejonwo who had earlier opposed the "spirit show" before her trip to bring Hindu from Ghana, suddenly changed and she too started to see "visions" like all others "possessed" by spirit.

During a 'trance' she claimed to have 'discovered' an international conspiracy to assassinate Fela during the up-coming Europe tour, chickens were slaughtered to appease the gods to give Fela victory over his alleged enemies. On the morning of our departure I woke up to find Fela standing outside his home and as expected, his presence outside his house drew the attention of passers-by.

A driver in an International Telegraph and Telephone (ITT) van, was attracted by Fela's presence and he slowed down his car to watch as the crowd started to gather. Unfortunately for the driver, one of the "spirit women" outside the house with Fela thought differently of the driver's intention and she raised alarm that he was out there to spy on Fela in view of the latter's song against ITT (International Thief-Thief).

Members of the organisation standing around, took chase of the car driver and the man had to accelerate his car to avoid being arrested, as expected the alarm plus the chase drew the attention of neighbours - one of such neighbours was Dr Fola Awosika (the man who borrowed us the use of his revolver for the Ajilete bullet-proof jacket test).

Unfortunately for him, he appeared at a wrong moment instead of getting a positive or better polite responds for his inquiry as to what was amiss, Fela pointed at him asking the boys coming back from the fruitless ITT car chase to drag him into the house. Dr Fola Awosika's "offence" was that he gave us "blank bullets" to test the jacket according to Fela. For me watching all these happen to a friend, I was speechless and to make matters worse it was the first time I was aware of any dispute as to the authenticity of the gun we used in Ajilete to test the bullet-proof jacket.

I was caught between two opposing streams - on the one hand was Dr Awosika appealing to me to say something in his defence, and on the other I was shocked to discover that Fela whom I thought I had his confidence believed the gun I brought to test the bullet proof jacket was fake.

Luckily Fela changed his mind and the doctor was set free but from that day on, Dr. Fola Awosika stopped talking to me or any member of the organisation. He kept his distance even after our return from the Europe tour when Fela asked me, to go and apologise on his behalf to the doctor. Shortly after this incidence, we all boarded our bus and proceeded to the Lagos airport to commence our Europe tour.

On our arrival at the airport instead of going into the building to check-in, Fela stood outside starring into the sun and at this point I felt I needed to talk to him to advice against anymore bizarre acts like we had witnessed since the beginning of the day. When I whispered to him that people would think he was out of his mind seeing him stare into the sun aimlessly, Fela's reaction was to admonish me and he asked me to apologise to his mother for making him disobey her instructions saying: "ID, my mother instructed me to look into the sun and you are asking me not to? Beg my mother!"

To avoid any arguments with him in public, I prostrated in the Yoruba traditional way to his unseen mother but after my apology he walked into the airport building as I had asked him.

Immediately he stepped into the building another of the "spirit women" standing close to him, whispered something in his ear and to the surprise of all around, Fela started to run from one end of the departure hall to the other. At a point in the ensuing pandimonium, I managed to catch up with him and again I opened my mouth to advice against such public display but like he did outside the airport building Fela again asked me to apologise to his mother.

I did as I was told to avoid any confrontation with him in public and he again stopped running but at that moment, a Nigerian immigration officer walked over to him to acknowledge Fela's presence.

To the man's warm greetings Fela's responds was "Catch fire!" This I presume was part of the "spiritual transformation" he was prophesied to go through. In one of the "prophecies" of one of the "spirit women," it was predicted that Fela would develop the ability to command anything to happen according to his wishes.

The immigration officer, who was shocked at Fela's "catch fire" responds to his greetings asked what all that was about. On my part in order to intercede, I explained the futility of Fela's action to him but he again asked me to apologise to his mother whom I was aware was long dead.

While all this was going on, it was announced over the public address system for all passengers travelling on our scheduled flight to proceed to the boarding gate. As expected Fela's presence anywhere in Nigeria usually draws the attention of people around, and with all the bizarre actions of his at the airport, a large crowd had gathered and to ensure an orderly passage for all passengers to the boarding point, the immigration officers on duty formed a human barrier insisting on allowing only passengers with boarding passes through.

Fela however saw this action as an attempt to stop him from travelling, and to ensure that everyone travelling with him went through immigration check safely, he prepared to force his way with the officers.

Unfortunately Fela's first wife Remi who had remained quiet while all these pandemonium lasted, shouted at him to behave himself. Instead of responding to her outcry, Fela called me aside and whispered in my ears: "ID, that woman is a CIA agent! Don't tell anyone!" For me this was the 'last straw that broke the camel's back', knowing Remi and Fela the way I do, I could not believe what I heard coming from Fela's mouth.

Remi had been with him since he was a student and in fact had his first three children, almost 21 years after staying married to him - she was being called a CIA agent? At this point I realised something had to be done urgently and it was clear Fela was no longer in control, but the reality of my position within the organisation made things delicate.

I know I am not a Kuti despite being a Fela close confidant, and I was aware I did not have the powers to commit him into a home for medical examination, the only person who could have done this legally was Remi being his married wife but to arrive at such a decision she would need the backings of almost all top members of our organisation - some of whom were playing the "spirit game".

Most of the top members JK included, chose to go along with the "spirit show" as some of us came to call it, without their support it would be difficult to convince him to subject himself to medical examination.

To compound my dilemma, behind the scene almost everybody in the organisation's leadership: JK, Duro, Femi Photo, agreed that the "spirit" affair was a hoax but in Fela's presence they acted differently.

My public opposition to the "spirit" issue, afforded me the opportunity to hear first hand how the people felt about it all. When I inquired why they were not voicing their disagreement, most of them pointed to the physical punishments dissenters were subjected to and my example that people like me couldn't be physically punished for opposing the "spirit show" was not reassuring to most of the people I spoke with in private.

Since officially I could not get Fela committed to a home to examine his mental state not being a Kuti, my position became more unjustifiable to make such a decision. The only person I could turn to was Remi but I was in a dilemma to discuss this line of action with her, I would have to tell Remi what Fela whispered in my ear in Lagos airport. How could I tell a woman that her husband for 21 years thought she was a CIA agent?

As a way out, I decided to keep my thoughts from everyone and I did my work moving around like one in a state of delirium during this tour. Paranoia was all over the place, everyone we came in contact with was suspect and for the first time I saw Fela perform without the precision and the particular attention he gave to the presentation of his shows.

Members of the organisation who had nothing to do on stage, were standing there in the name of protecting him from an alleged assassin's bullet and on the final leg of the tour, we had a week's stay in Paris to record the album ORIGINAL SUFFER-HEAD for Arista Records in England.

Despite all the "prophecies" there was no attempt on Fela's life but to bring that up, is to give credibility to the "sacrifices" and slaughtering of chickens made to the gods before our departure. It was obvious something had to be done, Fela was all the time trying to convince everyone around him of his impending "spiritual transformation" and in the end, I had to go to Remi who from the first performance of Hindu at the Shrine, made it clear that she did not believe in the man's magical ability.

As I had expected she wanted to know first what it was Fela whispered to me in Lagos airport. To convince her of the need for concrete action, I told her what he said and I impressed it on her that she should not take this seriously since this was not the real Fela we both know so well.

With regards to a solution, we both agreed to leave things until I came back from London as I was due to leave the next day to deliver the final mix of the album recorded for Arista Records and to collect £25,000 Fela's advance royalty for the record which we needed to pay bills the tour budget couldn't pay.

I left the hotel in Paris the next day for the airport in one of the most frightening thunderstorm I ever experienced, it rained heavily that day otherwise my flight to London was relatively uneventful. At the airport in London, I phoned the record company and made an appointment for the following day.

I checked into my hotel and with the rest of the evening free, I chose to visit an old friend whom I knew lived not too far from my hotel. We went to a concert at the Brixton Academy and had a good time having fun in the swinging London night life.

I returned to my hotel room in the wee-hours of the morning to find messages from the hotel reception asking me to call Fela in Paris no matter how late I got back. I dialled his hotel room number and he picked up the phone at the first ring an indication that he was waiting for my call. He immediately wanted to know the position of things, with regards to my appointment with the record company.

I assured him that my meeting was not until later in the morning and that was the reason why I went out all night but to my surprise, he changed the subject of discussion by asking why I revealed what he told me about Remi in Lagos airport to her.

Though I was disappointed that Remi told him what I had revealed to her in confidence, I realised it was best to bring-up the issue of him seeing a doctor for medical examination. I explained that he was no longer the Fela I used to know, pointing to all his bizarre actions since the advent of the "spirit saga". As a reproach, he said if he thought I was loosing my mind he would not consult with my immediate family like I did his, he went on to say he would have taken me to see a doctor if he had the feeling that I was loosing my mind.

I tried to make him see the futility, of me unilaterally taking such a decision in his case as the leader of our organisation. He finally attributed, my divulging of the "secret" as my lack of understanding of the "spiritual transformation" he was going through.

He cited the thunderstorm that accompanied me on my way to the airport earlier in the day as a sign of protection for me from his mother. According to him, the thunderstorm was to protect me and the 25,000 pounds (cash) I was collecting from Arista records. After taking care of business, I flew immediately back to Paris to find out how things had turned for the worse, Remi had left for Lagos with her two daughters in protest to Fela's CIA accusation. The following day, we all returned to Lagos and we found-out she had moved out of the house.

I felt my divulging the CIA accusation must have pushed Remi to finally leave him, and Fela on his part did not forgive me for this. I believe he held me responsible for her departure and my argument that I had to tell Remi to impress on her, the need for an urgent solution to this "spirit drama" did not absolve me from his blame.

With everyday that passed it became obvious to me that our struggle was loosing its focus, our search for physical proof as stated at the beginning of this chapter was getting more side tracked and word was getting around, people within and outside the organisation were talking about the crazy change going-on in Fela's commune.

Fela himself began to loose interest in going on the lecture and symposium circuits, that was helping us to put our ideas across to the student community and the Nigerian press that saw Fela as the only voice of opposition against the military dictatorship, suddenly stopped going to Fela for commentaries on various issues happening in the country. Since it was my duty to work with the press, it became more indefensible for me to explain the crazy happenings in Fela's house and anytime a member of the press stopped for commentaries on any issue, Fela's prime interest was to talk about his "spiritual transformation".

The sad aspect of this was that there was no visible transformation that one could point to, and some of the press personnel ended up asking me if I was sure Fela was sane?

How could I admit to anyone that I thought the man I represent was insane? The only option I had was to explain it in terms of human psychology and even with this, I had to be careful so that my own sanity would not be questioned. My position became less credible as things continued and I felt we were loosing our direction, but I could not abandon Fela and everybody in view of his: "ID, If you YAP Boys ever leave me…" statement two years earlier.

Finally, things came to a head for me with an unexpected police raid on the house. Unlike previous encounters the police stormed the house this time around, forced everyone outside the building and made us sit on the floor. At a point while all this was going on, the thought crossed my mind that the police raid was illegal (not sanctioned by police headquarters) particularly since, Fela rarely commented about the politics of the Shehu Shagari civilian regime.

Also the nature of previous raids where we were usually forced out of the house into waiting vans and driven to the police headquarters, reassured me in this line of thinking and in case we wanted to press charges against the police, I decided to memorise the registration number of the police vehicle close to me. Unfortunately I could not see the rear of the vehicle from where I was sitting, so I stood-up and instead of getting a reprisal from the police for standing up, they jumped into their waiting vans and left as suddenly as they came.

Sewa one of Fela's "spirit women" later thought differently of my standing up during the police raid, according to her it was a pre-arranged signal between me and the police as to where to search in the house. She accused me of playing on the anti-Ghana sentiments prevailing in Nigeria at that time, with a mass exodus of Ghana citizens from Nigeria.

All the economic and insecurity problems that reigned in Nigeria were blamed on the presence of "foreigners" mostly Ghanaians, hence the government of Shehu Shagari ordered all foreigners out of the country. Kalakuta had quite a large Ghana community, hence Sewa's fear when the police came raiding the house. To my surprise, Fela believed this allegation and he again cited my telling Remi of his CIA accusation as evidence of my diabolical acts within the organisation.

After almost a decade with this organisation, if my loyalty becomes a matter of question I guess it was time for me to move on. I realised as a folly my insistence on staying around because of the: "ID! If you YAP Boys ever leave me" statement from Fela. It was obvious to me that there was no basis for trust between us anymore and I made this clear to him.

I remember walking over to him sitting in the living room surrounded by his women. I thanked him for all he had taught me and I also told him I was withdrawing my services with the organisation in view of our mutual lack of trust. Thus ended my almost a decade of association with Fela and his Africa 70 Organisation.

In my attempt to explain the sequence of events that led to my parting of ways with Fela, I guess I must have presented the picture of a crazy man but despite the bizarre nature of my story I can say with all conviction that Fela was not crazy.

Though I am not a professional psycho-analyst and I do not have any medical report from a doctor who has had the opportunity to examine Fela during the "spirit saga", despite all these I still believe he was not crazy. With a hind-sight it was clear to me he was only disillusioned with the Nigerian people who sat arm-crossed while the system did everything to destroy him.

I have had the privilege to watch Fela perform on several occasions since our parting of ways and from my observation, his artistic genius was still very much intact. What then could one attribute to the cause of the turn of events?

The only person capable of explaining his state of mind was Fela himself, and a song he wrote shortly after the advent of the "spirit saga" could help us define correctly how the man felt then and towards the end of his life.

Fela in the song titled LOOK & LAUGH sang:
"Since long time I never write new song
Since long time I never sing new tune
Many of you go dey wonder why
Your man never write new song
Many of you go dey wonder why

Fela never write new tune
No be say I no want write new song
No be say I no want write new tune
To make you think and happy
Wetin I dey do be say
Wetin I dey do be say
I dey look and laugh (Chorus)"

Meaning: "many of you must have been wondering why, your man has not written new songs! It is not that I don't want to write new tunes to make you think and happy...what I am doing is just look and laugh". Fela went on to explain his contributions and sacrifices for the cause of black emancipation and the countless beatings and arrests from the Nigerian police and army, his trials and tribulations, his ultimate sacrifice the burning down of Kalakuta by the Nigeria army.

Despite his sacrifices and sufferings like million other Africans, he felt it was obvious that things were not getting better for the average man on the street. There are still injustice everywhere, no freedom, no happiness and despite his outspoken criticisms, the people seem not to want to do anything to change the situation - all these made him feel disillusioned and all he could do about the situation was to Look and Laugh. By 1981 when Fela wrote and started to perform live the song 'Look and Laugh' he was living a life that could be described as a recluse.

Fela who loved to go out for public lectures, symposiums, clubs, suddenly was always found sleeping or playing sax at home with women around him or performing at the Africa Shrine. His old attitude of keeping abreast of events giving lectures at universities and institutions of higher learning suddenly stopped, he rarely gave press conferences or press releases like he used to do.

His refuge in a "spiritual transformation" was understandable if one considers the price the man had paid for the struggle: several beatings and arrests from the police and army, plus the fact that he was not getting any younger. Be that as it may, my position regarding all this was I do not believe after all his contributions, that he should take the posture of LOOK & LAUGH.

It will amount to putting to waste a life of service to his people.

If he was disillusioned about the lack of a mass revolt in support of him during his many trials and tribulations, he should realise that this was because of the lack of an organised mass movement, out to educate the people on their rights like we tried with YAP before the movement was proscribed by the Obasanjo regime.

With my departure from the organisation, it was obvious I did not have anymore clout to give an opinion and whenever we met and I tried to bring issues like this up, Fela's responds was always "all that one nah gbe! Gbe! Gbe!" In Yoruba it means "all that is just talk".

Despite this I believed what was important for Fela at that point was to clean up his acts, he already had the ability and credibility of not being a part of the system that was exploiting the masses, the social rebellion that Kalakuta represented should be put to more positive work.

It was my conviction that most of the inhabitants of his home after finding work and freedom within his organisation waste away smoking marijuana. I felt instead of "Look and Laugh," it was time for him to educate his followers on the ways of revolutionaries and their methods, I remember we YAP boys brought this issue up with Fela shortly before the house was burnt down in 1977. Lemi, Duro, and I, noticed more than six months after the launching of the Young African Pioneers movement that there were few people within Kalakuta that were registered as members of YAP.

Kalakuta residents believed that as members of the Africa 70 organisation, they were automatic members of the movement. It became evident to us in the Care-taker committee of the movement from an incidence I noticed and later discussed with my two other friends while I was in the YAP office.

On the day in question, I suddenly saw a rush of some female members of Kalakuta to the office asking to be registered, though I complied with their requests I wanted to know the reason behind the sudden rush. One of the women explained to me that Fela was having an interview with a journalist covering FESTAC'77 and according to her, the journalist asked Fela what steps he was taking to organise the Nigerian masses to effect a change in our society, in responds he mentioned the founding of YAP.

He then asked, some members of his house sitting-in during the interview for an example of the YAP membership card. Unfortunately there was no one in the house with a YAP membership card and Fela was so embarrassed, to save face some of the women rushed to the YAP office situated in the Shrine just across the street to register as members and show their membership cards to Fela and his interviewer.

This incident more than proved to us the lackadaisical attitude of Kalakuta inhabitants to Fela vision of a Pan-African society. It was obvious that with some encouragement and pushing from him, people in his house could be organised to form the vanguard of a movement that would explain his ideas to the people. We discussed this with him, and he always said we should wait until he had money and could re-build the house with an auditorium where we could hold regular lectures with members of the organisation.

Also shortly before my parting of ways with Fela I remember making a criticism of one of his female dancers that she was no longer the fiery dancer she used to be and in responds, she asked me if I would encourage my daughter to take up a dancing career with Fela's organisation as it was.

Though I did not give her any answer, I went to think her question over in my solitary moments and I remember saying loud to myself NEVER! For me to encourage my daughter to take a dancing career with Africa 70 Organisation as it was, I would be failing in my duties to her as a father.

I have nothing against dancing as a career, rather my disagreement was that Africa 70 dancers needed to have a school that will enable them learn all the art and discipline of dancing to a professional level. My reason was based on the fact that there was no career guidance and advice within the organisation. In view of the failure of the Nigerian system as pointed out by Fela in the last three decades, people would have been more proud to identify with him and his African ideas if he presented his organisation as an alternative.

If his son Femi had to teach himself music, what then is the purpose of Fela's knowledge of music? There are thousands of semiliterate, but intelligent youths milling around then and what remains today of Kalakuta republic. Many of them, apart from working within the organisation sell marijuana on the side to make ends-meet financially.

They profited from Fela's influence in the area without trying to profit with his knowledge to become somebody in the society - these able bodied men and women who could contribute more positively to the propagation of his Pan-African ideas through their participation in lectures, seminars and other community services.

I believe this was the idea Femi was trying to impress on his father at the beginning of the "spirit saga" unfortunately he was not coherent enough to explain his ideas clearly.

I believe the young Kuti wanted to see more coherent actions in the organisation like he did with the financing of the YAP movement publishing and distribution of 80,000 copies of the YAP NEWS all-over the country every month. I remember on several occasions before my departure from the organisation, several conversations with Femi and his mother and the issue of convincing Fela to surround himself with people who want to work to realise this Pan-African goal.

We felt that he should set up schools that would study our culture and develop it as a vehicle of thought and agent of our civilisation. Like he himself used to say, it was not his duty to put in place all these social services if we have the right people and government in power.

However if they are not living up to expectations, we doing criticisms, can also create alternative examples for people to see with an exemplary organization like Africa 70 Organization. Also the physical proof his audience were asking for as explained at the beginning of this chapter are readily available in books.

For example, Cheikh Anta Diop in his book Civilisation or Barbarism clearly explains the origin of today's civilisation as we know it in the World. There are several other books published, that point to the same African origin of civilisation all we needed to do was find arrangements with the publishers to make them available.

But like I said earlier, all the years of persecutions were beginning to take its toll on the man, the financial squeeze did not help matters as the least Fela needed to do was to find the means to make the books available to his students' audience.

Like he sang in the song MISTAKE:

"Mistake you go make, people go laugh at you! After they laugh at you they keep laughing at you! Na bad mistake! (Chorus) Mistake you go make you no go fit stand like man! Na bad mistake" (Chorus).

This song is about perseverance, Fela said even if misunderstood and persecuted for one's believes, the most important thing is believe in the justness of one's cause. It was clear to me that at this time in his life Fela had become a phenomenon despite all his setbacks, hence it did not make sense for him to sit back after all the problems he sang and spoke about in the last three decades.

I felt it will amount to a big mistake (like he sang) on his part, to allow the system frustrate him to sit back and only look & laugh. This was how I felt for years after my departure from the organisation, I kept visiting the Shrine like members of the public and visited him at home in the company of his daughters Yeni and Sola who at this time were living with their mother Remi.

She had rented an apartment in Shomolu area of Lagos Mainland, from her Taylor family heritage after her departure from Fela. Many times she re-assured me that my telling her of Fela's comments at Lagos airport was not the reason why she left, for her she couldn't imagine that Fela would be that gullible to the spirit hoax.

I hope her children would one day publish her 'memoires' because I remember reading scripts from her talking about this episode before I left Nigeria to live in Europe.

While he did not openly admit this it was clear Fela did not believe Hindu and the "spirit transformation" hoax, his action in 1984 before his departure on an American tour would confirm this. But before going into details, it should be noted that Fela's visionary nature of condemning the transformation from military to civil rule in Nigeria as an 'Army Arrangement was confirmed despite the "spirit show".

The civilian rule was short-lived, Shehu Shagari was deposed in a military coup in December 1983 replaced by General Mohammed Buhari as head of state.

Also visionary was Fela's sarcasm about the introduction of "Austerity" measures by Nigerian government, in the wake of International Monetary Fund's (IMF) imposition of devaluation of the currencies of African nations in the 1980s.

Despite criticisms of this measure in songs like Look and Laugh, Authority Stealing, and his public statements, there was no reaction against IMF devaluation then by the leadership in Africa and in Europe.

Today (2011) austerity is installing in Europe with crises of unemployment, cuts in social spending, escalating national debts, and movements of young people who want change. Who is still saying the phenomenon that was Fela is not visionary?

Front cover album design Authority Stealing

Front cover album design Beasts of No Nation

BEASTS OF NO NATION

Like I mentioned at the end of the last chapter, while he did not openly admit this it was clear Fela did not believe Hindu and the entire "spirit transformation" facade that he tried to make believe, his action before the group's departure on an American tour would confirm this.

On September 4, 1984 Fela and forty-one members of his organisation were on their way to New York to do a US tour, this would have been his first trip to the US since his March 1970 return to Nigeria after his ten month stay in the United States of America.

Fela for many years escaped conviction in any law court because he was always thinking ahead of the law - he missed the jail sentence until the 8th November 1984, when he was sentenced to a ten-year jail term for allegedly contravening the exchange control (anti sabotage) decree.

Travelling on a Nigeria Airways flight from Lagos, he was arrested at the Murtala Mohammed International Airport for being in possession of £1,600 contrary to the directives of Decree 7 of 1984, promulgated by the new military regime headed by General Mohamed Buhari and his deputy Major General Tunde Idiagbon, to stem the flow of the Nigerian currency from being taken out of the country in large quantity as was the practice by many rich citizens.

According to people around him at this period, Fela who was aware that the new military regime would jump at the possibility of a contravention from him to make of him an example to the Nigeria public. Before his departure with his group to the airport, Fela was said to have given the $1,600 to Hindu asking the Ghanaian 'magician' to use his skills to make the money disappear while going through customs.

This incidence was a pointer that Fela, did not believe in the "spirit saga" despite his make believe attitude as we shall discover along this narrative. As his usual attitude while travelling with his group, Fela always made sure everybody travelling with him went through custom before passing through himself. On this day it was not different, all the other members travelling with him had gone through custom with the exception of Hindu who was being searched by a custom agent.

According to people around, Fela suspected that Hindu must have hidden the money in a winter coat he was carrying instead of making the money disappear as he pretended to. To avoid the money being found on Hindu, Fela called-out to the "magician" to pass the winter coat he was carrying to facilitate his body search. Hindu complied, handing the coat over to Fela and shortly after the "magician" was let through by the Nigerian Custom agent.

Meanwhile, Fela known generally never to carry anything on him not even money - his clothes were sewn with just one inner pocket that can only contain a "joint" as he usually did travelling in aeroplanes. This time carrying a winter coat as he tried to pass through security check, a custom agent who saw Fela collect the coat from Hindu earlier demanded to examine the coat before letting Fela through.

In compliance he handed the coat over and the custom agent while searching, pulled out the wads of note from the winter coat pocket. Fela immediately claimed ownership of the £1,600 pounds as security agents were called in and to avoid the whole group missing the flight, Fela instructed JK to take charge of the rest members of the group, while he ordered Femi to lead the band if he did not arrive on time before the first show in New York.

He was shortly after detained and three days after on September 7, he was arranged before a Nigerian High Court Judge Fred Anyaegbunam charged with illegal possession of foreign currency and he was accorded bail after his passport had been confiscated by the authorities.

Meanwhile as earlier mentioned forty-one members of his organisation had left for the US in anticipation that Fela would be set free, and in an attempt to publicly appeal to the government to step-in to help pave the way for him to honour his contractual agreement abroad, Fela called a press conference at his Ikeja residence.

He was re-arrested, in the middle of the press conference by plain clothe security men. The news of Fela's arrest in Nigeria deeply affected his tour in the United States and the band lead by Femi, were able to do just two shows before they were forced to return to Nigeria as a result of cancellations from other venues.

After the interruption of his press conference and his arrest on 13th September 1984, Fela was charged before the Port Harcourt Zone of the Exchange Control (anti sabotage) tribunal on a two count charge:

1. That he attempted to export £1,600 without permission from the ministry of finance as stipulated by the decree.

2. That he failed to declare on a prescribed blue form that he was in possession of the money before attempting to leave the country.

The tribunal was headed, by a high court judge Justice Gregory Okoro-Idogu. Twelve prosecution witnesses from the Customs, Police, Nigerian Airways, and the Nigerian Security Printing and Minting Company, were called to testify and eleven exhibits were tendered to prove Fela culpable. Fela was represented by Kanmi Ishola-Osobu before the tribunal. The latter, had kept his 'friendly' relationship with Fela despite Kanmi publicly declared membership of National Party of Nigeria (NPN party of deposed civilian government headed by Shehu Shagari).

Despite their separation of ways after the Kalakuta attack in 1977, Kanmi tried to re-new his friendship with Fela years after. He solicited Fela's musical skill for the political campaigns of NPN in the 1983 election, and he arranged a meeting in his Ebute Meta office with Umaru Dikko Minister of Transport and Chairman of NPN presidential campaign committee. At the meeting, Fela turned down the invitation to perform for NPN on ideological grounds, and he told Dikko he did not share the NPN ideology despite the huge financial benefits promised him.

Shehu Shagari was re-elected despite Fela's refusal to participate in his campaign, but the election crystallised the ambiguity of an attempt to implant a western style democracy in an African society. The ruling NPN party, claimed to have won with twelve-two third percentage of the votes counted while the opposition cried foul. The end result, further instability and insecurity reigning all over the federation - a perfect excuse for a military intervention.

Within a year of Shagari's re-election, the army again seized power and most of the civilian administration members went into exile - among them Umaru Dikko.

He demanded political asylum in England, and in their attempt at bringing members of deposed civilian regime to trial for plundering Nigerian treasury, the Buhari–Idiagbon regime kidnapped Umaru Dikko outside his London home and attempted to export his drugged body in a crate to Lagos.

A Nigerian Airways plane was waiting to transport the human 'cargo,' but Dikko was saved by vigilant British security agents at the airport. The incident would cause a big diplomatic dispute between the British government and the Nigerian military regime, a raw that lasted and probably accelerated the overthrow of the regime by General Babangida a little over a year after seizing power.

While the handing over of power by General Obasanjo to Shagari civilian administration in 1979 was hailed in the west, Fela called it an "army arrangement" and subsequent political scenarios of coup and counter coup d'état in 1984 and 1985 justified Fela's position.

Going back to his 1984 appearance before the tribunal in Fela's defence, Kanmi called four witnesses and tendered three exhibits. Addressing the court, Kanmi Osobu pleaded that: "The case presented by the prosecution suffers debilitating and incurable procedural defects which were fatal to the prosecution's case.

The decree made it mandatory on the Federal attorney general or by such officer subordinate to him as he may authorise, to commence the trial of offences under the decree by way of application supported by proof of evidence, where there is neither proof of evidence nor copies of evidence through an affidavit, the prosecution's trial suffers from major incurable and fatal defects".

Kanmi argued that the question of affidavit was obligatory because the word used in the decree is "shall", and he said the prosecution failed to invoke section (3) of the decree which required the accused to show 'cause' why he should not be punished.

Osobu said: "The procedure had been flagrantly departed from, the prosecution by taking steps contrary to the clear provisions of the decree had not made matters clear either generally or particularly enough to the defence case. Furthermore, there was no investigation done as is known in criminal procedures in this case".

Kanmi Osobu submitted that the Force CID hijacked the case from the Board of Custom and Exercise and he referred to the evidence of the 1st, prosecution witness Assistant Commissioner of Police Yaro Tarfa who said the police did "partial investigation," after himself had watched the report of a related press conference on television.

Osobu added "there is no iota of evidence of what the police investigation did on the important document that is vital to the prosecution of the case. For example, there was no direct positive, clear and unambiguous evidence on the 'yellow form' of the accused. The 'blue form' of the accused (the currency registration register–exhibit J), other than that he Mr Tarfa collected same almost six or seven days after the event".

Mr Osobu said the prosecution took no statements from any of the witnesses when the matter was still fresh and clear to them, "thus when they were asking for statements from the accused, they were either being oppressive and unfair and or guilty of double standards". However Osobu admitted, that there was an investigation of some sort which he said was carried out by the Board of Custom and Excise.

This investigation he claimed was favourable to the accused and for this reason the police took over and submerged it. Osobu said the prosecution refused to bring all the 'blue forms,' collected on the day of the incident because "they knew that the accused form was in the pack".

He affirmed that Fela's evidence that he filled the 'blue form' was collaborated by the 2nd prosecution witness who said it was impossible for anyone to pass through customs without filling the 'blue form'. Osobu also claimed that the prosecution did not adduce any evidence to prove that Murtala Mohammed Airport Ikeja was a custom airport, which by law is the only place from which anyone could travel abroad.

This lack of evidence he said, further compounded the fact that the date on the manifest tendered as exhibit was different from that of the boarding pass also admitted as exhibit. Osobu argued that although the decree put a ceiling of $50 on the amount a traveller could take abroad, the blue form also carried a foot note saying that a family travelling together could fill one form.

He said "on that date in question Fela was travelling with 41 members of his organisation, they included his wives and children - the evidence before the tribunal is that the amount was shared amongst them all one by one and every member of the group shall be entitled to an amount less than $40, an amount that by law and regulation can be legitimately taken out without the minister's consent".

Osobu submitted that Fela was not in the class of persons the decree had in its view to punish or even make a defendant, judging from the fact that he paid $14,000 American dollars to the nation's carrier (Nigeria Airways Limited) in New York for tickets – a patriotic act on the part of the accused. He urged the tribunal to acquit Fela, because of the "multiple discrepancies and gaping evidence of the prosecution".

However sentencing Fela to a ten year prison term, in his judgement the tribunal Chairman explained that the offending act was Fela's failure, to obtain permission from the minister of Finance before attempting to re-export the £1,600 pounds he had imported into the country a few days earlier.

Taking into account the argument from the tribunal anyone who has ever had to obtain such permit, would testify that it could never have been possible to complete the transactions involved within the 48 working hours Fela had to spend within the country after his return from London where he went to conclude arrangements for the tour. The bureaucratic procedures one has to wade through before getting to the "appropriate authorities" in most of Nigeria's public establishment, are hardly conducive to such speedy transactions.

This fact unfortunately, does not seem to have been taken into consideration by the tribunal. Further a foreign diplomat in Lagos said in sympathy to Fela's predicament that the American Embassy should have turned down Fela's visa application or better still, issued him the visa on the very day he applied for it if they were aware he was carrying the money with him on the trip.

With this Fela would have beaten the 48 hours deadline stipulated by the decree, and this was the same expressed opinion of majority of Nigerians who saw the verdict of the tribunal as one of those cases in which an undue concern with technicalities of law, ultimately leads to a verdict that is unfair if not entirely unjust.

The decree which Fela was convicted was aimed at combating economic sabotage, while his actions may have gone contrary to the letters of the decree, that action certainly could not be termed an act of economic sabotage. The money he was attempting to re-export according to his charges, was his legitimately earned money drawn from the Lloyd Bank account in England where his royalties were paid.

Fela neither bought the money from illegal currency market nor did he ever engage in the trade in exchange for Naira. Ultimately, Free Fela benefit concerts were organised world-wide and demonstrations against the Nigerian regime were held in many European capitals before the Nigerian embassy.

Meanwhile the show must go on as the saying goes, in the Shrine to support the large dependants and members of the organisation following Fela's instructions, Femi lead the band on stage and tried to re-organise the organisation relatively in line with his idea before the "spirit saga".

He however had an obstacle in his way in the person of his uncle Beko, but before we go into details it will be appropriate to note the reaction of Africa 70 members towards Hindu shortly after Fela's conviction – another indication that majority of the people in Kalakuta too did not believe in the "spiritual transformation".

Hindu had sensed the hostility of Kalakuta residents towards him from the moment they all arrived in Lagos from the cancelled US tour. The hostility came to a head, when the Ghanaian 'magician' refused to attend the tribunal session on the judgement day.

Anticipating a conviction for Fela, Hindu profited with the presence of Kalakuta members in court, to try and escape before their return. Unfortunately for him, the group arrived just as the 'magician' was leaving the commune.

Angered by Fela's conviction the common opinion was that Hindu was responsible for making Fela believe he could make the money disappear. His alleged 'magical' powers, could not foresee that the members will catch him trying to escape from Kalakuta. Hindu was beaten by the angry members who profited from Fela's absence to deal with the Ghanaian 'magician', thus ended the "spirit-saga" in Kalakuta and Hindu's final departure from the community.

With Fela away in prison for ten years, he gave a 'power of attorney' to Beko to administer the Africa 70 organisation in his absence. The arrangement was that Femi would lead the band on days the group performed and report to Beko, who was responsible for the over-all administration of the organisation.

Problem started between Femi and his uncle over disposability. Beko wanted Femi to report to him every morning after each concert, while the young Kuti after performing till the wee-hours of the morning, found this arrangement not convenient and he told Beko this.

I guess Beko was trying to be difficult with Femi because he held the young Kuti culpable for the "spirit saga" that contributed to Fela ending-up in jail. This point of view is based on the fact that despite my departure from the organisation I kept abreast of events by visiting Remi, her mother, and the two Kuti daughters (Yeni and Sola) at their Somolu residence.

With these visits I kept abreast of events within the organisation. Despite his mother's enstrangement with Fela, Femi also visited his immediate family regularly before Fela was sent to jail. During the trial however, Femi renounced his marriage with Sewa (the Ghanaian spirit woman), and moved out of Fela's (JK's) residence because he didn't feel comfortable with many things in the organisation as he had tried to impress on everyone at the beginning of his 'high fever' that was later recuperated by his father's wives who had other objectives in mind as earlier stated.

While living with his mother in Somolu, Femi kept his part of the bargain leading Fela's band and trying to improve the organisation. He gave-up smoking marijuana and was particularly heavy on the many hanger-on's, who profited with their connection with members of the organisation to deal 'marijuana'.

The young band leader prohibited the sale of marijuana inside the Shrine contrarily to what transpired while Fela was around, and the changes made by Femi made the headlines in many Nigerian newspapers with most of them favourable in opinion to the cleaning-up within his fathers organisation.

Beko however was not happy with the changes Femi was trying to make within the organisation, he criticised the young Kuti accusing Femi of trying to destroy his father's image, thus started a clash of interest that would eventually lead to a family discord carried on even after Fela's death many years after.

With this conflict of leadership within the organisation Femi, accompanied by his two sisters and the author, decided to inform Fela of developments in Maiduguri prison where he was serving his jail sentence. Femi informed Fela of the steps he took - justifying it by making his father understands the need for a clean-up within the organisation.

However Fela assured Femi that he understood the need for the clean-up, but he advised that it was better for the young Kuti to wait until he came-out of jail. To calm his children, he told them not to worry about Beko's high-handedness and he assured them that things would be rectified soon as he was released from prison. The four of us returned to Lagos and Femi tried to do his best cleaning-up the organisation's acts, and performing regularly with the band despite constant obstacles from Beko.

Things did not improve between the two and in the cause of Fela's two years stay in prison, I was privy to and accompanied his children on four visits to Maiduguri and Benin prisons where the children were forced to seek their father's mediation in the impasse. Keeping his promise to his father, Femi continued to work with the band recruiting news musicians to bring new energy to the Egypt 80 group.

I was always present during the group's performance despite my official departure from the organisation. Fela' was aware of my regular visits as I had the opportunity to visit him in Maiduguri Prison alone when I went to ask for his written authorisation to publish my first book, "Fela Why Blackman Carry Shit" required by my Nigerian publisher – Opinion Media Limited.

The military regime meanwhile, continued with its relative contradictions and double standards. It was no surprise when General Buhari's regime was deposed in a military coup headed by Major General Ibrahim Babangida in July 1985.

Fela however, would remain in jail until a news scoop published in the 21st April 1986 issue of the weekly magazine – NEWSWATCH, would reveal that the judge that convicted Fela paid him a visit in jail to apologies. The news scoop credited it's source of information to Beko.

It disclosed that Justice Okoro-Idogu the tribunal chairman responsible for the pronouncement of the 10 year jail sentence he was serving, visited Fela at the Maiduguri Teaching Hospital where he was temporarily admitted for urinal problems in company of the Chief Superintendent of Maiduguri prison Mr P. Goji. The visit took place shortly after dusk on September 24, 1985 and according to Fela, Justice Okoro-Idogu explained that he had intended to visit Fela earlier.

The purpose of his visit, was to apologise to the prisoner for the sentence passed which he (the judge) believed was unjustified. The judge also said it was not his desire to jail Fela but he had to because of the circumstances surrounding the case.

Particularly Justice Okoro-Idogu confessed, that he had been severely pressured by officials at the highest levels of government to make sure a jail sentence was pronounced. It was his earnest hope that Fela bore no malice the judge added.

Stunned by this admission, Fela said he courteously thanked the judge for his courage to admit this guilt but he felt relieved to hear at last that he had not been jailed because he had committed an offence contrary to the law. Fela added that from that moment, he no longer regarded himself a convict but a detainee that would soon be released.

All along my narrative I have made reference to the inexcusable interference in the Nigerian judiciary by the executive arm of the government, the disclosure by Justice Okoro-Idogu very well confirm the lack of independence of the Nigerian judicial system. Thanks to Fela's popularity, this miscarriage of justice would have gone unnoticed if it happened to someone less popular.

How many poor Nigerian citizens had been sentenced with the same bias and disrespect for justice? Considering that Nigerian military government still adheres to the capital punishment, if the offence had carried the death penalty Fela could have been subjected to such capital punishment.

This was the expressed general opinion of the Nigerian public. After this revelation in the NEWSWATCH, everyday that passed more and more word started to get around so much that it became highly embarrassing to the new

Babangida regime. How could the General sit back and do nothing in the wake of NEWSWATCH magazine's scoop?

A statement from the office of the Head of State released to the press, claimed that an investigation was underway to ascertain the facts of the case to verify if the judge did apologise or not to Fela. Thus started the count-down to his release from prison. Fela was finally released on Wednesday April 23, 1986, with a statement from the cabinet office that said it was established during government investigation, that the judge did visit Fela at the Maiduguri Hospital and had discussion with him.

The cabinet office statement further revealed, that the circumstances surrounding the visit clearly indicated improper and unethical conduct on the part of Justice Okoro-Idogu. As a result, the Federal Military government has decided to retire Justice Okoro-Idogu from the Judiciary with immediate effect and in the interest of justice and fair play. Also retired, was Mr. P. Goji Chief Superintendent of Maiduguri prison who was present at the meeting with Fela.

The statement further added that the misconduct of Justice Okoro-Idogu in this case, has raised doubts as to the impartiality of tribunal decisions and in all such case where there is doubt such doubts are resolved in favour of the accused. To this effect, the government is ordering the release of the accused Fela Anikulapo-Kuti.

He stepped into freedom finally in the early hours of Thursday 24th, April 1986 saying: "I won't thank government for releasing me but I thank all Nigerians, Africans, Europeans, Asians, and Americans, who have in one way or the other called for my release. To all of you, I thank from something deeper than the bottom of my heart". Back to familiar grounds, Fela started to perform at the Shrine Beasts of No Nations (BONN).

This was the first song he wrote in 1986, after he was liberated from prison. According to him in the song, everywhere he went after his release from prison people were questioning him what he was going to sing about ('Fela wetin you go sing about ? Them go worry me!') People wanted to hear him sing about his prison experience like he had done with songs like Alagbon Close, Kalakuta Show, and Expensive Shit.

Finally, he decides to sing about the world we live in with particular reference to Nigeria. In the song, he said when he was in prison he called it 'Inside world' and out of prison he called it 'Outside World' - but it is actually a 'Craze World' we live in he reflects. Otherwise what name can one give a world with police brutality, army oppression, courts without justice, magistrate who are supposed to up-hold the law, bend the law to please some special interest?

As further proof of the craze world we live in he sang about the judge who sent him to jail for ten years on a trumped-up charge, the same judge went to visit Fela in a prison hospital two years after and he apologises claiming he was under pressure from government to convict - this could only happen in a 'Craze World' Fela reasoned. It is only in a craze world, people sit and watch governments shoot-down protesting students in Soweto (South Africa), Zaria and Ife (Nigeria) with impunity.

Bearing in mind that Nigeria, like all the craze world countries condemn the apartheid regime in South Africa, while they all commit worse crimes against humanity in their respective countries.

Turning to another aspect of what he calls the craze-world policy of Nigerian governments, in 1984 the Buhari/Idiagbon military regime launched a public campaign dubbed: "War against Indiscipline". This was the regime's solution to corruption, inherent in the Nigerian society since independence.

To justify this campaign the Nigerian head of state General Buhari and his deputy General Idiagbon, publicly used words like: "my people are useless, my people are senseless, and my people are undisciplined" to describe the Nigerian people's attitude to governance.

According to Fela, only in a craze-world can such remarks be made and such statement could only come from an 'animal in human skin'. How could these two 'animals' (to quote Fela), use such words to qualify a people who feed them he asks in the song?

Also, other leaders from other countries must be animals themselves to associate with or accept to co-habit under such umbrella as the United Nations (UN) with a head of state that considers his people "useless, senseless, and undisciplined".

Turning to the United Nations, Fela see's it as an unhealthy organisation that suffers major inadequacy in its organisational principles. According to him, it is absurd to organise the UN principle bodies (the Security Council and the General Assembly) in such an undemocratic manner, where one member vote could veto the decision of majority members of the assembly. Is this democracy or Deem-all-crazy? Fela demands.

Fela asks, what is united about the United Nations? Thatcher went to war with Argentina over Falkland yet both countries are members of the same world body. Reagan and Libya went to war despite their respective countries being members of the UN. Israel versus Lebanon, Iran versus Iraq, East-West versus West–East block (cold war).

According to Fela with all these in-fightings, the UN looks more of a disunited than United Nations. He demands how such a body can work to promote and encourage respect for human rights? Talking about human rights, Fela said that this is another kind of animal talk. How can people talk about 'individual' rights?

According to him, no one has the right to deprive the other of what belongs to the individual. He emphasised that only an animal would try to take away another person's legitimate rights.

People who heard Fela say things like these, reminded him that it was because of such views that he was jailed. In his defence, Fela said it was not him to call members of the UN animals - it was Pik Bortha. According to Fela at the peak of the anti-apartheid struggle, the former South African President in reaction to the persistent riots against the racist regime, came out with the statement saying his regime will come-out more brutal if the riots did not stop: "this uprising will bring out the beasts in us" Bortha was quoted to have said.

Fela's argument in the song Beast of No Nations, is that President Reagan of the United States advocated "constructive engagement with the apartheid regime", it was also the same approach among majority of other member nations of the UN particularly the British government of Prime Minister Margaret Thatcher - an indication that they share the same friendship and animal characteristics like Bortha. In conclusion, Fela said if this is so the UN can only be an assembly of Beasts of no nation.

Another song he wrote shortly after his release from prison was, OVERTAKE DON OVER-TAKE-OVER-TAKE (ODOO) an expression in Pidgin English, meaning events have overtaken events in the daily existence of the average man's life in Africa.

In ODOO, Fela sang about the effects of military usurping power and the destruction of African young democracy since independence. Particularly, young democracies that were lead by leaders who fought and won independence, after long confrontations and sometimes wars with the colonial powers.

Describing their manner of seducing the public he said when they come to power, the military coup plotters assume such names as: 'Nigerian Supreme Military Council', 'Ghana Redemption Council', 'Libyan Revolutionary Council', etc. Most times he emphasize, that the coup plots were planned and financed by former colonial powers.

He added, that to those who are not aware the arrival of the military in the political arena creates the illusion of a peaceful 'democratic' participation and functioning of government. Particularly since most of the daily running's of government are performed by civilians who reported to military bosses. For Fela because it has no political mandate under normal circumstances, the duty of the armed forces is to defend, and support the civil government not to overthrow it or usurp the duties of any branch of government. To do the contrary, means 'Over-Take-Don-Overtake-Overtake.

Any idea of a prosperous, peaceful, country with the military at the realms of power is nothing but an illusion. Judging by the Nigerian experience with persistent scandals and corruption at the highest level of power, a hall mark of each and every successive regime since independence - all these helps put Fela's disillusion and distrust of the military in perspective.

Pointing to the ambiguity of modelling newly independent African nation's constitution after those of the departing colonial masters as the root cause of Africa's problems, Fela in his sarcastic manner calls what passes as government in Africa as "soldier go, soldier come" meaning, the institution that created the military structure purposeful put the army there to continue their colonial work.

To paint a clear picture of the plight of Africans under such dictatorship, Fela mentions a list of songs he had written criticising the wrongs of the system: Kalakuta Show, Mr Follow-Follow, Zombie, Suffering and Smiling, Authority Stealing, etc. Unfortunately, it is the poor masses who suffer most from these mismanagement and corruption in government Fela stressed.

According to him, from an early age African children are forced to learn how to survive in a system where you don't know where your next meal is coming from, social security are non existent, no education, etc. Despite all these setbacks, African parents still try to educate their children - teaching them the essential traditional values.

The children grow-up taking steady jobs to better their lives, saving money here and cutting edges there just to survive. In the end Over-Take Don Over-take Over-Take, because effects of the mismanagement from various administrations, render all sacrifices and cutting edges the individual makes to better his life useless.

Looking back to the epoch shortly after my departure from the organisation, it is clear to me that the entire "spirit saga" was a smoke-screen from a tired Fela. He was tired from putting his life, career and personal property on the line for a people who would sit back while the system rides-over them without rising-up against such oppressive system. His songs, were always attacking all the ills of government and society despite the semi-recluse way of life he lived in the last two decades of his existence.

On the family front shortly after his release from prison, Femi brought-up again the idea of cleaning-up acts within the organisation as promised by Fela during our visits to him in prison. Unfortunately, Fela obviously was tired as stated earlier and some of his inner circle believed the young Kuti's insistence for a clean-up, was direct contradiction to Fela's established way of doing things and they managed to convince Fela to this effect.

Thus developed an estrangement between father and son, leading to the young Kuti quitting his father's organisation. Femi shortly after resigned from the Egypt 80 and found his own group he called Positive Force. Thanks to his mother, he was able to buy some musical instruments that he could work with.

Fela's illness from the HIV malady, would finally prevent him from engaging actively in the struggle as he was known to do. Unfortunately; since there was no medical examination of his health after his release from prison, he wasted away with his infection not knowing himself that he carried the decease.

The possible origin of him contracting the malady are numerous as he was known, to pay the prison warders to procure women for him during his two year prison experience. Also women nurses in various hospitals where he was transferred to unofficially, to ameliorate his detention conditions recounted stories of his sexual passes and in cases where he had his way Fela never had protected sex.

With a hind-sight despite their respective medical experiences, and the impression of a close family bond that existed between the Kuti family, I am surprised his two brothers did not see it right to sit him down and convince him to see a doctor as his physical state deteriorated.

Agreed, that he was not a child who needed to be sat down and advised about his health, but judging from the involvement of his brother Beko in Fela's business interest and his desperate attempt to be included on the estate decision body after Fela's death, I am amazed to think someone like Koye and Beko with their medical experiences could fail to notice the physical deterioration of their brother's health.

Be that as it may, it will be appropriate at this point to talk about Fela's relationship with his siblings. Contrarily to the impression of a united family professed publicly, the Kuti family is like any other family with their harmony and discords. To underline this point, I remember Fela narrating his encounter with his two brothers after receiving his first professional big check. According to him, his brothers particularly Beko used to criticise him for running to their mother whenever he needed money in those early "struggling" days.

After the success of his first hit Jeun Ko Ku, EMI issued Fela a check worth 25,000 Naira (about $35,000 US). Filled with pride in his achievement, he went to his brother's to show them the cheque and asking them if in their so-called academic careers any of them had ever received a check with that amount of money in their respective names.

Though the three laughed over this, according to Fela his two brothers didn't like the remark. The Kuti family is a perfect example of the Nigerian colonial heritage and its contradictory values in the African society.

From the African stand-point, parents are to aid and support their children so that when they are too old to work the children will reverse roles taking responsibility for their aged parents. It is a kind of 'social security' therefore it should not be a surprise if Fela went to his mother for financial assistance in his early struggling days.

He would later compensate her with cars, and other kinds of gifts when he became more successful. Yoruba tradition justifies this practice saying: "Ti Okété ba d'agba omu omo re l'ọnmu" (meaning when the hair get's old it feeds on the milk of its children). While Fela distinguished himself as champion of the African personality, his other siblings can be considered as products of the system that he would condemn through-out his militant career.

Starting with the only female member of the Ransome-Anikulapo-Kuti siblings, Fela considered the strict Christian values of their parents as responsible for their older sister Dolu's choice of alcohol as a refuge to hide her disappointments in life. Considering that Western educated African elites from their parent's generation, tried to emulate and adopt English family lifestyle for themselves.

The education of women from this generation, consist of preparing young girls for a cultural life in which they could engage in agreeable and intelligent conversation with their husbands and devote their time to their families.

They were taught to write, read, paint, play the piano and on the humanitarian front raising funds for churches, schools and Christian relief. This was the education Funmilayo (their mother) was raised with, even if she went beyond these expectations with her political activities.

She and her husband chose the same way of education for Dolu Ransome-Kuti. "Auntie Dolu" as we all called her including Fela, was a large-bone strong masculine looking woman, inherited from their father. Despite her education background, she was cares-less about her looks and she went around with some front teeth missing and most times walked around bare feet.

After Obasanjo's regime attack on Kalakuta and the deterioration of their mother's health, auntie Dolu resigned her nursing job with the Lagos State Ministry of Health to take care of their aged mother.

I remember Fela in one of those criticisms of his siblings', remark that his brothers seem not to appreciate this sacrifice from their sister. To buttress his point, he mentioned an incidence shortly after the death of their mother when Beko took control of the administration of their mother's estate.

According to Fela without informing Dolu in advance of his intension, Beko drove to the Awolowo Road Ikoyi residence of her daughter and son-in-law Frances and Tunde Kuboye, where she usually stayed whenever she visited Lagos from her Abeokuta base.

Beko without any explanation, asked his older sister to get into the car and drove her all the way back to Abeokuta just to re-claim their late mother's gold trinkets in her charge. Despite her Christian education and the cultivation of Western values, auntie Dolu was not a material oriented person - this would accounts for Beko's treatment of her with levity. He probably thought in one of her drunken moment, she could give out to her friends or anyone around her those trinkets.

With her heavy drinking habits, and two children from her liaison with an Abeokuta lawyer and a former Nigerian Ambassador to United Kingdom, for a woman twelve years Fela's senior I guess health-wise she was not doing too badly for her age. Considering also that life had not been fair with the seventy-seven year old lady, her daughter Frances Koboye a dentist and musician died shortly after Fela in 1997.

Her death coming shortly after her uncle's, was shocking to everyone particularly those aware of the active role Frances played in the funeral rights of Fela. Auntie Dolu's son Yomi Ogundipe who lives in the United States used to play the guitar in Fela's Egypt 80 band.

Olikoye Ransome-Kuti, the second child of the Kuti siblings had a ten-year age difference between him and Fela, so it was no surprise that Fela addressed him too as "Brother Koye" in keeping with the tradition among Yoruba people. Unlike Fela who managed to discard most of his colonial education heritage,

Koye was an embodiment of the Ransome-Kuti educated middle-class Christian values.

In 1975, when Fela and his mother changed their middle name to Anikulapo, Koye would keep the name - he seemed to adore the "Ransome-Kuti" name. He belongs to that generation of African educated elite like Wole Soyinka, who are aware of the authenticity of Fela's claim of Africa's contribution to civilisation but constrained by the handicap of a colonial legacy to acknowledge and assume this fact. That generation, and those before them laid the foundation of blind acceptance of the superiority of Western and Arab values in post-colonial Africa.

As symbols of an acquired civilisation, some of them abandon their native and picturesque costumes to assume the hats and breaches of the Christian, they renounce their language as vernacular and even their traditional names for those of their Christian and Arab colonial masters. Fela's message in "Follow Follow" where he sang "…my brother make you no follow book oh, read am and use your sense" did not mean anything to most of them from that generation.

As earlier mentioned, the practice by successive regimes to reward prominent political activists with appointments but reduce their likely effectiveness caught up with most of the so-called intellectual elite of Fela's generation. It is a practice put in place by departing colonial administrations for "good" services rendered, some were rewarded with memberships of various institutions considered "prestigious" such as the Académie Française.

This was the case with Leopold Senghor for his "emotion is black and intellect is Hellenic (Greek)" negritude advocacy. And according to Fela, Wole Soyinka was awarded the Nobel price for "speaking oyinbo pass English man" (meaning for "speaking English better than the English man").

Despite his reputation of strong defence of his conviction brother Koye like most of the educated elite of his generation, was unable to resist the trappings of power and its accompanying gains for his liberty of speech. Before he became member of the Babangida regime, he was said to have uncompromisingly defended the transmission of one of his films depicting the deplorable health situations in Nigeria on a Scandinavian television when some Nigerian diplomats tried to accuse him of being unpatriotic. However, in 1985 he was appointed Nigeria's Minister of Health by the Babangida government and while his participation could be considered as "if you can't beat them you join them", Fela constantly decried Koye's participation in the administration.

He remained minister until Babangida was forced to step down from power in 1993. With criticisms from many people who revered the Kuti name, Koye's participation in such administration lives much to be desired. Brother Koye, justified his participation in Babangida's administration with his conviction for the need to improve the health-care system in Nigeria.

Looking back, little seem to have changed in the health-care system despite his participation. Also to be noted, Babangida's administration is on record as one of the most blatantly inept and corrupt in the history of the Nigerian federation.

With two physicians as brothers, for a man like Fela to die from the AIDS virus albeit one of them Nigeria's former Minister of health calls to question the publicly professed Kuti solidarity. According to Olikoye Ransome-Kuti at a press conference held at the Africa Shrine on Pepple Street in Ikeja Lagos shortly after Fela's death in August 1997: "if Fela knew he had AIDS, he would have made it public knowledge".

The former Nigerian health minister added, that the decision to take Fela to the hospital was made by members of his immediate family after he fell into a comma. This should not come as surprise, in view of Fela's belief that western trained medical practitioners are biased towards traditional medical practices and beliefs.

However, his refusal to be diagnosed or treated by any western trained medical practitioner is not enough justification for him not to be informed by his doctor siblings that he physically looked like one suffering from the symptoms of HIV.

While the responsibility of his contraction of the HIV virus laid most part with Fela himself, the professed Kuti solidarity makes it imperative for the two Kuti physicians to point this out to their ailing sibling.

Probably Fela would still be alive today, if his physician brothers had taken the pains to point out to him the necessity to do an HIV test. With the state of medicine and its current treatment of the virus, Fela could afford the cost of the popular 3-therapy treatment.

Another point to note that can very-well underline Fela's sexual suicide in my opinion, is his condemnation of the use of preservatives in sexual intercourse as he did in the song "CONDOM SCALIWAGY." This is another un-recorded song he wrote before his passing. From all indications as enumerated all along this volume, Fela was a well informed man he read books and was conversant with what was considered actuality. Looking back after his death, it is obvious to the writer that he was tired of it all and this accounted for his "sexual suicide".

Towards the end of his life, sex and music, were the only realities that counted. Fela an adept reader, who was always searching for information had stopped to read in the last two decades of his life because he was loosing his sight and due to personal vanity he did not want to wear glasses - symbol of the aged. Apart from his saxophone practice, he was in the habit of watching television particularly CNN channel (named "C (see) No News" by him). He was also a strong believer in family bond even if he criticised his brothers publicly, he usually did making it sound like a joke.

Many times during his "yabbis", some members of the public would point to his brother whenever he criticised the government. In reply, Fela would ask them to go say it direct to his brother if they ever get access to the minister. "Look at you! Foolish man! You fit talk to me but you no fit go talk to my brother for Ikoyi! Meaning: "look at you! Foolish man! You can talk to me but you cannot go and complain to my brother in Ikoyi" residential area where the government personalities used to live before the administrative capital was moved to Abuja.

Brother Koye's silence in view of the legal battles between Fela's heirs over the administration of his estate, and Beko backing Seun left much to be desired in view of Fela's commitments to family. Many times during their life times after some disagreement with Beko, Fela made comments like "I don't want to fight with my brother because nah my family" to underline his commitment to family bond.

I believe if it was Fela that found himself in the situation Beko was regarding

Fela's estate, he would have done everything possible to resolve the problem amicably within the family instead of going to court.

According to records from the family diary, a child named "Hildegard" was born in 1936 to their parents and the child died shortly after birth. Named after a German friend of the family, Fela with his strong African believe in re-incarnation, claimed that the child was him and in rejection of a foreign name at birth he chose to die to be re-born again two years after.

Bekololari Ransome-Kuti, the youngest of the Kuti siblings whom Abeokuta citizens of their parent's generation gave the name "Beni–Beko" (meaning in Yoruba "It is–It isn't") from an alleged rumour that their mother Funmilayo, was seduced by Oba Ladapo Ademola and the result of their liaison was the birth of the son contested by the father and affirmed by the mother.

Confronted by this family "controversy" Fela said affirmatively, that there was never any dispute between their parents regarding any of the four Kuti siblings. According to him, of the four Kuti siblings, Beko facially resembles their father more than the three others.

He stressed that the rumour emanated from the family affectionately, calling their youngest by the shortened version of his name "Bekololari" (it isn't the way riches are in Yoruba). Beko has been described in the Nigerian media circles as a determined fighter like Fela. While I concede the right to hold opinions to those who make this observation in my opinion, the youngest Kuti siblings was a body of many contradictions.

If there were any of the Kuti children that suffered psychologically from the legendary Ransome-Kuti pioneering notoriety it was Beko. Their grand parents as stated earlier, were pioneers of the protestant Christian education in Nigeria and their parents kept this tradition alive making them unique among their peers.

This was the education their parents tried to inculcate in their children. Koye as earlier stated, at the peak of his medical career left service as a Federal Minister of Health. Fela would even take this legendary Kuti name higher, by his pioneering contributions beyond the African shores with his international acclaim.

With a long list of pioneers before him, I believe Beko's many contradictions stemmed from this challenge.

Though he was raised like his other siblings with the Kuti middle class Christian values, Beko was an atheist and at the same time an embodiment of Western educated values and its contradictions. I lived with Beko for about six months at his Glover Road Ikoyi residence when he was working for the Lagos State Ministry of Health. This was shortly after the burning down of Kalakuta in 1977. It afforded me the opportunity to discus Fela's ideology with Beko and his opinion of his older brother.

There were issues concerning Fela we discussed, that we both were in total agreement. For example, Beko was convinced that Fela surrounded himself with "hanger-on" who hardly believed in his Pan-African ideology. According to him, most of these people were parasites feeding on his brother's generosity than people who could advance his struggle.

He was particularly critical of JK whom he detested from their London days. Despite Fela's insistence on having JK around for what he described as, JK's connection with people in the establishment and the social circle that counted, Beko's opinion of JK is the contrary. JK's gambling habits did not ameliorate Beko's opinion of him, the later was convinced that JK fed his habits with money from Fela.

The author was also privy to many conversations with Beko concerning the African personality and I can very-well say he was never convinced. Rather he believed our pride in African personality is taking us back to the middle age. His position is based on the standard impression of African being civilised by the West. Before the 1977 army attack on Kalakuta, and the physical injuries he sustained along with other Kalakuta residents Beko was never actively engaged in any publicly stated cause.

The media attention accorded him after, probably galvanised Beko into engaging in the battle for social reforms as he was never involved in issues like this before the Nigerian Army attack in February 1977.

He would later contest and become the 1979/80 Secretary General of the Nigerian Medical Association (NMA). Thanks to the notoriety he built from his

NMA activities, the military regime of General Olusegun Obasanjo and his immediate civilian successor Shehu Shagari had several clashes with the union. Several industrial actions embarked upon by the NMA in order to improve working conditions for Nigerian medical doctors, were motivated by Beko and others like him within the association.

In 1990, Beko with some associates found a movement called Campaign for Democracy in Nigeria. The movement's criticisms of the actions and policies of the most repressive military regimes in Nigeria - the Babangida and Abacha regimes, landed Beko and some of his associates in prison from many brushes with the security agents.

Beko in 1995 was sentenced to 15 years imprisonment, for an alleged involvement in a military coup attempt against the Abacha regime. Before Beko's prison sentence, Fela openly criticised his younger brother's involvement with General Obasanjo, who also was accused and sent to jail by Abacha regime for alleged complicity in the coup plot.

Hopefully, records of all the coup trials ever held in Nigeria would be made public to clarify to what extent those accused of complicity in coup attempts were actually involved. For now under the guise of "protection" of state secrets, many Nigerian ex-leaders practically got-away with murder in my opinion.

Most of the army personnel and civilians tried, and condemned for attempted coup d'état by special military tribunals, were educated and trained with the Nigerian tax payers money it is imperative to render account for those wasted lives. Thanks to public out-cry and mobilization, Beko, Obasanjo, and others charged with coup plots, could have been executed for their alleged crimes.

Beko was in-fact serving the jail sentence from the tribunal in 1997 when on his birthday August 2, Fela died. In view of his position in the legal battles of Fela's heirs after his liberation from prison, it might as well be said that it was good for Fela's children that Beko was not around immediately after Fela's demise.

Particularly his insistence on being included on the board responsible for the administration of Fela's estate. Like I underlined earlier as a doctor and general practitioner, Beko conveniently observed Fela's physical state and health deteriorate without action while after his death he insisted on being a board member of the Fela Anikulapo-Kuti estate.

His insistence to represent Seun's interest, as a member of the board administering Fela's estate to me as an observer close to the family I believe lives much to be desired. Beko, had no place in the administration particularly since Fela had adult children who could take care of business.

I believe if Fela wanted his brother to administer his estate, he would have signed a power of attorney to that effect. His insistence reminds one of his attitudes shortly after Fela's first musical break. Beko an ardent critic according to Fela proposed the latter to take-over his career as manager. Fela turned down the proposition from Beko saying a doctor cannot handle music business and in an attempt to prove Fela wrong, Beko would later manage Tee-Mac and Afro Collection".

Beko's desire to manage Fela however yielded dividends with his brother's incarceration in 1984 by the Buhari/Idiagbon military regime. Fela needed someone to run his organisation while in jail, hence he gave Beko "power of attorney" while Femi lead the band in his father's absence. The reader, will re-call all the problems between Beko and Femi over the latter's attempt at reforming Fela's organisation. After Fela's release from prison and Femi's departure from his father's organisation, Beko continued to manage Fela's business and the arrangement continued with Fela's renewal of the "power of attorney" in 1987.

However Beko's alleged engagements with Obasanjo would anger Fela to openly criticise his younger brother. For him it was ridiculous for Beko in his desperate search to be recognised as a national leader, to get involve with Obasanjo who was responsible for the burning down of Kalakuta. With his "power of attorney" long expired, and Fela's refusal to sign the new contract proposed by Beko's daughter Nike, there was no obstacle for Femi and the other Fela siblings to take over their father's estate after his death.

His backing of Seun against other Fela children and even going to court, lives much to be desired in view of him doing nothing to prolong Fela's life as a doctor. Also his political associations, re-enforces my conviction of Beko feelling psychologically 'lesser archived' than his other siblings.

Their mother from the narrative of her early carrier, was a pioneer and active member of NCNC a party headed by an Igbo man - Dr. Azikiwe in a Yoruba dominated region. While I concede to Beko his right to association his involvement with the Oduduwa People's Congress (OPC), a movement violently dedicated to champion the cause of Yoruba people in a federal setting boils-down to the actions of a man looking for fame and probably wealth by any means.

From many conversations with him, I know he was not convinced about Fela's Pan-African ideology and Beko's insistence to control Fela's business interest during his lifetime and even after his passing, boils down to "appreciating the milk and not the cow that produces the milk".

While it is not the intention of the author to dictate how he should live his life, my involvement with Fela and commitment to preserve the ideals he lived for compels me to speak-out against actions that could tarnish the Fela phenomenon and legacy.

Dispute over his material legacy, cannot come before the cause he lived and sacrificed for. Instead of the Balkanising court disputes, the family should be working with like minds to create a Fela foundation that would assemble all aspects of the icon's phenomenal life for posterity. Today, I am happy that after Beko's demise, Fela's heirs are getting along without those early divisions, something not too good for the image that was the phenomenon FELA.

For the European and subsequently American audience discovering the Fela phenomenon, it is sad that the people who presented Fela internationally did not take the time to understand the Fela phenomenon.

They lacked the professionalism necessary, to expose a multifaceted phenomenon such as Fela to a public with a colonial relationship with Africa and Africans.

In my opinion, most of Fela's European representatives were too much concerned about their financial interests to see what Fela represents to humanity in general. Martin Meissonier, Pascal Imbert, Francis Kertekian, Rikki Stein and even the Afro-Cuban journalist Carlos Moore, did not take the time to understand where Fela was coming from before attempting to represent him.

Contrarily to the image some would try to portray, Fela was not anti-White rather he did not believe in the superiority of Western so-called civilisation to the African traditional values. From the narrative the reader will agree with me, that Fela was a personified search for an answer to colonialism, and his lifestyle was a responds to the conflict of imposition of cultures in Africa.

Since Fela's demise moral judgements of him brings to mind, attempts by respective governments in the Western hemisphere to find an answer to the problem of delinquency among youths. As a solution to this problem, the Western approach of more police on the streets, curfew for youths below the age of thirteen, increase in defence budgets, more police surveillance in the neighbourhood and in schools - they call it "police by proximity".

Both left and right wing governments have attempted some of these solutions to the problem without much success. This is the issue Fela highlights in his song Everything Scatter.

These draconian policies, designed to enforce family values based on the statistics that claim that the major causes of delinquency among youths are high rates of divorce and out-of-wedlock births, television culture, time-constrained and usually absent parents, etc.

A Yoruba saying literally translated says: "Educate your child and he will give you a peace of mind". The question, we should address our minds is are we giving our children the right education that enables them to respect others in our today's individualistic capitalist system?

Before colonialism, most African kingdoms and Empires were organised on the basis of communalism - that collective value that imposes on the individual to be his sister's or brother's keeper. Fela's answer to Western governments is telling them to learn from the black African folks, to better explain this the author would suggest his experience as an example.

My father, died while I was nine years old the second of four children. In my growing-up days, I have missed the fact that I couldn't say like many other kids growing up around me: "my dad did this for me" or "my dad did that for my brother". Despite this, I have never felt short-charged for belonging to a single parent home.

We had scores of aunts and uncles blood and non-blood relatives, who had as much rights to reproach me or any other kid resident in our neighbourhood if they found us doing anything wrong. These myriad "family" members, "raised" me like many other young folks of my generation and provided us that protective web against any form of youth's delinquency.

While I am not saying there is no form of delinquency among African youths of today (thanks to television culture), I can very well say this African tradition is in practice among Diaspora Africans who grew-up even far away in the USA where black folks still keep this great African heritage of being our brother's and sister's keeper. Our urban social problems we might as well try to find solutions to, from cultures and traditions than increasing police presence in our neighbourhoods.

The history of Africans people largely omitted from textbooks and portrayed as barbaric to justify colonialism, is rich with cultural and traditional values that are relevant to cure most modern-day urban social problems. It will be a big surprise for most Westerners, when an African commuting in metro or other forms of urban public transport gives his seat to elders in crowded public transports, or an African who offers to help lift a nursing mother's baby-pram where electronic escalators are not functioning or not available.

African ancestors had well defined ideas of nature, human life, existence, social relations as well as of man himself. It is on the basis of these well defined ideas, that the fundamental elements of human civilisation and education were developed.

Though with the evolution of Western ways of life and its attempts at dominating other cultures, little is done to evelaute these cultural values and their importance to modern ways of life. Fela was very critical of some African American attitude to neglect these traditional values in their several generation struggles to be assimilated into the white American system.

However, the continuation of that tradition by some of them of being their brother's keeper is worth commendation. I am not sure whether the new America, the more divers America like the rest of the Western hemisphere will embrace our "extended family" concept as we become more different from our neighbours with each passing day.

We can collectively trigger change, by committing to being part of an extended family that will protect and nurture the child next door or around the corner no matter who his or her "people" are. That is the essential message of the Fela phenomenon and legacy.

Take for example, the French socialist government's attempt in the year 2001 to resolve their age long colonial problem with Algeria with a football (soccer) match. Unfortunately, the objective of organizing the event was not reached as national sentiments took the better of the public.

The root cause of the conflict of the Algerian people with France boils down to the respect in the difference that exits in the human family, to co-exist with our neighbours we have to recognise and respect this difference. Organising a football match without walking the path of history and admitting our respective wrongs, won't heal the wounds of colonialism. This was proved with young Franco-Algerians, and their fellow youths from other ex-French colonies whistling while the French national anthem was being played.

To make my point more clear, I remember once attending a concert at Le Palais des Congrés in Paris. Billed to perform was Ibrahim Ferrer and the famous Cuban Buena Vista Social Club. The venue in my opinion was the wrong place to programme dancing music like salsa. I was clapping my hands to the group's music, when suddenly a French couple seating in the row in front of me turned to ask me to stop clapping my hands.

Quietly, I told them we were not in a class room where we are all subjected to the same rules and regulations. I continued to appreciate the music the way I knew how to given the restrains of space. Towards the end of the concert, I noticed the French couple that had earlier reproached me, clapping their hands to the music like majority of the public.

At the end of the concert, I called their attention to this and the man's remark was: 'it is simple respect'. I told him I was not being disrespectful towards them rather, it was the couple trying to be disrespectful towards me. I underlined that if they had respect for me like they wanted me to do to them, they should have understood the different ways of our appreciating music - particularly since we were in a concert hall and not a classroom.

The French couple must have been raised to appreciate music quietly applauding the music while as an African, I was raised to clap and scream and dance to music in a public place. For us to be able to match onward towards a new world order with mutual respect among our human family, we have to recognise and respect that difference in humanity - that is the core of Fela's message. Unfortunately his European handlers missed this aspect in their dealings with Fela.

From Martin Meissonier the first European to present Fela to the French public, to those currently handling his affairs after his demise, I believe his European handlers have other things in mind than presenting the real FELA. Martin Meissonier for example wanted to sell Fela to the French public in the manner Chris Blackwell sold Bob Marley - a rebel (Rasta) non-conformist.

While his Kalakuta Republic notion can be considered a form of rebellion, the phenomenon that was Fela was more in his message than his life-style. Though there are common grounds in the ultimate goal of the Rasta revolution and Fela's ideal of the African personality, there are also big difference in Fela's opinion of venerated leaders of the Rasta revolution.

Like all Rasta man, Fela venerated Marcus Mosia Garvey while the Rasta veneration of Haille Selasi as the "king of kings, lord of lords" he considered as "substituting one form of slavery for another". The veneration of Emperor Haille Selasi can be seen in the same light, as the African American substitution of Christianity for Islam - in their search for a true African religion.

Musically Fela was presented in Europe like a rebel musician - a non conformist, who openly admitted the use of marijuana contrarily to the law, and was also projected with his marriage to 27 women as an African male sexist who treated his women like sex objects. Politically, he was presented in the manner of an African Che Guevara.

Fela was neither a male sexist nor an African version of El Ché, the essential part of his message was the emancipation of the African personality - men and women with their distinct personalities proud of their culture without feeling inferior to another culture as the legacy of colonialism in Africa would want Africans to believe.

Unfortunately his European handlers did not grasp the essence of this message. Some of them were too concerned with their personal interest to see the importance of Fela's overall vision. The reader will recall that at the end of Fela's Italian tour, Martin Meissonnier proposed to bring Fela and his band on a tour in France. The first tour he organised with the group was a media success, as he used his press connection to rally the French media to Fela's press conferences during the tour.

Fela's first concert attended by a public of about ten thousand strong was in a "chapiteau", a huge tent mounted in Pantin area of Paris. During the concert, Fela was criticised by musician Manu Dibango and Martin Meissonnier present backstage for keeping his public waiting. Fela refused to go on stage despite the public assembled calling out fervently for him.

Minutes before he was to go on stage, Femi who was performing for the first time before a largely European audience, suddenly developed stage fright from consuming too much "Fela Goro" a marijuana derivative made into paste. Martin Meissonnier and Manu Dibango, thought it was unwise to keep the public waiting but Fela felt otherwise and he insisted on taking care of Femi before he went on stage.

Finally when Fela managed to calm him, young Femi at the age of 17 had so much stage fright that he did not see the microphone when it was his turn to take solo in the band. Fela had to physically, guide him like a blind man towards the microphone during the concert. The media success of this tour however, would cause Fela not to believe Martin Meissonier when the latter attempted to cancel Fela's second tour in France. According to him, there were not enough dates to ensure a financial success of the tour.

Fela's position was re-enforced by an article published in the Paris based journal 'Actuel', a special edition titled "Almanac Des Annees 80" (Almanac of the 80's) with the heading: "Fela, The Black President!" Written by Patrice Van Eersel one of the first French journalists to interview Fela in Nigeria, the piece explained Fela's struggle and his Pan-African convictions. Fela was convinced that if Martin Meissonnier, had worked with conviction and underlined to the French public ideas such as those expressed by journalist Van Eersel there was no justifiable reason not to have enough dates to pay the cost of the second tour.

Eventually, the second tour was organized half-heartedly by Martin and the outcome was a financial disaster for the group and the organizer. They both parted ways in not too friendly manner as Martin was blamed for the out-come of the tour. "Fela, everybody thinks I am an arsehole! Even Pascal" was his comments referring to Pascal Imbert, another French citizen he had engaged to co-ordinate the two tours from Lagos.

Most of these Europeans around Fela, at this period were relatively novice in the music industry. Thanks to the exposure their contact with Fela provided, they would eventually become well connected with the leading figures in the industry, the case of Martin Meissonier could be considered as a good example. When he met Fela, Martin did not have any specific professional formation, except playing music and trying to become a tour agent. He claimed to Fela he represented an agency Martin/Daniel Promotions. According to him they had organised tours in Europe with Dizzy Gillespie, Don Cherry, and The Chicago Arts Assembly among others.

Instead of him working on the big media success of the first tour of Fela in France, highlighting Fela's message and image of an Africa personality with a solution for the world, Martin and the French press presented Fela to the French public as a male sexist and marijuana smoking rebel.

The second tour, Martin wanted to cancel at the last minute because he did not have enough financial guarantees to put a group of about seventy people on the road. He informed Fela who was deep in the "spirit saga" as explained earlier. A professional booking agent would have insisted on cancelling the tour despite Fela's opinion to the contrary.

On his part, Fela influenced by his "spiritual advisers" saw this move from Martin as an attempt to sabotage an opportunity to make a break in Europe. He insisted on doing the tour and even agreed to pay the flight fees for his group, despite the advice from Martin that he did not have enough dates to cover tour cost.

Fela managed to convince the young tour agent, who went along either with the hope that things would turn-out positive or as a novice in the business who did not know how to put his foot down.

From the reception of his first tour, Fela couldn't understand why Martin could not put enough dates to cover tour cost. For him it was either incompetence on the part of Martin, or an attempt at sabotage judging from the prevailing paranoia within his organisation during the 'spirit saga'. To cover hotel bills and other deficits from the financially disastrous tour, Fela had to hastily record "Original Suffer Head" for Arista records in London.

Despite the £25,000 pounds advance royalty paid for this album and the co-mission Fela paid him, Martin Meissonnier couldn't save his company from bankruptcy.

Financially in debt, and emotionally heart-broken and blamed for the turn-out of the tour, disillusioned Martin tried to replace Fela with Sunny Ade - a popular juju musician in Nigeria whom he signed with Island Records.

Unfortunately Sunny Ade was not Fela, the record sales from the album Sunny made with Chris Blackwell was a financial disaster for the record company. Chris Blackwell did a "disco" mix of Sunny's album, with the hope of breaking into a new market.

However Sunny Ade would not agree to the release of this version. For him the re-mix was no longer his concept of juju music, and the company renounced their contract and they went their separate ways. With his move towards Sunny Ade, Martin Meissonier lost Fela's confidence despite his attempt at rallying all hisFrench associates in Nigeria together to work on the Sunny Ade project.

This second tour in France by Fela would also coincide with the arrival of François Mitterrand and the Socialist government in power in 1981. Carlos Moore, an afro-Cuban journalist with the French magazine 'Jeun Afrique' would later attempt bringing Fela and his group on another tour in Europe. Fela got to know Carlos Moore for the first time in Lagos in 1975 during preparations for the Second World Black Festival of Arts and Culture (FESTAC).

He was introduced to Fela by the Nigerian film maker Ola Balogun. Many years after, Carlos would narrate his first meeting with Fela in a Radio Nova interview in Paris. According to him in the interview, he was shocked to discover a star like Fela living in the heart of the Lagos slum despite his international recognition.

During his first meeting with Fela, Carlos Moore presented himself as a Cuban dissident and he also informed Fela that he was forced into exile as a result of his criticisms of Fidel Castro and his Spanish – Cuban hierarchy of racism against "Afro-Cubans". Carlos Moore got back close to Fela during the first tour organised by Martin Meissonnier in France. During this tour he proposed to do a book "Fela, This Bitch of a Life". I remember giving him the manuscript of my first book "Fela, Why Blackman Carry Shit" to help him prepare his book.

I was present in all his interviews with members of the organisation and he would later describe me in the book as Africa 70 administrator because of my responsibilities with the administrative affairs or the organisation. Since he was regularly in Fela's company during this tour, he was privy to all the problems with Martin Meissonnier.

Carlos would later jump on his friendship with Fela, to propose organising another tour for the group in Europe. The tour was originally planned by him to coincide with the publication of his book. Despite his journalist credentials, he was not a booking agent and Carlos Moore's attempt at booking a tour for Fela was a disaster. He wanted to use his connection in the music industry to do a tour he didnot know how to organize. He didn't have enough dates and the few dates he proposed were not financially sufficient to pay the cost of the tour.

Learning from the risk he took with Martin Meissonnier, Fela refused to take same risk with Carlos thus putting the Cuban's credibility with people he was in contact with as organiser of the tour on the line. Unfortunately for Carlos Moore, it was also the peak of the 'spirit saga' within Fela's organisation. With the proposed tour impracticable, one of Fela's 'spiritual' advisers accused Carlos Moore of being a double-agent.

His sojourn in the US a bastion of anti Castro Cubans and marriage with an Asian instead of anAfro-Cuban like himself, were cited as justification for this double-agent accusation. His representation of Fela was withdrawn, and Fela would later authorise Pascal Imbert to represent him in Europe.

As earlier mentioned, Pascal Imbert was engaged by Martin Meissonnier to work on the tours the latter organised with Fela in Europe. Pascal was introduced to Martin in a kind of 'French connection' scenario in Lagos.

They were French citizens, who went separately on visits to Nigeria and they all were united by one phenomenon – Fela. The first of the French Connection, was Martin Meppiel who had gone on a mission to Nigeria with one of those French companies prospecting for off-shore oil in Nigeria. He worked with the company as a diver in Port Harcourt and visited Lagos whenever he was free.

With Fela as the major musical attraction in Nigeria, it was not long before Martin Meppiel was initiated into the community of expatriates who visited Fela and the new Shrine in Ikeja. Not long after, Martin invited his older brother Stephane Meppiel to come over to Nigeria.

He proposed his brother the possibility to work with the company prospecting for oil. Stephane, who had just got out of prison for drug traffic was tired of the French system and with his love for adventure decided to make the journey to Nigeria driving across the Sahara desert.

His adventure was temporarily halted when his car broke down in the middle of the desert. Waiting for a chance that another motorist wouldshow-up, Stephane waited in the desert for about three days. As luck would have it, Pascal Imbert too had learnt of the promising economic advantages in Nigeria with the advent of the oil boom.

He too was heading for Lagos driving through the Sahara. He ran into Stephane Meppiel with his broken-down car in the middle of the desert. Since both were driving 'Peugeot' pick-up vehicles, Pascal and Stephane were able to repair the latter's car and later continue their journey together.

They also discovered that they were both heading for Lagos where Stephane assured his new companion that his brother Martin Meppiel was waiting. Thanks to French expatriate community working in the embassy in Lagos and their regular visits to Ikeja shrine, most of these French visitors discovered through the Fela community the swinging Lagos night life of the 80's.

Apart from the Shrine, they discovered "ARIYA" night-club where Sunny Ade was the resident band and "BLACK PUSSYCAT" where Orlando Owo and his African Canneries performed regularly. In what would turnout a coincidence, it was the same period Martin Meissonnier arrived in Lagos to propose Fela the first tour.

He would later engaged Pascal Imbert and the Meppiel brothers to work with him on the logistics of the tours. As part of the media success of the first tour the French television Anten 2, would later do a 52 minute documentary of Fela titled "Musique Au Pong" (Music Is the Weapon) produced by Jean-Jack Flori and aired on the French national television. Seen as a public relation success in France for Fela, the documentary was the only attempt at presenting Fela in the context of an African personality.

Unfortunately, by the time it was aired in France there was no management structure in place to co-ordinate these media presentation of the man. Martin Meissonnier was in deep shit with his bankruptcy problems and Carlos Moore playing on Black sentiments, was insinuating caution towards the French community hanging around Fela.

The fact that most of these French guys too were novices in the business did not alleviate our suspicion towards them. As young adventurers, most of the French guys took advantage of the corruption in Nigeria to trafficsome marijuana. The Meppiel brothers would later buy a house boat from their many trips to Lagos.

Despite our knowledge of their extra activities, officially we dealt with them purely on the musical engagements they could propose. Particularly since none of them had any business structure to handle a big group like Fela's. Shortly after Fela dropped Carlos Moore, Pascal Imbert tried to represent the group as booking agent in Europe. Teaming up with the Meppiel brothers and another friend René Lenoble a photo-journalist with "Actuel magazine", they tried to set up a structure to tour Fela in Europe.

An apartment belonging to Jacqueline Meppiel (the mother of Stephane and Martin) situated on 18, rue de Reuilly in the 12 arrondissement (district) in Paris was taken over by the new structure they called Yaba Music Production (named after a popular area in the heart of Lagos).

Jacqueline Meppiel, a professor of cinematography had moved to Cuba to work with the Cuban government. Her two sons, installed with their friends their new company in her vacated apartment. With a large group like Fela on tour, it was obvious that an organised structure was necessary to make things run correctly.

By 1983 when I left the organisation, most of the French nationals working with Fela had become disillusioned and considered Fela and his aids as a bunch of "trade unionists using culture as bargaining power". The 'spiritual saga' around Fela, would later contribute to their non-comprehension of Fela and what he stood for.

While preparing their return to France, they convinced some of Fela's musicians to desert the group. With the promise of a management structure in Paris, the musicians left Egypt 80 to form the Group Ghetto Blaster.

Ghetto Blaster, was Stephane Meppiel's idea. He and his other French associates considered Fela difficult to deal with. They were also aware that the French market was getting hip to afrobeat music. He came-up with the idea of setting-up an afrobeat band resident in Paris.

Secretly he broached the subject with Udoh Essiet (conga), Kiala Njavotunga (guitar) and Nicolas Avom (drums) from Fela's Egypt 80 band. Inviting a few other French speaking African musicians like Willy Nfor, and Frankie Ntoh Song, resident in Lagos and playing in Sunny Okosun's band the group moved to the Black Pussycat. Tony Allen also auditioned, at the early stage with the group but the core members preferred Nicolas Avom as drummer.

From all indications, these young African musicians did not necessarily understand what it took to set-up an Afrobeat band in Paris. They were only content to leave Africa and her misery behind for Europe. The band would later move to Paris, they took residence on the Meppiel's house boat named "La Chine".

Unfortunately for the group shortly on their installation in Paris, Stephane Meppiel had a car accident that took the life of the passenger next to him. Some 'cocaine' was also found in the car by the police and it landed him back in jail.

With the group's 'connector' out-of circulation, Martin Meppiel (Stephane's younger brother) would take over the group's management. He signed the band to Island records in 1984, with the album "Preacher Man/Efi Ogunle". Ghetto Blaster disintegrated, after their second album titled "People" was released in the French market in 1986.

Despite their disillusion with Fela and his ways of doing business, this opinion did not discourage the French-Armenian neighbour of the Meppiels' Francis Kertekian, to join Yaba Music Production and later represent Fela's business interest. Francis got to know the Meppiel brothers after they bought their boat and took residence on the Seine at Porte d'Austerlitzs area of Paris.

As a neighbour of the Meppiels, he was privy to all the problems and good times they encountered on their trips to Lagos. Good times in the sense that Martin Meppiel for example, met the mother of his only daughter named Tania around the Fela community.

Catherine Leserve, a French sound engineer was earlier married to a traditional 'Chief' from a village in Benin Republic. She was the only White among the 'Chief's many wives. At his death, the other wives ganged-up against Catherine accusing her of putting witch-craft on their late husband.

With the help of a female Benin Republic singer Betty Ayaba, Catherine migrated to Lagos and eventually ended-up at Fela's Ikeja Shrine, where she met the French community and Martin Meppiel. She returned to Paris with them pregnant with Tania. With Stephane in prison, Martin had to take care of business with the group Ghetto Blaster.

All these were stories they brought back to Francis Kertekian. Francis first visit to Lagos was in 1975, at the peak of the 20 million ton cement scandal that rocked the Gowon regime at the height of the oil-boom in the early 70's. The reader will recall that the military regime of General Yakubu Gowon, embarked on the construction of prestigious projects like the national stadium in Suru-lere and the national arts theatre Iganmu (among many other projects of that nature), thus creating a construction boom in the Nigerian economy. Overnight, young able-bodied Nigerians farmers were abandoning their villages for the cities, inorder to become emergency contractors with the construction boom.

In their attempt to meet the demands for the boom, large quantities of cement were imported from Europe to meet the demand on the home market causing big port congestion in the Nigerian ports. Out of frustration from the port congestion, many boats discharged tons of cement in the sea after waiting for months to gain entry into the Lagos port to discharge their cargo.

In their attempt to decongest the Lagos Apapa port in 1975, the new military regime headed by General Murtala Mohammed called for aide from Europe. Charged with the decongestion of the Apapa port was Alex Bouri an Arab-Israeli. He introduced the use of badges attached to the narrow landing platforms in the Lagos port, to off-load the many boats anchored on the Atlantic waiting to discharge their cement cargo. Francis Kertekian, was employed by Alex Bouri to work on the decongestion program between 1975-1976.

On his return from his trip, Francis bought a 240 ton boat and installed his family in Porte d'Austerlitz in Paris. He had as neighbours, the Meppiel brothers who also had bought a boat from their trips in Nigeria. Returning to Paris, these French guys shared their respective experiences in Nigeria with special reference to Fela. Despite the disillusion of the Meppiel brothers in doing business with Fela, this did not stop Francis Kertekian from trying out his luck like other French guys before him.

Deciding to set-up office in another apartment also belonging to Jacqueline Meppiel, Francis proposed to take-over Yaba Music with René Lenoble. He flew to Lagos and with the connection of Jacqueline Grandchamp-Thiam a staff of the French embassy in Lagos, he was presented to Fela. Jacqueline Grandchapm-Thiam at her posting to the French Embassy in Lagos, was writing her doctorate theses on Pan Africanism and Resistant music - with particular reference to Fela.

When Jacqueline met Fela and told him the subject of her University thesis, Fela referred her to me and since this 1979 meeting we have remained friends. In her research, she frequented the Fela community regularly and she presented Francis Kertekian to Fela when the later arrived in Nigeria.

Francis proposed to represent Fela for a trial period of six months. Within this period in 1984, he managed to sign Fela to EMI in London. Fela would later tour Europe with Francis and YABA music production. It was during one of these tours that he recorded "ARMY ARRANGEMENT".

Unfortunately, the song was not mixed before Fela was arrested and jailed for currency violation by the Buhari/Idiagbon regime. Francis and Pascal Imbert would later sell this album to CELLULOID France after EMI refused to release without a final mix from Fela.

The un-mixed album was finally produced with the participation of Bill Laswel and Wali Badaru while Fela was in prison. Fela, was very much against this version of the song carrying his name because he did not like the final mix.

This album release, will serve to confirm my earlier allegation of his European representatives being more concerned about their financial interest than the over-all interest of Fela. Neither Francis nor Pascal, took the pain to visit Fela in jail in Nigeria before they decided to release their version of "Army Arrangement".

As earlier mentioned, none of these Europeans had the experience as artist manager or producer before their initial contact with Fela. However, their business association with Fela yielded big dividend. Professionally, it opened doors for them even if they rarely admit this. On the other-hand, Fela's believe in giving people the opportunity to prove their capabilities prompted him to work with these people.

From my understanding of the man, despite him being aware of the need for competent people to handle his affairs, the need to get his message across weighed more in his choice of representatives. Judging from what he went through, only people who had nothing to loose professionally or those who genuinely were convinced of his struggle took the risk to be associated with him.

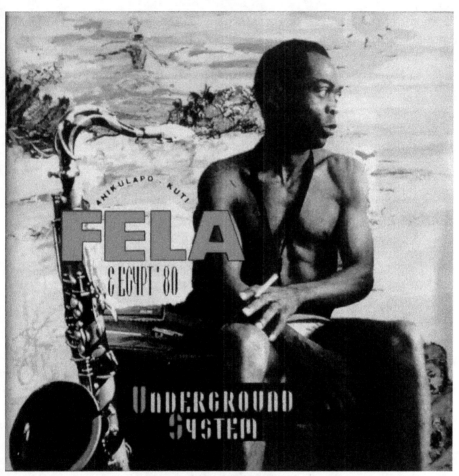

Front cover album design UNDERGROUND SYSTEM

UNDERGROUND SYSTEM

In the cause of this narrative I have talked about Fela's evolution from a colonially educated tea drinker, into a fiery anti-colonial advocate of an African personality. Also mentioned are his betrayals from trusted friends, legal representatives and associates. His disillusion with a people he sacrificed for with trials and tribulations as proof.

Fela also used the betrayal of Thomas Sankara, to underline his personal let downs from trusted friends and associates as he sang: "since I dey young nah to trust people I understand! Since I dey grow-up to find people to trust hard! Meaning "while growing-up to trust is what I was educated with, but since my adulthood to find people to trust is difficult".

The song titled "Underground System" stressed that in his tributes to great African men Kwame Nkrumah, the first President of Ghana was the greatest of all. In the same breath, he had sung songs against African thieves Olusegun Obasanjo a former Nigerian President and M.K.O. Abiola, late Chairman ITT Middle East and Africa are the biggest thieves he sang against.

Fela went on to explain that many young folks in Africa today, may not know about Kwame Nkrumah because of the diabolic conspiracy to keep Africans away from knowing the truth about who they should look-up to as role-models.

For Fela, those who know or read about Nkrumah will agree that there are not many like him in the history of Africa. He was African personality personified. He worked throughout his adult life for black-pride and African unity.

Unfortunately because of the Underground System in the lives of African leadership, whenever Africa finds a charismatic leader determined to change things on the continent other stooges passing as leaders will conspire to destroy such leader. Fela mentions how Nkrumah was destroyed by the Western powers who want to keep Africa latched to their colonial masters.

He mentioned how Sekou Toure suffered the same faith, Ahmed Ben Bella, Patrice Lumumba, Modibo Keita, and Gamel Abdu Nasser. Even Mandela they don't want him to arrive as head of a free South Africa he sang.

Claiming that every-where in the world, people look up to their role-model for inspiration. This brings us to the story of Thomas Sankara the assassinated President of Republic of Burkina Faso.

Fela sang:

"Africa since the passing of the leaders mentioned above the continent had not seen a charismatic leader like Sankara, he was one of the few leaders who was not afraid to speak the truth. Calling on other African heads of state to come together and unite". Sankara lived a modest life, compared to other African heads of state whose only pre-occupation is to line their pockets with money stolen from their respective countries.

Despite the attempt by corrupt African leaders to protect their crime against Sankara in what he called an Underground System, Fela say's everything in the world is in turns, they can conspire to kill Sankara today but can never kill the ideals he lived and was murdered for. Fela who met Sankara at the Presidential Palace in Burkina Faso was writing the song as homage to the young head of state, about the time he was assassinated by his close associates.

CLEAR ROAD FOR JAGA JAGA

The reader will recall my explanation earlier in this volume regarding Fela's ability to use music to provoke violence among his Nigerian audience, for example whenever he performed live the song Fogo Fogo (break bottle–break bottle in Yoruba), the public seemed to react violently towards each other breaking bottles. Though there was no where in the song, where he said they should attack each other but the Nigerian public usually reacted in a violent manner.

The lyrics of Fogo Fogo mentioned how he had sung songs like "Jeun Ko Ku, Na Fight Oh, Who Are You and Alu Jon Ki Jon." He insinuated that with all these songs he tried to raise their consciousness to reasons behind their daily sufferance, and not only that he also gave part of him entertaining his public with combative songs and catering for them. He underlined how he entertained his audience with music and all kinds of drinks (whisky, ogogoro – a locally brewed gin) and how he lost his money in the process.

In return, the beneficiaries of these entertainments broke bottles all over the place incurring more debts to the already long list of debts.

He concluded that to break bottles meant to react violently and that would be an apology - sung in Yoruba:

"Mo lanu mo ko'rin! Mo ko Jeun Ko ku!
(I opened my mouth! I sang Jeun Koku!)
Mo lanu mo ko'rin! Mo ko Na Fight oh!
(I opened my mouth! I sang Nah fight oh!)
Mo lanu mo ko'rin! Mo ko Who Are You re!
(I opened my mouth! I sang Who Are You!)
Gbese te fe ko mi si ni mo fe ko leseyi oh !
(The debt you want to commit me to is what I want to sing about)
Ebe ni o! Fogo Fogo! Ebe nio!
(It's apology! Breaking bottle is an apology!)
 Mo ra beer! Ti enfi wenu!
(I bought beer that you wash your mouths with)
Mo ra whisky ti en sha!
(I bought whisky that you get 'high' with)
Mo ra Ogogoro! Ti enfi wenu!
(I bought Ogogoro that you wash your mouths with)
Mo wo apo mi! Apo mi gbe!
(I checked my pocket, my pocket is dry)
Emu ti e mu! Ti efi fogo sile! Ti efi da gbese simi lorun!
(The drinks that made you break bottles which caused me so-much debt)
Ebe nio! Fogo Fogo Ebe nio! (It is an apology breaking bottles is an apology).

In retrospect, Fogo Fogo was Fela's visionary and prophetic reflection of his life and the people he fought for. Written in 1973, a period when he did not know how to put his concept of African personality into words, it was his prediction of a tomorrow the sacrifices he would make for the struggle and the price he would eventually pay.

The song re-enforces my opinion of Fela's disillusion in his Nigerian public particularly, their sit-back attitude in view of the mismanagement of their lives by successive regimes. Make no mistake about it, he never abandoned the struggle despite his disillusion with the Nigerian people.

This point can best be illustrated with another song he wrote towards the end of his life that provoked equal violence among his Nigerian audience titled Clear Road for Jaga Jaga (meaning - get reed of all these non-sense). Unfortunately he never recorded the song before he died. This song covered all his criticisms of the Nigerian leadership including their choice of name.

According to Fela, Alhaji Abubakar Alhaji literally translated signifies "Stranger Abubakar Stranger" (Alhaji or El Haj in Arab is the title given to those who made the pilgrimage to Mecca). He called on his listeners to get reed of such foreign values "Clear Road for jaga jaga oh" he sang - a cry that usually provoked his Nigerian public into a violent frenzy with knives, cutlass and bottles serving as weapons to attack each other.

However soon as he gets to the part where he sang "E je ka ma ba faji wa lo" (meaning lets continue to amuse ourselves), the violence would subside and everybody would continue to dance as if there was nothing to the earlier violent aggression let loose among the crowd.

Musically the song was Fela's testament as a musical phenomenon. Inter-weaving between his old highlife jazz days style and afrobeat, Clear Road For Jaga Jaga remains one of his all time musical classic. The message of the song is equally a direct attack on the personalities that constitute the jaga jaga (nonsense) successive regimes in Nigeria represent he named them all: Obasanjo, Abiola, Babangida, Falaye, Chiroma, Abubakar Alhaji, Abacha etc.

He accused all of them, of plundering the Nigerian treasury and he called on the people to "clear road for jaga jaga oh! Abacha! Abacha oh!" (Meaning: "get reed of all these non-sense oh! Discard our society of all these scum oh! Abacha in Yoruba means scum).

Fela's Nigerian public, could react violently to a song like this because they could see in their daily existence what he was singing about, despite the attempts by the 'leaders' above to give him a different image. This aspect of Fela never manifested itself outside the Nigerian shores, not even in Europe where he became eventually very popular. The only reason one could aduce to this no reaction must be language barrier.

A very important point to note here is that every song of Fela Anikulapo-Kuti from his Africa 70 to Egypt 80 works like I have all along underlined, are narratives of Nigeria's contemporary history.

From his 1973 Confusion, with his Pan-African solution - critical of what transpires as government on the continent, to his Army Arrangement – a narrative of how the military institution have high-jacked the people's clamour for freedom and democracy, all of Fela's songs are nothing but Nigeria's contemporary history – an actuality today and tomorrow as everyday is a testimony of all what he sang about.

Since the arrival of the military in the political scene, the aspiration of Nigerian people has over the years been transformed into nightmare with the military taking the country through a civil war and the spectre of another looming as we see from events in the Northern parts of Nigeria.

Nigeria's so-called peaceful transition from military rule to a democratic civilian regime is nothing but an illusion. The army is still very much in control – all the registered political parties are controlled by former army generals. Today they put-on civilian clothes and use religion to create a political base. There is even more talk from some of the leaders of the registered parties of dividing the country – with the North breaking away from the rest of the Nigerian nation.

North/South dichotomy talk in Africa is as old as colonialism - the policy that created the military institution. It is nothing but diversion that enabled the colonialist like the ex-generals to continue to divide and rule like Fela sang in Colo-mentality. Where is the opposition in Nigeria's so-called democracy? Instead of Nigeria's political class encouraging the masses to overcome years of fear and apathy and take to the streets like the case with Arab streets, they prefer like Fela sang in Sorrows, Tears & Blood: "I no want die! Papa dey for house! I want enjoy!" In a 21st Century Nigeria, we can see politicians talk about Balkanizing the country.

In this age of globalization, it is clear that no nation can survive without a continental approach hence the setting-up of world bodies such as World Trade Organization (WTO), Regional Trading Arrangements (RPTAs), Asia-pacific Economic Cooperation (APEC), Association of South/East Asian Nations (ASEAN), etc.

Those talking about partitioning Nigeria for example, are only doing so to divert the people from what they should be demanding like Fela sang in his un-recorded song: 'Clear Road for Jaga Jaga!' We have to get reed of the scum that is Nigeria and indeed African political elites. Nigeria is considered as the "giant of Africa" with a population of about 150 million inhabitants. In the last twenty–thirty years, oil and gas revenues have contributed more than 300 billion into Nigerian coffers.

Where has all that money gone? Again can someone please ask these Army Generals for an account of our oil revenue from the end of the Biafra war in 1970? With such daily income, there is no justified reason for the millions of unemployed Nigerians milling around our urban centres hustling for a living. Judiciously managed, Nigeria could feed her millions of population and sister countries. Corruption is the only reason.

In order to enrich them, the military regime of Gen. Yakubu Gowon for example, embarked on prestigious ventures as solution to solve the mounting economic problems of the nation. Building suspended highway networks to "decongest" the Lagos traffic, constructing a national theatre, and subsequent regimes building a new capital city in Abuja, importation of food, all in order to take the ten percent cut. Scandals and accusation of corruption became the hall mark of the regimes.

This corrupt practice was epitomized by the placement of an order worth 20 million United States dollars, for the importation of cement from Europe. Paying two-way transport charges to the shipping companies, who were not attracted to bring the cement to Nigerian shores only to return empty because the country was not exporting anything of interest to the shipping lines apart from oil. The cost of this senseless importation of cement was more than enough to develop the Nigerian cement industry, which would in turn provide jobs for the unemployed.

Commissions of enquiry were set-up regime after regime to investigate what has become the hall mark of every successive regime like Fela sang in Army Arrangement: "…2.8 Billion Naira oil money is missing, them set-up enquiry, supervisor Obasanjo, Yar'adua road manager. Money no lost them shout again!"

Today after more than three decades of military rule, everyone agrees that corruption has led the country into a fantastic anarchy like Professor Théophile Obenga mentioned in his book 'Appel a la Jeunesse Africaine' (Clarion Call to African Youths):

- A site designed to house a project worth 18 billion US dollars has never been found and cannot be located despite payment of the total cost as mobilization fees and despite setting-up of commission of enquiry.

- Millions were spent for paper mills never built talk less of producing any paper.

- At least not less than eighteen projects worth about 836 million dollars are neither completed nor operational: as of date nobody was ever arrested or worried of the potentials of arrest either.

- Between 1985 and 1992, Nigeria launched twenty other projects the same fate, non viability in spite of the NGO (Non-Governmental Organization) Transparency International present in the country.

The external debt of Nigeria is estimated 32 billion dollars (If we take into account the amount of money recovered from Abacha's family after his death, five of Nigeria's ex-Generals could conveniently pay back this debt). Nigeria's leadership, claims to fight against corruption by creating "Global Rights" an association for democracy. With the setting-up of anti-corruption commissions already 85 indictments, dismissal of the Minister of Housing who sold public goods dirt-cheap, detention of the head of the police for money laundering. While all these are going-on, imitated and counterfeit drugs flood the Nigerian and indeed African markets because they are not seized in airports, ports, etc.

There are even secret laboratories in some countries. One agrees that when one fights against corruption the risks all around the world are high: physical threats, resistance of armed gangs and protection thanks to certain collusive officials. The suitable way or rather fair distribution of the national income, is a policy which demands and encourages collective effort to make a success of the development of the country.

The energy of our young people cannot be mobilized with so much corruption but inevitably of a dialectical necessity by concrete examples of patriotism, dedication without compromise like Professor Obenga concluded in his book quoted above.

This is the Pan-African patriotism of Marcus Garvey it is Nelson Mandela's inflexible resistance, and it is the Pan-African aspiration and total faith of Kwame Nkrumah, the Pan-African nobility of soul of Julius Nyerere, the Pan-African vision high as the Mount Kilimanjaro of Jomo Kenyatta and Tom Mboya, the fertile blood of martyrs of the likes of Patrice Lumumba and Thomas Sankara.

It is the African Renaissance of Cheikh Anta Diop. "Globalization" is a fight, a strategic fight of diverse interests sometimes very opposite like Fela sang in (ITT) International Thief Thief. It is little necessary to recognize in the current world, that there is not either "concert of nations" or "international community" really fair nor democratic again apology Fela - 'Beasts of No Nation'.

What is at stake is political, economic, military, linguistic, cultural interests, appropriate for every State or Nation, for every region, for every civilization that make the weft of "globalization" which is nothing else than one contemporary "world-economy".

"Globalization" strengthens those that are already strong, and weakens those that are indifferent to the governance of the world. A united, Pan African Africa is the solution like Fela sang in 'Who No Know Go Know'. This is what our politicians should be talking about - not North/South dichotomy which is nothing but diversion.

Like Fela sang in: 'Clear Road for Jaga Jaga,' we have to get reed of the scum that is Nigeria and indeed African current political class.

Back cover album design Underground System

Front cover album design Black President

THE FELA PHENOMENON

Since Fela's demise as part of preserving the icon's legacy were initiatives like the "Fela Project", an exposition that opened at the New Museum of Contemporary Art, Broadway NYC between July 11-19th September 2003. Titled "Black President: The Art and Legacy of Fela Anikulapo-Kuti". The exposition presented the many sides of the Fela phenomenon and legacy particularly with the book titled: 'Fela Kuti, From West Africa to West Broadway'.

Though it must have taken a long gestation by Trevor Schoonmaker and his team with regards to planning, organising and fund-raising, it brought to life all the colours that are the Fela phenomenon. The "Fela Project," afforded some of those who had direct contacts with the man to clear the air about his person and those with opinions of him to air them. It was previewed, to be exposed in major European capitals after the New York opening.

During his life and in death, Fela has been maligned by those who did not really know him as macho or anti feminist. To those who really knew him, he was never anti feminist as he was only saying African women have always made the decisions in African traditional homes, today's African woman doesn't need 'feminist cause' to be in-charge. Fela's endorsement of polygamy is not anti feminist as polygamy is not unique with African men.

Europeans and European-Americans, who marry under Christian laws at the same time keep mistresses are only being hypocrites. They should learn from Africans who keep all their women under one roof to avoid any ambiguity.

On a serious note, while this exercise is not to defend polygamy it should be noted that African ancestors who introduced polygamy into their respective societies did so to re-populate a depleted community victims of slavery. For those who cannot align themselves with time to understand the tragedy of slavery and its effect on a people, the closest tragedy of that magnitude in the last century that came close enough to be compared to the crimes of slavery is the Jewish holocaust.

While this is not intended as a revisionist exercise, the Fela phenomenon is calling on humanity to bear in mind that for almost ten generations, the African society was systematically depleted of its able-bodies citizens aged between 15 to 45 years (thanks to Arab and European slave traffic) and that speaks volumes.

As an agrarian society, polygamy was also introduced to create room for a labour force that was needed to cultivate the fields in order to feed their families. The same can be said of the facial marks practised generation after generation - they cannot be considered as scarification. At the time of the practice, there were no identity cards in existence. With wars and the constant displacement of populations, facial marks and tattoos were invented to provide the people with a means of identification. I believe like Fela, that all cultures are subject to evolution and change only an imbecile remains un-changed.

While there are a lot of traditional practices in Africa that needs to be discarded at the same time like Fela tried to impress on the world, there are a great deal of value in the African culture and tradition. Historians without the Western bias, agree that African ancestors had well defined ideas of nature, human life, existence, social relations as well as of man himself. It is on the basis of these well defined ideas that the fundamental elements of human civilisation and education were developed.

These values are relevant to our collective advancement in the world as human beings, but they are systematically ignored because we are too egoist to admit that a people whom we once called barbarians have for so long been the masters of our today's civilisation – that is the essence of the Fela phenomenon and legacy.

The year 2010 saw the extraordinary explosion of the brand name FELA with the re-issue of his life's work and the media success of the musical from Broadway to a London theatre. With all the euphoria around FELA (the Broadway musical), one major aspect missing is the emphasis on the man and what he stood for as I have tried to present all along in this volume. From reports, Bill T. Jones did a great job with the musical from an aesthetic point of view however his representation of the man has nothing to do with Fela Anikulapo-Kuti. Fela (in the musical) is portrayed as championing polygamy which was not the reason for his mass marriage to his singers and dancers.

He was also projected as an indecisive man running to his mother for assurance and inspiration – this also was not Fela to those of us who knew him.

Fela at the launching of his political party Movement of the People (MOP) at the Tafawa Balewa Square Lagos in 1978.
Photo by Femi Bankole Osunla Africa 70 Photo Agency.

Fela performing at the launching of his political party Movement of the People (MOP) at the Tafawa Balewa Square Lagos in 1978.
Photo by Femi Bankole Osunla Africa 70 Photo Agency.

Fela addressing the public at the launching of his political party Movement of the People (MOP) at the Tafawa Balewa Square Lagos in 1978.
Photo by Femi Bankole Osunla Africa 70 Photo Agency.

Without any prejudice to the legal battle between Carlos Moore and the producers of the musical, I believe Bill T. Jones and the producers of the musical were hoodwinked (like most readers) into believing Carlos Moore with his self proclaimed "authorized biography of Africa's musical genius" in his re-edited work.

My book 'Fela, Why Blackman Carry Shit' too was published with a written authorization from Fela, and I did not portray Fela as an indecisive man nor sell it as THE authorized biography despite going to jail on countless occasions with Fela as part of our struggle. As a Fela biographer and Egypt 80 administrator at the time 'This Bitch of Life' was written and published (see page 148 new edition), I can say with certitude that Carlos Moore does not have any exclusivity to that claim of "authorized biographer" and I challenge anyone to say the contrary.

In fact, Fela was not pleased with the way he was portrayed in the book and it was one of the reasons he broke contact with Carlos Moore until his demise. Since my criticism of the musical on my website:www.radioshrine.com, I have had some feed-back saying it is OK to criticise the misrepresentation of Fela in the Broadway musical, but my criticism of Carlos Moore is seen as "divide and conquer".

Again without any prejudice to his legal battle, I affirm that I thought I was dealing with a brother when I made my opinion clear to Carlos Moore in long-distance phone conversations and exchanges of e-mails about the musical being a wrong representation of Fela. He confirmed his total agreement with my views (I have e-mails and my phone bills to substantiate this fact).

Hence my utter disgust after his hob-nobbing with the producers of the musical and later turns round to claim that their production was inspired by his work 'This Bitch of Life'. Does this mean he is the origin of the misrepresentation of Fela Anikulapo-Kuti? I am in no way saying that Carlos, cannot express an opinion of Fela because it is a right that no one can take away from him.

Same question was posed to Femi Kuti in the French version of my book Fela, Le Combbattant: What is your opinion of ID's book Fela, Why Blackman Carry Shit. Does the book represent the image you want people to have of Fela?

Femi replied:
"I read the first version (published in Nigeria while Fela was still alive). I think it is a good book it is interesting but I have never thought of it in the terms of how I want my father to be represented. ID was close to Fela like some others, Fela was aware about him publishing the book. That is ID's views about my father, people will always present Fela from their point of view, I guess that is how ID sees Fela. My mother was writing a book on Fela before she died, I guess it can be considered as my mother's view of Fela, If I ever write a book about Fela it will be my own personal view too it is an interesting book but I cannot say how I want Fela to be represented since I cannot be in everybody's head. We all see and think differently that is why we are human beings".

The presentation of Fela Anikulapo-Kuti in the Broadway musical if it was inspired by 'This Bitch of Life' is the problem of Moore and the producers, but what people like me who lived the experience and was witness to all the events cannot let pass is the misrepresentation issue.

"This is a historiographical combat" like the one I consider as my philosophical guru professor of Egyptology, linguist, and philosopher, Théophile Obenga, is appt to say when it comes to defending our ideas and struggle. This is no attempt to 'divide and conquer'. How long shall they kill our prophets while we stand aside and look? (Apology Bob Marley).

Marcus Garvey, Kwame Nkrumah, were maligned as a dictators despite their idea of African Unity: unique monetary and defence system for all Africa in a continental federal state being primordial actuality for the survival of the African continent today as Fela too sang in Confusion. Charlie Parker, in the film 'BIRD' was projected as a drugged-out drunken looser despite him being a musician's musician to several jazz icons like Miles Davis and John Coltrane.

Today his concepts and ideas are transcribed, studied, and analyzed, by a great deal of jazz students and are part of any player's basic jazz vocabulary. Charlie Parker, contributed a vast rhythmic vocabulary to the modern jazz solo despite the negative image of him projected in the film 'Bird'.

Malcolm X, was considered as the man who could start or stop a race riot and called all sorts of names in the American press.

Image of him from his childhood in Omaha up to his assassination in New York in 1965, Malcolm X's life was projected as the charismatic and controversial leader of Black Muslims who after a delinquent youth fought up to his death for the equality of his African American brothers and sisters.

An important evolution of his life, the formation of the Organization of Afro-American and African Unity was to a large extent played down until the film by Spike Lee helped the African and Diaspora African to identify them in Malcolm X.

Unlike when pioneering what is today known as RAP music in the early '70s; accompanied by congas and bongo drums, Gil Scott-Heron in his album 'Small Talk at 125th and Lenox' declared: "The Revolution Will Not Be Televised". Thanks to Internet and social networks, the revolution is being televised and people can communicate without waiting for their information from their national "official" media only.

It is widely accepted that the spark for the dramatic events in Egypt in 2011, came from the uprising in Tunisia. If people's power could bring down one regime perhaps it could do the same elsewhere. Many of the necessary conditions are already in place: public fury at years of political repression, economy that rewards corrupt elites and keep a majority in poverty, widespread loathing for leaders clinging to office (apology Fela Authority Stealing and ITT! International! Thief! Thief!)

Fear is one factor that has kept black people in bondage for so long people using family bonds, as justification for their non involvement in the struggle. Fela states in (STB) that individual fears will not make the fight for progress, freedom, happiness and injustices disappear - for as long as there is fear, police and army brutality will always be a part of our daily lives leaving in its wake, Sorrows Tears and Blood (STB).

Could other African countries like Egyptians, be persuaded to overcome years of fear and apathy and take to the streets? It is no accident that this question has been answered emphatically, the people's stride for true democracy has begun – this is not "dem-all-crazy" apology Fela, this is the people's true democracy! Let the wind of change blow from Cairo to Cape Town!

Since Fela' demise in 1997 and from the details and anecdotes about his life and times enumerated above, the reader will agree that the issues the phenomenon that was Fela protested all his life about are not only relevant in the Nigerian polity today, but they are a part of the global problems still facing the human society.

One of 20th Century Jazz music icons in: "MILES – The autobiography" by Quincy Troupe, affirmed that 'the music of one Fela Anikulapo-Kuti from West Africa would be the music of the 21st Century'. In 1989 when the book was first published, who would have thought Miles would be so right in his predictions? Today, the certitude of Miles Davis can be seen and heard from all the hues and cries of Fela and afrobeat music around the world.

Apart from Cheikh Anta Diop, Dr. Ivan Van Sertima, and Theophile Obenga, Fela Anikulapo-Kuti is also another personage that have contributed immensely towards African awareness in the last half of the 20th Century and beginning of the 21st Century. Using music as a weapon in his special musical creation called afrobeat, Fela invited Africans and Diaspora Africans to be proud of their African heritage as he sang in Blackman's Cry.

The production of the new Broadway musical "FELA" in New York and later in the year in London, featuring dancers in the aisles of a theatre decorated like his Nigerian nightclub with the music and choreography of the show, a testimony to the employ that Fela's name is taking. It is great to see Fela becoming a household name, but with all the hues and cries we should not forget the essential part of FELA'S message: "My music is not for entertainment! My music is to spread a message!"

Africa the mother of civilization has remained for over two thousand years and still remains the Dark Continent like Fela sang in COLOMENTALITY. There is no justifiable reason, not to recognize a dark part of one's past except if the person is ignorant or doing so for personal reasons. Like the author of CIBA SYMPOSIA, Dr. Victor Robinson felt obliged to say: "It is one of the paradoxes of history that Africa the mother of civilisation, remained for over two thousand years the Dark Continent.

To the moderns, Africa was the region where ivory was sought for Europe and slaves for America.

In the time of Johathan Swift (1667-1745), as the satirist informs us geographers in drawing African maps would fill in the gaps with savage pictures - where towns should have been they placed elephants". (Listen to Fela - Africa Centre of the world & Roy Ayers – 2000 Blacks).

What is meant by the "Dark Continent?" There is no precise established meaning for this phrase, each writer has his or her definition but in general, it can be considered a degrading phrase to describe a continent and her people. Down through the ages, there are of course equal amounts of adverse comments against Africa and her indigenous sons and daughters.

To some extent, most part of humanity only knows the adverse comments without knowing that the opposite exists. There are those who don't care one iota about the cultural genocide, that the Africans suffer at the hands of Western so-called authorities on African history.

Over the last five hundred years, from the vicious slave trade to the wanton partition of Africa and the subsequent so-called independence, right-up till now in the 21st century nothing much has changed to either rectify nor stop this cultural genocide despite the cries of people like Fela and those before him. There is no doubt that this opinion of Africa as the 'Dark continent,' is a creation based on religious bigotry and politically racist hypothesis to justify slavery (Why Blackman Dey Suffer – Fela).

However, other views of the continent by those who were opportune to know the truth are affirming the contrary. This is the case with the writer of the book, History of Nations published in 1906: "The African continent is no recent discovery it is not a new world like America or Australia…While yet Europe was the home of wandering barbarians, one of the most wonderful civilizations on record had begun to work its destiny on the banks of the Nile".

We are able to say today with all certainty that mankind was born in Africa – along the region that covers present-day Eritrea, Ethiopia, Kenya all along to Tanzania right down to South Africa. Also, it is clear that any member of the human community born in that region (south of the equator) could not have survived without the pigmentation of skin. Scientifically speaking, it is known with all certainty that nature doesn't create anything by chance.

It is for that reason, that humans born in a sub-equatorial region was given melanin to protect his or her skin hence the first-man had to be BLACK. At the time human anthropology had not quit evolve to the extent at which it is today, there were two theories confronting each other regarding the origin of man.

The mono-genetic theory, had its defenders who claim one source of origin for mankind. The idea is that man was born in one place and as he moved to other parts of the world, subjected to different atmospheric changes he became transformed. The second is the poly-genetic theory, which contended that man was born in Africa like in other continents such as Asia and Europe. Defenders of this theory pointed to the physical differences in humans to justify their claim.

On the surface it makes sense, looking at the different external characteristics of man. However under a close scrutiny, this theory falls apart if we remember that scientifically speaking nature does not create the same being twice. In the animal world through-out evolution of animals when it is created, it evolves either to become something else in the process of survival or disappears – but he is never created a second time.

The defenders of poly-genetic origin of man, based their scientific claims on the Piltdown man - a fossil fabricated piece-by-piece in 1912 by an English geologist Charles Dawson who claimed he dug them in the fields at Sussex, England.

Like modern man, his fossil had a fore-head and eyes of man but his mandible is that of a monkey. From this fabrication developed the poly-genetic theory to establish the existence of "pre-sapiens man". Many Western anthropologists defended this theory, basing their argument on the fossil of Piltdown man despite being aware that it was falsified.

We know today that it was false because in 1954, a British anthropologist Professor Oakley, working with the British museum tested the fossil and found it to be false. However the damage had already been done, for more than fifty years the scientific community was divided into two – one defending monogenetic origin of man while the other defended poly-genetic theory using Piltdown man as their reference.

No other continent in the world other than Africa so far, have been discovered the six series of Human fossils. All evolutionary information regarding man's origin was un-earthed along the Olduvai Gorge in Tanzania for this reason, scientists are able to say with certainty that man has a mono-genetic origin. Other fossils found outside Africa, have proved under scientific scrutiny to be of resent origin.

For example when we say the Americas is a new world, it is because the only human specimen (fossil) found in America is that of homo-sapiens sapiens. America was peopled through the Bering Strait at the end of the final glaciations, hence it can only have homo-sapiens sapiens. In Asia we have fossils of Homo erectus, the Neanderthal man, and Homo sapiens sapiens. Equally in Europe there are fossils of Homo erectus, the Neanderthal man, and Homo sapiens sapiens.

The man called in pre-historic history the Grimaldi Man, left Africa about 40,000 years ago for Europe. He lived between 40,000 and 20,000 years, adapting and transforming at a time when the climate was extremely cold – much colder than what it is today. This man would later transform into what is known as Cro-Magnon Man.

It was the last glaciations period that lasted for 100,000 years. Leaving Africa, some of them passed by what is called today the Suez Canal or the Isthmus of Suez to go and populate Asia and Eastern Europe while others left for Europe through the Strait of Gibraltar.

Count C. F. Volney, a member of the French delegation that visited Egypt in 1787 wrote a first-hand account of what he saw and published in 1890 titled "Ruins of Empire" and "Oeuvres" published in 1825. This is what he wrote: "There a people now forgotten (who) discovered while others were yet barbarians, the elements of the arts and sciences.

A race of men now rejected for their sable skin, and frizzled hair, founded on the study of the laws of nature, those civil and religious systems which still governs the universe". To deny Africa's role in history irrespective of religious affiliation, economic circumstance, or political attachment, is participating in genocide against a people.

Scientific and archaeological facts are abounding today pointing to Africa as the origin of civilization. To mention a few, the colloquium on the population of ancient Egypt and the decrypting of Meroe scripts for the production of a general history of Africa held in Cairo, Egypt from January 28–February 3rd, 1974 under the auspices of UNESCO validates this claim.

As members of the international scientific committee at the Cairo colloquium, the interventions of Dr. Cheikh Anta Diop assisted by Théophile Obenga, were considered in the final report as meticulously prepared and invite the scientific community to re-write universal history of humanity granting Black Africa her primordial role that she has effectively assumed in the edification of civilization.

Today one can see little-by-little, how history and science has departed from so-called reality proclaimed by "authorities on Africa". This move is commendable, in view of certain political views notoriously hostile to the approach to recognize a dark part of history (like the Dakar discuss of French President Sarkozy).

In the same spirit of not giving credit where it is due, while Fela was accused by music critics in Europe that he did not care about the rules of musical composition (see above accounts of Berlin Jazz Festival 1978), in North America Afrobeat is considered to be influenced by Western particularly American sounds - all these to justify the claim of a diversion through a European or American career.

One who knows, can say with certitude today that despite his education at the Trinity College of Music in London, the inspiration behind Afrobeat music came from the traditional Yoruba 'Apala Music'. The way the bass, tenor, and rhythm guitars, work in short phrases criss-crossing in unison in Afrobeat, it is parallel to those of the talking-drum family (omélé, dundun and bata) in Yoruba traditional music.

In view of the above let us like the German Leo Frobenius, who furthered the work of Count C. F. Volney in the year 1910 titled: UND AFRIKA SPRACH (AND AFRICA SPEAKS).

He urged his fellow Western colleagues to: "Let there be light! Light in Africa! Light in that portion of the globe to which the stalwart Anglo-Saxon Stanley gave the name "Dark" and "Darkest". Light upon the people and children we are accustomed to regard as types of natural servility with no recorded history. But the spell, has been broken the buried treasures of antiquity again revisit the sun."

In the same spirit with which the buried treasures of antiquity revisits the sun - thanks to archaeological excavations and works of people like Count C.F. Volney, Cheikh Anta Diop continued by Theophile Obenga, we know with certitude today that world civilisation in general owes a huge amount to African tradition - an essential part of Fela's message. Thus, Fela the man or the musical from Broadway to London or where else, the commercial success of the brand name FELA should not be lost in the Bling! Bling! Of six-figure Dollar signs.

The man himself when he was alive was very aware of his financial potentialities it is not the Knitting Factory team, the first to see the financial potentials of Fela. As far back as the early '80s Chris Blackwell of Island records, shortly after the demise of Bob Marley approached Fela to buy his back catalogue. Fela in return asked for $10,000,000 which Chris Blackwell thought was a crazy amount for Fela to ask at that time. Today, with all the Broadway and Hollywood talks around Fela, we know that the brand name plus his back catalogue is worth big money.

To the Knitting Factory guys who have succeeded in bringing Fela the Natty Dread main-stream I can only say like the French 'Chapeau Bas' (doff my hat). But with all the commercial success, let us not forget Fela's message: "my music is not for entertainment, my music is to spread a message".

The 21st century message of Fela to a capitalist world is: capitalism where morality is not capital is a shame and got to stop. It is not morally right to use the social welfare contributions of the masses to bail-out big banks during economic crises, while the same system considers providing health care for all as socialism. This is the important part of afrobeat message, Fela should not be only a commercial success on Broadway and Wall Street, Fela' ideas should be heard on Pennsylvania Avenue, Downing Street, Elysée, and all the seats of power around the globe.

A Welfare State where everyman is his neighbour's keeper is the future of man. From all enumerated above, the reader will agree with me that the issues Fela protested are still relevant in the Nigerian and indeed world polity today.

Also another essential part of Fela's message to the African, African-Caribbean, and African-American, is that at this point in our history isn't it time to look at what unites us as a people than what will potentially tear us apart. If people's power could bring down draconian regimes as we can see in the mass uprising in the Arab world, it could do the same elsewhere in other parts of Africa.

This is a legitimate democratic aspiration of any people under subjugation. Many of the necessary conditions are already in place: public fury at years of political repression, economy that rewards corrupt elites and keep a majority in poverty, widespread loathing for leaders clinging to office, etc. The only thing missing is educating the people to fight for their rights.

Echoing Dr. Yosef Ben-Jochanna in his epic work titled, Black Man of The Nile: "If the European Jews can fight for an arid piece of desert, the Irish for a small emerald Island, the British for a barren Island of misery, protestant Anglo-Saxon Americans for their stolen "Indian" empire, why should the Black man (the African, African-Caribbean and African-American) not fight for the richest piece of real estate on the planet earth his original homeland – mother Africa?"

Remember the age long saying of our ancestors: "A man who does not know where he is coming from can never know where he is going".

Talks of North / South dichotomy, are nothing but diversion. Abraham or Ibrahim - the patriarch of both Christian and Moslem religions was not born when our black ancestors built the pyramids.

All the great monuments Egypt is renown for today: Sphinx, Pyramids, etc., were already constructed during the reign of Pharaoh Neimer (called Aha by other writers) 2,800 BC. In the case of Nigeria the hieroglyphic writings of Isibidi people of Cross River State, and Nok culture of Plateau State, are perfect examples of our common ancestry with Egypt of the Black Pharaohs.

The cultural, linguistic, and religious unity, of all Africa is no longer in doubt thanks to archaeological excavations and the works of Africans the likes of Cheikh Anta Diop continued by Theophile Obenga.

Cosmogony mythologies play an important role in African societies. Though creation myths in African societies are as varied as the many cultures existing in the continent, some scientists and writers without the bias of Africa being the cradle of today's civilisation, are of the opinion that various groups of Africans originated from the Great Lakes and the Nile valley region, particularly Ancient Egypt.

Among the chain of evidence leading to this conclusion like Fela enumerated during his University of Ife debate in Nigeria are: similarity of language, traditional beliefs, ideas and practices, religion, plus the survival of customs and names, etc.

Concerning the Yoruba, one of the three major groups of people that inhabit present-day Nigeria, archaeological discoveries come in support of this theory. The Yoruba progenitor, Oduduwa, is said to have come from Ancient Egypt. This belief is based on the similarity of works of art (mainly sculptures), discovered in Ile-Ife the mythological centre of Yoruba land with those found in Egypt. Furthermore, some words belonging to the Egyptian language are also found in other African languages.

An example is the word "Ye", which means "to exist". Differences do sometimes occur, when "e" becomes "a" or "i" or "o" or "u" or these vowels are nasalized in some of the languages considered such as Tshi, Ewe, Ga, Yoruba, Edo. Other examples are: the word "amon" which means "to conceal" or "concealed" in ancient Egyptian language, it has the same meaning in Yoruba language. For example: "fi p'amon" means "conceal it" or "regard it as hiding". "Wu" which means "rise up" or "swell". "Miri" signifies water in Yoruba but is used only as an adverb viz "miri-miri" - "dazzling like water".

Also among the Igbo people the next-door neighbours to the Yoruba, "miri" is used to denote water (see - The Religion of The Yoruba, by Olumide Lucas). Most of the Ancient Egyptian principal Gods were well known at one time to the Yoruba's.

Among them are: Osiris, Isis, Horus, Shu, Thoth, Khpera, Amon, Anu, Khonsu, Knum, Khopri, Hathor, Sakaris, Ra, Seb. Most of them survive in name or attributes, or in both. "Ra" for instance, survives in name for the majority of the present–day Yoruba people are no longer Sun worshippers. Yet words like "Irawo", "Ra-ra", preserve the idea. The literal meaning of "Irawo" (a star) is that which appears when "Ra" (the sun) has set ("Wo" means set). The Yoruba expression "Ra-ra" (Not at all, or no-no), is probably an old form of swearing by the sun-God, Ra.

The word "amon" exists in the Yoruba language with the same meaning as it has in the language of the Ancient Egyptians. The God Amon is one of the Gods formally known to the Yoruba. Moreover, the Yoruba word "Mon" (or "Mimon"), which means holy or sacred, is probably derived from the name of the God Amon.

Also, "Thoth" was the Ancient Egyptian God of truth or righteousness. If the initial letters 'th' become's 't', and the final 'th' is dropped, the word thus become "to" – which in Yoruba means "right", "fair", or "just". Other words presumed to derive from Thoth are "O-ti-to", truth, or that which belongs to truth. Also the word: "E-to", rights, fairness or justice.

The apparent survival of indigenous African words in both the Greek and Latin languages lends credence to the impress of African high culture (civilisation) on both Greek and Roman culture and civilisation. The Latin word: "Fere", which means almost, survives in its entire form in the Yoruba language and has the same meaning. This exercise, shouldn't be persived as an over-kill from the part of the author since Fela in the previous chapter enumerated all the examples above.

I believe it is important to lay emphasis on these words to trigger in our collective conscience the need to find what unites than divids us. A common phenomenon, among the various groups of people that constitutes the federation of Nigeria is their shared cultural heritage. Be it among the Igbo, Hausa, or Yoruba, the naming of a child for example calls for celebration. Be it weddings, deaths, the award of chieftaincy titles, etc. These occasions are celebrated with traditional music and musicians with the heavy rhythms of the talking drum and other types of drums and percussion instruments.

Praise singers or griots, add their historic insights to the meaning of the ceremony by either singing in praise of or recounting the lineage of those present at the ceremony. Though the instruments played by the musicians are as varied as the ceremonies, the 'Talking Drum' is an instrument commonly used by musicians from most regions. Called 'Iya Ilu' 'mother drum' by the Yoruba, 'Kalangu' by the Hausa, it has existed since faraway times not only for entertainment but also as an instrument of communication.

Before the invention of the telephone technology, the 'talking drum' used to serve as a means of communication between communities. In Yoruba land played by 'Onilu Oba' (the Oba's drummer), it was used in the same manner as carrier-birds to convey messages from one king's messenger to the other or from one point of the kingdom to the other. 'Apala' music, sometimes called 'Sakara' music because of the leading role of the sakara drum – a round hand-drum made from cow or goat skin. Firmly secured or attached to a pottery top, the sakara drum is played with the fingers putting pressure on the skin to change tones like the strings of the 'mother drum', pulled or released to change tones and sounds.

It has the sound of the talking drum and can talk like the Iya Ilu (mother drum). It leads the rhythm and other percussion follows. Be it traditional 'Apala' music which serves as the root or the base of Yoruba urban dance music or its derivatives 'juju' or Fuji 'music', the talking drum sets the pace or can be described as the heart of the rhythm. As the evolution of apala (sakara) music has influenced both juju and fuji in the present day Yoruba urban music, the same can be said of its influence on Diaspora Yoruba music - particularly in the rumba, salsa and samba music.

Despite the presence of bata drums, congas or Latin percussion as they are known in the Diaspora Yoruba music (like in Haiti, Cuba, or Brazil), where they tend to mystify more the bata drum the important role of the Iya Ilu cannot be over-stressed here. The bata drum called the same name, conga-drums, or Latin-percussion, the samba-drums called bembe by the Yoruba, and other instruments figure prominently in apala music. The heart of apala music is percussion and the call and respond vocal style of the musicians add beauty to the music.

A first time visitor to present-day Yoruba land will notice this heritage in the richness and variety of its culture.

This heritage is part of the urbanised social structure in most of the Yoruba settlements. Present-day Yoruba land is situated below the river Niger, starting at the fringes of the northern savannah grassland in the western part of Nigeria, and covering the western high plains, right to the tropical rain forest in the south. Yoruba cosmogony tells us about a God, Olodumare, who lowered a chain from the sky at Ile-Ife, down which came Oduduwa, the progenitor of all Yoruba people. Another story tells us that Oduduwa came from the East. He, alike several other African people, were forced to migrate from the great lakes region and the Nile valley as a result of wars.

This assumption is based on the resemblance between sculptures and other works of art found in Ile-Ife and those found in temples and pyramids in Egypt. Today, Yorubas still refer to themselves as 'Omo Oduduwa' ('the children of Oduduwa'.) After his death, his vast kingdom was divided up among his seven sons that were later divided into numerous independent kingdoms that share a cosmogony origin. The Yoruba kingdom broke up into numerous empires after several internecine wars – for which the slave trade was largely responsible.

A major factor in Nigeria's political dynamics is the similar cosmogony myth shared by the other two major peoples, notably the Hausa and the Igbo. Hausa cosmogony tells of the 'Hausa Bokwai' or the 'seven Hausa states', and the 'Banza Bokwai' or the 'seven bastards' – referring to the 'seven legitimate' and 'seven illegitimate' children of the Hausa progenitor. After his death, like the progenitor of the Yorubas, his vast kingdom was shared among his children and later broken up into several geographically diverse and culturally varied states and empires – for which the Arab slave trade, or the 'Jihad' were largely responsible.

Present-day Hausa land is situated immediately above the Niger River, from the fringes of the northern savannah grassland in the western part, to the eastern end of Nigeria with a frontier with the republic of Cameroon above the river Benue, up to the fringes of the Sahara desert in the north.

The Igbo people of present-day Nigeria, occupy the eastern half of the southern part of the country. Historically, they reside in villages and towns smaller than those of the Hausa or Yoruba.

Most of these towns and villages are headed by 'chiefs' called 'Obi' or 'Eze', who don't have the same statute as the kings in Hausa land and Obas in Yoruba land. In present-day Nigeria, the existence of a Yoruba civilisation is an undisputed reality, alike the civilisations of the remnant states of the Hausa and Igbo kingdoms.

One can appreciate the strength and refinement of their legacies, considering the fact that from the 16th up to the 19th century, the Atlantic slave trade dramatically affected all of Africa.

Yoruba slaves for instance forcibly taken and resettled in Cuba, Haiti, Brazil, the United States, Trinidad and Tobago, still adhere to and keep alive basic principles of the Yoruba tradition and mode of worship that have existed through all the passing centuries in Africa.

The cultural, linguistic and religious unity of all Africa is no longer in doubt this in my opinion should be our focus not organizing us in little groups. Talks of North/South dichotomy are nothing but diversion. If I take it on me to draw our attention to what is necessary to do at this stage, it is because I have experience to draw our attentions to.

In the 70's when we were publishing monthly and distributing for free 80,000 copies of YAP NEWS (Young African Pioneers news letter), we didn't have all the social networks available today. Maybe if we had, the more than 40,000 civilians standing and watching while 1,000 Nigerian Army soldiers were burning down in broad-day-light Fela's Kalakuta Republic would have reacted differently.

Social networks, would probably have paved the way for and encouraged the masses to overcome years of fear and apathy and take to the streets like the case with Arab streets demonstrating and calling for change. Like I mentioned earlier without any vanity, I think I am a great person and I am sure that every African thinks of themselves as great people. What is there to be proud about today as a Nigerian? Abroad, people are afraid to visit Nigeria because they believe it is dangerous to visit.

This last October (2011), I had to cancel a charter flight trip I was organizing for Felabration 2011. I had managed to secure 50 passengers from different parts of Europe who had inscribed to be a part of the project.

Unfortunately, the attack on the United Nations building in August by Boko Haram forced 39 of the inscribed passengers to withdraw because of fear for their safety. I guess we can see what's going on around us again, Egyptian streets are clamouring and calling for the Army to go back to the barracks where they belong. Today Tahrir (Freedom) Square is full with Egyptians who don't want the Nigerian style "Army Arrangement".

Without over-emphasising as mentioned through-out this volume, January 15, 1966 saw Nigerians from all works of life trooping to the streets to welcome the first ever military coup d'état in the country. Their jubilation stemmed from the aspiration that the military will deliver them from the persistent wave of corruption and political gangstarism, burning down of homes of those considered as opponent – a common scene in the Northern and Southern parts of the country (News: Nigerian Parliamentarians in fists fights – 'Noise for Vendor Mouth' apology Fela).

The climate of insecurity which was the order of the day in the Nigerian contemporary politics of the early sixties, paved the way for the arrival of the military in the political arena. Since their arrival in the political scene, the aspiration of Nigerian people has over the years been transformed into nightmare with the military taking the country through a civil war and the spectre of another looming as we see from events in the Northern parts of Nigeria and the on-going military uprising in the oil producing regions. There is no doubt that haven tasted power they are finding it hard to relinquish it.

The army is still very much in control, all the registered political parties are controlled by former army generals. Today they put-on civilian clothes and use religion to create a political base and continue to divide and rule. Have we stopped to ask who is behind Boko Haram? How do they have access to arms and bombs? Suicide is not a part of the African tradition because we believe in reincarnation – that is why we have names like Yetunde, Babatunde, Malomo, Otolorin, etc., in the Yoruba tradition and it is the same with Hausa and Igbos.

Like I wrote in an article published in my radioshrine.com website titled, Arab Streets – Lesson to African Youths: There has been a long held stereotypical view that the Arab world has a social and cultural identity often associated with violence, extremism, and a mistrust of democracy western style.

But as the up-rising across the Arab world have shown, this view is largely inaccurate. This is a far cry from the stereotype image of the Arab youth, whose only aspiration is to wrap his body with explosive and kill infidels to become martyred with a thousand virgins waiting for him in paradise.

The introduction of Islamic fanaticism in our culture calls for concern. Same can be said of Christian fanaticism. Abraham or Ibrahim - the patriarch of both Christian and Moslem religions was not born when our black ancestors built the pyramids. Nok culture and the hieroglyphic writings of Isibidi people of Cross River State are perfect examples of our common ancestry with Egypt of the Black pharaohs. The cultural, linguistic, and religious, unity of all Africa is no longer in doubt thanks to archaeological excavations and the works of Africans the likes of Cheikh Anta Diop continued by Theophile Obenga.

Granted, the level of political awareness of our people in Africa is hampered by their religious believes and the will to fight for our rights are still yet to be a motivating factor, we can learn from our North African neighbours whose motivation is the chronic economic malaise and the growing disparity between rich and poor.

Democratic aspirations is common to all people under subjugation - the youths today have no jobs and nothing to do, economic conditions, racism, and police brutality are reasons for the mass uprising of youths world-wide. The demands for change, in the way politics is done in the 21st century is what is pushing the youths into the streets.

Thanks to social networks we can see this with the movement of indignant youths in Europe, the 'Occupy Wall Street' movement in North America, and those of North Africa and Arab streets. Social networking, has enabled exchange of information and helped avoid the classic diversions that takes away people's focus. They are perfect mediums, for us to investigate why 99% of our people are suffering while 1% are smiling (apology Fela-Suffering and Smilling).

The exchange of information via social networks, allows the masses to see diversions such as that of British historian David Starkey's "the whites have become black" comments on BBC's "Newsnight" program. For one who claims to be a historian, is he not aware of Linton Kwesi Johnson (LKJ) and his 'Time Come' message?

Instead of asking questions, and finding answers to how we got here, in a discussion on the 2012 violent riots in the United Kingdom we hear David Starkey and others like him hit out at the "destructive nihilistic gangster culture which has become fashion."

In an article published in my website titled "England Riots: Payback Time Come" I drew attention to this evergreen message from LKJ. The poem was a warning to the authorities, the police in particular, that Blacks in London were on the edge. When the poem was published, sure enough the authorities did not pay attention until Swamp 81 that resulted in the Brixton riots which later spread all across the UK. The then Prime Minister Margaret Thatcher, described the uprising as the greatest violence on the streets of Britain since World War 2. As we have seen with the 2012 UK uprising, it is not only Blacks on the edge.

It is exactly that sort of black / white discus that polarises the debate into nothing and history keeps repeating itself. Perhaps if the authorities concerned, had paid attention to LKJ and not tried to terrorize Blacks out of the UK, the riots would not have occurred in the first place. The thing that makes 'Time Come' a classic, is that even though it refers to a specific time and place when riots occurred, it is also timeless and universal in its "warning". Unfortunately the authorities never listen, they only react when there is another uprising.

In the last three decades, countless artists of different origins and social callings, have lent their voices to this "warning" and yet the authorities fail to do something about the root cause of such uprising. To mention a few, Steel Pulse's "Hanswort Revolution", Bob Marley's "Burning and Looting", Nyabinghi "Burn Down Babylon", Fela Kuti's "Everything Scatter" and we must not forget Birmingham's march for peace against gun shootings within and around the community.

Femi Kuti also sang in "Fight to Win": "There is suffering in the streets! Our leaders say let it be! We the people don't agree! For these suffering there is no need! But they'll wait until there is revolution everywhere! Burning of properties! More homeless people lying in the streets…"

While the authorities fail to address the root-cause, every uprising seems to be more devastating than those preceding. The 2012 uprising in UK, was described as the greatest violence on the streets of Britain since the last three decades.

Again instead of asking the question how we got here, Prime Minister David Cameron tells MPs the government will do 'whatever it takes' to rebuild communities and ensure order is restored. He also promised a series of tough measures to be unveiled, to fight crime and reclaim the streets from rioters, looters, and gangs.

Measures such as "zero tolerance" - a tough system of policing first popularised in the United States, which sees even minor offences prosecuted vigorously to send out the message that no form of law-breaking will be tolerated. While all these tough talks are going on, it seems convenient to side-step the cause and origin of the uprising - growing inequality in the United Kingdom and other parts of the world.

But the British Prime Minister David Cameron, blamed the violence on "the mindless selfishness" of looters. How about cleaning up the inequality in U.K. society? Did it ever cross the Prime Minister's mind, that it is likely some rioters in Britain believe there's a possibility the havoc they were wreaking might force a political change?

Frankly, instead of all these promised series of tough measures to be unveiled to fight crime and reclaim the streets from rioters, looters and gangs, doesn't it make more sense to ask what policies of the British government have led people to have that level of outrage? The News International phone-hacking scandal is one example of the inequality in U.K. society.

The controversy involved the News of the World, a British tabloid newspaper formerly published by News International. Employees of the newspaper were accused of engaging in phone-hacking, police bribery, and exercising improper influence in the pursuit of publishing stories. Investigations conducted from 2005-2007 concluded that the paper's phone-hacking activities were limited to celebrities, politicians, and members of the British Royal Family.

However in July 2011, it was revealed that the phone of murdered schoolgirl Milly Dowler, relatives of deceased British soldiers, and victims of the 7/7 London bombings were also accessed, resulting in a public outcry against News Corporation and owner Rupert Murdoch.

The UK parliamentary expenses scandals, and those involved in other corruption related scandals like the phone-hacking scandals, were never treated as propagating destructive, nihilistic, gangster culture of corruption? The scandal aroused, widespread anger among the UK public against MPs and a loss of confidence in politics. It also created pressure for political reform, extending well beyond the issue of expenses and led to the Parliament elected in 2005 being referred to as the 'Rotten Parliament'.

Despite all these, has anything really changed with the way politicians do business in the 21st Century? The answer is NO? Instead of putting the blamed of the violence on "the mindless selfishness" of looters, crashing banks, golden parachutes, and the compensation arrangements for executives of big banks and other financial firms should come under scrutiny. I don't hold a degree in economics but like Fela used to say "I have PhD common sense". How can we justify the millions paid to CEO's as compensation after heading a company that is bankrupt?

Another issue that needs to be reviewed is bank client relations. 90% of all legal transactions pass through banks, this makes 99% of the population in every society major auctioneer of all the banks operating in that society - the rest 10% we can assume belongs to the rich and private fortunes that constitute 1% of the society.

To avoid incidence of crashing banks and repetitive economic crises, legislation should be put in place that obliges banks to invest the savings from the 99% on social welfare, health, education, retirement schemes, etc. If the rest 1% investors want the banks to gamble and play casino and lotto with their fortunes, it is their problem – otherwise whenever there is bank crisis, the savings from the majority should in no way be used to bail-out the minority.

Bankers' excessive risk-taking is a significant cause of the current financial crisis and has contributed to others in the past. Mortgage lenders blithely lent enormous sums to those who could not afford to pay them back, dicing the loans and selling them off to the next financial institution along the chain which took advantage of the same high-tech securitization to load on more risky mortgage-based assets.

Financial regulation, will have to catch up with the most irresponsible practices that led banks down this road in hope, of averting the next crisis which is likely to involve different financial techniques and different sorts of assets. It is worth examining too, the root problem of compensation schemes that are tied to short-term profits and revenue and thus encourages bankers to take irresponsible levels of risk.

From the popular uprising picking momentum all over the world, the world has to get its priorities right. It is abundantly clear that the system capitalism, where morality is not capital is a shame and got to stop. It is not morally right, to use the social welfare contributions of the masses to bail-out big banks during economic crises while the same system considers providing health care for all as socialism.

The social welfare system, a good mixture of socialism and capitalism has served well the UK for the past 70 years - government healthcare, schools, police, fire, public services, mixed with free markets. What has failed, is that sections of the market have become more liberalised and less regulated. I'm in no way saying that people should be encouraged to live on government hand-outs. To get people back to work, governments can impose the employment of two people on the job.

We are generally employed and paid for eight working hours per day. However the time we spend on the job, is less than five hours per day if we take into consideration the time we spend getting on the job, time we spend to make piss and cigarette breaks, the time we spend to chat with colleagues (of course this depends on the nature of job), etc.

If each worker spends four hours on the job, the person can give his or her maximum giving room for the substitute to give another maximum of four hours on the same job.

It will put people to work, and give room for self improvements from the working pull. People will have the option to spend the extra four hours available to them on advancing their studies and skills, or simply spend time with family or friends like Linton Kwesi Johnson sang in 'More Time'.

In this age of globalization, it is clear that no nation can survive without a continental approach - that is why such bodies as United Nations (UN), World Trade Organization (WTO), Regional Trading Arrangements (RPTA's), Asia-pacific Economic Cooperation (APEC), Association of Southeast Asian Nations (ASEAN), are in place. We have to level the playing field, sections of the market have become more liberalised and less regulated since capital went global in search for cheap labour and maximum profit.

"Globalization" today is a fight, a strategic fight of diverse interests, sometimes very opposite. It is little necessary to recognize in the current world that there is not either "concert of nations," or "international community" really fair nor democratic as decried Fela in 'Beasts of No Nation'.

What is at stake is political, economic, military, linguistic, cultural interests, appropriate for every State or Nation, for every region, for every civilization, that make the weft of "globalization", which is nothing else than one contemporary "world economy". "Globalization" strengthens those that are already strong, and weakens those that are indifferent to the governance of the world.

The suitable way or rather fair distribution of the national income is a policy which demands and encourages collective effort, to make a success of the development of the country. The energy of our young people cannot be mobilized by examples of decadence and corruptions but inevitably of a dialectical necessity by concrete examples of patriotism, dedication, without compromise, as enumerated all along this volume with the example of Fela and other Pan-Africanist like him.

Austerity is installing in Europe with crises of unemployment, cuts in social spending, escalating national debts, and movements of young people who want change. Instead of looking for the root of all the problems, authorities use their spin-doctors to divide and rule with statements such as that of David Starkey's "the whites have become black" comments.

A parallel, that could be drawn as reasons for the current mass uprising worldwide is that many of the necessary conditions are already in place in Europe, Africa, China or anywhere else: public fury at years of political repression, economy that rewards corrupt elites and keep a majority in poverty, widespread loathing for leaders clinging to office.

We have mass uprisings in Tunisia, Egypt, Greece, Portugal, Ireland, Spain, France, Israel, Argentina, United Kingdom, United States of America and where next?

In the case of Spain, statistics show that one out of every four Spanish youth is unemployed, and the majority in Europe blame the problem on the system. Particularly the system put in place by the World Bank, and the International Monetary Fund (IMF).

It is interesting to note this development, and the bond it is creating among the youths of today who are feeling the brunt of the economic measures. Africa, was the laboratory in the early 80s of IMF's structural adjustment program responsible for the economic crises that are engulfing the world today.

I remember in 1980, paying hotel bills in Naira (Nigeria's currency) during our stop-over in Amsterdam while travelling with Fela and the Africa 70 to perform at the Communist Party festival L'Unita in Italy. Today, if I present the same Naira to pay my hotel bill, the answer would be "what currency is this?"

Thanks to the IMF and its Structural Adjustment Program, in a little over three decades the Naira that was exchanged in the world's market for sixty Kobo (the Nigerian decimal currency) to one United States dollar, is today exchanged between one hundred and eighty to two hundred Nairas to the dollar.

Unfortunately in Europe there was not much resistance to the devaluation of African country's money then. Today, IMF and the World Bank, are proposing the same structural Adjustment program to European and other governments like China.

While Europe cannot say no to IMF, the Chinese are resisting for as long as possible – how long depends on when the system will collapse.

Europe cannot resist, because their society is producing less and becoming more and more service economy, since when capital went global in search for cheap labour and maximum profit, hence their leaders choice of austerity measure. With this comes like Fela sang in Authority Stealing, crises of unemployment, cuts in social spending, escalating national debts.

For now on the surface this is not the case with China, that was subjected to all kinds of economic sanctions because of alledged human rights abuses some years back. Made in China goods up till about a decade ago was synonymous with counterfeit product, today majority of everything is made in China. For how long can the Chinese government resist?

Many of the necessary conditions leading to the current mass uprising are already in place in China like anywhere else: public fury at years of political repression, economy that rewards corrupt elites and keep a majority in poverty, widespread loathing for leaders clinging to office etc.

British officials believe social media, particularly Black Berry messenger, helped to ignite and organize rioters in Britain but experts say such tools are now a fact of life and simply alternative forms of communication. The social network finger pointing aspect is actually another distraction from deep-rooted issues.

As earlier mentioned, the real problem lies in the chronic economic malaise and the growing disparity between rich and poor in Britain just as was the case in the Arab uprising. It's no coincidence, this would happen so soon after the world-wide freak-out about stocks and the economic crisis.

In Tunisia, Egypt, and elsewhere during the 'Arab Spring' social networks were the tools that made the popular uprising against dictators possible, today protesters in the western countries are considered as rioters, looters, and violent enemies of the state and social networks are seen as the "catalyst".

When mainstream medias were shut out earlier in 2011, and the social networks were providing citizen journalism, they (social network) were seen as helping in the overthrow of corrupt regimes in the Arab world and lauded as tools of democracy. However, when the same methods are used in a scenario like the England uprising they are seen as disturbing.

Listening to the local voices (on social network media) in London who are not represented by mainstream media for the most part, they are talking about the lack of jobs, inequality, funding for youth clubs that were cut, etc. The youth have no jobs and nothing to do, economic conditions, racism, and police brutality, are also the real reasons for the uprisings. To put the blame of these uprisings on social networks is nothing but diversion.

Thanks to social networking and their alternative forms of communication, society is getting away from the stereotype aptly described in George Orwell's classic: "1984". Remember, those who make peaceful change impossible make a violent change inevitable. It time to stop the diversions and disinformation, the uprising on the world's streets can be described in street parlance as: Pay-Back Time Come! Unfortunately for now, it is the innocents that are paying for Babylon sins!

Like I have reiterated on numerous occasions; apart from Cheikh Anta Diop and Theophile Obenga, Fela Anikulapo-Kuti is also another personage that have contributed immensely towards African awareness in the last half of the 20th Century and beginning of the 21st Century.

In their quest to economically reap the fruits of the extraordinary explosion of the brand name FELA in this capitalist world where morality in not capital, we believe it is also important to do everything to avoid sweeping under the carpet the emphasis on the man and what he stood for.

We don't want to see all what we stoically suffered and stood for as part of our struggle in Kalakuta, reduced to: "WE LOVE FELA" written on T-Shirts, underpants and g-strings, in-order to sell their brand name. Hence, we need to watch out what kind of image of him is being touted out there. Since his demise and the extraordinary explosion of his name world-wide, there is this tendency to present all kinds of image of him from those who claim to know him.

A lot of un-truths about him are out there circulating. This was the case with the facebook debate, where the creation of the music classic called afrobeat today and drum-beat were credited to Orlando Julius Ekemode and Tony Allen respectively.

My intervention setting the records straight, and the prompt intervention of Yeni Anikulapo-Kuti with her: "thank God ID people like you are still alive...." the debate was quickly put to rest as my big brother OJ had the decency, to admit that he never claimed to be the originator of afrobeat but journalist who put that claim out in the press.

When it comes to defending our ideas and struggle, people like me who lived the experience and witness to all the events revealed in this book cannot let pass any misrepresentation of Fela.

From the moment I discovered his unique and uncompromising use of music in disseminating wisdom and the enlightenment of the ordinary man in Nigeria, Africa, and the Diaspora Africa in general, it has remained almost like an apotheosis in me, a supreme or ideal example of the kind of wisdom that must propel a society.

Thanks to Fela, afrobeat in my heart is beyond mere music, it has become a profoundly educational theme. This is a historiographical combat! How long shall they kill our prophets while we stand aside and look? (apology Bob Marley).

Front cover album design Overtake Don Overtake Overtake (ODOO)

Album design Fight To Win

FEMI ANIKULAPO-KUTI AND POSITIVE FORCE

Fela lives! Though physically he is no longer with us, yet his legacies are very much a part of us. As I wrote in the text accompanying Femi Anikulapo-Kuti's second major-label album titled "FIGHT TO WIN" (Universal Music France), Femi not only picks off where his previous CD - Shoki Shoki left off, it has also gone further to confirm him as the undisputed new King of Afrobeat music.

An album that can aptly be described in Yoruba language as 'Omo d'agba tan' (which literally means 'a child has come of age' or 'a child has attained adulthood'). Considering that at his age (born 16th June 1962) he can no longer be considered as a child, however the 'lager-than-life' image of his legendary father Fela Anikulapo-Kuti places him in the minds of Afrobeat die-hards as a child from whom are expected great deeds.

It has become a tradition, where siblings of great achievers all over the world are subjected to rigorous scrutiny and are expected to surpass the legacies of their parents. This was the case with Ziggy Marley after the passing of his father Bob Marley, alike Andrew Tosh the son of Peter Tosh and many others not necessarily children of musical icons.

For Femi at an early stage in his life, he realised this great expectation and chose long before the passing of his father to be his own man. This led him to quit his father's band in 1986 to found his group Positive Force.

A decision that has served the young man well by the look of things, it helped prepare him as the heir to the Afrobeat throne and wither the storm of criticisms from Fela's fans. Die-hard Fela fans criticised him for quitting Fela's Egypt 80 band and for many years, there were criticisms of him not following Fela's path by being as forceful or not playing Afrobeat the way Fela did. Some said his music was too fast or too jazzy. Others said he was not as militant as his father and his music, is devoid of the outright attacks on the system like Fela.

Since Fela's passing, some of the icon's fans claim Fela's other son Seun sax player and lead singer in Fela's Egypt 80 band, is a better representative of Fela than Femi. If I may ask, are these fans expecting another Fela in the person of Femi? Stepping into Fela's shoes? What a big expectation!

While it is impossible to have another Fela, nature has its ways of giving answers to human expectations hence the inequality of their shoe sizes. Fela wore size 43 shoes while Femi a head taller than his late father, wears size 44/45 shoes - for him his feet are too big for Fela's shoes.

With regards to comparing Femi with Seun in my opinion as one who lived the Fela experience, I can boldly state that there is no basis for comparison with both Fela siblings. There is a difference in their ages that shows a big gap in their respective knowledge, education, maturity, personality and achievement.

On all these subjects, there is no basis for comparison even if Seun is leading Fela's old band. As stated earlier, Femi is playing his own original interpretation of Afrobeat music while Seun is trying to copy Fela – albeit a poor imitation of the icon in my opinion. Seun does not have Fela's charisma on or off stage, and his attempts at reproducing Fela gimmicks on stage for those die-hard Fela fans looks to me nostalgic.

Despite the advantage of playing with members of Egypt 80 the group that backed the icon, watching Seun and Egypt 80 perform since Fela's passing reminds me of The Wailers without Bob Marley. There is the permanent absence of the fire and precision from Fela particularly, those of us who know how much trouble Fela went through keeping the band in tune during concerts. The icon was known to replace some of his musicians on stage for playing out of tune.

With Fela gone, I am sure it is not Seun that could keep that band in tune and he does not for now have that competence. I heard the young Seun singing out of tune many times in concerts. On the other hand, Femi has never pretended to be another Fela.

To his credit, he has been able to create a personality for himself and as a saxophone player developed a voice that those who know his music can call the "Femi voice" on alto sax. I saw the young man practice his saxophone for hour's on-end during the period I worked with the or- ganisation and years after we all left.

Despite all the criticisms, Femi has tried to remain true to him - focusing his attention on adding his own in-put to his Afrobeat heritage.

Criticisms are good particularly if they are objective, from my involvement and understanding of the young Femi from my working relationship with him, he has always paid attention to objective criticisms. His close maternal family circle (his grandmother affectionately called nanny, his mother Remi and his two sisters Yeni and Sola) saw to that. Though like any other child a 'part' on-the-back from his 'larger-than-life' father could be re-assuring.

On this point though Fela never publicly acclaimed him as the Afrobeat heir apparent, I believe he considered Femi his heir to the Afrobeat thrown. His reaction and comment at the Shrine in 1993 shortly after his reconciliation with Femi and the latter's return with Positive Force to play the regular Sunday jump in place of Fela confirms this.

Fela usually attended Femi's Sunday concerts to jam with Positive Force. On this day, the band was playing Femi's new composition titled "Mind Your Own Business" (MYOB) publicly for the first time.

After jamming with the band on the song MYOB, Fela remarked: "Femi! I must say you have the tightest horn-section in town" to the hearing of all at the jump. For the icon to make such a remark, he must have taken into consideration the efforts he had to make to keep his own horn-section in the Egypt 80 in tune.

For people like me hearing Fela publicly make comments like this, can only indicate his satisfaction at Femi's originality and the direction he was taking the music. Fela's fans who want to cling to the cherished memories of the musical icon, and who expect to see them transformed in the music of Femi I guess they were not disappointed with Femi's work in the Fight To Win album.

Alike I guess they were able to discover the Femi touch in Afrobeat. The album for me is an indication of the progression and future direction of this musical classic. There is no doubt that Fela never wanted another Fela of any of his children.

If he were around today, Femi's second outing with Universal Music France, would be considered by the late musical icon as a 'back to the roots' musical master piece. Rich with political motivations and cultural interests, the two important reasons behind the explosion of Fela and Afrobeat music as the weapon of the future, Femi in this album can be said to have conveniently re-assured Afrobeat die-hards of the safe future of the protest music.

He has not only sustained his father's heritage, he also has improved on the musical legacy bequeathed him. Packaged with messages in the spirit of a return to the roots and spiced with rich melodies of traditional African music, it is a big credit to the young man's musical capabilities despite not being raised with the real traditional Yoruba musical experiences of Fela who grew-up listening to traditional rhythms like 'Apala' or 'Sakara' music in his early days in Abeokuta.

Like his father, Femi has transformed the repetitive phrases of the talking drum sound in apala music, into short phrases for the bass and rhythm guitars in Afrobeat music, a perfect example of this apala rhythm influence is Eko Lagos – a perfect 'woro' as the style of playing between rhythms is called in Yoruba. For those critics who say Femi's songs are not as forceful and critical of those in power they should listen to "Traitors of Africa".

TRAITORS OF AFRICA

Written and performed live in Nigeria in 1992 during the regime of General Ibrahim Babangida, considered to head the most corrupt regime ever in Nigeria. His administration's inability to find solutions to basic national problems, the mindless, corrupt, vision-less and narrow minded attitude and policies of his and other members of his government are responsible for the slide into the abyss of poverty from which Nigerian is yet to recover.

Babangida's government was particularly marked for its cynical destruction of the inalienable rights of his people 'Traitors of Africa', is an outright condemnation of the regime and others like him who are responsible for the instability and strife currently tearing the African continent apart.

Femi starts the song by looking around him and seeing his people crying and he asks why? The answers are there to see: relentless sufferings and miseries of a people living in abject poverty in an oil rich country, held hostage by the corrupt practices of army generals and civilian allies who usurped power without a mandate from the people.

Rendered in the manner of his father an outright bold attack on the bad ways of governance on the African continent, Femi names chain of policies and decisions made by Babangida's regime to justify the culpability of the General: "he cancel election, him bring corruption and spoil the Naira...Babangida oh ! Cause the cry..." Referring to the election sham and gross violation of democratic practice of the General, when in 1993 he annulled a free and fair presidential election.

Femi further undelines how Babangida's government through corrupt practices siphoned off revenues from Nigeria's natural resources, and how his government forced the devaluation of the national currency – the Naira in the world's foreign exchange market.

Femi concludes that men like Babangida are abounding on the African continent men put in power to serve the interest of their colonial masters, men who for little money in foreign bank accounts, a small house abroad sell their countries away to foreign interests, such men should be known by their names as the "Traitors of Africa" he concludes.

In the album title FIGHT TO WIN, Femi addresses again the issue of the relentless sufferings of the African masses, how the leadership fail to see reason and the signals of a coming revolution in the air.

African dictators seem to say "Let it be!" sings Femi, they continue to rule in a manner reminiscent of a 'banana republic' - gross violations of democratic process, destruction and violation of individual inalienable rights, appointments and dissolution of national electoral bodies, under-estimation of the people's resolve and determination to be free.

Despite advice from street veterans for these leaders to listen to the cry of the people and to see reason for change, they wait until the people disgracefully eject them from power. Usually the eventual chage arrives through riots, fighting in the streets, blood-shed and people dying in the streets.

Femi believes this blood letting could be avoided if the leadership would listen to the people's cry. Instead of listening, they continue to rule like they are not accountable to anyone forgetting that the people will "Fight to win" Femi concludes.

In the song DO YOUR BEST, Femi addresses himself to the realities of the numerous problems that pervades Africa and the need for leaders with the courage and vision to bring about significant changes in the way people live and think on the continent. Instead of the present compendium of colonial politics considered irrelevant to Africa's present predicament as a people, Femi sings that one of the biggest obstacles to progress on the continent is the absence of motive and dynamics that drives a people in doing things for their country.

The reasons for this according to him, is that people see their hopes of a democratic Africa constantly being killed, banished, or forced to languish by misrule and corruption in high places. Femi accepts the fact that these problems are too numerous to resolve at once, but if leaders can 'Do their Best' in their attempt to find solutions to problems on the continent, it would amount to something – a concrete step to finding solutions to the problems.

Rendered in the characteristic cynical and sometimes sarcastic manner reminiscent of Fela's songs, Femi' sings: "Ask your mama! She self go tell you! When I ask my Papa! Himself tell me! Na so-so problems dey Africa! To solve the problems, na wahala!" Meaning if you ask your parents like he did his, they will tell you that it requires a lot of efforts to solve the African continent numerous problem. As solution he advises leaders to try and "Do Your Best and Leave the rest".

STOP AIDS: As the death toll from AIDS recedes in the Western hemisphere, Africa is reeling from an epidemic of a catastrophic proportion. The continent, can conveniently be called 'continent left to die' considering recent reports that AIDS will kill more people on the continent in the next two decades than war or famine.

The religious prohibition of the use of preservatives in sex – notably by Christianity and Islam, should be held responsible for the wide-spread of the HIV virus on the African continent. The Catholic Church expressly forbids adherents from the use of condoms, saying such teachings about 'safe sex' are dangerous and immoral. It considers such policy as based on the 'deluded theory' that the condom can provide adequate protection against the AIDS virus.

While adherents in Europe and America practice safe sex despite the Papal decree, there are at least 122 million Catholics in Africa whose source of information is the church. Religion and its attendant contradictions of "do what I say and not what I do", is responsible for the detonation of the AIDS time-bomb on the Black continent.

While the threat of the spread of HIV virus was the worst fears of the 1980's in the Western hemisphere, it is just being realised in Africa – particularly among a sexually active population. STOP AIDS is Femi's contribution to AIDS awareness. Sub-titled "Ma l'abo" in Yoruba language literally translated, means "don't suck pussy" or "don't lick vagina", an advice based on the reality that there are yet to be condoms for the tongue. Ma l'abo is an advice to practice safe and protected sex.

WALK ON THE RIGHT SIDE:

If Fela could be considered as ideological and musical role-model and mentor for Femi, his mother Remi and her mother Sadie Eileen fondly called 'Nanny' by her grandchildren can be considered as his moral mentors. Walk on the right side, written in Femi's early struggling days when he quit Fela's band, is his tribute to these two women who helped shape his morale vision and encouraged him to resolve to be his own man.

He narrates in the song how his mother taught him not to hurt another person because everything he does in life will come back to him, how she taught him to be humble and avoid the diversions that can only make him loose his direction.

He sang: "she said walk on the right side, in your life-time you will find that shinning star…." As an example of the two women's influence on Femi, the author remembers the reaction of 'Nanny' when she was told Fela's comments about Femi having the "tightest horn section in town". His maternal grandmother turning towards Remi remarked: "Rem, I hope Femi won't start getting big-headed with such compliment".

Without waiting for his mother to reply, Femi interjected saying "I can never get big headed because of remarks like that, but it is good and assuring to hear comments like that from someone who knows better".

Femi Kuti commenting about his parents some years after their demise said: "They (Fela & Remi) were different, my father was very liberal and my mother was more careful and strict. So to put it as short as possible, my mother was a little-bit strict because she was very afraid for us. My father was more liberal, he gave us everything we wanted especially when he became a little-bit rich. At the beginning he was never at home but by the time we were teenagers, he had money and we could practically do whatever we wanted. If we wanted to drive any of his cars he allowed us to despite our not being of age, my mother used to get angry with him about this asking Fela why he would permit children to drive a car. So in short, my mother was more careful and strict while my father was more liberal".

Walk on the right side serves as the young man's testimony to his complete education, an engagement in the struggle from his father and moral equilibrium from his mother and grandmother.

The year 1997 (called NINETY–SEVEN in this song), will go down in the annals of the Kuti family history as the year of deaths. It was a year, when successive deaths of three members of the family caused people to ask if the family were jinxed.

It started with the passing of Fela on 2nd, August 1997 and less than a month after his death one of Femi's favourite cousins Frances Kuboye, the daughter of Fela's sister died. Her death came as a shock to the family, judging from the fact that she was actively involved in all the burial arrangement of her uncle Fela.

As if all these successive deaths would know no bounds, death again struck the family this time it was the turn of Femi's younger sister, Olusoladegbin Anikulapo-Kuti fondly called 'Sola'. She died 9th, October 1997 after being wrongly diagnosed and operated on for ailments that had nothing to do with the real cause of her death - Cancer.

The timing of these deaths in quick succession caused people to ask if the family were jinxed. Ninety-seven, is Femi's tribute to these members of his family and also his way of expressing his gratitude, to friends and numerous fans of Fela who turned-out in large number to pay tribute to the musical legend.

EKO (LAGOS) as mentioned earlier in this volume, was the indigenous name the natives called Lagos before Portuguese colonialist re-named it Lagos. This Eko, is the focal-point of Femi's dream as he sings in this track.

The Eko (Lagos) in his dream is presented as a new dawn in the world, where there are no-more relentless sufferings of a people, a peaceful world where people are motivated with ideological dynamics, driving them to do great things for their country, a world where there are significant changes in the way people live, where instability and strife are things of the past. In Femi's dream, Eko in a new era and order will be without leadership that remain vision-less, narrow-minded, and corrupt.

Suddenly Femi woke-up and realised that he was living a dream Lagos, like the rest of the world are still the same place, where there are gross violation of people's inalienable rights, there is corruption and relentless sufferings of the people. He concludes by saying how important it would be, to have a world like Eko (Lagos) of his dream.

In the song ALKEBU-LAN, Femi explains how Europe underdeveloped Africa starting with name. Names have meanings and are believed to live out their meaning in many African traditions, thus serious thought is put into the naming of a new baby. As the saying goes in Yoruba: 'ile ni a'nwo, ki a to so omo l'oruko'. Meaning: 'we have to pay attention, to the traditions and history of a family before we give name to a child'.

Scientists and writers without the bias of Africa being the cradle of civilisation, say Alkebu-Lan was the name of the continent before the Portuguese gave the name Africa. The propagation of a so-called Western Civilisation, is responsible for the colonial-era erosion of African culture through name and to some extent it continues till date.

Both European and Arab colonisers on the continent, educated Africans to abandon their native and picturesque costumes, to assume the hats and breaches of the Christian and Moslems as symbols of being cultured and to even renounce their names for those of their colonial masters, as the author has tried to explain all through this volume – defining the Fela phenomenon. In keeping with the recommendations of the Colloquium On Black Civilisation and Culture, held in Lagos Nigeria in 1977 that advised: "…that African education system be directed towards African needs and not according to the needs of her ex-colonial masters." Femi calls on Africans to stop carrying around slave names. All those African states and individuals, with colonial names should discard them he advises.

ONE DAY SOME DAY is Femi's answer to the questions: "When Will Africa be free?" "When will Africa Unite?" From problems of instability and strife tearing Africa apart, to the relentless sufferings of a large part of the population, the use of religion as a political tool to separate and divide the people, problems of corrupt, vision-less, narrow minded, mindless leadership. These seemingly insoluble problems, prompts Femi to ask "When Will Africa be free?" "When will Africa Unite?"

He re-counts, statements from anti-African unity advocates who use these numerous problems as justification for their conviction. For Femi even if their convictions are based on some superficial witchery, he is convinced that if their is the will to unite among African leaders and all black people are truly dedicated to this cause, he is confident that Africa will free itself from the relentless and seemingly insoluble problems that is keeping the continent from having a United States Of Africa. One Day Some Day is Femi's optimistic clarion call for unity in Africa.

Femi in the song DO THE RIGHT THING, is calling on individuals to do the right thing in life particularly those in position of power. "Do the right thing and let us all be happy" he sang. To give opportunity to all in the process of doing the right thing, Femi says there will reign in our world a perfect peace and a world without stress. He calls on those in positions of power, to show good examples by using power to make life easy for people, by taking the people right to the top of the tower. He concludes that "the choice is yours to either do the right thing and let us all be happy".

Femi's music mirrors Fela in terms of musical style and message, he doesn't shy away from addressing social issues such as (Stop AIDS), nor political issues (African Unity A Must, Traitors of Africa), confirming his engagement as a protest singer like his father. Also the success of Shoki Shoki featuring title like 'Beng Beng Beng' (a major European club hit), can be measured by the number of re-mixes dubbed "Shoki Re-mixed." Nuyorican Soul, François Kevorkian, Ashley Beedle, Dixon (Jaazzanova), Joe Clausell, Sofa Surfers, Kerry Chandler, and Seven Dub all these guys making their remix version of the song.

These projects show how seriously Femi is regarded by electronic music's toast-makers, and it further confirms African music influence on all today's urban dance music. In the US and Europe, the sound of Afrobeat music inspires and fuels musical genres from hip-hop to house.

This return "back to the roots" is in step with a new movement among African and the Diaspora African musicians, they all seem to be convinced like Femi that "music will bring Africa back on the world map".

Certainly all the black music classics like jazz, reggae and recently afrobeat are testimonies to that. Despite their musical collaboration in Femi's album "Fight to win," Mos Def's song "Fear not for man" was inspired by Fela's song of the same title, same with Common's album "Like Water For Chocolate", and listening to D'Angelo's "Spanish Joint" or Mos Def's "Umi Says," the Afrobeat sound is unmistakably present. It is also there in the music of Antibalas the Brooklyn based Afrobeat Orchestra.

All these are testimonies to the arrival of Afrobeat as a world classic.

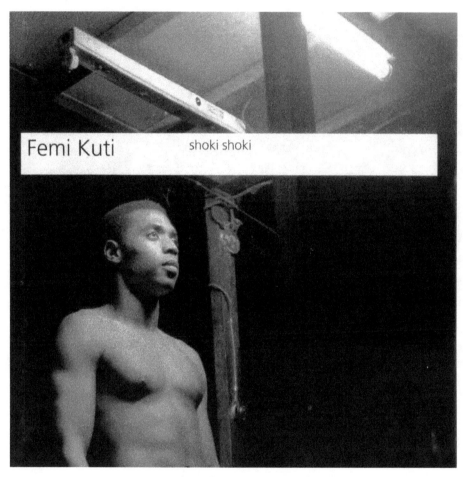

Front cover album design Shoki Shoki

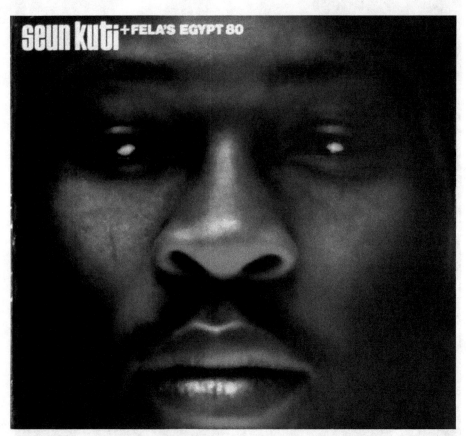

Front cover album Seun Kuti + Egypt 80

SEUN ANIKULAPO-KUTI & EGPYPT 80

Seun Anikulapo Kuti is claimed particularly among those who never saw the King to possess the grace, the energy, and the fury of Fela. Performing with the Egypt 80 the legendary group of Fela, Seun's showmanship has been described in the media as "relive the most original embodiment of Afrobeat". His gestures and mimicks of Fela on stage, plus all the comments about him being a Fela reincarnate, prompted me to ask him the following questions after his show at the New Africa Shrine during Felabration 2009.

ID: I see you trying to play like Fela on stage, when are we going to see Seun Kuti himself doing his own thing and not imitating Fela? Because I heard you doing some new things in Paris – like Afrobeat Hip Hop, with Monkobe and the buzz I am hearing which is a generation thing is that the young folks who listen to hip hop, want to see you do more things in that direction. For me it gives a generational thing to Afrobeat.

Seun: For me afrobeat is not about generation, afrobeat is the sound and music itself. I know what I believe in, most people think when I am on stage I am being Fela. To me NO, I am performing afrobeat the way the master said it should be. The way Bach has written classical music that is how people like classical music to be played. Rock n'Role legends – that is why Rock'n'Role stars have that craziness about them on stage, because there are certain traits that goes with certain genres that you have to keep alive.

Me I am not from the school of thought that says afrobeat is old music like you say generation thing. I still believe that afrobeat is well ahead of it's time, even if it is becoming a global-phenomenon. Even I don't know where afrobeat is going to be by the time my children are going to be playing afrobeat. For me the way I am doing my own afrobeat now is what I believe in and what I believe afrobeat should be.

I don't think afrobeat should be influenced by any Western culture, I don't want to see Soul Afrobeat, etc…No, and this Western music should be putting afrobeat in their music, not afrobeat putting Western influence in it music. I believe afrobeat is greater than all those music.

ID: Yeah! I believe and agree with you absolutely in fact talking the way you just did confirms something, people always said that afrobeat was influenced by James Brown, funk, but we see that "Apala Music" the original apala rhythm of our ancestors were what Fela put together in afrobeat and it is also what you guys are trying to continue in your own ways.

However for me when I am talking about when will we see the real Seun Kuti, I am making reference to when are we going to see the original you? You must have been very young or not born when Bob Marley died. They were pushing after Ziggy as a kind of replacement to Bob Marley – and we know we cannot have two Bob Marley's. You just said you are doing Seun Kuti thing and not copy Fela...

Seun: If I wanted to be like my father, I would have released my first album when I was sixteen or seventeen. People were pushing me to do an album because I am Fela's son, but I didn't want to do an album because I am Fela's son I wanted to do an album when I feel I am a good musician – good enough to do an album.

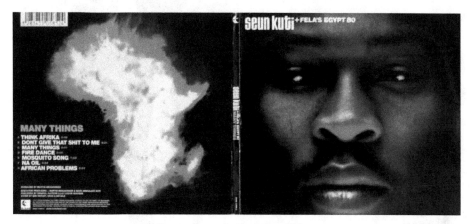

Cover album design Many Things

Front cover album design Who Is This America

ANTIBALAS AFROBEAT ORCHESTRA

Antibalas, the Spanish word that has the double meaning of anti-bullet and bullet-proof vest, considered a little over a decade ago as 'cool' name for a band during a chance visit to Mexico City by Martin Perna a founding member of the group, has done it again keeping afrobeat alive and underlining their claim as the North American afrobeat orchestra. When I first heard of the Antibalas, as a largely white American band I was filled with scepticism. Can these non-African guys play Afrobeat? Their broad cultural and racial background, a microcosm of the cultural mix that is America - amplifying the country's diversity did not alleviate this feeling.

During the fall of 2003, I was opportuned to watch the orchestra perform at the New Brooklyn Museum and twice at the No Moore club in lower Manhattan. I discovered that they pay obvious tribute to Fela – staying true to his musical roots, rhythm, and soul. Watching them perform and talking with individual members of the group, I discovered that they are a group of talented musicians who have strong thoughts and opinions.

Undoubtedly, they have learned from listening to Fela's several albums and his political ideals relevant to the world and community in which they live. But this is no justification to dismiss them, as taking credit for being a repertory group as some critics of the band tend to. Afrobeat is about rhythm and Antibalas is doing a great job with their assimilation, despite them not being of Yoruba origin. Hearing the band play without seeing the musicians, one who knew Fela's band would think they were old members from Fela's Africa 70 or Egypt 80 bands.

After seeing Antibalas perform, I believe it is a misconception on my part to think Afrobeat can only be played meaningfully by people of African origin. Since the inception of the group in 1997, critics never seize to claim that one would be hard-pressed to determine exactly, what political message they want to pass across due to their broad cultural and racial background.

However keeping with the tradition of 'engaged music', this claim can be put to rest with their album 'WHO IS THIS AMERICA', a politically progressive song without being dogmatic talking about the ills of American society in general terms.

Listening to the album particularly as a Fela biographer, ideologue, and associate for almost a decade, I can confirm that the Afrobeat sound is unmistakably present and the group is living-up to their mission of preserving Fela's music and style. In keeping with this tradition songs like Filibuster, Sanctuary, Hilo, Obanla'e, Elephant and "Sister" mirrors and carries on the tradition and musical style created by Africa's activist and musical icon Fela Anikulapo-Kuti.

SECURITY another albums from Antibalas musical stables, underlines the fact that security comes from mutual respect of the difference in human beliefs and not the investments of billions of dollars in home-land security. Hearing messages such as this, it is most encouraging that Antibalas are living-up to and are present as a restorative force, for people who need some fun to support their ideals and a big challenge to musicians who were in Fela's band to keep Afrobeat alive.

I consider members of Antibalas as a restorative force, because of their humility towards ex-Fela musicians. As members of a younger generation, they consider the presence of ex-Africa 70 or Egypt 80 group at their concerts as an honour.

Martin Perna underlined this humility when he said "they are our elders in every sense, they played on most of those recordings we can only dream of playing on. In that sense, it is an honour than disappointment. Just to meet them, shake their hands, look them in the eyes and thank them for the music they made. We've had similar experiences with musicians who played with James Brown, incredible performances on the albums and masters of their respective instruments".

Antibalas no doubt has a whole new perspective on Afrobeat, and only posterity can judge them for their contribution. Understandably working within the framework and form laid down by Fela, they are bound to sound similar to the icon. Particularly with 'Who Is this America' and 'Security' albums, they are building on the legacy of Fela – carrying on the Afrobeat tradition with an almost obsessive attention to accuracy.

Their contribution to the spread of Afrobeat to their credit, should be viewed more positive as preservationist. Same way as Wynton Marsalis and the Lincoln Centre Orchestra are keeping older forms of jazz alive.

Or those playing those funky beats inspired by James Brown and Funkadelic Parliament. Antibalas is keeping Afrobeat Alive, and for a new generation of musicians who discovered Afrobeat from samples and not direct live performances from Fela, in view of their energy on stage I can only say posterity will judge their role in keeping afrobeat alive. Today, it is most encouraging that Antibalas is living-up to their name as the leading Afrobeat orchestra in North America.

Front cover album design Security

Front cover album design COUP DE GUEULE (FIT OF RAGE)

COUP DE GUEULE (FIT OF RAGE)

Tiken Jah Fakoly's song 'Fit of rage' (Coup de gueule in French) as an album title, can only come from an artist with a political motivation and cultural interest. He is courageous enough to call African nations to recognize firmly that their so-called debts to world bodies like IMF and the World Bank are obnoxious, inequitable, and it is immoral to demand their repayment. Courageous, if we remember that statements such as this was the motivation of the West to sponsor the coup d'état, that toppled the Pan-African Government of Kwame Nkrumah in Ghana in 1966 after the Ghanaian leader published: Neo-Colonialism, last stage of Imperialism in Africa – the first to call the world's moral attention to Africa's debt issue.

Corruption the cancer that is devouring the African society and impedes the continent's progress, has been lavishly treated in this volume particularly Fela's denunciation of African leadership and their complicity in the wide-spread. Majority of the finger-pointing of the politico-financial corruptions are directed at those persons in charge of politics on the African continent, but from all indications this bad decease emanated from the Western Hemisphere and today it has spread almost everywhere in the world becoming a contemporary universal reality.

In view of its recurrent nature, one can ask where is the African money from corruption banked? And to answer one can say - of course in the banks in Western countries! After making the same analysis of the African continent's situation, Tiken Jah Fakoly asks the same question as Kwame Nkrumah in this song titled: L'Afrique Doit Du Fric? (Does Africa owe any debt?) With his typical West African reggae flavour he sings "Africa enslaved, colonized, tortured, and ransacked! Does Africa owe any debt?"

Like Fela with afrobeat and Bob Marley with reggae music, it appears that Tiken Jah too sees music as the best way to bring his contribution to the awakening of the consciousnesses of youths of this generation to the problems of Africa and their cause.

Asked if he nurtures any political ambitions, his consistent answer is: "It does not interest me to have a political career in any country in particular, I play reggae which is already politicized music.

The advantage with reggae is that I can put a lot and carry my projects on the scale of the continent, because to awake the consciousnesses of a people one has to show an example." As we can see, music is becoming a weapon like Fela affirmed and like he sang in ITT globalization is a fight, a strategic fight of diverse interest sometimes very opposite.

It is little necessary to recognize in the current world, that there is not either "concert of nations" or "international community" really fair nor democratic as enumerated over and over again through-out this volume.

What are at stake are political, economic, military, linguistic, cultural interests, appropriate for every State or Nation. This is the message of Pan-Africanist Théophile Obenga in his book: "Appel A La Jeunesse Africaine", and it is the same message from Tiken Jah in his album 'fit of rage' (Coup de gueule in French).

Already half a century after Independence in Africa (granted or acquired by liberation struggles), young people like Tiken Jah Fakoly can sing haven made the same analysis of the African situation like Fela and Obenga. Another good example of these analysis, apart from his fit of rage song title is
PLUS RIEN NE M'ETONNE (NOTHING AMAZES ME ANYMORE).

He sang:
"Ils ont partagé le monde, plus rien ne m'étonne.
Si tu me laisses la Tchétchénie,
Moi je te laisse l'Arménie
Si tu me laisses l'Afghanistan,
Moi je te laisse le Pakistan
Si tu ne quittes pas Haïti,
Moi je t'embarque pour Bangui.
Si tu m'aides à bombarder l'Irak,
Moi je t'arrange le Kurdistan
Ils ont partagé le monde, plus rien ne m'étonne.
Ils ont partagé Africa sans nous consulter".

Literally translated:
"They shared the world,

nothing more amazes me.
If you leave me Chechnya,
I leave you Armenia
If you leave me Afghanistan,
I leave you Pakistan
If you do not leave Haiti,
I'll embark you for Bangui
If you help me to bombard Iraq,
I arrange you Kurdistan
They shared the world,
nothing more amazes me.
They shared Africa without consulting us..."

Listening to his first major-label album titled "FRANCEAFRIQUE," Tiken Jah confirms his statue as an engaged artist with a statement like to quote him: "…a capitalist society where morality is no more capital is a shame".

Rendered in a mix of French and Djoulla, a language spoken widely among the Mandingo people of West Africa, Tiken Jah describes the French and American politics in Africa as "blaguer tuer," (literally translated means a "murderous joke"). "How they cultivate and encourage dictators.

How they plunder African riches and bury Africans alive – by inflaming the Congo, burning down Angola, and causing genocide in Rwanda" the Ivorian musician sang.

He went further to sing about how, as soon as Africans found solutions to these problems, they again impose on Africans "co-operation" in the name of "Independence". Soon again as their "co-operation" was exposed, they impose "Globalisation" all these in whose favour? Africa always in deep-shit (Afrique toujours dans la merde) he sang.

Hearing messages such as these in an album, reminds one of the fighting spirit of Fela and those before him particularly this track titled "ON EN A MARRE" meaning "We are sick and tired":
"We are sick and tired.
Africa is sick and tired…
After abolition of slavery

They created colonisation
Soon as we found the solution
They created co-operation
Soon as we denounced their co-operation
They created globalisation...."
We are Sick and tired
Africa is sick and tired..."

Political and cultural interests, that underlined Fela's musical career and also led him to sacrifice so much can be found in Tiken Jah's lyrics and actions. The Fela phenomenon in Africa, paved the way for all those generations of engaged artists after Fela even if he paid dearly for this. Asked in an interview what Fela represents to African youths Femi Kuti replies:

"If it wasn't for Fela, many people will not be talking about Nigeria today! If it wasn't for Fela, many African bands will not be known or be touring around Europe and America today. He opened many doors for Africans. I am not saying he was perfect but if it wasn't for Fela, the scandalous schemes and machinations perpetrated by those in government in Africa would not be known as what it is corruption and exploitation of Africans by Africans.

If that is what they mean by "Fela corrupted the youths", opening their eyes enlightening them about how their leaders have mismanaged their lives etc. If marijuana smoking can enlighten you, is marijuana smoking good or bad? If marijuana can make you reflect: "Waoh! Our leaders are not giving us our dues" Is that bad or good?"

"I mean, all those name calling is just what I term as hypocrisy. It is the excuse by those in power for not doing things right. You cannot fault Fela's marijuana smoking after all the sacrifices he made and paying with his personal freedom for the ideals he stood for. It was the same criticism "Fela wore under-pants" but if White folks go on African beaches and swimming pools in their pants and topless they are not considered to be mad.

But Fela who has never stepped-out of his house without being dressed, whose only "offence" was to sit in his house in his under-pant, they say he is mad and corrupting the youths. It is all hypocrisy to cover the truth Fela was talking about.

You know very well people don't like the truth that's how I see it. Please don't get me wrong I am not saying my father was perfect, he had his ups-and-downs but that is no excuse to condemn his contributions to the African society by labelling him a "marijuana smoker".

Except if we want to be hypocrites like the Greeks who once condemned their great citizens as propagators of foreign values only to later make an about-turn and hail the same citizens as great Greek philosophers" concludes Femi.

Like Fela, some of the new generation artist who are courageous enough to speak-out get beat, jailed, or forced to exile, because of their commitment and engagement in raising awareness among Africans. Tiken Jah's home, was burnt down in Abidjan during the rebellion in Ivory Coast and was forced to go on exile in France as he sang in his 'Coup de Gueule' (Fit of rage) album. The trac titled, Ou veux tu que j'aille? (Where do you want me to go?)

He sang:
Où veux que j'aille?
Pourquoi veux-tu que j'm'en aille ?
T'as brûlé ma maison d'Abidjan,
Parce que je ne suis pas de ton clan
Mon grand-père t'a tout donné,
Mon papa a tant sué
Moi je suis né la.
Pourquoi veux-tu que j'm'en aille ?
Front la racaille !

Literally translated:
Where do you want me to go?
Why do you want me to go away?
You burnt my home in Abidjan,
Because I don't belong to your clan
My grandfather gave everything for this country,
My dad so much sweated
Me! I was born here.
Why do you want me to go away?
Forehead of the villain!

As we can see from the above accounts, it is most encouraging today to hear musicians like Tiken Jah Fakoly identifying with Fela's legacy of music of contestation and commitment. Tike Jah see's himself, as a member of that generation first to be free on the continent and decolonized only 50 years ago.

That generation, strongly believes that education is going to change things. His motivation he told me, comes from the fight of people before him against lack of education and the non-evolution of African mentality against illiteracy which prevents young Africans to take their destiny in their hands.

He is appt to point-out, when asked about the disunity on the African continent: "in Europe also there are problems and Africa is not an extraterrestrial continent, if Europeans are talking to each-other to find solutions to their problems then Africans have to come together to find solutions to our problems".

Also reassuring, is that most of these engaged artists are not contented to just sing about the issues they are doing positive things towards making changes. The famous reggae musician, performs all-over France for his association "A concert A school". They have as objective, the construction of schools in remote villages in Africa. According to him, this will give a chance of schooling to the children living in remote and isolated villages.

My only point of discord with this idea, is the issue of what type of education will be passed in such schools. An education, that will continue to perpetuate colonialism is not the right thing. What we need in Africa is education which talks of our culture, environment, and our past. This last point is crucial, because if we don't know where we are coming from, we can never know where we are heading.

Hence I believe the need to co-ordinate all these efforts into a non-governmental associations, organizations, and movements inorder to be effective. Ideas are abounding with everyone doing their thing separately. Initiatives like "A concert A school", should be actively coordinated with other positive ideas from engaged artists, writers, and other professionals out there who want to make a change.

Asked why he built the New Africa Shrine, Femi Kuti replies: "the most important reason was that I built the Shrine to provide the space to accommodate the legacies that is the teachings of the philosophies of great-men like my father, Kwame Nkrumah, Marcus Garvey, Malcolm X, Martin Luther King, and provide in large quantities history books on the African heritage and also to continue the struggle for African Unity using the Shrine as a political base to spread the message of Pan Africanism and the ultimate universalism".

As we can see, initiatives to solve the African problems are abounding, if it is difficult to do business with African governments because of their so-called corrupt reputations, do the people of Africa deserve double punishment? If the leadership is not leaving-up to expectations and there are individual initiatives to make a change, I believe everything should be done to help such initiative to archive its goal. Like Femi did with the Shrine, it is great to construct schools with the association "A concert A school" but the million dollar question is, what kind of school curriculum, what kind of education, are we going to teach in those schools?

Today's African Universities, are considered by Black intellectuals as degree producing factories. As underlined all-along this volume, the discipline required to think and act big, has not yet become a part of the neo-colonial academic and intellectual tradition on the continent. African current education system, has to a large extent excluded the study of her heritage, and their development, as vehicles of thought and agent of civilisation.

Is this the education system we intend to continue in the "A concert A School" project? In my opinion, this will amount to keeping the old unproductive system going. The advantage with projects such as Tiken's "A concert A school" is that if co-ordinated with Black intellectual's world-wide, it will provide a platform to assemble and carry the idea on a continental scale.

All like minds agree, that to awake the consciousnesses of a people one has to show example. Many intellectuals are abounding still alive of African and Diaspora Africa origin, who can contribute their knowledge and professional competence if asked to participate.

Africa united as one country, all Pan-African politically, and economically, can only come from working together. Since, we agree as solution to the academic and intellectual problem of Africa, the conclusion of Cheikh Anta Diop enumerated in his epic work 'Civilization or Barbarism':

"For us, the return to Egypt in all domains is a primordial condition to reconcile African civilization with history, to be able to build a corpus of modern human sciences to renew African culture. Far from delectation with the past, a look towards ancient Egypt is the best way to conceive and build our cultural future. Egypt will play in a newly thought African culture, the same role the ancient Greco-Latin played in Western Culture".

People who can help us attain that primordial condition necessary to reconcile African civilization with history are still very much around either physically or with their legacies: works of art, music, research, etc., why don't we use the platform FELABRATION festival provides to coordinate all these efforts? We shall discuse this in the chapter ahead.

Back cover album design COUP DE GUEULE (FIT OF RAGE)

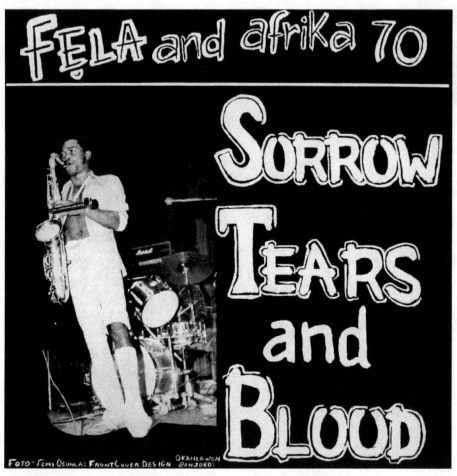
Front cover album design Sorrows Tears and Blood

FELABRATION: ONE OF THE SOLUTIONS

FELABRATION FESTIVAL, since 1999 is an annual event of music and arts taking place at the New Africa Shrine in Lagos Nigeria to commemorate, the life and times of Nigeria's foremost musical icon Fela Anikulapo-Kuti. As part of the festival's programme, a carnival procession is organised annually to re-create the atmosphere of the funeral procession of 1997.

Almost a million Nigerians participated in the funeral procession - a seven kilometre march from Tafawa Balewa Square on the Lagos Island to his residence in Ikeja on the Lagos mainland. During the burial ceremony despite the non-official participation from the government, an entire nation rendered homage not only to an exceptional musician and creator of Afrobeat music, but also to an untiring combatant for the dignity of Black people. What is the state of afrobeat today in Nigeria more than a decade after the demise of its originator?

Annually all through the week-long events, Fela' lyrics that were banned on air in Nigerian radio and television stations for more than two decades during his life time, resound in a beautiful manner and due to security concerns from the government and logistic reasons, Felabration carnival has since been reduced from the march across Lagos to cover only Ikeja, Ojota, Maryland, and Agidingbi areas of Lagos mainland.

In the future with giant puppets, traditional dancers, and drummers in attendance, the street carnival can be transformed into a measure to access the state of the music – while it allows those who lived the Fela experience to relive his crowd pulling effects on Nigerian streets and for the new generation to discover something new.

In 2008 over 50 artistes came together from the United States, Great Britain, France, and Senegal, to participate in the festival. Felabration 2009, despite the constraints of Lagos State Government to limit the events to inside of the New Africa Shrine unlike previous years when the concerts were held outside in the street, the festival still managed to draw more than 20,000 people and more than 100 artists performing. The festival over the years has attracted many highly popular musicians from all-over the world, the role call includes: Hugh Masakela, Lucky Dube, Baba Maal, and many others.

The venue unique in every sense of the word, today more than ever is fast becoming legendary in Africa as a platform for artist from all horizons from traditional music, to rap and hip-hop, break dance and theatre musicals. What impact has afrobeat world-wide as protest music?

For an answer to this question I guess apart from all the artists mentioned above, there are afrobeat groups springing-up all over the world in all major cities.

How has Fela made the consciousness of the average Nigerian, to understand political and social issues? The Fela Debates' part of Felabration festival an event that invites the public to choose a defining topic which will always reflect Fela, his philosophy, his career, his politics and whatever else, could serve as a regular forum to measure the continuous impact of afrobeat as protest music.

This forum that also gather's together every year a selection of notable speakers that can shed light on subjects like the social and political influence of Fela on African society, how it affects the paradigm for social awareness and mobilization on the continent, in my opinion if well coordinated could help a great deal in bringing like minds together to access the progress of the struggle and map-out concrete plans for the future.

Other initiatives that deserve to be indicated in this gloomy landscape of general demobilization characterizing African officials, is that of the late President Omar Bongo of Gabon creating an Institute dedicated to researches on Bantu people (The Institute is headed by Théophile Obenga, a great disciple of Cheikh Anta Diop).

Also in existence, the radiocarbon laboratory of the Institute Fundamental of Black Africa Dakar Senegal, (Le laboratoire du radiocarbone de l'Institute Fundamental d'Afrique Noir), founded by Cheikh Anta Diop. These institutes, could serve as a base for future research works and training African scientists covering all disciplines.

We cannot forget to add the team from the Journal of African Civilization created by the late Dr. Ivan Van Sertima, author of the epic work: "They Came before Columbus" – African presence in the Americas before Christopher Columbus.

For those who don't know him he was a literary critic, a linguist, an anthropologist, and made a name in all three fields. His legacy which corresponds with the theme of the annual Fela Debate and his works, could serve ideas such as Tiken Jah's "A concert A School" initiative.

Dr. Van Sertima, talking about the works and legacy he intend to leave after him said:
"Our urgent concern is to ensure the use of these books as texts in high schools and universities. The audio tapes, soon to also become CDs issued through our Legacies Series, are equally important since those tapes bearing the book titles summarize, and crystallize, the most important elements in the texts and give to teachers and students alike, a more thorough understanding of the subject matter. The work of a whole generation of scholars, will go to waste unless these works can enter "the curriculum of inclusion" or, as it is known in some circles, "the multicultural curriculum. This is the beginning of a major revolution in thinking, which goes beyond mere protest rhetoric which attempts with the utmost seriousness, to change the perception everywhere of the role of people of African descent in the history of the world. This cannot be accomplished without the help of many people. We therefore, urge you to join in this crusade. You can do this simply by completing your own library of books and audio tapes, by alerting family and friends, local bookstores and libraries, and your school systems at all levels, so that we may continue this critical revision of history".

Future Felabrations, as a festival that assembles all groups playing all forms of protest music, particularly afrobeat groups world-wild at the Africa Shrine Lagos Nigeria, in a-week long musical pilgrimage and street carnival has a promise to bring annually more than one million people on the street. It will also provide, a regular way to access Fela's continuous impact and opportunity for the new generation to discover the phenomenon that was Fela.

The festival could also help like Dr. Sertima urged above, "by alerting family and friends, local bookstores and schools" to all the efforts put in place already, and those yet to materialise but under consideration.

All the events from Felabration filmed, and recorded, with the objective of producing CDs and DVDs annually that would be sold world-wide.

Also plans should be put in place, for two-way charter flights from for example New York, London, and Paris, for interested individuals, associations, or groups, in a package including hotel accommodation and ground transport, for participants at a price to be determined. Obviously the more people inscribed the cheaper the price will be, and the merrier of course and it is one of the best ways to pay respect to the sacrifice made by Fela and a way to keep his legacy alive. Femi Kuti asked about Fela's legacy and the influence on the public everywhere he performed in Africa and other parts of the world, replied:

"There is this warm reception for me and my band, I think that people are getting aware of his legacies it is good the audience are coming to our shows, I can use the opportunity to further expose the extent of corruption in Africa, talk to people in-order to find solutions and means to rectify the problems. For me it is a challenge and I believe as a professional musician, I will do my best to spread the message for the uplifting of the African and underprivileged in the world.

This is what Fela's legacy stands for and I believe in the same values. It is clear that somebody has to do it, and I believe I am just playing my part as an African. The total unity and independence of Africa, the choice to determine our destiny cannot be compromised. Also fighting for the under-privileged is why I took-up the struggle, it is my personal conviction and I sincerely believe in the justness of the cause. To start at this stage, thinking of the warm reception I get as a sign of people getting aware of Fela's legacy is not very wise we still have more work to do spreading the message".

The reader will agree, with Femi's statement above and the insight into the Fela phenomenon enumerated all along this volume, that it is evident the situation on the African continent is getting worse. Many people have died for the cause trying to change things in Africa, and for me I think it will amount to a more worse crime to let great people die in vain without any attempt to give fulfilment to the cause they lived and died for. The work of a whole generation of scholars will go to waste, unless these works are channelled through African school curriculum and education system.

One good thing about finding answers to the issues raised is that as long as these problems persist on the continent, people will always refer us to solutions put forward by notable Pan Africanists.

Pan Africanism is a way of life, a concept for the advancement of Africa from an African stand-point, propagated by people before our times and for people coming after us to find rallying-point.

Pan Africanism, is a concept based on the total economic and political unity of Africa and the Diaspora Africa, one unique monetary system for the entire continent, open trade, education system based on the needs of the African environment.

The idea has been well treated in the books published by Kwame Nkrumah, and as a champion and pioneer of Africa's Independence, he proposed among other things our own technology, medicine, that is what Pan Africanism is about. Let us use FELABRATION as a forum to find solutions to the problems of Africa and her leadership.

Fela with his pet donkey Yakubu named after General Yakubu Gowon.
Photo by Femi Bankole Osunla Africa 70 Photo Agency

Fela Anikulapo-Kuti (Oct. 15, 1938-Aug. 2, 1997) Discography and Summary

YEAR	TITLE	SUMMARY
1960	Fela Ransome-Kuti and His Highlife Rakers: **AIGANA** **Fela's Special** (7" UK, Melodisc)	**Aigana:** A popular highlife music tune in Nigeria of the 60's was composed by Victor Olaiya. Sung in Igbo language, aigana means "We are Going". The song is about musicians who have been performing all night and have no more strength to continue. "Ike agwu l'ayin" means in Igbo language "we have no more strength". Fela Ransome-Kuti who played occasionally with Victor Olaiya's orchestra before his departure in 1958, to study music at the Trinity College of Music in London did this 'cover' version of Aigana in a highlife-jazz fashion – a style of music that would become his trade mark for many years after. Highlife Rakers was the name of Fela's first band.
1960	Fela Ransome-Kuti and His Highlife Rakers: **Wa Ba Mi Jo Bonsue / Calypso N°1** (7" UK, Melodisc)	**Wa Ba Mi Jo Bonsue** in Yoruba language means "come dance bonsue with me". Bonsue was a popular dance style in English West Africa of the 60's made popular by many highlife bands. During his music student days in London at the time he started to play 'Wa bami jo bonsue' at Nigerian students parties, Fela had built up some road experience by playing with different student groups mostly of West Indian origin. This was when he formed his first group named Highlife Rakers – playing jazz, highlife and calypso like the song **'Calypso N°1'**. The group covered the repertoires of bands like Lord Kitchener and Mighty Sparrow as well as Fela's compositions. Most of his songs were covers from popular highlife tunes rendered in Yoruba and Igbo languages.

YEAR	TITLE	SUMMARY
1960	Fela Ransome-Kuti and The Highlife Jazz Band: FERE or "Onifere" (7" Nigeria, Phillips, 1960s).	**Fere** or **'Onifere'** (literally means horn player) in Yoruba language, it represents all wind instruments like the horn (trumpet) or whistle. This recording with The Highlife Jazz band was Fela's attempt to show his dexterity as a trumpet player and the song is talking about how the sound of horn made him dance and the sound of drum beat made him shake vigorously. "Féré ti mo gbo s'eti! L'ojé ki n'jo! Ilu ti mo gbo s'eti sé! L'ojé ki n'mi jigi jigi!"
1960	Fela Ransome-Kuti and The Highlife Jazz Band: **YESE** (7" Nigeria, Phillips)	**Yésé** is another song in Yoruba language by Fela talking about man woman relationship. "Yeshe" means "don't continue" or "stop". He sang: "Yéshé! Yéshé! Yé oh! Owo ti o'fin rinmi oh! O'nsé mi giringirin yéshé!" Meaning: "Don't continue! Those hands that you tickle me with! Makes me tremble!"
1963 - 1964	Fela Ransome-Kuti and Koola Lobitos: **BONFO / FERE** (7" Nigeria,The RK label)	**Bonfo** also sung in Yoruba is talking about the "mini skirt" that was in fashion in Nigeria like most parts of the world in the 60's. As can be scene from the evolution of fashion, generation after generation fashion is a continuous mix of the past to make the present – prompting the idiom in Yoruba "ko si ohun tuntun, labé orun" meaning: "there is nothing new under the sky". In Bonfo Fela sang: "Arabirin! Esé ré da! Arabirin! Sé Bonfo ni? Yé oh ma baa élo! Meaning: "Young lady! You got beautiful legs! Young lady! Is it "mini-skirt?" Yeah oh! I will go with you! Even if it is London or America! Bonfo too was a popular highlife tune in the 60's covered by many musicians. This was one of the first recordings of Fela, after his return to Nigeria in 1963 following his graduation from London's Trinity College of Music. Recorded with his new band named Koola Lobitos. **Fere** (see column above).

YEAR	TITLE	SUMMARY
1963 - 1964	Fela Ransome-Kuti Quintet: **GREAT KIDS / EKE** (7" Nigeria, Phillips).	**Great Kids** is a modern highlife jazz instrumental piece featuring: **Fela Ransome-Kuti on trumpet, Medonal Amaechi guitar, E. Ngomalloh bass, T. Adekoya drums, Ayinde Folarin conga.** **EKE** written by Isaac Olashugba and vocals by Ezekiel Hart, is a highlife jazz tune sung in Yoruba taking about morals in the society. "Lo wa isé sé ore ko yé mura éké! Ronu lati sé otito ko yé mura éké! Eké ma n'pa ni oh! Esan ma n'bo oh! Itiju ni o! Fimi s'ile baby aséwo lé ju oh! Ayiri ni ko mo kan! Iku leri yen ké ya sa! Fi aiye mi s'ile oh! Jowo mo fé lo oh! Bye bye loda oh! Meaning: "Go find some work to do instead of gossiping about! Think to be always forthright and say the truth all times! Back-biting kills and payback day is coming! It brings shame! In the same breath, he bemoans prostitution singing: "Baby please leave me alone, prostitution is not good! She is ignorant and crazy, a walking death that deserves to be run-away from! Please leave my life and go away, please let me keep on with my life! It is good-bye time! Leave my life alone!" This recording with the Quintet was before Fela put together the group Koola Lobitos.

YEAR	TITLE	SUMMARY
1963 - 1964	Fela Ransome-Kuti and His Koola Lobitos: **OLORUKA / AWO** (7" Nigeria, The RK label)	Generation after generations, many Nigerian song-writers use elements of social commentary or social cliché as the basis of their songs. **Oloruka**, like most of Fela's early compositions is about daily life in a Nigerian society - someone taking another man's wife. The moral message of the song is that, the same woman could also leave the second man in-order to return to her first man from whom she was taken away - leaving the former empty handed. Sung in Yoruba language: "Aya wa ni! E sé lo fé! Oloruka gb'oruka! Owo awe dofo oh! Meaning: "She is our wife! Why did you marry her! The owner of the ring takes back his ring! Leaving the man empty handed! **Awo** in Yoruba language means cult or Masonic culture. Fela in Awo would like to pass the message that a person protected by the cult and culture of his people can never be conquered – he sang:"Yeah lé lé éyin awo léri! Gbogbo ohun ti asé awon to fé wa o dun mon won! Awa ko binu enikan! Bi eniyan binu awa ko mo! Oja Oyingbo (Oyingbo Market) ko mo pe enikan ko wa oh! Bi oko kan ko re Ejinrin égbé gbérun re aalo! Sugbon ti aba sé won oh éyin agbagba éfi oriji wa oh Awo! Meaning; "Shame on you! You can only see the back of a cult plate! All we have done is a pleasure to those who love us! We hold no grudge against anyone, if someone is holding grudge we are not aware! Oyingbo market is full of people to notice the absence of one person! If one train doesn't go to Ejinrin, there are thousand others that will go! However if we make offence to anyone, we apologise to the elders around!"

YEAR	TITLE	SUMMARY
1964 - 1965	Fela Ransome-Kuti and His Koola Lobitos: **YESE / EGBIN** (7" Nigeria, Parlophone)	**Egbin** in the traditional worldview of the Yoruba people is considered the most beautiful animal in existence. Fela in Egbin is talking about a woman named Aduke that is beautiful like the égbin. He sings: "Aduke dara o wun mi bi égbin lori! Odara o léwa osé omo jéjé. Awa la fo Marina loju awa oni lu! Eyin le fo Marina loju eyin oni jo! Ajuwa yéyé sawa sawa! Meaning: "Aduka is beautiful and pleases me! She is not only beautiful but also nice and cultured! He then went on to sing about Marina a popular Lagos street - how it was blinded by musicians and dancers. One of those goodtime dance music that didn't say much ideologically but melodious to dance to. **Yésé** (see above)
1964 - 1965	Fela Ransome-Kuti and His Koola Lobitos : **OMUTI TI DE** (7" Nigeria)	**Omuti Ti Dé** in Yoruba language means: "here comes the drunkard". "Omuti ti de o" (here comes the drunkard). "E wa wo aiye omuti" (come see the life of a drunkard). "Ofi isé silé o wa beer lo" (he abandons his job in search of beer). "Isé wa bo oh, o n'ronu oh" (he lost his job and now he is thinking). "E jé ka sora ki a maa k'abamo" (we have to be careful so we don't have regrets). Fela in this song bemoans the habit of neglecting responsibility due to alcoholism.
1964 - 1965	Fela Ransome-Kuti plays with The Koola Lobitos : **DIE DIE / KUSIMI LAYA / FIRE / ONI MACHINI** (7" Nigeria, Parlophone)	

YEAR	TITLE	SUMMARY
1965	Fela Ransome-Kuti and His Koola Lobitos: **A.** **Signature Tune / It's Highlife Time / Lagos Baby / Omuti / Ololufe / Araba's Delight** **B.** **Wa Dele / Lai Se / Mi O Mo / Obinrin Le / Omo Ejo** The re-edited CD version titled "Koola Lobitos / The '69 Los Angeles Sessions" (Barclay, France 2001) Contains 6 tittles from this album: **Highlife Time** **Omuti Tide** **Ololufe Mi** **Wadele Wa Rohin** **Laise Lairo** **Wayo-otherwise called:** **Mio Mo** (2nd version LP Nigeria, EMI)	**SIDE A: Signature Tune** – is a strictly highlife jazz instrumental piece that Fela had the attitude at that time to open his concerts with. A way of giving to his public a taste of what is yet to come. **It's Highlife Time** is sung in English, it is about highlife music and how from morning time people jump for joy listening to the music. Fela underlines in this song how highlife music got the beat and how it makes its listener heat-up particularly at the brand new place where he was performing called 'Kakadu Night Club'. He sang: "At this swinging Club, that makes the craze" – the latest craze he concludes. **Lagos Baby** is a song about the social cliché in Nigeria that tends to look at Lagos women as 'money lovers' and not lovers from the heart. Sung in Pidgin English: "Lagos baby na so so money" (Lagos women only care for money). "Because of money oh, my baby run away. "Lagos baby oh na so so money". Fela in the same song bemoans Lagos men: "wetin you be oh, you be woman wrapper" (what are you, you are nothing but women's wrapper) – another social cliché about men who run after 'anything' in skirts. **Omuti Ti Dé** – here comes the drunkard (see above). **Ololufe Mi** sung in Yoruba language, is about a repentant lover appealing to his woman to hold him in her arms. "Ololufemi ti ré ni mo fé! Alayanfe mi, mio sé ti won mon! (My love, it's only you I want! My chosen one, I have nothing to do with them anymore!) "Wa fi énu ko mi l'énu! Wa fi ara romi l'ara" (come kiss me and rob your body against me). Basically a love song, that Fela like most musicians at the early part of their careers would like to project the 'lover boy side'.

YEAR	TITLE	SUMMARY
1965	**Araba's Delight** Part of the re-edited CD version titled: **Koola Lobitos / The '69 Los Angeles Sessions** (Barclay, 2001)	Fela's **Araba's Delight,** is a cover from the song with the same title composed by the veteran highlife music star J. O. Araba that bemoans abortion among women. The song's idea is based on the social cliché that children are the fruits of ones labour in life. JO (as he was known to his pears) was to highlife music, what Miles Davis was re-known for in Jazz music – the maker of great musicians. The famous bandleader and impresario, club-owner Bobby Benson, played in J.O. Araba's band in the late 40s. Same with Fatai Rolling Dollar, who latter taught the popular Juju music star Ebenezer Obey how to play the guitar. Members of Koola Lobitos featured in this recording included Tony Allen (drums), Ojo Okeji (bass), Yinka Roberts (guitar), Isaac Olasugba (sax), Tunde Williams (trumpet), Eddie Aroyewun (trumpet), Tex Becks and Uwaifo (tenor sax), Fred Lawal (guitar). All the tracks except for **'Araba's Delight'** (by J. O. Araba) were written by Fela.

YEAR	TITLE	SUMMARY
1965 - 1966	Fela Ransome-Kuti and His Koola Lobitos: [A] **Everyday I Got My Blues / Mo ti Gborokan / Waka Waka** [B] **Ako / Oloruka / Lai Se** Recorded Live at the Afro Spot Lagos, Nigeria (10" Phillips/Polydor PLP001)	**MO TI GBOROKAN** and **Waka Waka** were songs, written by Fela with a theme like most Nigerian song-writers of the 60's based on elements of social commentaries or social cliché – the sayings, slangs, and even popular phrases from the streets and night clubs, were used as moral guidelines for the society. **Mo ti gborokan**, sung in Yoruba language is talking about, hearing the news that someone is planning to take his "wife" and the husband sure of himself says: "Ko le shé sheé! Laiyé yi o!" Meaning: "It will not be possible! Not in this world!" **Waka Waka** is about walking thousands of miles in search of his lover the clear skin lady. How lover boy was prepared to borrow, big agbada (Yoruba traditional dress) to be able to go on the journey in search of his love girl. **Everyday I Got My Blues** unlike other songs written in highlife style, this tune was purely soul. Fela was in this song, keeping in touch with the wave of soul music invading the continent in the late sixties. He sang: "Everyday, I got my blues! I'm a little baby! Everyday I got My blues! On the B side is is another version of **Ako** which in Yoruba language means 'bluff'- another social cliché addressed to women. "We asked her to be our wife she refused! Let her go get married to director, civil servant or bank manager! One day she will regret and come back to beg". **Lai Se** is about the broken hearted man who felt cheated and unjustly treated. Without doing anywrong they took my wife, without doing anywrong, I was locked in detention. A song about injustice, based on elements of social commentaries about the powerful and rich taking advantage of the poor.

YEAR	TITLE	SUMMARY
1965 – 1966	Fela Ransome-Kuti and His Koola Lobitos: **ONIDODO / ALAGBARA** (7" Nigeria, Phillips West Africa Records PF383 620)	**Onidodo** another piece sung in Yoruba language is about a street vendor that had spent the whole day walking all-over Lagos in an attempt to sell her wares. She arrives in Lafiaji area in the heart of the Lagos slum, she puts down her wares in a little corner by the roadside. Another street hawker with same story tries to push the first street vendor from the little space she is occupying – in the process hell is let loose! The moral lesson of this song is that a hungry man is an angry man! **Alagbara** in Yoruba language mean "someone powerful". In this song Fela sings:"You cannot punish me unjustly forever without my mother knowing". "Oni f'iya jemi ki iya mi ma mo! Oni f'iya je mi gbe!" O'lagbara si mi! E w'oku olé o! Meaning: "Look at this so called powerful man flexing his lazy muscles! One of those songs denouncing the inequalities of society – the rich and powerful taking advantage of the helpless poor.
1965 - 1966	Fela Ransome-Kuti and His Koola Lobitos: **ABIARA / AJO** (7" Nigeria, Phillips West Africa Records PF383 622)	**Abiara** is about trust between friends - rumours of one friend having affairs with the other friend's wife. The friend in return dismisses all the back-talks as nothing but rumours – with all the back talks and suspicions, who are we going to have a relationship with he asks? "Abiara, éru re m'nba mio! Maa ma fémi l'aya! Maa ma fémi l'alé! Ewo ni ka fé l'area yio! Won soro l'eya! Abiara won soro l'eya! **Ajo** is all about nostalgia, a young folk trying to assure his parents that he is well and safe while away on a journey. Sung in Yoruba language: "Iya mi osé o mé ku o ajo moré! Baba mi osé o mé ku o ajo more! Meaning: "My mother thanks to you I am not dead! I am only on a journey! My father thanks to you I am not dead! I am only on a journey! "They are lying and gossiping I am not dead! I am on a journey! "Iro ni won pa! Eké ni won n'sé mé ku o ajo more!

YEAR	TITLE	SUMMARY
1965 - 1966	Fela Ransome-Kuti and His Koola Lobitos: **IKILO / EKO** (7" Nigeria, Phillips West Africa Records PF383 800)	**Ikilo** in Yoruba language means 'warning'. **Eko** is the traditional name of Lagos before the Portuguese re-named it after her sea-side look-alike city with the same name in Portugal. Fela in this song projects the pride of Eko citizens in their city – how you will travel home anywhere in the country affirming Eko as the home of knowledge and the best of the best. He sang in Yoruba language: "Wa délé wa royin! Wa délé wa fo sé! Eko l'ogbon wa sé wa royin! Won gba wa l'oga wa royin!" Eko is the home of intelligence you will go home and tell he concludes.
1966 - 1968	**Fela Ransome-Kuti and His Koola Lobitos:** Waka Waka / SE E TUN DE (7" Nigeria, Phillips West Africa Records PF383 802)	**Waka Waka** (see above - live recordings at Afro Spot Lagos, Nigeria). **SE E TUN DE** in Yoruba language means "Are you here again?". Fela in this song tries to mystify the musical power of his band Koola Lobitos. He sings: "Lobitos, are you here again? Was it not you that sent telegraph to heaven and God sent telegraph back saying there is no snake in the dawn. "Lobitos sé étun dé! Eyin le té waya s'orun, Olorun wa té waya pada pé éjo si larimo!" One of those songs that did not mean much in message, but show great musical dexterity in direction of jazz-highlife.

YEAR	TITLE	SUMMARY
1967 – 1968	**Fela Ransome-Kuti and His Koola Lobitos:** **MY BABY DON LOVE ME / Home Cooking** (7" Nigeria, Phillips WA425004)	Listening to Fela in **MY BABY DON LOVE ME,** one can hardly identify the later years Fela who affirmed that "my music is not for entertainment my music is to spread a message". He sang: "My baby don love me. Oh yeah! She makes me cry all day yeah! My baby don't care. Oh yeah! I'm going to tell to mama!" Like most band leaders of that epoch Geraldo Pino, Orlando Julius Ekemode, Easy Kabaka, etc. - American soul music was coming back to its source like most style of music in the Black Diaspora – rumba, jazz, soul and later reggae. And all them bandleaders were jumping on the "soul music" band-wagon. My baby don't love me, was part of those self searching songs written before Fela's eye opener trip to America in 1969. **Home Cooking** is a highlife-jazz tune with lyrics that are self explicit: "Let's have a ball to this home cooking tune! It's a hell of a tune, it makes me move! It makes you move! It makes me jump, it makes you jump too! So when I say wail, say wail!"
1968 - 1969	**Fela – Koola Lobitos:** **The '69 L.A. Sessions / AKO 2" 40**	**Ako** track 10 from the '69 L.A. Sessions, is about bluff. Ako in Yoruba language is about bluff: "Ako ko pe! Bobo ti onfi s'ako simi! Bobo o'to!" Meaning "showing off or bluffing doesn't pay! The guy you showing off with is not up to my standard!
1968 - 1969	**Fela Ransome-Kuti and His Koola Lobitos:** **ONIFERE No. 2 / OYEJO** (7" Nigeria, The RK label RK4)	**Fere or Onifere** (see above). **Oyejo** otherwise titled **Ako** which in Yoruba language means 'bluff'- another social cliché addressed to women (see above).

YEAR	TITLE	SUMMARY
1968 - 1969	**Fela Ransome-Kuti and His Koola Lobitos:** **WA DELE / LAISE** (7" Nigeria, Parlophone NPJ514 --7XNPS1575/1576)	Cosmogony beliefs and myths handed down from generation to generation, play a big part in the larger part of the Yoruba society. There is this believe that those given the powers of "Egbe" can appear and disappear at will. Gbe **WA DELE** in Yoruba language means "carry us home". In this song Fela calls on 'egbe' to take him and his band member's home: "Gbe wa delé o! Kélélé! Egbé gbé wa delé o! Aiyé ti mo wa o! Kélélé! Gbé wa lo lé o!" Meaning: "Carry us home! Straight home! Egbé carry us home! In this life that I live! Carry us straight home!" **LAI SE** in Yoruba language means "without doing any wrong". Fela sings: "lai se lai ro! lai se ogba mi ni iyawo ! O fi mi si itimole ! lai se !" Meaning "without doing any wrong! He took my wife! Without doing any wrong! He puts me in jail!" Another song based on elements of social commentaries about the powerful and rich taking advantage of the poor.
1968 - 1969	Fela Ransome-Kuti and the Koola Lobitos: **ORISE / EKE** featuring **VC 7** (7" Nigeria, Parlophone)	**ORISHE** an Ishekiri song is written by Ojo Okeji and vocals by Ezekiel Hart. (**EKE** see above)
1968 – 1969	Fela Ransome-Kuti and the Koola Lobitos: **VC 7 / I Know Your Feeling** (7" Nigeria, Parlophone)	**I KNOW YOUR FEELING** was writen by Ojo Okeji and vocals by Ezekiel Hart. A song about a heart broken man that believes his woman is cheating behind him – another of those social cliché songs. **VC 7** written by Ojo Okeji and Isaac Olashugba with Ezekiel Hart on vocals is about a popular dance in Nigeria in the late 60's called VC 7. "Swing, dance to the VC7! Turn around and shake-up, dance to the VC7 brothers! Let go now let's do it, to the VC7..."

YEAR	TITLE	SUMMARY
1968 – 1969	**Fela Ransome-Kuti and His Koola Lobitos:** **Voice of America Sessions** **Ironu / Magbe Yen Wa / Iro / Ojo (Part 1) / Ojo (Part 2) / Oyejo / Igba L'aiye**	**Ironu Ko papo** literally translated signifies "we don't have the same worries". Fela in this song portrays the feeling of 'a hungry man is an angry man" – sung in Yoruba language he sings: "Ironu ko papo sé égbo! We don't have the same worries do you hear! Fi mi silé jé ki n'mi! Leave me alone and give me some breathing space! Ko s'owo l'apo mi sé égbo! Fi mi s'ilé je ki n'mi! I have no money in my pocket do you hear, leave me alone and give me some breathing space!" In Yoruba language **Ma Gbe Yen Wa** can be literally translated as "don't bring that". The song is about a young girl warned by her parents not to go into dark corners with men. She affirms her virginity to the man trying to entice her to go to bed with him saying: "Oséré nimi mio sé ma ko mi! "I am a virgin, I don't want don't teach me!" Iya mi ni ki n'ma ma sé s'ogbo! Baba mi ni ki n'ma ma sé s'ogbo o! "My mother told me not to! My father told me not to, do you hear!" Oséré ni mi ma gbe yen wa o! I am a virgin don't bring me that! **Iro** in Yoruba language means 'lies' but in this song Fela literally uses 'Iro' to signify empty threats. "Iro l'eda n'pa, éké l'eda n'sé! All these humane threats are nothing! B'aiye sata pelu ésu! If humans are full with evil! Eyi ti Oluwa ba wi ni yio sé! It is what God has ordained that will prevail! Igi ti Oluwa ba gbin, iro l'eda n'pa éda ko lé wo! Tree planted by God can never be uprooted by human! A song based on spiritualism and faith in the almighty.

YEAR	TITLE	SUMMARY
1968 – 1969	**Fela Ransome-Kuti and His Koola Lobitos:** Voice of America Sessions **Ironu / Magbe Yen Wa / Iro / Ojo (Part 1) / Ojo (Part 2) / Oyejo / Igba L'aiye**	**Ojo (parts 1&2)** is about a common Yoruba expression that talks about 'let it be', whatever is ordained to happen will come to pass. Ojo is rain, and in this song Fela sings about dark clouds and threats of rainfall: "Ojo to su, to su dédé oh! Rain with so much dark clouds in the sky! Ojo ro bo maa ro bo de ro ko kasé! Rain if you want fall go ahead and if you don't want you can disappear! **Oyejo** otherwise titled **Ako** which in Yoruba language means 'bluff'- another social cliché addressed to women, is about a man sure of himself. Talking to a woman he made passes and the woman turns him down. To console himself, the man says let her go she will regret even if she marries to a bank manager, civil servant, or whatever – she will one day regret her refusal and comeback to beg for forgiveness. **Igba Laiye** in Yoruba language can literally be translated as "everything in life has it's time." Fela's message in this song is that whatever position one finds his or herself, the person should do everything not to take too much advantage. Stay upright and do the right thing. The same people rolling for you today could turn against you tomorrow.

YEAR	TITLE	SUMMARY
1963 - 1969	**Fela Ransome-Kuti:** **LAGOS BABY** (from jazz and highlife to soul and afrobeat VAMPICD 097)	**Mio Mo** in Yoruba language means "I am not aware", Fela in this song is addressing the cliché of trust between friends. Mio mo pe oni wayo ni é (I am not aware that you are not trust worthy). Mio mo pe oni jibiti ni é (I am not aware that you are a dupe). Mio mo pe olé ni é se (I didn't realise that you are a thief). I am not aware at all (mio mo rara, mio mo). Trust plays an important part in African culture and it is more important in the Yoruba tradition. For example, if a man travelling between villages arrives in a farm with ripe fruits and he is hungry. Tradition permits that he can help himself with the fruits without taking extras with him. So long as you eat all the fruits you need on the spot, it is not considered as stealing from the farm. **Obirin Lé** is a social commentary or social cliché about women. Sung in Yoruba Fela affirms: "O le gboju le won (you cannot rely on them). Lai ma f'iya je é (without making you suffer). Eé o wo aiyé o (look at life). Ewa ni wo'nta (they are only selling beauty). Obirin lé o (women are difficult). Won lé oh (they are really difficult)." **Omo Ejo** is a typical social education elders give to the younger generation on the dangers in life. Ejo in Yoruba language means snake. Fela in this song warns about looking down on fellow humans no matter how lowly placed the person is. The danger a little snake poses is as great as a snake ten times larger. He sang: "Ma sé f'omo éjo séré (don't play with a child snake). Ma sé dan wo (don't even tempt it). M'élé f'omo éjo sere (I can't play with a child snake). M'élé dan wo (I can't tempt to). Won gé ni je (they can bite). Won bu ni je (they bite). A morale song about looking down on people we think are too little or inferior.

YEAR	TITLE	SUMMARY
1969 - 1970	**Fela Ransome-Kuti and The Nigeria 70:** **VIVA NIGERIA / FUNKY HORN/ WITCHCRAFT / OBE/ My Lady's Frustration** (7" Nigeria, The Duke Records) 4 titles included in the re-edited CD Koola Lobitos / The '69 Los Angeles Sessions (Barclay, 2001)	The '69 Los Angeles Session recordings, were a collection of songs that reflect Fela's musical and political evolution from a musician entertainer with a style of music called 'highlife jazz' to a fighter of a black cause with music as a weapon. Coming to America, he overestimated the power of his 'highlife jazz' style of music. He forgot that America expected something more authentic from an African band than jazz - of which America has produced the greatest maestros. Fela recounts his experience: "My American tour in 1969 was a turning point in my way of thinking and approach to life. America is a great country it made me jealous that we don't have today that kind of greatness in our country. It was also in America that I was exposed for the first time to a lot of black history - that background knowledge about Africa which I did not have before. I was exposed to the teachings of Marcus Garvey, Malcolm X, and also the Black Panther Party". With a new thinking, he realised he had to write and arrange his music in a way more relevant to the environment he came from - something with the African background. During a rehearsals in Los Angeles, after smoking a joint (marijuana) for the fist time, he said he heard this heavy bass line vibrating in his head in the form of sakara (apala rhythm), a traditional Yoruba music from the West of Nigeria. The result: **My Lady's Frustration** an instrumental piece dedicated to Sandra Iszidore (nee Smith) - the lady who stood by him during his troubles and evolution in the US. According to Fela, she felt frustrated with all the problems encountered by him in his musical search for greener pastures. Finally finding his feet, he wrote this song as a tribute to her.

YEAR	TITLE	SUMMARY
	Fela Ransome-Kuti and The Nigeria 70: VIVA NIGERIA / FUNKY HORN/ WITCHCRAFT / OBE/ My Lady's Frustration (7" Nigeria, The Duke Records) 4 titles included in the re-edited CD Koola Lobitos / The '69 Los Angeles Sessions (Barclay, 2001)	**Viva Nigeria** or **Keep Nigeria One** written in his new style of music called: 'Afrobeat' is about the Biafra civil war going on in Nigeria and calling on Nigerians to unite and resolve their differences in more amicable ways than war. Other tittles from these sessions are songs talking about social issues like **Obe** in Yoruba language - literally translated means soup or source. In street parlance it means 'don't give that crap or bullshit. Fela sings: "Mi olé jé Obe ti ko lata (I can't eat soup without pepper). Mi olé jé obe ti ko n'iyo (I can't eat soup without salt). Mio lé jé obe ti ko ni epo (I can't eat soup without oil). Mio jée(I don't want to eat) Ma fi lo mio Obe ti ko dun (Don't propose to me soup that is not sweet). To many Yoruba folks, soup without the basic ingredients mentioned in the song is not considered as good soup. **Funky Horn** is Fela's attempt to show his dexterity as a trumpet player – an instrumental piece. **Wichcraft** (see below).

YEAR	TITLE	SUMMARY
1969 - 1970	**Fela Ransome-Kuti and The Nigeria 70 :** **LOVER / WAYO / WITCHCRAFT** 3 titles included in the re-edited CD Koola Lobitos / The '69 Los Angeles Sessions (Barclay,2001) (7" Nigeria, The Duke Records)	**Wayo** (1st version otherwise titled **Mio MO** – see above). Wayo in Hausa language means dishonest, though sung in Yoruba language it conveys the same meaning of dismay at the discovery that a person you trust is dishonest, a cheat, and a fraud. It is all about being upright in society. **Wayo** (2nd version) is about forthrightness and speaking the truth. Sung also in Yoruba language: "Opuro o sé o k'abo (stop lying thanks and welcome). Gbemi s'ilé osé (drop me down from your high lyings). Enu opuro ki n'sejé (a lire's mouth never bleeds). Wayo oh (it all lie and tricks)." **Lover** (otherwise titled Ololufe Mi – see above). **Witchcraft** is about Yoruba beliefs in the mystical powers that could transform a human into an unseen bird that could fly anywhere at will without being seen with natural eyes. This power is called "égbé". Fela in this song is calling on the mystical powers to bring them home safely and surely.
1970	**Fela Ransome-Kuti and The Nigeria 70:** **JEUN K'OKU PART 1 & 11**	**JEUN KO KU (CHOP'N QUENCH)** this piece was Fela's first musical success in Nigeria. It paved the way for his eventual popularity throughout Africa. Within six months of its release, this track sold more than two hundred thousand copies - a reason why it remains one of the most exploited (instrumental/vocal versions) of Fela's repertoires. Jeun Ko Ku is about a glutton - who eats himself to death.

YEAR	TITLE	SUMMARY
1970 - 1971	**Fela Ransome-Kuti and The Nigeria 70:** **Blackman's Cry / Beautiful Dancer** (7" Nigeria, Pathe Marconi).	**BLACK MAN'S CRY** is about identity. 'I am Black and proud' Fela sings in Yoruba. 'Who says Black Is Not Beautiful? Bring that person out let me see! - He challenges. 'There is nothing as beautiful as the black skin! Look at me! Look at me very well! There is nothing as beautiful as the black skin! Look at me very well. A song to rid the black mind of inferiority complex. Particularly Africans who use chemical products to bleach their skin, or Africans who feel inferior to the White folks. **Beautiful Dancer** is Fela's first tribute to his female afrobeat dancers. He sings in Yoruba language: "Look at this beautiful dancer! Come see her beautiful legs! See her beautiful backside shaking rhythmically! Come with me! Come with me! There is no doubt that Fela was with this song, preparing his public for what he would later call the "fire dance" of the African woman.
1970 - 1971	**Fela Ransome-Kuti and The Nigeria 70:** **WHY BLACK MAN DEY SUFFER** (LP Nigeria, African Songs)	**WHY BLACK MAN DEY SUFFER** (see below)

YEAR	TITLE	SUMMARY
1971	**Fela Ransome-Kuti and The Nigeria 70:** **WHO ARE YOU PART 1 & 2** (7" Nigeria, EMI)	There was this incident at the Afro Spot not long after the success of **Jeun Ko Ku**. Fela arrived at the club to find an Alhaji (as those who have made the pilgrimage to Mecca in Saudi Arabia are called) insisting on not paying to enter the club. Fela asked the Alhaji why he did not want to pay to see him play. According to Fela, if the man could afford to pay to make a pilgrimage to Mecca just to worship a black stone paying to see a concert shouldn't pose any problem. To the contrary either as a result of alcoholic confidence or share madness, the man in responds pushed Fela on the chest demanding at the same time **"Who Are You?"** The Alhaji got slapped in the face by young guys who accompanied Fela. Without being told he took to his heels running away as fast as his legs could carry him to avoid getting more slaps. Fela later wrote the incident into a song he called **WHO ARE YOU**, in the lyrics he narrated his experience with the Alhaji and how the latter got beaten.

YEAR	TITLE	SUMMARY
1971	Fela Ransome-Kuti and The Africa 70: **ARIYA PART 1 & 2** (7" Nigeria)	**ARIYA** in Yoruba language means 'good times'. Fela, in Ariya tries to convey the celebration of good times saying: '...we are having a good time! It is no one's business! What we get high on doesn't concern them. It is a party song for everyone to get together and have good times.
1971	Fela Ransome-Kuti and Nigeria 70: **LONDON SCENE/ JEHIN-JEHIN** (LP Nigeria, EMI)	Compared to the one-song lengthy vinyl that characterised Fela's musical works the last two decades preceding his demise, **J'EHIN J'EHIN (gnashing of teeth)** was part of a collection of short songs Fela recorded at the EMI Abbey Road studio in 1971 titled: **LONDON SCENE**. Afro Beat was born in this epoch, and Fela could identify with Malcolm X and Black Panthers but, ideologically he did not know what to sing about hence songs like this talking about an insatiable person that was given everything and still was not satisfied. Fela concludes in Yoruba asking the person to go away as their ways are not the same (maa lo, ona wa ko papo he concludes in Yoruba language).

YEAR	TITLE	SUMMARY
1972	Fela Ransome-Kuti and The Africa 70: **OPEN AND CLOSE** (LP Nigeria, EMI) A. Open and Close / Swegbe and Pako B. Gbagada Gbagada Gbogodo Gbogodo	**OPEN AND CLOSE** is teaching its listeners how to move to his Afrobeat song - a dance choreography with a lot of African vitality. **SWEGBE AND PAKO** sung in 'broken-English' is about good and bad. Competence and its opposite incompetence according to Fela, a carpenter who does not know his trade is 'Swegbe'. A tailor who sews like someone in the carpentry trade is another 'Swegbe'. A doctor acting like a lawyer is 'Swegbe' same with a lawyer trying to act like a doctor. On the other hand, a carpenter competent at his work is 'Pako' alike the tailor, lawyer and doctor. The message of the song is that if you are in a position of responsibility and you do your work with competence then you are 'Pako'. On the other hand, if you do it bad you are 'Swegbe'. "If you are good you are Pako and if you are bad you are Swegbe". **GBAGADA GBAGADA! GBOGODO GBOGODO!** Is another folk song recounting the war gallantry of the Egbas against the colonial forces and their agents on the coasts of West Africa. The Egba war with the British colonial force was led by Adubi a renowned Egba war General. Fela starts the song by calling on his listeners to please help him sing this folk song "Gbagada Gbagada! Gbogodo Gbogodo!" With pride the people marched and went to war. This is a tale of pandemonium caused by attacking colonial British forces. Egba forces believed they were not only resisting for themselves, but also for the love of their children "Oh! Oh! Oya oh! Eni omo wun oya kalo oh!" Meaning, if you love your children! Let us go to war!

YEAR	TITLE	SUMMARY
1972	**Fela Ransome-Kuti and The Africa 70:** **LIVE With Ginger Baker** **A. Let's Start / Black Man's Cry** **B. YE YE DE SMELL** (LP UK, Regal Zonophone)	**LET'S START**: "Let us start what we've come into the room to do' is telling it as it is another graphic and explicit song about sex, sung in Yoruba with some broken English explanations. Fela calls on his partner in the room to get on with it, 'don't play the innocent... let's start! Take off your clothes! Let's start!' The recording has Ginger Baker, of the former English pop group 'Cream' playing live as guest drummer on some tracks like Let's Start in place of Tony Allen, the regular drum player in Fela's Africa 70 band. The album, titled 'Live With Ginger Baker' was recorded in the sixteen track mobile studio Ginger Baker sold to Polygram Nigeria in 1972. **Black Man's Cry (see column above).** **YE YE DE SMELL** is about people getting what they deserve - reaping what you sow. If you flirt with another person's wife, you shouldn't feel bad if people do the same to you. Literally meaning bullshit stinks. It implies that if you give people bullshit, you should not be surprised if you get the same back from others.
1972	**Fela Ransome-Kuti and The Africa 70:** **JE'NWI TEMI (DON'T GAG ME)**	**JE'NWI TEMI (DON'T GAG ME)** is the first of Fela's attacks at the Nigeria 'powers that be'. A strong message that he is not one to be gagged. Sung in Yoruba language, it says: "Even if you jail me, you cannot shut my mouth! I will open my mouth wide like basket! You cannot shut my mouth!" He goes on to stress that the truth is bitter, but it remains what it is - the TRUTH. Hence, he will not stop talking and singing about the truth.

YEAR	TITLE	SUMMARY
1972	**Fela Ransome-Kuti and The Africa 70:** **Alujon Jon Ki Jon Part 1 & 2** (7" Ghana, 1972).	**ALU JON JON KI JON** is a traditional moonlight tale made into a song. Yoruba mythology makes constant references to inter-reaction between the human and the animal world, a co-habitation between the two worlds. Once there was a great farming that ravaged the entire world, so goes the tale. To survive this farming, all animals agreed to sacrifice their mothers in the collective cooking-pot in-order to save the population. When it came to the turn of the dog, the other animals discovered that he had secretly hidden away his mother in heaven. Alu Jon Jon Ki Jon, the other animals chorused after the dog treating him as a selfish and dishonest comrade.
1972	**Fela Ransome-Kuti and The Nigeria 70:** **SHENSHEMA PART 1 & 2** (7" Nigeria, 1972)	**SHENSHEMA**: Sung in broken English signifies different things, it could mean a shameful thing if addressed that way and it could mean out of use or out-of-service if used to describe a problematic machine. Fela sings: "a car you have to push to start is Shenshema, same for a woman who has thirty-nine men because she feels thirty-six is not enough. A man, who has thirty-three women and complains he cannot get ninety-nine is regarded as Shenshema. A man or woman who uses chemical products to bleach her skin in order to lighten his or her skin is Shenshema. Same for the man or woman who wears a wig to cover his or her natural hair".

YEAR	TITLE	SUMMARY
1972	Fela Ransome-Kuti and The Nigeria 70: **MONDAY MORNING** PART 1 & 2 (b/w 7" Nigeria)	In swinging funky Lagos City, Fela sings that Saturdays are reserved for tent makings in preparation for Sunday parties where people drink to life's beauty. However on Monday Mornings the partying is over, no more room for credits, Mr. Inflation is all over town and if you demand to be paid for debts owed, you get a negative responds. To the Western mind it is called superstition, but to most Africans – Lagosians in particular asking to be paid back a debt on a Monday Morning is asking for trouble. Everyone believes that it is the way you start the week that it will end. So don't go asking for credits or payment of debt from anybody on any Monday Morning Fela advised.
1972	Fela Ransome-Kuti and The Nigeria 70: **FOGO – FOGO** Part 1 & 2 (b/w 7" Ghana)	**Fogo Fogo** (meaning in Yoruba language "break bottle") is an example of how Fela could incite his audience into violence with music. Whenever he performed the song live, the public seemed to react violently against each other breaking bottles and there is nowhere in the song where he called for violence. He never said they should attack each other but the public usually reacted in a violent manner. The first time Fela played Fogo Fogo at the University of Ibadan "Havana Night", the students attacked each other with bottles.
1972	Fela Ransome-Kuti and The Nigeria 70: **COMING IN & GOING OUT** PART 1 & 2 (7" Nigeria, EMI)	Fela in **Coming in and Going Out** affirms that anything that goes in must come out, the laws of laws that cannot be changed. If you enter any room you will come-out again, also if you enter a prison you will come-out again and he affirms that if you go inside a woman, you will come-out again. Meaning that anywhere you enter you will have to com-out again. However Fela' says if you enter somewhere and you fail to come-out of the place, it means that the person is dead (you will RIP - rest in peace).

YEAR	TITLE	SUMMARY
1972	Fela Ransome-Kuti and The Africa 70: **EGBE MI O** (7" Ghana, Stateside 7" UK, Regal Zonophone)	**EGBE MI O** in Yoruba language means Carry Me. In this song Fela is singing about the different kinds of things that happen to you while you dance. How you could go into trance while dancing. How in a state of musical trance, the traditional beads women wear under their skirts break without the woman noticing. How a man's hat would fall off his head, while dancing without him noticing. All kinds of things happen to you doing the dance - but you are not alone! '...be ke iwo nikan ko.' Fela ends this track with a general chorus calling everybody to sing together with the band: Egbe Mi O!
1972	Fela Ransome-Kuti and The Africa 70: **SHAKARA / LADY** (LP Nigeria, EMI, 1972)	**SHAKARA** in Pidgin English, is a loud mouth braggart who can talk but cannot act. Fela as a social critic, condemns in his habitual sarcastic manner Africans who cannot fight for their rights. Instead, such folks boast and pretend (shakara) to be what they are not. In the song **"LADY"** Fela criticised the use of White Western values and standards of feminine beauty in Africa. However to his detractors songs such as this are interpreted as anti-feminist or simply "macho".

YEAR	TITLE	SUMMARY
1973	Fela Ransome-Kuti and The Africa 70: **A. HE MISS ROAD** / **Monday Morning in Lagos.** **B. He No Possible.**	**HE MISS ROAD**: Africans emerging from colonial rule don't have the benefit of job satisfaction. Most Africans find themselves in work places that pay the bills, not jobs that give them personal satisfaction. Most Africans take up professions because it gives them status for example students attend law schools to become lawyers, because their parents feel that such a profession is ideal compared to music. Condemning this approach to professional life, Fela in He Miss Road, compares a person in the wrong profession to a gentleman who instead of taking his clothes to the laundry for washing, gives them to a shoe-maker to be washed or to an accused person who drives counter direction in a one-way traffic, only to collide with a magistrate who probably would judge his case in court - He Miss Road. **Monday Morning** (see above). **He No Possible** is about trust between two adults each giving and expected to get back. Fela sings in this track: "You are you, I am me. We both share things sometimes, you need my help – I give you all the help you need. It's my turn to need your help you start to turn and twist left and right, without giving me any help. Fela says now you want to be my friend – it not possible. A friend does not do things the way you do. Another issue of trust he raised is about two car drivers driving on a street in opposite direction. They both collided in an accident. One driver admits that it was his fault, signing an unofficial account of accident and promising to repair the other driver's car the following day. Unfortunately the guilty driver never kept his promise – he disappeared. But as luck would have it, his victim finds him and won't let him run away the second time. Fela say: " a real man will strive to keep his promise (man no dey do the things the way you do) It is no possible.

YEAR	TITLE	SUMMARY
1973	Fela Ransome-Kuti and The Africa 70: **SWEGBE AND PAKO**	**Swegbe & Pako (see above)**
1974	Fela Ransome-Kuti and The Africa 70: **A. Noise For Vendor Mouth** **B. Mattress** (LP Nigeria)	**NOISE FOR VENDOR MOUTH.** The Nigerian establishment label Kalakuta Republic inhabitants as 'hooligans', 'hemp smokers', etc. Noise For Vendor Mouth is Fela's indifference to all those name-calling, because for him people in Kalakuta are really a bunch of hard working citizens, trying to survive in a society riddled with corruption and mismanagement. He adds that the real hooligans are those in authority who resort to political gangsterism and sometimes military coups, in order to resolve constitutional issues. He considers their criticisms as nothing but the noise made by street vendors to sell their wares. **Mattress** (see column below).

YEAR	TITLE	SUMMARY
1974	Fela Ransome-Kuti and The Africa 70: **CONFUSION** **A. Confusion (Instrumental)** **B. Confusion (Vocal).** (LP Nigeria, EMI)	An American journalist in 1977, writing in the New York Times described Fela as: ".... musically, Fela is James Brown, Bob Dylan and Mick Jagger all rolled into one. Politically, he is Stokely Carmichael, H. Rap Brown and Huey Newton all rolled into one". While Fela cannot be described, as an African Che Guevera with a band of armed freedom fighters, his ideological clarity based on Pan African concept as propagated by Kwame Nkrumah cannot be faulted. In 1962, Kwame Nkrumah (who led the nation of Ghana to independence) championed a group of newly independent African nations in a demand for the formation of a United States of Africa. As a convinced Pan Africanist, Fela describes the non-existence of a United States of Africa and a sole monetary system for the continent as **Confusion**: "Them be three men wey sell for roadside! Them three speak different language! One White man come pay them money! Him pay them for Pounds! Dollars! and French money! Me I say! Na Confusion be that oh!" In his characteristic satirical and sarcastic manner, he compares what transpires as 'government' in Africa, to a popular cross-road junction in Lagos called 'Ojuelegba Confusion Centre'- a cross-road with a permanent traffic jam.

YEAR	TITLE	SUMMARY
1974	Fela Ransome-Kuti and The Africa 70: **ALAGBON CLOSE** A. Alagbon Close B. I No Get Eye for Back (LP Nigeria, Jofabro Nigeria)	The 30th of April 1974, Fela was attending to some guest in his house when suddenly some policemen walked into the living room demanding that every one should subject them to on the spot search, they produced a signed warrant by a high court judge authorising the search and they went through the house searching every room until they were satisfied they had what they came looking for. After the search Fela was arrested along with other persons found with him in the house. The police claimed they recovered some weed suspected to be "Indian Hemp" from the house, and all the arrested persons from the house were taken to the Force Criminal Investigation Department (CID) at Alagbon Close on the Lagos Island. At the CID head-quarters Fela was detained in a cell named KALAKUTA by previous occupants, and he was latter charged to court for possession of prohibited substance suspected to be "Indian Hemp" and "abduction" of juveniles. The last charge, was included because of teenagers arrested along from the house. After his release from police custody, Fela would chronicle police methods of torture in the song titled **ALAGBON CLOSE**. It was also the beginning of Fela using visual art designs, to illustrate his message on album covers. 'Alagbon Close' album cover, was the first of the series from the artist Ghariokwu Lemi - one of the pioneers of visual illustrations in Nigeria. Ghariokwu Lemi, my friend who introduced me to Fela did a great job with Alagbon Close album

YEAR	TITLE	SUMMARY
1974	Fela Ransome-Kuti and The Africa 70: **ALAGBON CLOSE** **A. Alagbon Close** **B. I No Get Eye for Back** (LP Nigeria, Jofabro Nigeria)	cover. Lemi tried to illustrate the message of police brutality in Alagbon CID jails and how Fela came-out of their jail still strong. Painted originally in poster colour, Lemi decrypted a scenario that had a rocky background with Fela's Kalakuta Republic home standing solidly on the left, and an Alagbon CID jailhouse in the last stage of decay with a broken chain. Half part of the chain, still attached to the left wrist of a dancing Fela triumphant over a capsized police patrol boat tipped over by an enormous whale. **I No Get Eye for Back,** is Fela's non-charlatan attitude towards those who nursed bad feelings towards him. Sung in Yoruba with a Pidgin English translation, he sang: "Mo n'rin lo mo ri iwaju mi (I am walking along I can see my front), mo n'rin lo mio rehin mio (I am walking along, I can't see my back), bi o fé sé mi lésé mio ri é o (whether you want to do bad for me I don't see), I don't know that you are behind me, I don't know if you have wicked mind towards me, I don't know that you are holding a knife behind my back, bi o fé semi lésé mio ri é o (whether you want to do me bad, I can't see), oju ti o'fin wo mi yen (those bad looks from you), maa danwo (don't use them) his chorus section replies.

YEAR	TITLE	SUMMARY
1974	Fela Anikulapo-Kuti and The Africa 70: **A. I GO SHOUT PLENTY** **B. Why Black Man Dey Suffer** (LP Nigeria, Decca-Afrodisia)	In the song **I GO SHOUT PLENTY**, Fela sings saying that there many things happening in life that aren't good and his chorus section replies: "Tell am, brother tell am" (say them brother say them). Sung in Pidgin English, this is the translation: "I know what I am seeing, someone wants to cover my face with clothe – I will shout oh! I know where I am going someone wants to tell me it is not the right road – I will shout oh! I know the kind of person I am, someone wants to make me look different – I will shout oh! Because I don't speak big English (Oyinbo) someone wants to say that I am not civilized – I will shout oh! All through the issues raised, the chorus section replies: "we will shout plenty" (we go shout plenty).
1974	**IGBE** B side Gentleman album (LP Nigeria, EMI)	**Igbe** in Yoruba language means shit, Fela in this song conveys moral judgement on those who abuse 'trust'. He says: "Ki lo jade lati inu ré ti o tadi mehin fun oh" (what comes out of your stomach that you stare-away from), the chorus section replies "It is shit". Ki lo té mole tio légun ti o'ntiro (what did you step-on without picks that makes you limp?) Chorus: "It is shit". Eda ti ko lowo fara re (someone without respect for himself – Is shit). Eda ti ko fowo fun ara re (someone that never keeps his words – is shit). A friend that back-bites behind his friend – Is shit (Ore t'on sé ofofo oré re – Igbe ni).
1974	**FEFE NAA EFE** B side Gentleman album (LP Nigeria, EMI)	Fela in **FEFE NAA EFE** is describing certain feminine gests as natural signs of beuty. Sung in Pidgin English, Yoruba, and Ashanti languages: "Fefe naa efe, this is an Ashanti proverb in Ghana that says "it is because of beauty, that is why a woman holds her breast when she runs and not because the breast is going to fall".

YEAR	TITLE	SUMMARY
1974	Fela Ransome-Kuti and The Africa 70: **EXPENSIVE SHIT** A. Expensive Shit. B. Water No Get Enemy (LP Nigeria, Soundwork)	**EXPENSIVE SHIT**: Fela in this song, compares the mentality of the Nigerian Police Force and the army as far below a goat's. For him, a goat would shit and walk away from it, same with a monkey and other 'normal' humans. However when a police man forces an accused to shit, and keeps such shit for laboratory test in-order to convict the latter, such mentality should be looked on as far below any animal level of thinking. Expensive Shit, was Fela's experience in the hands of the Nigerian police force looking for a way to convict him as it was public knowledge that he smoked "marijuana" a 'crime' that used to carry a ten year jail term in Nigeria. In November 1974, the police came to search Fela's house bringing their own exhibits of marijuana in case they did not find any in Kalakuta Republic. When he was confronted with their 'find' Fela managed to swallow the exhibit. Although deprived of their 'sole' evidence, the police arrested Fela keeping him in jail until he gave them specimen of his faeces (shit) for laboratory test. It took three days and a lot of trouble, for the Nigerian police to obtain his faeces! What an EXPENSIVE SHIT!

YEAR	TITLE	SUMMARY
1974	Fela Ransome-Kuti and The Africa 70: A. KALAKUTA SHOW B. Don't Make Ganran Ganran (LP Nigeria, Kalakuta)	**KALAKUTA SHOW**: The release of this album, was Fela's undaunted manner of extracting revenge on the military regime that attacked and brutalised him in 1974. Using the police as cover the second of such attacks in a space of eight months, Kalakuta Show, was an attempt by the Nigerian police to influence the cause of justice. After the first police raid on Kalakuta in April 1974, Fela was charged to court for 'possession of dangerous drugs' and abduction of 'minors'. However, the evidence presented by the prosecution was easily explained away by the defence who claimed that the drugs found in the premises belonged to Junction Clinic a government licensed clinic situated inside Kalakuta Republic and run by Fela's younger brother Dr. Beko Ransome-Kuti. On the 'abduction of minor' charge, all the young girls arrested in Fela's house denied they were under-age nor abducted, and they claimed in court they went to Fela's house of their own accord. With no substantial evidence to convict Fela in this highly publicised trial, the police chose to raid Fela's residence a second time, one week before judgement on the first case with the hope to find evidence this time around. The result, is the narrative of the gruelling and brutal manner the police treated their victims. They lost the case, and Fela appearing in court with scalp-wounds and a broken arm, drew more sympathy from the judge than the contrary. A crowd of more than fifty-thousand Lagos youths, waiting outside the court hause carried Fela from the Apapa area of Lagos, to Kalakuta Republic - a distance of about six kilometres. During this jubilation, traffic was at a stand-still for several hours in the central part of Lagos mainland.

YEAR	TITLE	SUMMARY
1974	**Fela Ransome-Kuti & Africa 70:** **A. WHY BLACK MAN DEY SUFFER.** **B. IKOYI MENTALITY VERSUS MUSHIN MENTALITY.** (LP Nigeria, Decca-Afrodisia).	There have been claims, that Africans sold themselves to slavery by historians who want to justify the holocaust committed against African people during slavery. But in **WHY BLACK MAN DEY SUFFER,** Fela takes on the role of the griot or musician as the custodian of history passing it from generation to generation. In the song he asks: "Why is the Blackman suffering today? Why doesn't the Blackman have money today? Why hasn't the Blackman gone to the moon today? This is the reason why he answers, Africans have been quietly living in their land minding their business. Some people came from far-away land, fought the Africans and took their land, took the people and spoilt the African land. Since then the African trouble started, her riches were taken away to foreign lands in return for colonies. Banned the practices of divers African cultures and imposed on her people, foreign cultures that are not understandable to the African. As a result, Africans don't know themselves and their history, we don't even know our ancestral heritage he underlines. This ignourance leads to Africans, fighting eachother everyday. We are never together at all, and that is why Blackman is suffering today" Fela concludes: "We have to think of the future (times to come), we have to think of the future of our children to come. We have to be together and unite.

YEAR	TITLE	SUMMARY
1974	**Fela Ransome-Kuti & Africa 70:** A. WHY BLACK MAN DEY SUFFER. B. IKOYI MENTALITY VERSUS MUSHIN MENTALITY. (LP Nigeria, Decca-Afrodisia).	The implantation of foreign cultures and the alienation, of African culture and traditions in Africa is the issue Fela is addressing in **IKOYI MENTALITY VERSUS MUSHIN MENTALITY.** (Ikoyi is the residential area of the rich, while Mushin is the core of the Lagos ghetto). Sung in Pidgin Enlish, this is a translation: "Let us hear how people are different in this our Lagos town. Some people are in Ikoyi and some people are in Mushin. Ikoyi man has travelled all over the world, he brought us a civilization we don't understand. Mushin man has never travelled anywhere at all, always stayed at home and understands his African language and culture. Ikoyi man when hungry will say give me my breakfast, lunch, and dinner with my fork and knife. When a Mushing man is hungry he does not call eating names like his Ikoyi opposite, he simply ask for his food and eats it with whatever he can find like his fingers for example. While talking, Ikoyi man will talk in what Fela call "big-big" English, the man would like to speak like an Oyinbo (English) man, while his Mushin opposite would talk naturally in Pidgin (broken) English". Fela concludes that the Ikoyi way of life and mentality is alien to African culture while the Mushin way is what he calls the "peoples".

YEAR	TITLE	SUMMARY
1975	Fela Ransome-Kuti and The Africa 70: **GENTLEMAN** A. Gentleman. B. Fefe Naa Efe / Igbe (Na Shit). (LP Nigeria, EMI)	Convinced of the authenticity of the African way of life Fela in the song **GENTLEMAN**, explained that the concept of Pan Africanism is about identity - the idea of Africans and Africans in the Diaspora, to be proud and seen as African personalities. The practice where Africans dress in western suits and ties, in a temperature more than 30 degrees hot is considered as stupid. "Gentleman" in the street terms, is the equivalent of an Uncle Tom or an African who prefers western mannerisms and values to original African traditional ways of life. A gentleman is also a black person, who turns the other cheek in a passive protest against oppression. By the time Fela recorded Gentleman, he had stopped playing the trumpet because according to him, he couldn't keep-up with the rigourous demands of the instrument. Listening to him play the alto saxophone in this track, one can hear Fela attack the alto saxophone like a trumpet player searching for high notes.

YEAR	TITLE	SUMMARY
1975	Fela Ransome-Kuti and The Africa 70: **ROFOROFO FIGHT** (LP Nigeria, Jofabro)	**Roforofo Fight** is about human intolerance towards each other, issues that could be resolved amicably usually end-up in fist-fights and sometimes such fights finish bloody or muddy. Dramatising the scenario that ensues before a fight particularly in a muddy place, Fela says it usually starts with words like: "You are crazy! I am not crazy! Get away, who are you? These are two people who could quietly resolve their differences, screaming and yelling at each other. Unfortunately for both of them, the area where the argument is taking place is full of mud, and within seconds their argument and exchange, draws the attention of passers-bye that would turn into a crowd. 'If you are among the crowd watching, and your friend is among the two yapping please tell him not to fight oh! Fela adviced. However because of human egos, instead of heeding the advice and walk away quietly both will feel disrespected and shamed and to settle scores, the two of them chose physical combat in the mud. A muddy fight follows and at the end of the fight, on-lookers couldn't differentiate the one from the other both of them looking like muddy twins. They won't get any sympathy from the people looking too because, '...you don tell am before make him no fight, roforofo dey for there!' Meaning you advised them not to fight because of all the mud around.

YEAR	TITLE	SUMMARY
1975	Fela Ransome-Kuti and The Africa 70: **EQUALIZATION OF TROUSER AND PANT** (LP Nigeria Opposite People)	The notion that all men are born equal is the issue Fela addressed in **EQUALIZATION OF TROUSER AND PANT.** To underline this notion, he compares the trouser to the underpant, saying there is not one of the two that is more important to the human than the other. Sung in Pidgin English this is a translation: "This is trouser, this is pant. Trouser has longer legs than the underpant anytime, trouser has decorations anytime like: button, like zip, like buckle and like some stupid trouser used to, it will have belt holes at it's head. In the case of the underpant it is smaller than trouser anytime, does not have decorations anytime: like button, like zip, like buckle, and as it is ten times smaller than trouser it will have rope by force. However as small as the underpant is, you can't look at it with disdain, as small as the pant is you cannot in anger take it off the way you like, you cannot out of anger take it off your body from your head, and neither can you take it off from the side. The pant has to travel right down you legs like the trouser. Mr. VIP that thinks he is more important than the poor man, I want Mr. VIP to hear me proper now! As small as the pant is, if you take off your trouser without a pant under: iho ho gédégbé (total nakedness) everything under your pant will be revealed in a total nakedness.

YEAR	TITLE	SUMMARY
1975	**Fela Anikulapo-Kuti & Africa 70:** **WATER NO GET ENEMY** A. Expensive Shit. B. Water No Get Enemy. (LP Nigeria, Sound Workshop)	Sung in Yoruba with a Pidgin English translation, Fela declares that **WATER NO GET ENEMY** (meaning water has no enemy). He sings: "Ti o ba fé lo wé omi loma lo (if you want to wash, you have to use water). Ti o ba fé sée obé, omi loma lo (if you want to cook soup, you have to use water). Ti ori ba n'gbona o, omi léro re (if your head is hot, it is water that can cool it down). Ti omo ba n'dagba, omi loma lo (if your child grows-up, the child will need water). Even if water kills your child, you will always need water (ti omi ba pa omo re o, omi na loma lo). Ko si ohun ti o lé sé ki oma lomi o (there is nothing you can do without using water) because water has no enemy. This is a song underlining the importance of one of the four elements indispensable to the existence of man: Water, earth, wind and fire.
1976	**YELLOW FEVER** (LP Nigeria, Decca-Afridisia)	The practice where Black people use all kinds of chemical products to lighten their skin in order to appear close to the White colour is called **YELLOW FEVER**. Describing such psychological and mental-block as a sickness or malady, Fela compares the lack of pride in the black identity (their colour of skin) as sickness like: jaundice, malaria, or influenza. However the sickness mentioned above are natural maladies that you get in natural situations. But the case of the malady called Yellow Fever by Fela, it is the victim that goes looking for the sickness by buying those chemical products.

YEAR	TITLE	SUMMARY
1976	Fela Anikulapo-Kuti and The Africa 70: **OPPOSITE PEOPLE** (LP Nigeria, Decca Afrodisia)	In every society or gathering of people there is always one person who as a laud mouth braggart, tries to disrupt such assembly for personal reason or just to be noticed - such person Fela calls: **OPPOSITE PEOPLE.** Sung in his habitual Pidgin English here is a translation: "they will show, they will show themselves clear clear they will show. Everyone is dancing for enjoyment, everyone is talking for communication, everyone is listening for ideology, everyone is thinking for their progress. But instead of dancing like everyone, opposite people will push, everyone is talking he will shout, everyone is listening opposite people will sleep, everyone is thinking he will drink. Called to question the loud mouth braggart starts to show off and cause all sorts of confusion – others will turn and say: look at him Opposite People.
1976	Fela Anikulapo-Kuti and The Africa 70: **JOHNNY JUST DROP (JJD** (LP Nigeria, Decca Afrodisia))	**Johnny Just Drop** is talking about Africans who travel abroad only to return home with new values and mannerisms. Since the advent of colonialism in Africa, the education system left Black people with an inferior perception of their culture. Those who are Western educated, are in the habit of repeating untruths about African traditions and heritage. This is because the discipline required to think and act big, has not yet become a part of Africa's present day academic and intellectual traditions. For example those trained in the use of English, Spanish, German, French or Portuguese languages, will argue forcefully that those are international languages in which alone science and technology can be intelligently studied. Fela in this song asks that if this is true, one wonders how the ancient Black Egyptians built the pyramids or how the guild of craftsmen in Benin and other parts of the continent created the works of arts produced over many centuries past. In JJD, Fela is reminding Africans travelling abroad in search of greener pastures to be proud of their original cultural values - those inherent values the JJD 'educated' elite have been brainwashed to despise.

YEAR	TITLE	SUMMARY
1976	Fela Anikulapo-Kuti and The Africa 70: **WHO NO KNOW GO KNOW** (LP Nigeria, Coconut)	Fela's message in **Who No Know Go Know** is in line with many Pan Africanist, who call for African Unity as the only solution to the continents problems. Based on the conviction that "Globalization" strengthens those that are already strong, and weakens those that are indifferent to the governance of the world, a united Pan African oriented Africa is the solution. This is a clarion call to all Africans and the African Diaspora, to heed the calls of all the leaders of the African struggle for emancipation. In this song Fela is saying that for many years Kwame Nkrumah was shouting for togetherness (Unity), we let him die without heeding his African Unity call. Sekou Toure shouted we didn't listen, even Idi Amin - as head of the Organisation Of African Unity (OAU), shouted and we did not listen. Fela concludes by saying: "who does not know today, will come to realise one day that only the blackman can fight for blackman and his salvation"

YEAR	TITLE	SUMMARY
1976	Fela Anikulapo-Kuti and The Africa 70: **MONKEY BANANA**	**MONKEY BANANA** is Fela's advice to those who want to work for the status quo, without social security, health insurance, job security, etc., to think twice before slaving for nothing. In his habitual manner of putting-down the Nigerian elite, he starts this song with the popular English expression: "A fool at forty is a fool forever" - implying that life begins for a man at the age of forty. Fela says he will not advice his brother to wait until forty, before the man realises he has been making a fool of his life. Twenty, for him is the limit to make a fool of one's life. After that age, a man is supposed to know how to take his destiny in his hands. He sings: 'book sense different from belly sense': meaning the reality of hunger, is not always the way the elites like to project it. How can the majority of the people in Nigeria still live below poverty line, despite the much publicised oil-boom? The Nigerian 'elites' who profit from the oil-boom, encourage the younger generation to be optimistic hoping the living standards of the average conscientious worker will improve one day. Fela advises the contrary, saying corruption and mismanagement of the Nigerian economy is responsible for the poor state of the social order. Calling on the worker to stop slaving for nothing, he compares the worker to a monkey that can only be enticed to dance if you offer it the banana. He concludes by saying: 'before I jump like monkey, give me banana' (before slaving for nothing, ask to be better paid).

YEAR	TITLE	SUMMARY
1976	Fela Anikulapo-Kuti and The Africa 70: **UNNECESSARY BEGGING** (LP Nigeria, Decca Afrodisia)	Fela says, **"UNNECESSARY BEGGING"** as an expression in the 'area' (ghetto) unspoken rules is not done and it is not necessary. In the ghetto if you give your word, people believe you for such words until you do otherwise. African ghetto thoughts and deeds, are the traditional way of life of the people. They are based on age-long belief that "words are like eggs, when they drop they cannot be taken back - and it is not necessary to take such words back". However today sings Fela, some of us in the spirit of trust believe in our governments. We go into agreement with them to provide us (the people) good houses, good roads, good health services in place, keep the economy buoyant, etc. What do the people get? No government, corruption at the highest level, etc. With all these, there are still some academics who preach patience, 'Intellectuals' and 'leaders of thought' who try to justify the mismanagement of African lives by those in government as 'problems of young democracies'. Fela says this is Unnecessary Begging. He calls on those in power, to beware of the day when the people will revolt against this situation. It will be a day to render accounts, there will be no room for any Unnecessary Begging.
1976	Fela Anikulapo-Kuti and The Africa 70: **MR. FOLLOW - FOLLOW**	Africans who look for ideas outside the African continent to solve her problem are those Fela calls MR. FOLLOW–FOLLOW. He sings that there is nothing wrong in following models found in books, but it is better to follow with some sense. Describing who Mr. Follow–Follow is: "Some follow with their eyes closed, those that follow with their mouths closed instead of speaking-out, some follow closing their ears, others follow closing their senses". Fela advises: "If you follow those books, you have to open your eyes, mouth, ears, and sense. That is when you won't fall, but if you follow blindly, you will fall into a cupboard where there is darkness, cockroach, and termite. My brother don't follow those books, read them and use your sense" he advices.

YEAR	TITLE	SUMMARY
1976	Fela Anikulapo-Kuti and The Africa 70: **UPSIDE DOWN.**	Sandra Smith, the woman who stood by Fela and also brought him in contact with African oriented books and knowledge about the Black Panther party, during his transformation years in the United States, came back to visit a highly popular and successful Fela in Nigeria in 1976. **Upside Down** was written by Fela to portray a worldly travelled African, who searches in the dictionary and finds the definition of upside down - a perfect description of the African situation. 'I have travelled widely all over the world like any professor' Fela made Sandra sing: "The thing I have seen I will like to talk about upside-up and downside-down, in overseas where I have been, everything is organise, their system is organise, they have their own names, etc. But back home in Africa where I expect to see our culture and tradition, everything is disorganized (head for down, yansh for up) meaning back home everything is totally Upside Down.
1976	Fela Anikulapo-Kuti and The Africa 70: **GO SLOW.**	**GO SLOW** is about the crawling bumper-to-bumper Lagos traffic-jam, that symbolises the confusion that reigns in Nigeria. Fela compares the traffic situation with a person in jail he says: "you have to be a man in life to support and survive while driving in Lagos". According to him survival is a natural instinct in any man, but when caught in Lagos traffic, all your aspirations, determination, and confidence to survive as a man will wither away. You feel suddenly incapacitated like a man in jail or how would you feel, driving on a Lagos road and suddenly in your front there is a lorry, to your left a taxi cab, all these vehicles in a standstill. Also to your right a tipper-truck, and behind you a'molues' passenger bus, to add to all these above you a helicopter flying to complete the picture of you imprisoned on the Lagos highway.

YEAR	TITLE	SUMMARY
1976	Fela Anikulapo-Kuti and The Africa 70: **QUESTION JAM ANSWER**	**QUESTION JAM ANSWER** sung in Pidgin English says: "When question drops in the mouth, answer will run after! When question jams answer on the road? Another thing will happen. Fela in this piece is singing about human nature, he says when people pose questions they definitely get answered back. The answer however, could result into something we never expect. Questions such as: "Why did you step on my leg? Didn't you see my leg on the ground?" Could be seen as obstinate questions that need answers equally obstinate. In the same obstinate manner, answer replies: "Why Did you put your leg in my way? Didn't you see me coming?"A song addressed to those who like to pose questions to always bear in mind, that they may not get the answers they expect to their questions.
1976	Fela Anikulapo-Kuti and The Africa 70: **TROUBLE SLEEP YANGA WAKE AM**	**TROUBLE SLEEP YANGA WAKE AM** an English translation literally means 'toying with a loaded gun' or 'playing with fire'. It is a song talking about the limit to human endurance. Mr. Trouble is lying quietly and Mr. Provocation (Yanga) goes to play around him, what else could he be looking for except palaver (trouble). A good example of such trouble-shooting is that of a man, who has just got out of prison and goes about desperately looking for work, in order to avoid what led him to jail. While at it, a police man stops and charges the man for wandering Fela asks, what could the police man be looking for but trouble? It is like when a cat is asleep, and a rat goes to bite its tail or a tenant who has just lost his job, sitting quietly thinking of where his next meal will come from, his landlord comes knocking demanding his rent. Of cause the landlord will get trouble, bigger than the rent he came to collect. Trouble Sleep Yanga Wake Am, simply means there is a limit to any human endurance.

YEAR	TITLE	SUMMARY
1976	Fela Anikulapo-Kuti and The Africa 70: **ZOMBIE** A. Zombie. B. Mr Follow Follow (LP Nigeria, Coconut)	Fela in his life time was never 'a good bed-fellow' of the military institution, and as a political activist he believed the army should operate under the mandate of a civil government. If national interest compels the armed forces to intervene in government, the army is obliged to hand over power to a new civil government elected by the people and enjoying their mandate. To do otherwise is to usurp power particularly, since a soldier's duty is not to seek a political mandate. For emphasis in the song, he narrates the military in motion, comparing their orientation to the **ZOMBIE** without minds of their own. Fela paid a big price for this bold condemnation of the military institution. One thousand members of the Nigerian army, attacked and burnt down his house after the release of the record. The tribunal set up to investigate the cause of the attack as a result of the public out-cry against the army, heard as part of the evidence presented by the Nigerian army an example of the Zombie album cover with the military uniform and boots displayed boldly. The army justification of the attack, was that Fela treated the military institution with levity.

YEAR	TITLE	SUMMARY
1977	Fela Anikulapo-Kuti and The Africa 70: **STALEMATE** A. Stalemate B. African Message (Don't Worry About My Mouth-O). (LP Nigeria, Decca Afrodisia)	**STALEMATE**: While a few VIP class live in luxury, majority of Africans live in abject poverty. Most of the people drown their frustrations in 'ogogoro' (a locally brewed gin) and other brands of alcohol. Those who don't spend their scarce kobo (little money) on alcohol, squander it gambling (football pools, lotto and lotteries). Survival has become imperative for most Africans, the deadly weariness of rural life where basic social services are non-existent, and the impossibility of making money in the country side which drives most young and able bodied Africans into city centres and alcohol. In this song STALEMATE, Fela underlines the plight of the black man with the example of two young men who have managed to buy a bottle of beer between them, and while enjoying their hard buy a young lady comes flirting at the same time demanding a bottle of beer from the young men. Both men took a long look at the woman their interest roused, but their economic reality could not meet her demand, what a Stalemate! In **AFRICAN MESSAGE (DON'T WORRY ABOUT MY MOUTH)**, Fela sings again about putting into value African things: "Don't worry about my mouth as I use chewing stick to clean my mouth every morning. You see I know what I am talking about, as an African man that is how it should be. No to all those tooth paste, I prefer those chewing sticks that my fore-fathers taught me in Africa to clean my teeth with. Tooth pastes makes my mouth un-clean, while chewing sticks makes my teeth very strong". "Don't worry about my yansh (back-side), I use water to clean it after using the toilet. I found-out that if I use toilet paper, my yansh (back-side) still smells". "Don't worry about my way of dressing, because Africans have been dressing in their big and colourful clothes before the Whiteman changed all that on the African continent. For proof, go and read the book, Blackman of the Nile by Yosef ben-Jochannan and many other books saying the same thing.

YEAR	TITLE	SUMMARY
1977	Fela Anikulapo-Kuti and The Africa 70: **FEAR NOT FOR MAN** A. Fear Not for Man B. Palm-Wine Sound (LP Nigeria, Decca Afrodisia)	**FEAR NOT FOR MAN:** After the attack and burning down of Kalakuta Republic by Nigerian soldiers in 1977, plus the subsequent pressure put on promoters and venues by the military authority to prevent Fela from performing live in public, he was advised by some of his friends like in the song No Agreement, to leave Nigeria on a self imposed exile or stop his criticisms of the military. Fela was urged by friends to move to Europe or the United States particularly since his music was becoming very popular in those continents. Fela again replied: "Dr. Kwame Nkrumah, the father of Pan Africanism says to Black people all over the world 'the secret of life is to have no fear' we all have to understand that!" Describing himself as a man and not a goat that runs away in fear, Fela emphasises in this song his determination to stay in Nigeria and make a strong stand against all forms of military dictatorship. **Palm-Wine Sound** is named after the traditional drink with the same name, sold in palm-wine bars mostly in the south of Nigeria.
1978	Fela Anikulapo-Kuti and The Africa 70: **OBSERVATION NO CRIME** (Recorded live at the Berlin Jazz Festival 1978)	Recorded live at the November 1978 Berlin Jazz Festival, Fela is singing about those who would like to stop him from giving his opinion on issues that involve the individual life. 'Na oil I dey carry, sand-sand man no come spoil my own! (Meaning he is carrying a barrel of oil on his head and he does not want any sand-carrying man around him that would try and make him tripple-over). Fela in **OBSERVATION NO CRIME,** is literally comparing the delicate nature of individual life to a delicate barrel of oil, when oil falls into a heap of sand it is difficult to recover the oil from the sand. Fela says he is given a mouth to say things he feels like saying, same thing for his eyes which are for him to see with. Turning to the government in Nigeria, who has always tried to silence him, he concludes by saying **'Observation Is No Crime'**.

YEAR	TITLE	SUMMARY
1977	Fela Anikulapo-Kuti and The Africa 70: **A. No Agreement** **B. Dog Eat Dog** (LP Nigeria, Decca Afrodisia)	After the burning down of Kalakuta Republic 'friends' and childhood acquaintances of Fela tried to talk him out of confronting the Nigerian military authorities, stressing that "government can do no wrong" or "government is too powerful to be confronted" etc. In a respond to their defeatist attitude, Fela in the song **NO AGREEMENT** stated clearly that he was in the struggle because he couldn't sit and watch fellow Africans going hungry or living homeless without talking against it. Particularly convinced that according to the estimation of Africa wealth, every Black man should be a millionaire - why is the black man poor? Using the legendary Kuti family contributions to the evolution of modern-day Nigeria as further justification of his resolve not to compromise, Fela sang: "my grand-papa talk, my grand-mama talk, my papa talk, my mama talk, those wey no talk them see. I no go gree make my brother hungry make I no talk! No agreement today! No agreement tomorrow! (Meaning: "my grand-father spoke, my grand-mother talked, my father talked, my mother spoke, those that didn't speak-out could see. I won't agree for my African brothers and sisters to go hungry without speaking out. No Compromise today!No Compromise tomorrow!

YEAR	TITLE	SUMMARY
1978	Fela Anikulapo-Kuti and The Africa 70: **SUFFERING AND SMILLING** SIDE A & B (LP Nigeria, Coconut)	Confrontation with police and military was not the sole combat Fela had to face in his active militancy as this song explains. Christianity and Islam, playing on the spiritual nature of the African traditional society, have been the major instruments used to exploit and colonise African people. In **SUFFERING & SMILING** Fela highlights the ambiguity of the Christian and Muslim doctrine of suffering in this world, in exchange for a 'glorious' place in 'heaven'. Pointing to the opulence and rich life of the Pope and his Episcopal followers as examples of people not suffering in this world and waiting to go to heaven. Fela questions why Africans would believe in a Jesus, whose blue eyes and blond hair disqualify him as a Black man's God-Head, same with Mohammed and his Arab looks. With a song like Suffering and Smiling, Fela was able to respond to the question "Were African ancestors ruling themselves before the White man and the Arabs came?"

YEAR	TITLE	SUMMARY
1978	Fela Anikulapo-Kuti and The Africa 70: **UNKNOWN SOLDIER** **A. Unknown Soldier (Instrumental)** **B. Unknown Soldier (Vocal)** (LP Nigeria, Phonodisk Skylark)	To the unsuspecting mind this song's title represents a homage to military 'heroes', in keeping with world-wide trend of erecting statues in memory of soldiers who lost their lives in wars. While Fela in his lifetime cannot be described as 'a good bed-fellow' of military orientation and approach in a civil society, his song **UNKNOWN SOLDIER** has nothing to do with homage to the memories of fallen soldiers. Rather, Fela wrote the song as a result of a controversy that 'rocked' the military regime of General Obasanjo in February 1977. One week after the end of FESTAC on 18th February, 1977, about one thousand armed members of the Nigerian army invaded Fela's Kalakuta Republic rapping the women, beating and arresting everyone within sight and finally burning down the house. Fela's 77 year old mother was thrown down from the first floor balcony of the house, the shock and trauma she suffered from this attack kept her in the hospital until her death a year after. Fela's pets, a family of four German Shepherds named Wokolo (meaning 'go find penis), Jokotobo (sit next to pussy), Gbangba lobo (widely open pussy) and Ido n'dun (clitoris is sweet) were burnt in the inferno that engulfed the house. A French speaking snake-charmer who wanted to discus the possibility of presenting his acts with Fela at the Shrine was trapped in the house along with everyone, he also was beaten and lost a finger and his snakes in the inferno. Fela was arrested and paraded naked throught the street to the near-bye Abaty Military barrack, where all the arrested persons were taken to.

YEAR	TITLE	SUMMARY
	Fela Anikulapo-Kuti and The Africa 70: UNKNOWN SOLDIER A. Unknown Soldier (Instrumental) B. Unknown Soldier (Vocal) (LP Nigeria, Phonodisk Skylark)	With Fela in their hands and the house on fire, the army soldiers moved into Kalakuta area getting drunk from the many abandoned illegal bars that dotted the area. Looting and stuffing their pockets, with all the abandoned marijuana and everything of value. The military regime was shaken by the outpour of public sympathy for Fela and his clan, soldiers tried to stop newspapers from carrying the news of the attack and they impounded printed copies of both Punch and Daily Sketch publications that carried news of the attack. Government owned Daily Times, which did not print any news of the attack hastily came out with a government induced explanation that "the soldiers had gone to Kalakuta to make a legitimate arrest". Contrary to what the Obasanjo regime (1976 -1979) would have people believe there is no doubt that Fela's refusal to participate in the FESTAC sham, the sea of black power salutes that surrounded him wherever he went in Nigeria, his uncompromising bold lyrics condemning government's corruption and his financing and publishing of YAP NEWS were the true reasons behind the Nigerian army attack. Fela in this song, tries to capture the event and the justification by the tribunal that the house was burnt by an unknown soldier.

YEAR	TITLE	SUMMARY
1978	Fela Anikulapo-Kuti and Africa 70: **VAGABONS IN POWER (V.I.P.)** **A. V.I.P. (Instrumental)** **B. V.I.P. (Vocal)** (LP Nigeria, Jofabro/ Kalakuta)	The abbreviation **V.I.P.** which means Very Important Personality in modern day society, is reserved for privileged persons - people who when they drive around in cities are accorded privileges and priority of passage because of their position of power. In his view of an egalitarian society, Fela draws a parallel with the contributions of all individuals in any society as deserving the same privilege. The truck pussher too should be accorded privilege like those in power. For him, people who enjoy privilege while others are barely surviving the poverty line should be seen as **VAGABONDS IN POWER**.

YEAR	TITLE	SUMMARY
1978	Fela Anikulapo-Kuti and Africa 70: PANSA PANSA (Recorded live at the 1978 Berlin Jazz Festival)	**PANSA PANSA**, was Fela's most defiant statement to the Nigerian military rulers of his determination to champion the cause of Pan Africanism. Mid 1976 when Fela started to play this track live, musically he was at his Zenith - extremely popular in Africa. Politically, his message was beginning to get across. Youths in Nigeria were beginning to identify with the Fela ideals and registering en-mass at the Africa Shrine head-quarters of the new grass-roots movement Fela had inaugurated and called Young African Pioneers (YAP). Economically, it was the peak of the oil-boom. Nigeria never had it better, careering along on at least two million barrels of sulphur-low oil, pumped daily and sold on the world market. Fela had just signed a twelve album a year deal with DECCA records. The record industry was booming - people were buying records. At government level it was corruption galore including those in the highest echelon of government. Denunciations and criticisms from Fela had brought him in open confrontation with the military rulers on previous occasions, some of which he had sang into songs: Alagbon Close! No Bread! Monkey Banana! Zombie! Go Slow! Kalakuta Show! The release of all these songs angered the military establishment in Nigeria, and most times prompted attacks on Fela and Kalakuta republic residents. For Fela however, despite all the repression he sang: 'as long as Africa is suffering! No freedom! No justice! No happiness! They will hear PANSA PANSA' (meaning they will hear more and more).

YEAR	TITLE	SUMMARY
1979	Fela Anikulapo-Kuti and The Africa 70	Fela in the song **ITT (INTERNATIONAL THIEF THIEF)**, condemns the diabolical role of multi-national corporations and their local collaborators in the politics of African states, calling them International thieves that should be fought with all strength and vigour. Their method is standard practice world-wide they employ a local citizen, who in turn warms his way up the ladders of power by bribing and ass-licking. Stressing the connection of such conglomerates with the secret police of their 'parent' state, like ITT (International Telegraph & Telecommunication) rumoured to be the electronic arm of the American Central Intelligence Agency (CIA). Departing from his habitual satirical reference to individuals in power, Fela in ITT named the local collaborators of such multy nationals: "....like Obasanjo and Abiola! International Thief Thief!
1979	Fela Anikulapo-Kuti and The Africa 70: **AUTHORITY STEALING** A. **Authority Stealing (Instrumental).** B. **Authority Stealing (Vocal)** (LP Nigeria, Kalakuta)	Violence a daily reality among most African ghetto dwellers, has its roots in the mismanagement of the economy of most African states. People have been lynched in African urban centres for stealing a chicken and despite the animal instincts in man, Fela sings in **AUTHORITY STEALING:** that no man is born criminal - society makes him so, no man (human that is), would enjoy sticking a gun in another man's head without reason or circumstances which force him to do so in order to survive. However, the masses watch as their leaders plunders and steal their respective national treasuries dry. 'Leaders' get away with crimes of mismanagement and corruption, while highway robbers forced by the hardships of society are subjected to a public execution for their crimes. In his sarcastic manners, Fela draws a parallel between robbery with the pen and robbery with a gun - he says Authority Stealing is bigger a crime than armed robbery.

YEAR	TITLE	SUMMARY
1980	FelaAnikulapo-Kuti and The Africa 70 / Roy Ayers: **MUSIC OF MANY COLORS** A. Africa - Center of the World. B. 2000 Blacks Got To Be Free. (LP Nigeria, Phonodisk)	Fela during his life time and in death touched many people, he collaborated with many artists musically and since his passing more and more musicians have been doing re-mixes and samplings of his musical legacy afrobeat. **MUSIC OF MANY COLOURS** is a result of one of such collaborations in Fela's life time. Co-produced with the African American funky-jazz man Roy Ayers in 1979, the album is rich musically and with a strong political message. **AFRICA CENTRE OF THE WORLD** is a song about Africa, the cradle of today's civilisation. Recorded twenty-one years after he left the Nigerian shores to study music in London Trinity College Of Music, according to Fela in this song the ignorance of the Western world at this time was still very much evident. English men, who were not aware of the ape-like origin of man, used to come-over to him to find-out if he got a tail like apes and monkeys. For him, it is only ignorance that could be the reason for such dumb question. He points to Africa's place, at the centre of the world map as not by accident, rather because we were the first people on earth. Territorial claims an old animal trait has always been to the advantage of the strongest in a contest. If black people live and habit in one of the most strategic and wealthiest part of the world, it must be because of Africa being the origin of the human race. If Africans occupy the best area in the world, this is not by accident. Africans must have been the strongest people to occupy the centre of the world. Fela calls on black people to see the advantage of living on the continent as strategic. **2000 Blacks:** Is Roy Ayers message to black people in Africa and the Diaspora to unite before year 2000.

YEAR	TITLE	SUMMARY
1980	Fela Anikulapo-Kuti and The Africa 70: **COFFIN FOR HEAD OF STATE** A. Coffin for Head of State (Instrumental) B. Coffin for Head of State (Vocal) (LP Nigeria, Kalakuta)	On February 18, 1977 one thousand armed members of the Nigerian army attacked, brutalised, raped, and burnt down Fela's commune Kalakuta Republic as earlier explained in the column Unknown Soldier. As a result of the public out-cry against this barbaric attack, a Federal government tribunal was set up by the Nigerian military regime to investigate the "cause" of the attack. The tribunal, headed by a Nigerian high court judge - Justice Agwu Anya, in it's final report, condemned the use of the name Kalakuta Republic by Fela to describe his domain, as a defiance of the Nigerian constitution - an indication of 'a state within a state'. The tribunal recommended the ban on the use of the name "Republic" and also the proscription of the Young African Pioneers (YAP) - a movement, created by Fela in 1976 with the aim of spreading economic, cultural and political awareness among black people in Africa and the Diaspora. As a sign of protest, Fela and members of the Young African Pioneers placed a coffin (not his mother's), on the balcony of the ruins of Kalakuta Republic with a banner stating: **This Is The Spot Where Justice Was Murdered!**

YEAR	TITLE	SUMMARY
1980	Fela Anikulapo-Kuti and The Africa 70: **COFFIN FOR HEAD OF STATE** A. **Coffin for Head of State (Instrumental)** B. **Coffin for Head of State (Vocal)** (LP Nigeria, Kalakuta)	For a period of one year, people walking or driving past the ruins saw this symbolic protest as a defiance of the military regime. In November 1978, Fela and sixty-nine members of his organisation left Nigeria to perform at the Berlin Jazz Festival in then West Germany. The military regime seized the opportunity of his absence from the country to evict, and demolish the Kalakuta commune, including the ruins of the burnt-down house causing a displacement of more than five thousand people. On his return back to Nigeria, Fela accompanied by members of his organisation and the Young African Pioneers, visited the site of the dispersed Kalakuta commune. They found the coffin placed on the debris of the demolished buildings and asked by members of the press present what he intended to do with the coffin? Fela replied: "...on or before 1st October 1979, we will deposit this coffin at the state house Doddan Barracks, as a parting gift to the Obasanjo regime who we hold responsible for this barbaric act". Keeping his promise on September 30th, 1979 accompanied by members of his organisation, the Young African pioneers, and the Movement of The People, a political party founded by Fela to contest the trumped-up election to civil rule that will replace the out-going military regime, they deposited the coffin despite security put in place all over the route to prevent them from getting to the seat of power. **Coffin For Head Of State** was Fela's parting gift to a corrupt and dictatorial regime.

YEAR	TITLE	SUMMARY
1981	Fela Anikulapo-Kuti and The Egypt 80: **SORROWS TEARS AND BLOOD (STB)** **A. Sorrow, Tears and Blood.** **B. Colonial Mentality.**	Fear, one factor that has kept black people in bondage for so long is addressed in the song. People using family bonds and personal ambitions, as justification of their non involvement in the struggle. Fela in **STB**, states that individual fears will not make the fight for progress, freedom, happiness and injustice disappear. For as long as there is fear, police and army brutality will always be a part of our daily lives leaving in its wake **SORROW TEARS AND BLOOD (STB)**. **Colo-Mentality,** Fela wrote in 1975 shortly after he dropped the "Ransome" from his family name and replaced it with "Anikulapo". The song is particularly critical of the African elites who prefer Western values and mannerisms to the African traditional way of life. As inheritors of the colonial administration left behind after independence, they propagate a culture that makes a great part of the African population develop negative images of their traditional values. Teaching Africans to consider themselves as inferior to other race and to develop a mannerism devoid of pride in their traditional heritage.

YEAR	TITLE	SUMMARY
1981	Fela Anikulapo-Kuti and The Egypt 80: **ORIGINAL SUFFERHEAD** **A.** Original Sufferhead **B.** Power Show (1. LP Nigeria, Lagos International. 2. LP UK, Arista)	Fela's message in **ORIGINAL SUFFERHEAD** is that, Africa possesses two-thirds of the world's natural resources and he asks why a people with such riches would sit back and watch her population wither away in poverty. He affirms that no prayers can change the mess that is Nigeria and indeed Africa: "Before we all are to Jefahead (enjoy) oh! We must be ready to fight for am now!" Everywhere in the world where they have the basic necessities of life: water, light, food and roof over their heads, it is the result of the people fighting for these basic necessities of life. If they have water, light, food and house in France for example today, it is because the French people in 1789 made a REVOLUTION. Since then, they organized themselves into workers unions and all sorts of unions and movements to keep pressure on their successive governments' in-order not to forget why those before them organized to make a revolution. We all know very well that revolution is not knitting embroideries, it's not having dinner parties, or praying to Allah and Jesus Christ. Fela affirms, that Africans should stop putting their hopes in prayers and individuals if they want to enjoy the basic things of life. Like they say in French: "union makes a force" remember: "before we all are to Jefahead (enjoy) oh! We must be ready to fight for it now!" Original Suffer Head is calling on African people to rise and fight the malady that is keeping them down poverty-lane. The use or misuse of power and privilege in Africa, is what Fela questions in the song **POWER SHOW**, people because of their privilege positions or power, tend to use such powers like tin-gods.

YEAR	TITLE	SUMMARY
	Fela Anikulapo-Kuti and The Egypt 80: **ORIGINAL SUFFERHEAD** **A.** **Original Sufferhead** **B. Power Show** (1. LP Nigeria, Lagos International. 2. LP UK, Arista)	This is a translation: I open my eyes I see for my land, (Na wrong show o - it is a wrong show) Chorus) Motor car owner, he will use his car to push the labourer down on the road. Then he starts to yap: Foolish labourer! Nonentity, he's got no money! Look at his sandals, they are worn completely! Look at his trousers; they are torn at the back! Look at his singlet, it is totally dirty! Look at his body, he did not take his bath this morning! Look at his pocket, it is empty! Don't you know who I am? I am a general at the army office! I am an officer at the police station! I am a secretary at the government office! You foolish labourer, you will suffer for nothing! Nonentity, you will suffer for nothing! That is the time they start their Power Show! (Na wrong show o - it is a wrong show) Chorus) Power Show is the wrong thing! Yes (chorus) It is a sad thing! (Na wrong show o - it is a wrong show) Chorus) Power is to help your land and to help your mates! Power that does not help mates and land! (Na wrong show o - it is a wrong show) Chorus).

YEAR	TITLE	SUMMARY
1981	Fela Anikulapo-Kuti and The Egypt 80: **GIVE ME SHIT I GIVE YOU SHIT**	**GIVE ME SHIT I GIVE YOU SHIT** is addressing Africans and the Diaspora to stop playing 'the second-fiddle' in life. Using a discussion between him and a European businessman to make his point, Fela sang "hear the discussion between European and myself." According to him the European in an attempt to show how important and well connected he is in Africa, talks of having so many companies with a lot of black people working for him. The European also claims to be a friend of African heads of state and how he was at a dinner last night with the President of Nigeria. To make the European tell more, Fela said he offered the man the last 'joint' (marijuana) in his pocket. The effect of the smoke further let-loose the European's tongue. After his long narrative Fela decided to ask if in Europe and America, any black man could have the same opportunity as he does in Africa. 'If black people own companies in Europe like he does in Africa? Fela also asked, if it is easy for black people to get invited to dinner with any European leader? He told the European that 'negritude' and colonial mentality, are responsible for the cause of African inferiority complex. For Fela, it is the problem of leadership in Africa where Africans don't like to do things for their own folks. He says he feels vexed that Africans in the twentieth century are still slaves of the system. For him, it is time to stand firm 'anybody that gives us shit! He go get shit back! Like Abiola him get! He go get shit! Ten buckets full of shit! He go get shit!

YEAR	TITLE	SUMMARY
1981	Fela Anikulapo-Kuti and The Egypt 80: **A.** **LIVE IN AMSTERDAM /** **MUSIC IS THE WEAPON** **B.** **GOVERNMENT CHICKEN BOYS**	Those Fela calls **GOVERNMENT CHICKEN BOYS** are what you could call 'establishment boys', believers of the system and establishment. Fela compares them with the chicken crowing at dawn like an alarm clock, waking people for the day's job ahead. He sings: "Su! Su! We dey chase chicken him dey run! Him go try to fly! Him go land with him mouth! Him mouth go dey drag for ground! Gerere! Gerere!" Government Chicken boys like the chicken, could be chased away from the grain at will and recalled back to share the same grain again. Like tools of the system they can be dispensed with at will, and Fela says if you ask him where to find 'government chicken boys?' The answer - in government ministries and establishments, civil servants, police, army, commissioner, minister, and the president. The news media he also calls 'government chicken boys' because of the way they depend on western sources of information. He also criticises their organisation structures and ethic - which he regards as not just a carbon copy of western news media, but a poor imitation of them. Finally, Fela says that among these 'government chicken boys,' you find some good people and bad people. For the good people, it is a big fight 'na wahala' for them to stay up-right and give good advice, but the bad people have a decease called 'shaky-shaky'. They are always trying to please the master even if they know, he is doing the wrong thing - like chicken, they shake and say yes to everything.

YEAR	TITLE	SUMMARY
1982	Fela Anikulapo-Kuti and The Egypt 80: **PERAMBULATOR** A. **Perambulator** B. **Frustration of my Lady** (LP Nigeria, Lagos International, 1983)	The effects of five hundred years of slavery and colonialism in Africa, is the issues Fela raises in **PERAMBULATOR**. How generation after generation, Africans have been programmed and conditioned to work and slave for the system. Sung in Pidgin English this is a translation: "My father, your father, African fathers must start to work at twenty. Success and riches are their entire target, everyday from six in the morning till six in the evening, going to work for a small salary. For fifty-five years, from sun-up to sun-down, he slaves for the system until he is tired or retired by force. And to compensate all these year of "meritorious" services, the enslaved man is given a 'gold wrist watch'. Apart from this, the only property he could point to from all the years of slaving for the system is an old bicycle. Fela adds that the conditioning and brainwashing of Africans into becoming certified slaves, started from the education system. Teaching them big grammar in English, to the detriment of their African languages, or brainwashing to believe in European medicine to the detriment of African medicine. For example in their school curriculum Africans, are taught to see European explorers as people who came to discover and save the population from savagery. Fela asks how is it possible to credit the discovery of the sauce of the Niger River to the British explorer Mungo Park? What about those fishermen, who have been plying the river's course from generation before the arrival of Mungo Park? Same can be said of other so-called explorers? He concluded that the European explorers may have "discovered" Africa for Europeans, but certainly not for the African people they met on the continent. He concludes by saying Africans started civilization and if the continent is behind in development, it is because of five hundred years of slavery and colonialism.

YEAR	TITLE	SUMMARY
1984	Fela Anikulapo-Kuti and The Egypt 80: **CUSTOM CHECK POINT**	From 1884-1885 colonial powers, met in Berlin to divide and share Africa among themselves, with this Balkanisation artificial boarders were created to separate African people. Come the so-called independence, most of the nations still respect and adhere to the frontiers created from colonial times. **CUSTOM CHECK POINT** is Fela's criticism of the system that still respects these artificial boundaries separating African people. Tracing the cultural, linguistic, and traditional unity of African people to an origin of same motherhood, Fela describes the men of customs and excise as humans who have been put in place to do the dirty works of those who want to keep Africans apart. He advises them to pack-up and allow our people to travel freely among sister nations.Cut down the barriers! Custom she kia kia kia! He asks them to hurry-up and get out of the way.

YEAR	TITLE	SUMMARY
1984	Fela Anikulapo-Kuti and The Egypt 80: **A. Army Arrangement** **B. Government Chicken Boys**	**ARMY ARRANGEMENT,** is about Nigeria's attempt at 'democracy' in 1979 after more than a decade of military rule. In 1970, Nigeria emerged from a three-year Biafra civil war with the largest standing army in black Africa, no financial debts - careering along on at least two million barrels of sulphur-low oil, pumped daily into the world market. With such revenue invested prudently in the Nigerian economy, there should be no reason for any Nigerian to live below the poverty line. Fela in this song affirms that, the arrival of the military in the political arena created the illusion of a peaceful 'democratic' participation in government. With the daily running of government carried out by civilians who reported to military bosses. With persistent scandals of corruption as the standard in every administration since independence, the army has lost all credibility to effect any change in the system. Fela, calls on the people to be bold enough to criticise the government, because fear of the man with the gun would not put an end to the sufferings of the masses, who eventually pay for government mismanagement. He points to the foreign exchange scandal that prompted the military regime to arrest highly placed Nigerians. Most of them, were tried and sentenced to jail terms ranging from five to fifteen years. But with the change from military to civil rule, most of the jailed socialites were released by the new administration - a preview scenario organised by the departing military regime Fela accuses. Turning to the election issue and how the military, manipulated the country by eliminating young political movements like The Movement of The People (MOP) calling for a change in the system. Fela points to the fact that the military handed power to the same elite politicians, who prompted the army to seize power earlier. He concludes that it is an arrangement from colonial rulers, who put the military in place to do their dirty work and calls the whole political manoeuvre an **Army Arrangement. Government Chicken Boys (see column above).**

YEAR	TITLE	SUMMARY
1985	MOVEMENT OF THE PEOPLE POLITICAL STATEMENT N°1	Despite the diabolic manner in which the military regime in their transition to civil rule programme, eliminated young political movements from contesting the 1979 general elections in Nigeria, Fela continued the struggle in the name of his unregistered party the Movement Of The People (MOP). He made political statements critical of the military and their civilian successors. **MOVEMENT OF THE PEOPLE POLITICAL STATEMENT N°1** is one of such stated opinion. In his habitual sarcastic manner, Fela starts the song saying: "Before they turn us into monkey with tail... Let us hear some important things that our governments are hiding from us – we will expose them ..." Delving into some history, he says: "We have to talk about long time ago" in reference to the history of Eko (Lagos), before the arrival of the British colonial administration. How the British used their 'divide and rule' tactics to gain foot-hold in the coastal regions, thus paving the way for their eventual colonisation of the entire country. After came the 'trading companies' such as United African Company (UAC), John Holt Company, etc., whose sole interest were to exploit the African people and their natural resources. To ensure their absolute control, the British like all the other colonialists, started to recruit some of the natives into their forces. Thus began the military and police institutions, who were trained to brutalise and suppress all forms of decent and oppositions. Unlike the United States, where the military institution provides poor families the possibility of an education, those who took up military careers in colonial times' were mostly 'never do wells', students whose school grades were below the average mark. These are the quality of men that made-up the colonial forces on the African continent.

YEAR	TITLE	SUMMARY
	MOVEMENT OF THE PEOPLE POLITICAL STATEMENT N°1	Before the arrival of colonial administration, there were no police and army institutions in the African society Fela reminds us in this song. If there was war, all the able bodied men and sometimes women volunteered to defend the nation while the wars lasted. As soon as the war is over, the warring men and women went back to their respective jobs. This is unlike the institutions created by the colonial administration with soldiers and police gallivanting around, doing the dirty works of their employers. The colonial administration started the police college and army schools to brainwash their new recruits, condemning the authentic traditions of the people as savage, and encouraging them to look up to the culture of the colonisers as superior. Fela says we should ask ourselves what is government? For him, government and the governed should have a father-child relationship with mutual love and concern for the welfare of both parties as their main focus. However in Africa, there is no father-child relationship between the government and the governed. Instead what we have, are men who like to lord it over the masses. Hence, when such government officials appear in public places they are surrounded by their police and army for protection. For Fela this is alienation. In conclusion, he says if those in government think first of the welfare of their citizens, they won't need all those security to move around among their own people.

YEAR	TITLE	SUMMARY
1986	Fela Anikulapo-Kuti and The Egypt 80: **LOOK AND LAUGH**	By 1981, when Fela wrote and started to perform live at the Ikeja Africa Shrine the song **LOOK AND LAUGH** he was living a life that could be described as a recluse. Fela who loved to go out in public places, clubs, suddenly was always found sleeping or playing sax at home with women around him, or performing at the Africa Shrine. His old attitude of keeping abreast of events, giving lectures at universities and institutions of higher learning stopped. He rarely gave press conferences, or press releases like he used to do. Finally he wrote the song to explain what was going-on with him. He sang: '......many of you go dey wonder, why your man never write new song! Wetin I dey do be say... I dey look and laugh. Meaning: ...many of you must have been wondering why, your man has not written new songs! ...what I am doing is just look and laugh! Fela went on to explain his contributions and sacrifice for the cause of black emancipation, the countless beatings and arrests from the Nigerian police and army, his trials and tribulations, his ultimate sacrifice being the burning down of Kalakuta by the Nigeria army. But despite his sacrifices and sufferings like millions of other Africans, it was obvious that things were not getting better for the average man on the street. There is still injustice everywhere, no freedom, no happiness, yet the majority of the people watch while a few profit from the situation.

YEAR	TITLE	SUMMARY
	Fela Anikulapo-Kuti and The Egypt 80: **LOOK AND LAUGH**	Today after more than three decades of military rule, everyone agrees that corruption has led the country into a fantastic anarchy. For proof, like Professor Théophile Obenga mentioned in his book "Appel a la Jeunesse Africaine" (Clarion Call to African Youths): - A site designed to house a project worth 18 billion US dollars has never been found and cannot be located despite payment of the total cost as mobilization fees and despite setting-up of commission of enquiry. - Millions were spent for paper mills never built talk-less of producing any paper. - At least not less than eighteen projects worth about 836 million dollars are neither completed nor operational. As of date, nobody was ever arrested or worried of the potentials of arrest either. - Between 1985 and 1992, Nigeria launched twenty other projects the same fate, non viability, in spite of the NGO (Non-Governmental Organization) Transparency International present in the country. The debt of Nigeria is 32 billion dollars (If we take into account the amount of money recovered from Abacha's family after his death, five of Nigeria's ex-Generals could conveniently pay back this debt). Fela concluded that all these seemingly endless culture of corruption, made him feel disillusioned and all he could do about the situation is to **LOOK AND LAUGH!**

YEAR	TITLE	SUMMARY
1986	Fela Anikulapo-Kuti and The Egypt 80: **Teacher Don't Teach Me Nonsense** **A. Teacher Don't Teach Me Nonsense (Instrumental)** **B. Teacher Don't Teach Me Nonsense (Vocal).** **C. Look And Laugh (Instrumental).** **D. Look And Laugh (Vocal)**	In **TEACHER DON'T TEACH ME NONSENSE**, Fela explains the role of the teacher in any society with the concept that 'all the things we consider as problems, and all the good things we accept from life as good begin with what we are taught. The individual teaching begins with when we are children, our mother is our teacher. When we come of school age, our teacher is the school-teacher. At the university, the lecturers and professors are our teachers. After university when we start to work, government becomes the individual's teacher. Who then is government's teacher? Culture and Tradition' say's Fela. This is the order of things everywhere in the world. However, it is the problem side of teacher and student that interests Fela in this song. Because every country in this world except in Africa, it is the respective culture and tradition of that country that guides the government on how to rule their people. Going for specifics, Fela mentions France, Germany, England, Korea, Japan, Syria, Jordan, Iran, and affirms that it is the culture of the countries that shapes and guides their respective government's decisions. The culture and traditions of these countries, serve as a teacher to their respective governments. Turning his attention to Africa and her problems. Problems which he had sung about: corruption, inflation, mismanagement, authority stealing, electoral fraud, the latest addition which even makes him laugh is – austerity.

YEAR	TITLE	SUMMARY
1986	Fela Anikulapo-Kuti and The Egypt 80: **Teacher Don't Teach Me Nonsense** A. Teacher Don't Teach Me Nonsense (Instrumental) B. Teacher Don't Teach Me Nonsense (Vocal). C. Look And Laugh (Instrumental). D. Look And Laugh (Vocal)	Fela say's if you ask him why 'austerity' makes him laugh. The answer is that it is beyond crying. Government steals money from the country, the same government is introducing austerity measures forcing the poor people to pay for their own greed and calling it 'austerity measures'. How funny if to say the least. Who taught African 'leaders' to rule the way they do today? 'Na the oyinbo' (meaning in Yoruba language: 'it is them white folks') referring to ex-colonial rulers of each country. Take electoral fraud, which is a true test of our democracy. Many African leaders rig elections with impunity and their respective ex-colonial rulers say nothing against this form of 'democracy'. While the same 'white folks' are quick to claim credit for Africa's 'civilisation' - which Fela disputes in this song. Is this democracy he asks? Turning to other problems like the ever-growing gap between the rich and the poor. Particularly, since the rich are the rulers and also the people stealing the country into poverty. Is this democracy? Or dem-all-crazy? In conclusion, as an African personality, Fela says he is not in the same league as those who believe in dem-all-cracy, so he calls on the western powers who claim to be Africa's teachers not to teach him nonsense - **Teacher Don't Teach Me Nonsense.**